W AROUND THE
ORLD
IN 450 RECIPES

W AROUND THE WORLD
IN 450 RECIPES

Delicious, authentic dishes from the world's best loved cuisines
with step-by-step techniques and over 1500 stunning photographs

EDITOR
SARAH AINLEY

HERMES HOUSE

This edition is published by Hermes House

Hermes House is an imprint of Anness Publishing Ltd
Hermes House, 88–89 Blackfriars Road, London SE1 8HA
tel. 020 7401 2077; fax 020 7633 9499

www.hermeshouse.com; www.annesspublishing.com

If you like the images in this book and would like to investigate using them for publishing, promotions
or advertising, please visit our website www.practicalpictures.com for more information.

Publisher: Joanna Lorenz
Senior Cookery Editor: Linda Fraser
Editor: Sarah Ainley
Design: Siân Keogh and Ian Sandom
Photography: William Adams-Lingwood, Steve Baxter, James Duncan, Amanda Heywood, Patrick McLeavey,
Thomas Odulate and Juliet Piddington
Recipes: Carla Capalbo, Kit Chan, Carole Clements, Silvana Franco, Rosamund Grant, Rebekah Hassan, Masaki Ko,
Elizabeth Lambert Ortiz, Ruby Le Bois, Sallie Morris, Laura Washburn and Elizabeth Wolf-Cohen
Illustrator: Madeleine David

ETHICAL TRADING POLICY
Because of our ongoing ecological investment programme, you, as our customer, can have the pleasure and reassurance of knowing that a tree
is being cultivated on your behalf to naturally replace the materials used to make the book you are holding. For further information about
this scheme, go to www.annesspublishing.com/trees

A CIP catalogue record for this book is available from the British Library.

Previously published as *The Around the World Cookbook*

PUBLISHER'S NOTE
Although the advice and information in this book are believed to be accurate and true at the time of going to press, neither the authors nor
the publisher can accept any legal responsibility or liability for any errors or omissions that may be made nor for any inaccuracies nor for any
harm or injury that comes about from following instructions or advice in this book.

NOTES

For all recipes, quantities are given in both metric and imperial measures and, where appropriate, measures are also given
in standard cups and spoons. Follow one set of measures, but not a mixture, because they are not interchangeable.
Standard spoon and cup measures are level. 1 tsp = 5ml, 1 tbsp = 15ml, 1 cup = 250ml/8fl oz
Australian standard tablespoons are 20ml. Australian readers should use 3 tsp in place of
1 tbsp for measuring small quantities of gelatine, cornflour, salt, etc.
American pints are 16fl oz/2 cups. American readers should use 20fl oz/2.5 cups in place of 1 pint when measuring liquids.
Electric oven temperatures in this book are for conventional ovens. When using a fan oven, the temperature will
probably need to be reduced by about 10–20°C/20–40°F. Since ovens vary, you should check with your manufacturer's
instruction book for guidance.
Medium eggs are used unless otherwise stated.

CONTENTS

Introduction

How often have you wished you could recreate in your own kitchen a favourite take-away dish or one once enjoyed while travelling abroad? Holidays in far flung places have increased our awareness of different foods, and restaurants on every street corner now offer dishes that not so long ago would have been unfamiliar. This cookbook takes its inspiration from some of the world's most exciting cuisines and brings together a collection which celebrates the diversity of traditional cooking styles around the globe. Most of the recipes use accessible fresh ingredients and store-cupboard staples, and even the more exotic foods are now commonly available from supermarkets and delicatessens. From Africa, India and the Orient, through Europe to the Americas, the classic cuisines of the world are at your fingertips.

AFRICA

Lamb, Bean and Pumpkin Soup

INGREDIENTS

Serves 4

115g/4oz split black-eyed beans,
   soaked for 1–2 hours, or overnight
675g/1½lb neck of lamb, cut into
   medium-size chunks
5ml/1 tsp chopped fresh thyme, or
   2.5ml/½ tsp dried
2 bay leaves
1.2 litres/2 pints/5 cups stock or water
1 onion, sliced
225g/8oz pumpkin, diced
2 black cardamom pods
7.5ml/1½ tsp ground turmeric
15ml/1 tbsp chopped fresh coriander
2.5ml/½ tsp caraway seeds
1 fresh green chilli, seeded and chopped
2 green bananas
1 carrot
salt and freshly ground black pepper

1 Drain the black-eyed beans, place
   them in a saucepan and cover with
fresh cold water.

2 Bring the beans to the boil, boil
   rapidly for 10 minutes and then
reduce the heat and simmer, covered
for 40–50 minutes until tender, adding
more water if necessary. Remove from
the heat and set aside to cool.

3 Meanwhile, put the lamb in a large
   saucepan, add the thyme, bay leaves
and stock or water and bring to the
boil. Cover and simmer over a
moderate heat for 1 hour, until tender.

4 Add the onion, pumpkin,
   cardamoms, turmeric, coriander,
caraway, chilli and seasoning and stir.
Bring back to a simmer and then cook,
uncovered, for 15 minutes until the
pumpkin is tender, stirring occasionally.

5 When the beans are cool, spoon into
   a blender or food processor with
their liquid and blend to a smooth purée.

6 Cut the bananas into medium slices
   and the carrot into thin slices. Stir
into the soup with the beans and cook
for 10–12 minutes, until the vegetables
are tender. Adjust seasoning and serve.

Assiette of Plantains

This melange of succulent sweet and savoury plantains makes a delicious crunchy appetizer.

INGREDIENTS

Serves 4

2 green plantains
1 yellow plantain
½ onion
pinch of garlic granules
salt and cayenne pepper
vegetable oil, for shallow frying

1 Heat the oil in a large frying pan over a moderate heat. While the oil is heating, peel one of the green plantains and cut into very thin rounds using a vegetable peeler.

2 Fry the plantain rounds in the oil for about 3 minutes, turning until golden brown. Drain on kitchen paper and keep warm.

3 Coarsely grate the other green plantain and put on a plate. Slice the onion into wafer-thin shreds and mix with the grated plantain.

4 Heat a little more oil in the frying pan and fry handfuls of the mixture for 2–3 minutes, until golden, turning once. Drain on kitchen paper and keep warm with the green plantain rounds.

5 Heat a little more oil in the frying pan and, while it is heating, peel the yellow plantain, cut in half lengthways and dice. Sprinkle with garlic granules and cayenne pepper and then fry in the hot oil until golden brown, turning to brown evenly. Drain on kitchen paper and then arrange the three varieties of cooked plantains in shallow dishes. Sprinkle with salt and serve as a snack.

Cameroon Suya

INGREDIENTS

Serves 4

450g/1lb frying steak
2.5ml/½ tsp sugar
5ml/1 tsp garlic granules
5ml/1 tsp ground ginger
5ml/1 tsp paprika
5ml/1 tsp ground cinnamon
pinch of chilli powder
10ml/2 tsp onion salt
50g/2oz/½ cup peanuts, finely crushed
vegetable oil, for brushing

2 Mix the sugar, garlic granules, spices and onion salt together in a small bowl. Add the crushed peanuts and then scatter over the steak, mixing well so that the spices are worked into the meat.

3 Thread the steak on to six satay sticks, pushing the meat close together. Place in a shallow dish, cover loosely with foil and leave to marinate in a cool place for a few hours.

4 Preheat a grill or barbecue. Brush the meat with a little oil and then cook on a moderate heat for about 15 minutes, until evenly brown.

1 Trim the steak of any fat and then cut into 2.5cm/1in wide strips. Place in a bowl or a shallow dish.

COOK'S TIP

If barbecueing the meat, try to avoid it cooking too quickly or burning.

Akkras

These fritters are almost always made from black-eyed beans. For a quicker version; after soaking the beans, drain them thoroughly and liquidize without removing the skins.

INGREDIENTS

Serves 4

250g/8oz/1¼ cups dried black-eyed beans
1 onion, chopped
1 red chilli, halved, with seeds removed (optional)
150ml/¼ pint/⅔ cup water
oil, for deep frying

1 Soak the black-eyed beans in plenty of cold water for 6–8 hours or overnight. Drain the beans and then, with a brisk action, rub the beans between the palms of your hands to remove the skins.

2 Return the beans to the bowl, top up with water and the skins will float to the surface. Discard the skins and soak the beans again for 2 hours.

3 Place the beans in a blender or food processor with the onion, chilli, if using, and a little water. Blend to make a thick paste. Pour the mixture into a large bowl and whisk for a few minutes.

4 Heat the oil in a large heavy saucepan and fry spoonfuls of the mixture for 4 minutes until golden brown.

Nigerian Meat Stew

This recipe was adapted from a Nigerian stew. It is made with meats of different flavours, such as beef, offal and mutton, along with dried fish or snails, and served with yam or rice.

INGREDIENTS

Serves 4–6
675g/1½ lb oxtail, chopped
450g/1lb stewing beef, cubed
450g/1lb skinless, boneless chicken
  breasts, chopped
2 garlic cloves, crushed
1½ onions
30ml/2 tbsp palm or vegetable oil
30ml/2 tbsp tomato purée
400g/14oz can plum tomatoes
2 bay leaves
5ml/1 tsp dried thyme
5ml/1 tsp mixed spice
salt and freshly ground black pepper

1 Place the oxtail in a large saucepan, cover with water and bring to the boil. Skim the surface of any froth, then cover and cook for 1½ hours, adding more water as necessary.

2 Add the beef and continue to cook for a further hour, until tender.

3 Meanwhile, season the chicken with the crushed garlic and roughly chop one of the onions.

4 Heat the oil in a large saucepan over a moderate heat and fry the chopped onion for about 5 minutes until soft. Stir in the tomato purée, cook briskly for a few minutes, then add the chicken. Stir well and cook gently for 5 minutes.

5 Meanwhile, place the plum tomatoes and the remaining half onion in a processor and blend to a purée. Stir into the chicken mixture with the bay leaves, thyme, mixed spice and seasoning.

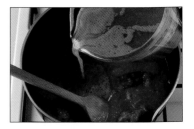

6 Add about 600ml/1 pint/2½ cups of stock from the cooked oxtail and beef and simmer for 35 minutes.

7 Add the oxtail and beef to the chicken. Heat gently, adjust the seasoning and serve hot.

Lamb Tagine with Coriander and Spices

Here is Rachida Mounti's version of a Moroccan-style tagine. It can be made with chops or cutlets, and either marinated or cooked immediately after seasoning.

INGREDIENTS

Serves 4
4 lamb chump chops
2 garlic cloves, crushed
pinch of saffron strands
2.5ml/½ tsp ground cinnamon, plus
   extra to garnish
2.5ml/½ tsp ground ginger
15ml/1 tbsp chopped fresh coriander
15ml/1 tbsp chopped fresh parsley
1 onion, finely chopped
45ml/3 tbsp olive oil
300ml/½ pint/1¼ cups lamb stock
50g/2oz/½ cup blanched almonds,
   to garnish
5ml/1 tsp sugar
salt and freshly ground black pepper

1 Season the lamb with the garlic, saffron, cinnamon, ginger and a little salt and black pepper. Place on a large plate and sprinkle with the coriander, parsley and onion. Cover loosely and set aside in the fridge for a few hours to marinate.

2 Heat the oil in a large frying pan, over a moderate heat. Add the marinated lamb and all the herbs and onion from the dish.

3 Fry for 1–2 minutes, turning once, then add the stock, bring to the boil and simmer gently for 30 minutes, turning the chops once.

4 Meanwhile, heat a small frying pan over a moderate heat, add the almonds and dry fry until golden, shaking the pan occasionally to ensure they colour evenly. Transfer to a bowl and set aside.

5 Transfer the chops to a serving plate and keep warm. Increase the heat under the pan and boil the sauce until reduced by about half. Stir in the sugar. Pour the sauce over the chops and sprinkle with the fried almonds and a little extra ground cinnamon.

--- COOK'S TIP ---

Lamb tagine is a fragrant dish, originating in North Africa. It is traditionally made in a cooking dish, known as a tagine, from where it takes its name. This dish consists of a plate with a tall lid with sloping sides. It has a narrow opening to let steam escape, while retaining the flavour.

Beef in Aubergine Sauce

When served with boiled yam or rice, this makes a hearty dish.

INGREDIENTS

Serves 4

450g/1lb stewing beef
5ml/1 tsp dried thyme
45ml/3 tbsp palm or vegetable oil
1 large onion, finely chopped
2 garlic cloves, crushed
4 canned plum tomatoes, chopped, plus 60ml/4 tbsp of the juice
15ml/1 tbsp tomato purée
2.5ml/¹⁄₂ tsp mixed spice
1 fresh red chilli, seeded and chopped
900ml/1¹⁄₂ pints/3³⁄₄ cups chicken stock or water
1 large aubergine, about 350g/12oz
salt and freshly ground black pepper

1 Cut the beef into cubes and season with 2.5ml/¹⁄₂ tsp of the thyme and salt and pepper.

2 Heat 15ml/1 tbsp of the oil in a large saucepan and fry the meat, in batches if necessary, for 8–10 minutes until well browned. Transfer to a bowl using a slotted spoon and set aside.

3 Heat the remaining oil in the saucepan and fry the onion and garlic for a few minutes, then add the tomatoes and tomato juice and simmer for 5–10 minutes, stirring occasionally.

4 Add the tomato purée, mixed spice, chilli and remaining thyme, stir well, then add the reserved beef and the stock or water. Bring to the boil, cover and simmer gently for 30 minutes.

5 Cut the aubergine into 1cm/¹⁄₂ in dice. Stir into the beef mixture and cook, covered, for a further 30 minutes until the beef is completely tender. Adjust the seasoning and serve hot.

Duck with Sherry and Pumpkin

INGREDIENTS

Serves 6

1 whole duck, about 1.75kg/4–4½lb
1 lemon
5ml/1 tsp garlic granules or 2 garlic
    cloves, crushed
5ml/1 tsp curry powder
2.5ml/½ tsp paprika
4ml/¾ tsp five-spice powder
30ml/2 tbsp soy sauce
salt and freshly ground black pepper
vegetable oil, for frying

For the sauce

75g/3oz pumpkin
1 onion, chopped
4 canned plum tomatoes
300ml/½ pint/1¼ cups medium-dry
    sherry
about 300ml/½ pint/1¼ cups water

1 Cut the duck into 10 pieces and place in a large bowl. Halve the lemon and squeeze the juice all over the duck and set aside.

2 In a small bowl, mix together the garlic, curry powder, paprika, five-spice powder and salt and pepper and rub into each of the duck pieces.

3 Sprinkle the duck with the soy sauce, cover loosely with clear film and leave to marinate overnight.

4 To make the sauce, cook the pumpkin in boiling water until tender, then blend to a purée with the onion and tomatoes.

COOK'S TIP

The back and wings of the duck are rather bony, so try and use just the fleshier parts or buy leg or breast portions.

---

5 Pat the duck pieces dry with kitchen paper, then heat a little oil in a wok or large frying pan and fry the duck for 15 minutes until crisp and brown. Set aside on a plate.

6 Wipe away the excess oil from the wok or frying pan with kitchen paper and pour in the pumpkin purée. Add the sherry and a little of the water, then bring to the boil and add the fried duck. Simmer for about 1 hour until the duck is cooked, adding more water if the sauce becomes too thick. Serve hot and hand soy sauce separately.

Joloff Chicken and Rice

Serve this well-known, colourful West African dish at a dinner party or other special occasion.

INGREDIENTS

Serves 4

1kg/2¼ lb chicken, cut into 4–6 pieces
2 garlic cloves, crushed
5ml/1 tsp dried thyme
30ml/ 2 tbsp palm or vegetable oil
400g/14oz can chopped tomatoes
15ml/1 tbsp tomato purée
1 onion, chopped
450ml/¾ pint/1⅞ cups chicken stock or water
30ml/2 tbsp dried shrimps or crayfish, ground
1 green chilli, seeded and finely chopped
350g/12oz/1½ cups long grain rice, washed

1 Rub the chicken with the garlic and thyme and set aside.

2 Heat the oil in a saucepan until hazy and then add the chopped tomatoes, tomato purée and onion. Cook over a moderately high heat for about 15 minutes until the tomatoes are well reduced, stirring occasionally at first and then more frequently as the tomatoes thicken.

3 Reduce the heat a little, add the chicken pieces and stir well to coat with the sauce. Cook for 10 minutes, stirring, then add the stock or water, the dried shrimps or crayfish and the chilli. Bring to the boil and simmer for 5 minutes, stirring occasionally.

4 Put the rice in a separate saucepan. Scoop 300ml/½ pint/1¼ cups of the sauce into a measuring jug, top up with water to 450ml/¾ pint/1⅞ cups and stir into the rice.

5 Cook, covered, until the liquid is absorbed, place a piece of foil on top of the rice, cover the pan with a lid and cook over a low heat for 20 minutes until the rice is cooked, adding a little more water if necessary.

6 Transfer the chicken pieces to a warmed serving plate. Simmer the sauce until reduced by half. Pour over the chicken and serve with the rice.

Chicken with Lentils

Kuku, this delicious tangy chicken stew, comes from Kenya. The amount of lemon juice can be reduced, if you would prefer a less sharp sauce.

INGREDIENTS

Serves 4–6
6 chicken thighs or pieces
2.5–4ml/¹/₂–³/₄ tsp ground ginger
50g/2oz mung beans
60ml/4 tbsp corn oil
2 onions, finely chopped
2 garlic cloves, crushed
5 tomatoes, peeled and chopped
1 green chilli, seeded and finely chopped
30ml/2 tbsp lemon juice
300ml/¹/₂ pint/1¹/₄ cups coconut milk
300ml/¹/₂ pint/1¹/₄ cups water
15ml/1 tbsp chopped fresh coriander
salt and freshly ground black pepper

1 Season the chicken pieces with the ginger and a little salt and pepper and set aside in a cool place to marinate. Meanwhile, boil the mung beans in plenty of water for 35 minutes until soft, then mash well.

2 Heat the oil in a large saucepan over a moderate heat and fry the chicken pieces, in batches if necessary, until evenly browned. Transfer to a plate and set aside, reserving the oil and chicken juices in the pan.

3 In the same pan, fry the onions and garlic for 5 minutes, then add the tomatoes and chilli and cook for a further 1–2 minutes, stirring well.

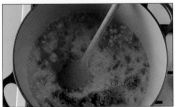

4 Add the mashed mung beans, lemon juice and coconut milk to the pan. Simmer for 5 minutes, then add the chicken pieces and a little water if the sauce is too thick. Stir in the coriander and simmer for about 35 minutes until the chicken is cooked through. Serve with a green vegetable and rice or chapatis.

Fish and Prawns with Spinach and Coconut

INGREDIENTS

Serves 4

450g/1lb white fish fillets (cod or
  haddock)
15ml/1 tbsp lemon or lime juice
2.5ml/½ tsp garlic granules
5ml/1 tsp ground cinnamon
2.5ml/½ tsp dried thyme
2.5ml/½ tsp paprika
2.5ml/½ tsp freshly ground black
  pepper
seasoned flour, for dusting
vegetable oil, for shallow frying
salt

For the sauce

25g/1oz/2 tbsp butter or margarine
1 onion, finely chopped
1 garlic clove, crushed
300ml/½ pint/1¼ cups coconut milk
115g/4oz fresh spinach, finely sliced
225–275g/8–10oz cooked, peeled
  prawns
1 red chilli, seeded and finely chopped

1 Place the fish fillets in a shallow bowl and sprinkle with the lemon or lime juice.

2 Blend together the garlic granules, cinnamon, thyme, paprika, pepper and salt and sprinkle over the fish. Cover loosely with clear film and leave to marinate in a cool place or put in the refrigerator for a few hours.

3 Meanwhile, make the sauce. Melt the butter or margarine in a large saucepan and fry the onion and garlic for 5–6 minutes, until the onion is soft, stirring frequently.

4 Place the coconut milk and spinach in a separate saucepan and bring to the boil. Cook gently for a few minutes until the spinach has wilted and the coconut milk has reduced a little, then set aside to cool slightly.

5 Blend the spinach mixture in a blender or food processor for 30 seconds and add to the onion with the prawns and red chilli. Stir well and simmer gently for a few minutes then set aside while cooking the fish.

6 Cut the marinated fish into 5cm/2in pieces and dip in the seasoned flour. Heat a little oil in a large frying pan and fry the fish pieces, in batches if necessary, for 2–3 minutes each side until golden brown. Drain on kitchen paper.

7 Arrange the fish on a warmed serving plate. Gently reheat the sauce and serve separately in a sauce boat or poured over the fish.

Tanzanian Fish Curry

INGREDIENTS

Serves 2–3

1 large snapper or red bream
1 lemon
45ml/3 tbsp vegetable oil
1 onion, finely chopped
2 garlic cloves, crushed
45ml/3 tbsp curry powder
400g/14oz can chopped tomatoes
20ml/1 heaped tbsp smooth peanut
  butter, preferably unsalted
½ green pepper, chopped
2 slices fresh root ginger
1 green chilli, seeded and finely
  chopped
about 600ml/1 pint/2½ cups fish stock
15ml/1 tbsp finely chopped fresh
  coriander
salt and freshly ground black pepper

1 Season the fish, inside and out with salt and pepper and place in a shallow bowl. Halve the lemon and squeeze the juice all over the fish. Cover loosely with clear film and leave to marinate for at least 2 hours.

2 Heat the oil in a large saucepan and fry the onion and garlic for 5–6 minutes until soft. Reduce the heat, add the curry powder and cook, stirring for a further 5 minutes.

3 Stir in the tomatoes and then the peanut butter, mixing well, then add the green pepper, ginger, chilli and stock. Stir well and simmer gently for 10 minutes.

COOK'S TIP

The fish can be fried before adding to the sauce, if preferred. Dip in seasoned flour and fry in oil in a pan or a wok for a few minutes before adding to the sauce.

4 Cut the fish into pieces and gently lower into the sauce. Simmer for a further 20 minutes or until the fish is cooked, then using a slotted spoon, transfer the fish pieces to a plate.

5 Stir the coriander into the sauce and adjust the seasoning. If the sauce is very thick, add a little extra stock or water. Return the fish to the sauce, cook gently to heat through and then serve immediately.

King Prawns in Almond Sauce

INGREDIENTS

Serves 4

450g/1lb raw king prawns
600ml/1 pint/2½ cups water
3 thin slices fresh root ginger
10ml/2 tsp curry powder
2 garlic cloves, crushed
15g/½ oz/1 tbsp butter or margarine
60ml/4 tbsp ground almonds
1 green chilli, seeded and finely
    chopped
45ml/3 tbsp single cream
salt and freshly ground black pepper

For the vegetables

15ml/1 tbsp mustard oil
15ml/1 tbsp vegetable oil
1 onion, sliced
½ red pepper, seeded and thinly sliced
½ green pepper, seeded and thinly
    sliced
1 christophene, peeled, stoned and cut
    into strips
salt and freshly ground black pepper

1 Shell the prawns and place shells in a saucepan with the water and ginger. Simmer, uncovered, for 15 minutes until reduced by half. Strain into a jug and discard the shells.

2 Devein the prawns, place in a bowl and season with the curry powder, garlic and salt and pepper and set aside.

3 Heat the mustard and vegetable oils in a large frying pan, add all the vegetables and stir fry for 5 minutes. Season with salt and pepper, spoon into a serving dish and keep warm.

4 Wipe out the frying pan, then melt the butter or margarine and sauté the prawns for about 5 minutes until pink. Spoon over the bed of vegetables, cover and keep warm.

5 Add the ground almonds and chilli to the pan, stir fry for a few seconds and then add the reserved stock and bring to the boil. Reduce the heat, stir in the cream and simmer for a few minutes, without boiling.

6 Pour the sauce over the vegetables and prawns before serving.

Fried Pomfret in Coconut Sauce

INGREDIENTS

Serves 4

4 medium pomfret
juice of 1 lemon
5ml/1 tsp garlic granules
salt and freshly ground black pepper
vegetable oil, for shallow frying

For the coconut sauce

450ml/¾ pint/1⅞ cups water
2 thin slices fresh root ginger
25–40g/1–1½ oz creamed coconut
30ml/2 tbsp vegetable oil
1 red onion, sliced
2 garlic cloves, crushed
1 green chilli, seeded and thinly sliced
15ml/1 tbsp chopped fresh coriander
salt and freshly ground black pepper

1 Cut the fish in half and sprinkle inside and out with the lemon juice. Season with the garlic granules and salt and pepper and set aside to marinate for a few hours.

2 Heat a little oil in a large frying pan. Pat away the excess lemon juice from the fish, fry in the oil for 10 minutes, turning once. Set aside.

3 To make the sauce, place the water in a saucepan with the slices of ginger, bring to the boil and simmer until the liquid is reduced to just over 300ml/½ pint/1¼ cups. Take out the ginger and reserve, then add the creamed coconut to the pan and stir until the coconut has melted.

4 Heat the oil in a wok or large pan and fry the onion and garlic for 2–3 minutes. Add the reserved ginger and coconut stock, the chilli and coriander, stir well and then gently add the fish. Simmer for 10 minutes, until the fish is cooked through. Transfer the fish to a warmed serving plate, adjust the seasoning for the sauce and pour over the fish. Serve immediately.

Donu's Lobster Piri Piri

Lobster in its shell, in true Nigerian style, flavoured with dried shrimp.

INGREDIENTS

Serves 2–4

2 cooked lobsters, halved
fresh coriander sprigs, to garnish

For the piri piri sauce
60ml/4 tbsp vegetable oil
2 onions, chopped
5ml/1 tsp chopped fresh root ginger
450g/1lb fresh or canned tomatoes, chopped
15ml/1 tbsp tomato purée
225g/8oz cooked, peeled prawns
10ml/2 tsp ground coriander
1 green chilli, seeded and chopped
15ml/1 tbsp ground dried shrimps or crayfish
600ml/1 pint/2½ cups water
1 green pepper, seeded and sliced
salt and freshly ground black pepper

1 Heat the oil in a large flameproof casserole and fry the onions, ginger, tomatoes and tomato purée for 5 minutes or until the onions are soft.

2 Add the prawns, ground coriander, chilli and ground shrimps or crayfish and stir well to mix.

3 Stir in the water, green pepper and salt and pepper, bring to the boil and simmer, uncovered, over a moderate heat for about 20–30 minutes until the sauce is reduced.

4 Add the lobsters to the sauce and cook for a few minutes to heat through. Arrange the lobster halves on warmed serving plates and pour the sauce over each one. Garnish with coriander sprigs and serve with fluffy white rice.

Tilapia in Turmeric, Mango and Tomato Sauce

Tilapia is widely used in African cooking, but can be found in most fishmongers. Yam or boiled yellow plantains are good accompaniments.

INGREDIENTS

Serves 4
4 tilapia
½ lemon
2 garlic cloves, crushed
2.5ml/½ tsp dried thyme
30ml/2 tbsp chopped spring onions
vegetable oil, for shallow frying
flour, for dusting
30ml/2 tbsp groundnut oil
15g/½ oz/1 tbsp butter or margarine
1 onion, finely chopped
3 tomatoes, peeled and finely chopped
5ml/1 tsp ground turmeric
60ml/4 tbsp white wine
1 green chilli, seeded and finely chopped
600ml/1 pint/2½ cups well-flavoured fish stock
5ml/1 tsp sugar
1 medium underripe mango, peeled and diced
15ml/1 tbsp chopped fresh parsley
salt and freshly ground black pepper

2 Heat a little vegetable oil in a large frying pan, coat the fish with some flour, then fry the fish on both sides for a few minutes until golden brown. Remove with a slotted spoon to a plate and set aside.

4 Add the turmeric, white wine, chilli, fish stock and sugar, stir well and bring to the boil, then simmer gently, covered, for 10 minutes.

1 Place the fish in a shallow bowl, squeeze the lemon juice all over the fish and gently rub in the garlic, thyme and some salt and pepper. Place some of the spring onion in the cavity of each fish, cover loosely with clear film and leave to marinate for a few hours or overnight in the fridge.

3 Heat the groundnut oil and butter or margarine in a saucepan and fry the onion for 4–5 minutes, until soft. Stir in the tomatoes and cook briskly for a few minutes.

5 Add the fish and cook over a gentle heat for about 15–20 minutes, until the fish is cooked through. Add the mango, arranging it around the fish, and cook briefly for 1–2 minutes to heat through.

6 Arrange the fish on a warmed serving plate with the mango and tomato sauce poured over. Garnish with chopped parsley and serve immediately.

Egusi Spinach and Egg

This is a superbly balanced dish for those who don't eat meat. Egusi, or ground melon seed, is widely used in West African cooking, adding a creamy texture and a nutty flavour to many recipes. It is especially good with fresh spinach.

INGREDIENTS

Serves 4

900g/2lb fresh spinach
115g/4oz ground egusi
90ml/6 tbsp groundnut or vegetable oil
4 tomatoes, peeled and chopped
1 onion, chopped
2 garlic cloves, crushed
1 slice fresh root ginger, finely chopped
150ml/¼ pint/⅔ cup vegetable stock
1 red chilli, seeded and finely chopped
6 eggs
salt

1 Roll the spinach into bundles and cut into strips. Place in a bowl.

2 Cover with boiling water, then drain through a sieve. Press with your fingers to remove excess water.

3 Place the egusi in a bowl and gradually add enough water to form a paste, stirring all the time.

4 Heat the oil in a saucepan, add the tomatoes, onion, garlic and ginger and fry over a moderate heat for about 10 minutes, stirring frequently.

5 Add the egusi paste, stock, chilli and salt, cook for 10 minutes, then add the spinach and stir into the sauce. Cook for 15 minutes, uncovered, stirring frequently.

6 Meanwhile hard-boil the eggs, stand in cold water for a few minutes to cool and then shell and cut in half. Arrange in a shallow serving dish and pour the egusi spinach over the top. Serve hot.

COOK'S TIP

Instead of using boiled eggs, you could make an omelette flavoured with herbs and garlic. Serve it either whole, or sliced, with the egusi sauce. If you can't find egusi, use ground almonds as a substitute.

Marinated Vegetables on Skewers

These kebabs are a delightful main dish for vegetarians, or serve them as a vegetable side dish.

INGREDIENTS

Serves 4

115g/4oz pumpkin
1 red onion
1 small courgette
1 ripe plantain
1 aubergine
1/2 red pepper, seeded
1/2 green pepper, seeded
12 button mushrooms
60ml/4 tbsp lemon juice
60ml/4 tbsp olive or sunflower oil
45–60ml/3–4 tbsp soy sauce
150ml/1/4 pint/2/3 cup tomato juice
1 green chilli, seeded and chopped
1/2 onion, grated
3 garlic cloves, crushed
7.5ml/1 1/2 tsp dried tarragon, crushed
4ml/3/4 tsp dried basil
4ml/3/4 tsp dried thyme
4ml/3/4 tsp ground cinnamon
25g/1oz/2 tbsp butter or margarine
300ml/1/2 pint/1 1/4 cups vegetable stock
freshly ground black pepper
fresh parsley sprigs, to garnish

1 Peel and cube the pumpkin, place in a small bowl and cover with boiling water. Blanch for 2–3 minutes, then drain and refresh under cold water.

2 Cut the onion into wedges, slice the courgette and plantain and cut the aubergine and red and green peppers into chunks. Trim the mushrooms. Place the vegetables, including the pumpkin in a large bowl.

3 Mix together the lemon juice, oil, soy sauce, tomato juice, chilli, grated onion, garlic, herbs, cinnamon and black pepper and pour over the vegetables. Toss together and then set aside in a cool place to marinate for a few hours.

4 Thread the vegetables on to eight skewers, using a variety of vegetables on each to make a colourful display. Preheat the grill.

5 Grill the vegetables under a low heat, for about 15 minutes, turning frequently, until golden brown, basting with the marinade to keep the vegetables moist.

6 Place the remaining marinade, butter or margarine and stock in a pan and simmer for 10 minutes to cook the onion and reduce the sauce.

7 Pour the sauce into a serving jug and arrange the vegetable skewers on a plate. Garnish with parsley and serve with a rice dish or salad.

COOK'S TIP

You can use any vegetable that you prefer. Just first parboil any that may require longer cooking.

Vegetables in Peanut Sauce

INGREDIENTS

Serves 4

15ml/1 tbsp palm or vegetable oil
1 onion, chopped
2 garlic cloves, crushed
400g/14oz can tomatoes, puréed
45ml/3 tbsp smooth peanut butter,
  preferably unsalted
750ml/1¼ pint/3⅔ cups water
5ml/1 tsp dried thyme
1 green chilli, seeded and chopped
1 vegetable stock cube
2.5ml/½ tsp ground allspice
2 carrots
115g/4oz white cabbage
175g/6oz okra
½ red pepper
150ml/¼ pint/⅔ cup vegetable stock
salt

1 Heat the oil in a large saucepan and fry the onion and garlic over a moderate heat for 5 minutes, stirring frequently. Add the tomatoes and peanut butter and stir well.

2 Stir in the water, thyme, chilli, stock cube, allspice and a little salt. Bring to the boil and then simmer gently, uncovered for about 35 minutes.

3 Cut the carrots into sticks, slice the cabbage, top and tail the okra and seed and slice the red pepper.

4 Place the vegetables in a saucepan with the stock, bring to the boil and cook until tender but still with a little "bite".

5 Drain the vegetables and place in a warmed serving dish. Pour the sauce over the top and serve.

Bean and Gari Loaf

This recipe is a newly created vegetarian dish using typical Ghanaian flavours and ingredients.

INGREDIENTS

Serves 4

225g/8oz/1¼ cups red kidney beans, soaked overnight
15g/½oz/1 tbsp butter or margarine
1 onion, finely chopped
2 garlic cloves, crushed
½ red pepper, seeded and chopped
½ green pepper, seeded and chopped
1 green chilli, seeded and finely chopped
5ml/1 tsp mixed chopped herbs
2 eggs
15ml/1 tbsp lemon juice
75ml/5 tbsp gari
salt and freshly ground black pepper

1 Drain the kidney beans, then place in a saucepan, cover with water and boil rapidly for 15 minutes. Reduce the heat and continue boiling for about 1 hour, until the beans are tender, adding more water if necessary. Drain, reserving the cooking liquid. Preheat the oven to 190°C/375°F/Gas 5 and grease a 900g/2lb loaf tin.

2 Melt the butter or margarine in a large frying pan and fry the onion, garlic and peppers for 5 minutes, then add the chilli, mixed herbs and a little salt and pepper.

3 Place the cooked kidney beans in a large bowl or in a food processor and mash or process to a pulp. Add the onion and pepper mixture and stir well to mix. Cool slightly, then stir in the eggs and lemon juice.

4 Place the gari in a separate bowl and sprinkle generously with warm water. The gari should become soft and fluffy after about 5 minutes.

5 Pour the gari into the bean and onion mixture and stir together thoroughly. If the consistency is too stiff, add a little of the bean liquid. Spoon the mixture into the prepared loaf tin and bake in the oven for 35–45 minutes, until firm to the touch.

6 Cool the loaf in the tin and then turn out on to a plate. Cut into thick slices and serve.

COOK'S TIP

Gari is a course-grained flour, used as a staple food, in a similar way to ground rice. Gari is made from a starchy root vegetable, cassava, which is first dried, then ground.

Efua's Ghanaian Salad

INGREDIENTS

Serves 4

115g/4oz cooked, peeled prawns
1 garlic clove, crushed
7.5ml/½ tbsp vegetable oil
2 eggs
1 yellow plantain, halved
4 lettuce leaves
2 tomatoes
1 red pepper
1 avocado
juice of 1 lemon
1 carrot
200g/7oz can tuna or sardines
1 green chilli, finely chopped
30ml/2 tbsp chopped spring onion
salt and freshly ground black pepper

1 Put the prawns in a small bowl, add the garlic and a little seasoning.

2 Heat the oil in a small saucepan, add the prawns and cook over a low heat for a few minutes. Transfer to a plate to cool.

3 Hard-boil the eggs, place in cold water to cool, then shell and cut into slices.

4 Boil the plantain in a pan of water for 15 minutes, cool, then peel and slice thickly.

5 Shred the lettuce and arrange on a large serving plate. Slice the tomatoes and red pepper and peel and slice the avocado, sprinkling it with a little lemon juice. Arrange vegetables on the plate. Cut the carrot into matchstick-size pieces and arrange over the lettuce with the other vegetables.

6 Add the plantain, eggs, prawns and tuna fish or sardines. Sprinkle with the remaining lemon juice, scatter the chilli and spring onion on top and season with salt and pepper to taste. Serve as a lunch-time salad or as a delicious side dish.

COOK'S TIP

To make a complete meal, serve this salad with a meat or fish dish. Vary the ingredients, use any canned fish and a mixture of interesting lettuce leaves.

Plantain and Green Banana Salad

The plantains and bananas may be cooked in their skins to retain their soft texture. They will then absorb all the flavour of the dressing.

INGREDIENTS

Serves 4

2 firm yellow plantains
3 green bananas
1 garlic clove, crushed
1 red onion
15–30ml/1–2 tbsp chopped fresh
   coriander
45ml/3 tbsp sunflower oil
22.5ml/1½ tbsp malt vinegar
salt and coarse grain black pepper

1 Slit the plantains and bananas lengthways along their natural ridges, then cut in half and place in a large saucepan.

2 Cover the plantains and bananas with water, add a little salt and bring to the boil. Boil gently for 20 minutes until tender, then remove from the water. When they are cool enough to handle, peel and cut into medium-size slices.

3 Put the plantain and banana slices into a bowl and add the garlic, turning to mix.

4 Halve the onion and slice thinly. Add to the bowl with the coriander, oil, vinegar and seasoning. Toss together to mix, then serve as an accompaniment to a main dish.

Cameroon Coconut Rice

This version of a favourite African dish, Coconut Joloff, can be left moist, like a risotto, or cooked longer for a drier result.

INGREDIENTS

Serves 4
30ml/2 tbsp vegetable oil
1 onion, chopped
30ml/2 tbsp tomato purée
600ml/1 pint/2½ cups coconut milk
2 carrots
1 yellow pepper
5ml/1 tsp dried thyme
2.5ml/½ tsp mixed spice
1 fresh green chilli, seeded and chopped
350g/12oz/1½ cups long grain rice
salt

1 Heat the oil in a large saucepan and fry the onion for 2 minutes. Add the tomato purée and cook over a moderate heat for 5–6 minutes, stirring all the time. Add the coconut milk, stir well and bring to the boil.

2 Roughly chop the carrots and chop the pepper, discarding the seeds.

3 Stir the carrots, pepper, thyme, mixed spice, chilli and rice into the onion mixture, season with salt and bring to the boil. Cover and cook over a low heat until the rice has absorbed most of the liquid. Cover the rice with foil, secure with the lid and steam very gently until the rice is done. Serve hot.

Chick-pea and Okra Fry

Other vegetables can be added to this stir-fry to make a pleasing side dish. Mushrooms, cooked potatoes, courgettes or French beans would all be suitable additions.

INGREDIENTS

Serves 4
450g/1lb okra
15ml/1 tbsp vegetable oil
15ml/1 tbsp mustard oil
15g/½ oz/1 tbsp butter or margarine
1 onion, finely chopped
1 garlic clove, crushed
2 tomatoes, finely chopped
1 green chilli, seeded and finely chopped
2 slices fresh root ginger
5ml/1 tsp ground cumin
15ml/1 tbsp chopped fresh coriander
425g/15oz can chick-peas, drained
salt and freshly ground black pepper

1 Wash and dry the okra, remove the tops and tails and chop roughly.

2 Heat the vegetable and mustard oils and the butter or margarine in a large frying pan.

3 Fry the onion and garlic for 5 minutes until the onion is slightly softened. Add the chopped tomatoes, chilli and ginger and stir well, then add the okra, cumin and coriander. Simmer for 5 minutes, stirring frequently then stir in the chick-peas and a little seasoning.

4 Cook gently for a few minutes for the chick-peas to heat through, then spoon into a serving bowl and serve at once.

Coconut Chapatis

INGREDIENTS

Makes 9–10

450g/1lb/4 cups plain flour
2.5ml/½ tsp salt
300ml/½ pint/1¼ cups coconut milk
vegetable oil, for shallow frying

1 Place the flour and salt in a large bowl and gradually stir in the coconut milk to make a soft dough. Bring together with your hand.

2 Turn the dough out on to a floured work surface and knead with your hands to form a firm but pliable dough, adding more flour if the dough is on the sticky side.

3 Break the dough into nine equal-size balls, and roll out each ball on a lightly floured surface to a 22cm/8½ in round.

4 Brush the rounds with oil, roll up and twist into a ring, tucking the ends into the middle. Place on a floured board and set aside for 15 minutes.

5 Roll out each of the dough rings to a 5cm/2in round. Brush a heavy frying pan with oil and cook the chapatis for 3–4 minutes on each side until golden brown. Serve hot as an accompaniment.

Mandazi

Serve these East African breads as a snack or as an accompaniment to a meal.

INGREDIENTS

Makes about 15

4 or 5 cardamom pods
450g/1lb/4 cups self-raising flour
45ml/3 tbsp caster sugar
5ml/1 tsp baking powder
1 egg
30ml/2 tbsp vegetable oil, plus oil for deep frying
225ml/7fl oz/⅞ cup milk or water

1 Crush each cardamom pod, shake out the seeds and grind the seeds in a small mortar and pestle, then place in a large bowl with the flour, sugar and baking powder. Stir well to mix.

2 Put the egg and oil in a small bowl and beat together, then add to the flour mixture. Mix with your fingers, gradually adding the milk or water to make a dough.

3 Lightly knead the dough until smooth and not sticky when a finger is pushed into it, adding more flour if necessary. Leave in a warm place for 15 minutes, then roll out the dough on a floured surface to about a 1cm/½in thickness and cut into 6cm/2½ in rounds.

4 Heat the oil in a heavy saucepan or deep-fat fryer and fry the mandazis for 4–5 minutes, until golden brown, turning frequently in the oil.

Fresh Pineapple with Coconut

This refreshing dessert can also be made with vacuum-packed pineapple. This makes a good substitute, but fresh is best.

INGREDIENTS

Serves 4

1 fresh pineapple, peeled
slivers of fresh coconut
300ml/½ pint/1¼ cups pineapple juice
60ml/4 tbsp coconut liqueur
2.5cm/1in piece stem ginger, plus
    45ml/3 tbsp of the syrup

1 Peel and slice the pineapple, arrange in a serving dish and scatter the coconut slivers on top.

2 Place the pineapple juice and coconut liqueur in a saucepan and heat gently.

3 Thinly slice the stem ginger and add to the pan along with the ginger syrup. Bring just to the boil and then simmer gently until the liquid is slightly reduced and the sauce is fairly thick.

4 Pour the sauce over the pineapple and coconut, leave to cool, then chill before serving.

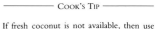

COOK'S TIP

If fresh coconut is not available, then use desiccated coconut instead.

Paw Paw and Mango with Mango Cream

INGREDIENTS

Serves 4

2 large ripe mangoes
300ml/½ pint/1¼ cups extra thick
  double cream
8 dried apricots, halved
150ml/¼ pint/⅔ cup orange juice or
  water
1 ripe paw paw

1 Take one thick slice from one of
  the mangoes and, while still on the
skin, slash the flesh with a sharp knife
in a criss-cross pattern to make cubes.

2 Turn the piece of mango inside-
  out and cut away the cubed flesh
from the skin. Place in a bowl, mash
with a fork to a pulp, then add the
cream and mix together well. Spoon
into a freezer tub and freeze for about
1–1½ hours until half frozen.

3 Meanwhile, put the apricots and
  orange juice or water in a small
saucepan. Bring to the boil, then
simmer gently until the apricots are
soft, adding a little more juice or water
if necessary, so that the apricots remain
moist. Remove from the heat and set
aside to cool.

4 Chop or dice the remaining
  mangoes as above and place in a
bowl. Cut the paw paw in half, remove
the seeds and peel. Dice the flesh and
add to the mango.

5 Pour the apricot sauce over the
  fruit and gently toss together so the
fruit is well coated.

6 Stir the semi-frozen mango cream
  a few times until spoonable but
not soft. Serve the fruit topped with
the mango cream.

COOK'S TIP

Mangoes vary tremendously in size. If you
can only find small ones, buy three instead
of two to use in this dessert.

Tropical Fruit Pancakes

INGREDIENTS

Serves 4

115g/4oz/1 cup self-raising flour
pinch of grated nutmeg
15ml/1 tbsp caster sugar
1 egg
300ml/½ pint/1¼ cups milk
15ml/1 tbsp melted butter or
   margarine, plus extra for frying
15ml/1 tbsp fine desiccated coconut
   (optional)
fresh cream, to serve

For the filling

225g/8oz ripe, firm mango
2 bananas
2 kiwi fruit
1 large orange
15ml/1 tbsp lemon juice
30ml/2 tbsp orange juice
15ml/1 tbsp honey
30–45ml/2–3 tbsp orange liqueur
   (optional)

1 Sift the flour, nutmeg and caster sugar into a large bowl. In a separate bowl, beat the egg lightly, then beat in most of the milk. Add to the flour mixture and beat with a wooden spoon to make a thick, smooth batter.

2 Add the remaining milk, butter and coconut, if using, and continue beating until the batter is smooth and of a fairly thin, dropping consistency.

3 Melt a little butter or margarine in a large non-stick frying pan. Swirl to cover the pan, then pour in a little batter to cover the base of the pan. Fry until golden brown, then toss or turn with a spatula. Repeat with the remaining mixture to make about eight pancakes.

4 Dice the mango, roughly chop the bananas and slice the kiwi fruit. Cut away the peel and pith from the orange and cut into segments.

5 Place the fruit in a bowl. Mix the lemon and orange juices, honey and orange liqueur, if using, then pour over the fruit.

6 Spoon a little fruit down the centre of a pancake and fold over each side. Repeat with the remaining pancakes, then serve with fresh cream.

Spiced Nutty Bananas

Cinnamon and nutmeg are spices which perfectly complement bananas in this delectable dessert.

INGREDIENTS

Serves 3

6 ripe, but firm, bananas
30ml/2 tbsp chopped unsalted cashew nuts
30ml/2 tbsp chopped unsalted peanuts
30ml/2 tbsp desiccated coconut
7.5–15ml/½–1 tbsp demerara sugar
5ml/1 tsp ground cinnamon
2.5ml/½ tsp freshly grated nutmeg
150ml/¼ pint/⅔ cup orange juice
60ml/4 tbsp rum
15g/½ oz/1 tbsp butter or margarine
double cream, to serve

1 Preheat the oven to 200°C/400°F/ Gas 6. Slice the bananas and place in a greased, shallow ovenproof dish.

2 Mix together the cashew nuts, peanuts, coconut, sugar, cinnamon and nutmeg in a small bowl.

3 Pour the orange juice and rum over the bananas, then sprinkle with the nut and sugar mixture.

4 Dot the top with butter or margarine, then bake in the oven for 15–20 minutes or until the bananas are golden and the sauce is bubbly. Serve with double cream.

COOK'S TIP

Freshly grated nutmeg makes all the difference to this dish. More rum can be added if preferred. Chopped mixed nuts can be used instead of peanuts.

Banana and Melon in Orange Vanilla Sauce

Most large supermarkets and health food shops sell vanilla pods. If vanilla pods are hard to find, use a few drops of natural vanilla essence instead.

INGREDIENTS

Serves 4

300ml/¹/₂ pint/1¹/₄ cups orange juice
1 vanilla pod or a few drops vanilla
  essence
5ml/1 tsp grated orange rind
15ml/1 tbsp sugar
4 bananas
1 honeydew melon
30ml/2 tbsp lemon juice

1 Place the orange juice in a small saucepan with the vanilla pod, orange rind and sugar and gently bring to the boil.

2 Reduce the heat and simmer gently for 15 minutes or until the sauce is syrupy. Remove from the heat and leave to cool. If using vanilla essence, stir into the sauce once it has cooled.

3 Roughly chop the bananas and melon, place in a large serving bowl and toss with the lemon juice.

4 Pour the cooled sauce over the fruit and chill before serving.

Banana Mandazi

INGREDIENTS

Serves 4

1 egg
2 ripe bananas, roughly chopped
150ml/¹/₄ pint/²/₃ cup milk
2.5ml/¹/₂ tsp vanilla essence
225g/8oz/2 cups self-raising flour
5ml/1 tsp baking powder
45ml/3 tbsp sugar
vegetable oil, for deep frying

1 Place the egg, bananas, milk, vanilla essence, flour, baking powder and sugar in a blender or food processor.

2 Process to make a smooth batter. It should have a creamy dropping consistency. If it is too thick, add a little extra milk. Set aside for 10 minutes.

3 Heat the oil in a heavy saucepan or deep-fat fryer. When hot, carefully place spoonfuls of the mixture in the oil and fry for 3–4 minutes until golden. Remove with a slotted spoon and drain on kitchen paper. Keep warm while cooking the remaining mandazis, then serve at once.

CHINA

Wonton Soup

In China, wonton soup is served as a snack or dim sum rather than as a soup course during a large meal.

INGREDIENTS

Serves 4

175g/6oz pork, not too lean,
   roughly chopped
50g/2oz peeled prawns, finely minced
5ml/1tsp light brown sugar
15ml/1 tbsp Chinese rice wine or
   dry sherry
15ml/1 tbsp light soy sauce
5ml/1 tsp finely chopped spring onions
5ml/1 tsp finely chopped root ginger
24 ready-made wonton skins
about 750ml/1¼ pints/3 cups stock
15ml/1 tbsp light soy sauce
finely chopped spring onions,
   to garnish

1 In a bowl, mix the chopped pork and minced prawns with the sugar, rice wine or sherry, soy sauce, spring onions and chopped ginger root. Blend well and set aside for 25–30 minutes for the flavours to blend.

2 Place about 5ml/1 tsp of the filling at the centre of each wonton skin.

3 Wet the edges of each wonton with a little water and press them together with your fingers to seal, then fold each wonton over.

4 To cook, bring the stock to a rolling boil in a wok, add the wontons and cook for 4–5 minutes. Transfer to individual soup bowls, season with the soy sauce and garnish with the spring onions. Serve.

Hot-and-sour Soup

This must surely be the best-known and all-time favourite soup in Chinese restaurants and take-aways throughout the world. It is fairly simple to make once you have got all the necessary ingredients together.

INGREDIENTS

Serves 4

4–6 dried Chinese mushrooms, soaked
 in warm water
115g/4oz pork or chicken
1 packet tofu
50g/2oz sliced bamboo shoots, drained
600ml/1pint/2½ cups stock
15ml/1 tbsp Chinese rice wine or
 dry sherry
15ml/1 tbsp light soy sauce
15ml/1 tbsp rice vinegar
salt and ground white pepper
15ml/1 tbsp cornflour paste

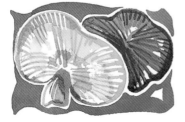

1 Squeeze the soaked mushrooms dry, then discard the hard stalks. Thinly shred the mushrooms, meat, tofu and bamboo shoots.

2 Bring the stock to a rolling boil in a wok and add the shredded ingredients. Bring back to the boil and simmer for about 1 minute.

3 Add the wine or sherry, soy sauce and vinegar and season. Bring back to the boil, then add the cornflour paste, stir until thickened and serve.

Crab Spring Rolls and Dipping Sauce

Chilli and grated ginger add a
hint of heat to these sensational
treats. Serve them as a starter or
with other Chinese dishes as part
of a main course.

INGREDIENTS

Serves 4–6
15ml/1 tbsp groundnut oil
5ml/1 tsp sesame oil
1 garlic clove, crushed
1 fresh red chilli, seeded and finely
    sliced
450g/1lb fresh stir-fry vegetables, such
    as beansprouts and shredded carrots,
    peppers and mangetouts
30ml/2 tbsp chopped coriander
2.5cm/1in piece of fresh root ginger,
    grated
15ml/1 tbsp Chinese rice wine or
    dry sherry
15ml/1 tbsp soy sauce
350g/12oz fresh dressed crab meat
    (brown and white meat)
12 spring roll wrappers
1 small egg, beaten
oil, for deep-frying
salt and ground black pepper
lime wedges and fresh coriander, to
    garnish

For the dipping sauce
1 onion, thinly sliced
oil, for deep-frying
1 fresh red chilli, seeded and finely
    chopped
2 garlic cloves, crushed
60ml/4 tbsp dark soy sauce
20ml/4 tsp lemon juice or
    15–25ml/1–1½ tbsp prepared
    tamarind juice
30ml/2 tbsp hot water

1 First make the sauce. Spread the
onion out on kitchen paper and
leave to dry for 30 minutes. Then half-
fill a wok with oil and heat to
190°C/375°F. Fry the onion in batches
until crisp and golden, turning all the
time. Drain on kitchen paper.

2 Mix together the chilli, garlic, soy
sauce, lemon or tamarind juice and
hot water in a bowl.

3 Stir in the onion and leave to stand
for 30 minutes.

4 Heat the groundnut and sesame
oils in a clean, preheated wok.
When hot, stir-fry the crushed garlic
and chilli for 1 minute. Add the
vegetables, coriander and ginger and
stir-fry for 1 minute more. Drizzle over
the rice wine or dry sherry and soy
sauce. Allow the mixture to bubble up
for 1 minute.

5 Using a slotted spoon, transfer the
vegetables to a bowl. Set aside until
cool, then stir in the crab meat and
season with salt and pepper.

6 Soften the spring roll wrappers,
following the directions on the
packet. Place some of the filling on a
wrapper, fold over the front edge and
the sides and roll up neatly, sealing
the edges with a little beaten egg.
Repeat with the remaining wrappers
and filling.

7 Heat the oil for deep-frying in the
wok and fry the spring rolls in
batches, turning several times, until
brown and crisp. Remove with a
slotted spoon, drain on kitchen paper
and keep hot while frying the
remainder. Serve at once, garnished
with lime wedges and coriander, with
the dipping sauce.

Dim Sum

Popular as a snack in China, these tiny dumplings are fast becoming fashionable in many fast-food, as well as specialist, restaurants in the West.

INGREDIENTS

Serves 4
For the dough
150g/5oz/1¼ cups plain flour
50ml/2fl oz/¼ cup boiling water
25ml/1½ tbsp cold water
7.5ml/½ tbsp vegetable oil

For the filling
75g/3oz minced pork
45ml/3 tbsp canned chopped
    bamboo shoots
7.5ml/½ tbsp light soy sauce
5ml/1 tsp dry sherry
5ml/1 tsp demerara sugar
2.5ml/½ tsp sesame oil
5ml/1 tsp cornflour
lettuce leaves such as iceberg, frisée or
    Webbs, soy sauce, spring onion curls,
    sliced fresh red chilli and prawn
    crackers, to serve

1 To make the dough, sift the flour into a bowl. Stir in the boiling water, then the cold water together with the oil. Mix to form a dough and knead until smooth.

2 Divide the mixture into 16 equal pieces and shape into circles.

3 For the filling, mix together the pork, bamboo shoots, soy sauce, dry sherry, sugar and oil.

4 Add the cornflour and stir well until thoroughly combined.

5 Place a little of the filling in the centre of each dim sum circle. Pinch the edges of the dough together to form little "purses".

6 Line a steamer with a damp tea towel. Place the dim sum in the steamer and steam for 5–10 minutes. Arrange the lettuce leaves on four individual serving plates, top with the dim sum and serve with soy sauce, spring onion curls, sliced red chilli and prawn crackers.

VARIATION

You can replace the pork with cooked, peeled prawns. Sprinkle 15ml/1 tbsp sesame seeds on to the dim sum before cooking, if wished.

Pork Dumplings

These dumplings, when shallow fried, make a good starter to a multi-course meal. They can also be steamed and served as a snack or poached in large quantities for a complete meal.

INGREDIENTS

Makes about 80–90
450g/1lb plain flour
about 475ml/16fl oz/2 cups water
flour, for dusting
salt

For the filling

450g/1lb Chinese leaves or
   white cabbage
450g/1lb minced pork
15ml/1 tbsp finely chopped
   spring onions
5ml/1 tsp finely chopped fresh
   root ginger
10ml/2 tsp salt
5ml/1 tsp light brown sugar
30ml/2 tbsp light soy sauce
15ml/1 tbsp Chinese rice wine or
   dry sherry
10ml/2 tsp sesame oil

For the dipping sauce

30ml/2 tbsp red chilli oil
15ml/1 tbsp light soy sauce
15ml/1 tbsp finely chopped garlic
15ml/1 tbsp finely chopped
   spring onions

1 Sift the flour into a bowl, then pour in the water and mix to a firm dough. Knead until smooth on a lightly floured surface, then cover with a damp cloth and set aside for 25–30 minutes.

2 For the filling, blanch the Chinese leaves or cabbage until soft. Drain and chop finely. Mix the cabbage with the pork, spring onions, ginger, salt, sugar, soy sauce, wine and sesame oil.

3 Lightly dust a work surface with the flour. Knead and roll the dough into a long sausage about 2.5cm/1in in diameter. Cut the sausage in about 80–90 small pieces and flatten each piece with the palm of your hand.

4 Using a rolling pin, roll out each piece into a thin pancake about 6cm/2½in in diameter.

5 Place about 25ml/1½ tbsp of the filling in the centre of each pancake and fold into a half-moon pouch.

6 Pinch the edges firmly so that the dumpling is tightly sealed.

7 Bring 150ml/¼ pint/⅔ cup salted water to the boil in a wok. Add the dumplings and poach for 2 minutes. Remove the wok from the heat and leave the dumplings in the water for a further 15 minutes.

8 Make the dipping sauce by combining all the sauce ingredients in a bowl and mixing well. Serve in a small bowl with the dumplings.

Deep-fried Ribs with Spicy Salt and Pepper

INGREDIENTS

Serves 4–6

10–12 finger ribs, about 675g/1½lb,
  with excess fat and gristle trimmed
about 30–45ml/2–3 tbsp flour
vegetable oil, for deep frying

For the marinade

1 clove garlic, crushed and
  finely chopped
15ml/1 tbsp light brown sugar
15ml/1 tbsp light soy sauce
15ml/1 tbsp dark soy sauce
30ml/2 tbsp Chinese rice wine or
  dry sherry
2.5ml/½ tsp chilli sauce
few drops sesame oil

For the spicy salt and pepper

15ml/1 tbsp salt
10ml/2 tsp ground Szechuan
  peppercorns
5ml/1 tsp five-spice powder

1 Chop each rib into three or four pieces, then mix with all the marinade ingredients and marinate for at least 2–3 hours.

COOK'S TIP

Ideally, each sparerib should be chopped into three or four bite-sized pieces before or after deep frying in a wok. If this is not possible, then serve the ribs whole.

2 Coat the ribs with flour and deep fry in medium-hot oil for 4–5 minutes, stirring to separate. Remove from the oil and drain.

3 Heat the oil to high and deep fry the ribs once more for about 1 minute, or until the colour is an even dark brown. Remove and drain.

4 To make the spicy salt and pepper, heat all the ingredients in a preheated dry wok for about 2 minutes over a low heat, stirring constantly. Serve with the ribs.

Deep-fried Squid with Spicy Salt and Pepper

This recipe is one of the specialities of the Cantonese school of cuisine. Southern China is famous for its seafood, often flavoured with ginger.

INGREDIENTS

Serves 4

450g/1lb squid
5ml/1 tsp ginger juice, see
  Cook's Tip
15ml/1 tbsp Chinese rice wine or
  dry sherry
about 575ml/1 pint/2¹/₂ cups
  boiling water
vegetable oil, for deep frying
spicy salt and pepper
fresh coriander leaves, to garnish

1 Clean the squid by discarding the head and the transparent backbone as well as the ink bag; peel off and discard the thin skin, then wash the squid and dry well on kitchen paper. Open up the squid and, using a sharp knife, score the inside of the flesh in a criss-cross pattern.

2 Cut the squid into pieces, each about the size of a postage stamp. Marinate in a bowl with the ginger juice and rice wine or sherry for 25–30 minutes.

3 Blanch the squid in boiling water for a few seconds – each piece will curl up and the criss-cross pattern will open out to resemble ears of corn. Remove and drain. Dry well.

4 Heat sufficient oil for deep frying in a wok. Deep fry the squid for 15–20 seconds only, remove quickly and drain. Sprinkle with the spicy salt and pepper and serve garnished with fresh coriander leaves.

----- COOK'S TIP -----

To make ginger juice, mix finely chopped or grated fresh root ginger with an equal quantity of cold water and place in a piece of damp muslin. Twist tightly to extract the juice. Alternatively, crush the ginger in a garlic press.

Crispy "Seaweed"

Surprisingly, the very popular and rather exotic-sounding "seaweed" served in Chinese restaurants is, in fact, just ordinary spring greens.

INGREDIENTS

Serves 4
450g/1lb spring greens
vegetable oil, for deep frying
2.5ml/¹/₂ tsp salt
5ml/1 tsp caster sugar
15ml/1 tbsp ground fried fish, to garnish (optional)

1 Cut off the hard stalks in the centre of each spring green leaf. Pile the leaves on top of each other, and roll into a tight sausage shape. Thinly cut the leaves into fine shreds. Spread them out to dry.

2 Heat the oil in a wok until hot. Deep fry the shredded greens in batches, stirring to separate them.

3 Remove the greens with a slotted spoon as soon as they are crispy, but before they turn brown. Drain. Sprinkle the salt and sugar evenly all over the "seaweed", mix well, garnish with ground fish, if liked, and serve.

Sesame Seed Prawn Toasts

Use uncooked prawns for this dish, as ready-cooked ones will tend to separate from the bread during cooking.

INGREDIENTS

Serves 4
225g/8oz uncooked prawns, peeled
25g/1oz lard
1 egg white, lightly beaten
5ml/1 tsp finely chopped spring onions
2.5ml/¹/₂ tsp finely chopped root ginger
15ml/1 tbsp Chinese rice wine or dry sherry
15ml/1 tbsp cornflour paste
115–150g/4–5oz/white sesame seeds
6 large slices white bread
vegetable oil, for deep frying
salt and ground black pepper

1 Chop together the prawns with the lard to form a smooth paste. In a bowl, mix with all the other ingredients except the sesame seeds and bread.

2 Spread the sesame seeds evenly on a large plate or tray; spread the prawn paste thickly on one side of each slice of bread, then press, spread side down, on to the seeds.

3 Heat the oil in a wok until medium-hot; fry 2–3 slices of the sesame bread at a time, spread side down, for 2–3 minutes. Remove and drain. Cut each slice into six or eight fingers (without crusts).

Chinese Sweet-and-sour Pork

Sweet-and-sour pork must be one of the most popular dishes served in Chinese restaurants and take-aways in the Western world. Unfortunately, it is often spoiled by cooks who use too much tomato ketchup in the sauce. Here is a classic recipe from Canton, the city of its origin.

INGREDIENTS

Serves 4

350g/12oz lean pork
1.5ml/¼ tsp salt
2.5ml/½ tsp ground Szechuan
   peppercorns
15ml/1 tbsp Chinese rice wine or
   dry sherry
115g/4oz bamboo shoots
30ml/2 tbsp plain flour
1 egg, lightly beaten
vegetable oil, for deep-frying

For the sauce

15ml/1 tbsp vegetable oil
1 garlic clove, finely chopped
1 spring onion, cut into short sections
1 small green pepper, seeded and diced
1 fresh red chilli, seeded and thinly
   shredded
15ml/1 tbsp light soy sauce
30ml/2 tbsp light brown sugar
30–45ml/2–3 tbsp rice vinegar
15ml/1 tbsp tomato purée
about 120ml/4fl oz/½ cup Basic Stock
   or water

1 Cut the pork into small bite-sized cubes and place in a shallow dish. Add the salt, peppercorns and rice wine or dry sherry and set aside to marinate for 15–20 minutes.

2 Drain the bamboo shoots, if canned, and cut them into small cubes the same size as the pork.

3 Dust the pork with flour, dip in the beaten egg and coat with more flour. Heat the oil in a preheated wok and deep-fry the pork in moderately hot oil for 3–4 minutes, stirring to separate the pieces. Remove and drain.

4 Reheat the oil until hot, return the pork to the wok and add the bamboo shoots. Fry for about 1 minute, or until the pork is golden. Remove and drain well.

5 To make the sauce, heat the oil in a clean wok or frying pan and add the garlic, spring onion, green pepper and red chilli. Stir-fry for 30–40 seconds, then add the soy sauce, sugar, rice vinegar, tomato purée and stock or water. Bring to the boil, then add the pork and bamboo shoots. Heat through and stir to mix, then serve.

Pork Chow Mein

A perfect, speedy meal, this family favourite is flavoured with sesame oil for an authentic oriental taste.

INGREDIENTS

Serves 4

175g/6oz medium egg noodles
350g/12oz pork fillet
30ml/2 tbsp sunflower oil
15ml/1 tbsp sesame oil
2 garlic cloves, crushed
8 spring onions, sliced
1 red pepper, seeded and roughly
    chopped
1 green pepper, seeded and roughly
    chopped
30ml/2 tbsp dark soy sauce
45ml/3 tbsp Chinese rice wine or
    dry sherry
175g/6oz beansprouts
45ml/3 tbsp chopped fresh flat-leaf
    parsley
15ml/1 tbsp toasted sesame seeds

1 Soak the noodles according to the packet instructions. Drain well.

2 Thinly slice the pork fillet. Heat the sunflower oil in a preheated wok or large frying pan and cook the pork over a high heat until golden brown and cooked through.

3 Add the sesame oil to the wok or frying pan, with the garlic, spring onions and peppers. Cook over a high heat for 3–4 minutes, or until the vegetables are beginning to soften.

4 Reduce the heat slightly and stir in the noodles, with the soy sauce and rice wine or dry sherry. Stir-fry for 2 minutes. Add the beansprouts and cook for a further 1–2 minutes. If the noodles begin to stick, add a splash of water. Stir in the parsley and serve sprinkled with the sesame seeds.

Peking Beef and Pepper Stir-fry

This quick and easy stir-fry is perfect for today's busy cook and tastes superb.

INGREDIENTS

Serves 4

350g/12oz rump or sirloin steak, sliced
    into strips
30ml/2 tbsp soy sauce
30ml/2 tbsp medium sherry
15ml/1 tbsp cornflour
5ml/1 tsp brown sugar
15ml/1 tbsp sunflower oil
15ml/1 tbsp sesame oil
1 garlic clove, finely chopped
15ml/1 tbsp grated fresh root ginger
1 red pepper, seeded and sliced
1 yellow pepper, seeded and sliced
115g/4oz sugar snap peas
4 spring onions, cut into 5cm/2in
    lengths
30ml/2 tbsp oyster sauce
60ml/4 tbsp water
cooked noodles, to serve

1 In a bowl, mix together the steak strips, soy sauce, sherry, cornflour and brown sugar. Cover and leave to marinate for 30 minutes.

2 Heat the sunflower and sesame oils in a preheated wok or large frying pan. Add the garlic and ginger and stir-fry for about 30 seconds. Add the peppers, sugar snap peas and spring onions and stir-fry for 3 minutes.

3 Add the beef, together with the marinade juices, to the wok or frying pan and stir-fry for a further 3–4 minutes. Pour in the oyster sauce and water and stir until the sauce has thickened slightly. Serve immediately with cooked noodles.

Stir-fried Beef and Broccoli

This spicy beef may be served with noodles or on a bed of boiled rice for a speedy and low-calorie Chinese meal.

INGREDIENTS

Serves 4

350g/12oz rump steak
15ml/1 tbsp cornflour
5ml/1 tsp sesame oil
350g/12oz broccoli, cut into small florets
4 spring onions, sliced diagonally
1 carrot, cut into matchstick strips
1 garlic clove, crushed
2.5cm/1in fresh root ginger, cut into very fine strips
120ml/4fl oz/½ cup beef stock
30ml/2 tbsp soy sauce
30ml/2 tbsp dry sherry
10ml/2 tsp soft light brown sugar
spring onion tassels, to garnish (optional)
noodles or rice, to serve

1 Trim the beef and cut into thin slices across the grain. Cut each slice into thin strips. Toss in the cornflour to coat thoroughly.

2 Heat the sesame oil in a preheated wok or large non-stick frying pan. Add the beef strips and stir-fry over a brisk heat for 3 minutes. Remove and set aside.

3 Add the broccoli, spring onions, carrot, garlic, ginger and stock to the wok or frying pan. Cover and simmer for 3 minutes. Uncover and cook, stirring, until all the stock has reduced entirely.

4 Mix the soy sauce, dry sherry and brown sugar together and add to the wok or frying pan with the beef. Cook for 2–3 minutes, stirring continuously. Spoon into a warmed serving dish and garnish with spring onion tassels, if liked. Serve on a bed of noodles or rice.

COOK'S TIP

To make spring onion tassels, trim the bulb base, then cut the green shoot so that the onion is 7.5cm/3in long. Shred to within 2.5cm/1in of the base and put into iced water for 1 hour.

Stir-fried Lamb with Spring Onions

This is a classic Beijing "meat and veg" recipe, in which the lamb can be replaced with either beef or pork, and the spring onions by other strongly flavoured vegetables, such as leeks or onions.

INGREDIENTS

Serves 4

350–400g/12–14oz leg of lamb fillet
5ml/1 tsp light brown sugar
15ml/1 tbsp light soy sauce
15ml/1 tbsp Chinese rice wine or
　dry sherry
10ml/2 tsp cornflour paste
15g/½oz dried wood ears
300ml/½ pint/1¼ cups vegetable oil
6–8 spring onions
few small pieces of fresh root ginger
30ml/2 tbsp yellow bean sauce
few drops of sesame oil

1 Slice the lamb thinly and place in a shallow dish. Mix together the sugar, soy sauce, rice wine or dry sherry and cornflour paste, pour over the lamb and set aside to marinate for 30–45 minutes. Soak the wood ears in water for 25–30 minutes, then drain and cut into small pieces. Finely chop the spring onions.

2 Heat the oil in a preheated wok and stir-fry the lamb for about 1 minute, or until the colour changes. Remove with a slotted spoon, drain and set aside.

3 Pour off all but about 15ml/1 tbsp oil from the wok, then add the spring onions, ginger, wood ears and yellow bean sauce. Blend well, then add the meat and stir for about 1 minute. Sprinkle with the sesame oil and serve.

Szechuan Chicken

A wok is the ideal cooking pot for this stir-fried chicken dish. The flavours emerge wonderfully and the chicken is fresh and crisp.

INGREDIENTS

Serves 4

350g/12oz chicken thigh, boned
  and skinned
1.5ml/¼ tsp salt
½ egg white, lightly beaten
10ml/2 tsp cornflour paste
1 green pepper, cored and seeded
60ml/4 tbsp vegetable oil
3–4 whole dried red chillies, soaked in
  water for 10 minutes
1 spring onion, cut into short sections
few small pieces of fresh root
  ginger, peeled
15ml/1 tbsp sweet bean paste or hoi-
  sin sauce
5ml/1 tsp chilli bean paste
15ml/1 tbsp Chinese rice wine or
  dry sherry
115g/4oz roasted cashew nuts
few drops sesame oil

1 Cut the chicken meat into small cubes, each about the size of a sugar lump. Mix together the chicken, salt, egg white and cornflour paste in a bowl.

2 Cut the green pepper into cubes about the same size as the chicken.

3 Heat the oil in a preheated wok. Stir-fry the chicken cubes for about 1 minute, or until the colour changes. Remove from the wok with a slotted spoon and keep warm.

4 Add the green pepper, chillies, spring onion and ginger and stir-fry for about 1 minute. Then add the chicken, sweet bean paste or hoi-sin sauce, chilli bean paste and rice wine or sherry. Blend well and cook for 1 minute more. Finally add the cashew nuts and sesame oil. Serve hot.

Peking Duck

This has to be the *pièce de résistance* of any Chinese banquet. It is not too difficult to prepare and cook at home – the secret is to use duckling with a low-fat content. Also, make sure that the skin of the duck is absolutely dry before you start to cook – the drier the skin, the crispier the duck.

INGREDIENTS

Serves 6–8

2.25kg/5–5¼lb oven-ready duckling
30ml/2 tbsp maltose or honey, dissolved in 150ml/¼ pint/⅔ cup warm water

For the duck sauce

30ml/2 tbsp sesame oil
90–120ml/6–8 tbsp yellow bean sauce, crushed
30–45ml/2–3 tbsp light brown sugar

To serve

20–24 thin pancakes
6–8 spring onions, thinly shredded
½ cucumber, thinly shredded

COOK'S TIP

If preferred, serve Peking Duck with plum sauce in place of the duck sauce. Plum sauce is available from oriental stores and larger supermarkets. Duck sauce can also be bought ready-prepared.

1 Remove any feather studs and any lumps of fat from inside the vent of the duck. Plunge the duck into a saucepan of boiling water for 2–3 minutes to seal the pores. This will make the skin airtight, thus preventing the fat from escaping during cooking. Remove and drain well, then dry thoroughly.

2 Brush the duck all over with the dissolved maltose or honey, then hang the bird up in a cool place for at least 4–5 hours.

3 Place the duck, breast side up, on a rack in a roasting tin and cook in a preheated oven at 200°C/400°F/Gas 6 for 1½–1¾ hours without either basting or turning.

4 Meanwhile, make the duck sauce. Heat the sesame oil in a small saucepan. Add the crushed yellow bean sauce and the light brown sugar. Stir until smooth and allow to cool.

5 To serve, peel off the crispy duck skin in small slices using a sharp carving knife or cleaver, then carve the juicy meat in thin strips. Arrange the skin and meat on separate serving plates.

6 Open a pancake on each plate, spread about 5ml/1 tsp of the chosen sauce in the middle, with a few strips of shredded spring onions and cucumber. Top with 2–3 slices each of duck skin and meat. Roll up and eat.

Special Chow Mein

Lap cheong is a special air-dried Chinese sausage. It is available from most Chinese supermarkets. If you cannot buy it, substitute with either diced ham, chorizo or salami.

INGREDIENTS

Serves 4–6
45ml/3 tbsp vegetable oil
2 garlic cloves, sliced
5ml/1 tsp chopped fresh root ginger
2 red chillies, chopped
2 lap cheong, about 75g/3oz, rinsed
    and sliced (optional)
1 boneless chicken breast, thinly sliced
16 uncooked tiger prawns, peeled, tails
    left intact, and deveined
115g/4oz green beans
225g/8oz beansprouts
50g/2oz garlic chives
450g/1lb egg noodles, cooked in
    boiling water until tender
30ml/2 tbsp soy sauce
15ml/1 tbsp oyster sauce
salt and freshly ground black pepper
15ml/1 tbsp sesame oil
2 spring onions, shredded, to garnish
15ml/1 tbsp coriander leaves,
    to garnish

2 Heat the rest of the oil in the same wok. Add the beansprouts and garlic chives. Stir fry for 1–2 minutes.

4 Return the prawn mixture to the wok. Reheat and mix well with the noodles. Stir in the sesame oil. Serve garnished with spring onions and coriander leaves.

1 Heat 15ml/1 tbsp of the oil in a wok or large frying pan and fry the garlic, ginger and chillies. Add the lap cheong, chicken, prawns and beans. Stir-fry for about 2 minutes over a high heat or until the chicken and prawns are cooked. Transfer the mixture to a bowl and set aside.

3 Add the noodles and toss and stir to mix. Season with soy sauce, oyster sauce, salt and pepper.

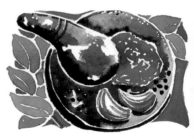

Egg Foo Yung

A great way of turning a bowl of leftover cooked rice into a meal for four, this dish is tasty and full of texture.

INGREDIENTS

Serves 4
3 eggs, beaten
pinch of Chinese five-spice
    powder (optional)
45ml/3 tbsp groundnut or
    sunflower oil
4 spring onions, sliced
1 garlic clove, crushed
1 small green pepper, seeded and
    chopped
115g/4oz beansprouts
225g/8oz/generous 1 cup white
    rice, cooked
45ml/3 tbsp light soy sauce
15ml/1 tbsp sesame oil
salt and ground black pepper

1 Season the eggs with salt and pepper to taste and beat in the five-spice powder, if using.

2 Heat 15ml/1 tbsp of the oil in a preheated wok or large frying pan and, when quite hot, pour in the egg. Cook rather like an omelette, pulling the mixture away from the sides and allowing the rest to slip underneath.

3 Cook the egg until firm, then tip out. Chop the omelette into small strips and set aside.

4 Heat the remaining oil and stir-fry the onions, garlic, green pepper and beansprouts for about 2 minutes, stirring and tossing continuously.

5 Mix in the cooked rice and heat thoroughly, stirring well. Add the soy sauce and sesame oil, then return the egg strips and mix in well. Serve immediately, piping hot.

Noodles in Soup

In China, noodles in soup are far more popular than fried noodles. This is a basic recipe which you can adapt by using different ingredients.

INGREDIENTS

Serves 4

225g/8oz chicken or pork fillet
3–4 dried Chinese mushrooms, soaked
115g/4oz can sliced bamboo shoots, drained
115g/4oz spinach leaves, lettuce hearts or Chinese leaves
2 spring onions
375g/12oz dried egg noodles
600ml/1 pint/2½ cups Basic Stock
30ml/2 tbsp vegetable oil
5ml/1 tsp salt
2.5ml/½ tsp light brown sugar
15ml/1 tbsp light soy sauce
10ml/2 tsp Chinese rice wine or dry sherry
few drops of sesame oil

1 Thinly shred the meat. Squeeze dry the mushrooms and discard any hard stalks. Thinly shred the mushroom caps, bamboo shoots, spinach, lettuce hearts or Chinese leaves and the spring onions. Keep the meat, the spring onions and the other ingredients in three heaps.

2 Cook the noodles in boiling water according to the instructions on the packet, then drain and rinse in cold water. Place in a serving bowl.

3 Bring the stock to the boil and pour over the noodles. Keep warm.

4 Heat the oil in a preheated wok, add the spring onions and the meat and stir-fry for about 1 minute.

5 Add the mushrooms, bamboo shoots and spinach, lettuce or Chinese leaves and stir-fry for 1 minute or until the meat is cooked through. Add the salt, sugar, soy sauce, rice wine or dry sherry and sesame oil and blend well.

6 Pour the "dressing" over the noodles and serve.

Red-cooked Tofu with Chinese Mushrooms

Red-cooked is a term applied to Chinese dishes cooked with a dark soy sauce. This tasty dish can be served as either a side dish or main meal.

INGREDIENTS

Serves 4

225g/8oz firm tofu
45ml/3 tbsp dark soy sauce
30ml/2 tbsp Chinese rice wine or dry sherry
10ml/2 tsp soft dark brown sugar
1 garlic clove, crushed
15ml/1 tbsp grated fresh root ginger
2.5ml/½ tsp Chinese five-spice powder
pinch of ground roasted Szechuan peppercorns
6 dried Chinese black mushrooms
5ml/1 tsp cornflour
30ml/2 tbsp groundnut oil
5–6 spring onions, sliced into 2.5cm/1in lengths, white and green parts separated
small fresh basil leaves, to garnish
rice noodles, to serve

1 Drain the tofu, pat dry with kitchen paper and cut into 2.5cm/1in cubes. Place in a shallow dish. In a small bowl, mix together the soy sauce, rice wine or sherry, sugar, garlic, ginger, five-spice powder and Szechuan peppercorns. Pour the marinade over the tofu, toss well and leave to marinate for about 30 minutes. Drain, reserving the marinade.

2 Meanwhile soak the dried black mushrooms in warm water for 20–30 minutes until soft. Drain, reserving 90ml/6 tbsp of the soaking liquid. Squeeze out any excess liquid from the mushrooms, remove the tough stalks and slice the caps. In a small bowl, blend the cornflour with the reserved marinade and mushroom soaking liquid.

3 Heat a wok until hot, add the oil and swirl it around. Add the tofu and stir-fry for 2–3 minutes until evenly golden. Remove from the wok and set aside.

4 Add the mushrooms and white parts of the spring onions to the wok and stir-fry for 2 minutes. Pour in the marinade mixture and stir for 1 minute until thickened.

5 Return the tofu to the wok with the green parts of the spring onions. Simmer gently for 1–2 minutes. Scatter over the basil leaves and serve at once with rice noodles.

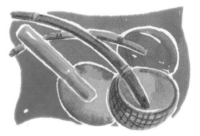

Braised Chinese Vegetables

The original recipe calls for no less than 18 different ingredients to represent the 18 Buddhas (*Lo Han*). Later, this was reduced to eight, but nowadays anything between four and six items is regarded as quite sufficient to put in a wok.

INGREDIENTS

Serves 4

10g/¼oz dried Chinese mushrooms
75g/3oz straw mushrooms
75g/3oz sliced bamboo shoots, drained
50g/2oz mangetouts
1 packet tofu
175g/6oz Chinese leaves
45–60ml/3–4 tbsp vegetable oil
5ml/1 tsp salt
2.5ml/½ tsp light brown sugar
15ml/1 tbsp light soy sauce
few drops sesame oil

1 Soak the Chinese mushrooms in cold water for 20–25 minutes, then rinse and discard the hard stalks, if any. Cut the straw mushrooms in half lengthways, if they are large, keep them whole, if they are small. Rinse and drain the bamboo shoot slices. Top and tail the mangetouts. Cut the tofu into about 12 small pieces. Cut the Chinese leaves into small pieces about the same size as the mangetouts.

2 Harden the tofu pieces by placing them in a wok of boiling water for about 2 minutes. Remove and drain.

3 Discard the water and heat the oil in the wok. a saucepan or a flameproof casserole. Lightly brown the tofu pieces on both sides. Remove with a slotted spoon and keep warm.

4 Stir-fry all the vegetables in the wok or pan for about 1½ minutes, then add the tofu, salt, sugar and soy sauce. Continue stirring for 1 minute, then cover and braise for 2–3 minutes. Sprinkle with sesame oil and serve.

Aubergine in Spicy Sauce

Aubergines are given a royal treatment in this recipe, where they are stir-fried with seasonings more commonly associated with fish cooking.

INGREDIENTS

Serves 4
450g/1lb aubergines
3–4 whole dried red chillies, soaked in water for 10 minutes
vegetable oil, for deep frying
1 clove garlic, finely chopped
5ml/1 tsp finely chopped fresh ginger
5ml/1 tsp finely chopped spring onion, white part only
115g/4oz lean pork, thinly shredded (optional)
15ml/1 tbsp light soy sauce
15ml/1 tbsp light brown sugar
15ml/1 tbsp chilli bean sauce
15ml/1 tbsp Chinese rice wine or dry sherry
15ml/1 tbsp rice vinegar
10ml/2 tsp cornflour paste, see page 30
5ml/1 tsp finely chopped spring onions, green part only, to garnish
few drops sesame oil

1 Cut the aubergines into short strips the size of chips – the skin can either be peeled off or left on, whichever you prefer. Cut the soaked red chillies into two or three small pieces and discard the seeds.

2 Heat the oil in a preheated wok and deep fry the aubergine chips for about 3–4 minutes or until limp. Remove and drain.

3 Pour off the excess oil, leaving about 15ml/1 tbsp in the wok. Add the garlic, ginger, white spring onions and chillies, stir a few times, then add the pork, if using. Stir-fry the meat for about 1 minute or until it becomes pale, almost white, in colour. Add all the seasonings, then increase the heat and bring the mixture to the boil.

4 Add the aubergines to the wok, blend well and braise for 30–40 seconds, then thicken the sauce with the cornflour paste, stirring until smooth. Garnish with the green spring onions and sprinkle with sesame oil.

--- COOK'S TIP ---

Soaking dried chillies in water will reduce their spicy flavour. If you prefer a milder chilli taste, soak for longer than the recommended 10 minutes.

Thin Pancakes

Thin pancakes are not too difficult to make, but quite a lot of practice and patience are needed to achieve the perfect result. Nowadays, even restaurants buy frozen, ready-made ones from Chinese supermarkets. If you decide to use ready-made pancakes, or are reheating home-made ones, steam them for about 5 minutes, or microwave on high (650 watts) for 1–2 minutes.

INGREDIENTS

Makes 24–30
450g/1lb/4 cups plain flour, plus extra for dusting
about 300ml/½ pint/1¼ cups boiling water
5ml/1 tsp vegetable oil

1 Sift the flour into a mixing bowl, then pour in the boiling water very gently, stirring as you pour. Mix with the oil and knead the mixture into a firm dough. Cover with a damp cloth and let stand for about 30 minutes.

2 Lightly dust a work surface with flour. Knead the dough for about 5–8 minutes, or until smooth, then divide it into 3 equal portions. Roll out each portion into a long "sausage", cut each into 8–10 pieces and roll each into a ball. Using the palm of your hand, press each piece into a flat pancake. With a rolling pin, gently roll each into a 15cm/6in circle.

3 Heat an ungreased frying pan until hot, then reduce the heat to low and place the pancakes, one at a time, in the pan. Remove the pancakes when small brown spots appear on the underside. Keep under a damp cloth until all the pancakes are cooked.

Red Bean Paste Pancakes

If you are unable to find red bean paste, sweetened chestnut purée or mashed dates are possible substitutes.

INGREDIENTS

Serves 4
about 120ml/8 tbsp sweetened red bean paste
8 Thin Pancakes
30–45ml/2–3 tbsp vegetable oil
granulated or caster sugar, to serve

1 Spread about 15ml/1 tbsp of the red bean paste over about three-quarters of each pancake, then roll the pancake over three or four times.

2 Heat the oil in a preheated wok or frying pan and fry the pancake rolls until golden brown, turning once.

3 Cut each pancake roll into three or four pieces and sprinkle with sugar to serve.

Almond Curd Junket

Also known as almond float, this is usually made from agar-agar or isinglass, although gelatine can also be used.

INGREDIENTS

Serves 4–6

10g/¼oz agar-agar or isinglass or
    25g/1oz gelatine powder
about 600ml/1 pint/2½ cups water
60ml/4 tbsp granulated or caster sugar
300ml/½ pint/1¼ cups milk
5ml/1 tsp almond essence
fresh or canned mixed fruit salad with
    syrup, to serve

1 In a saucepan, dissolve the agar-agar or isinglass in about half the water over a gentle heat. This will take at least 10 minutes. If using gelatine, follow the packet instructions.

2 In a separate saucepan, dissolve the sugar in the remaining water over a medium heat. Add the milk and the almond essence, blending well. Do not allow the mixture to boil.

3 Mix the milk and sugar with the agar-agar, isinglass or gelatine mixture in a serving bowl. When cool, place in the refrigerator for 2–3 hours to set.

4 To serve, cut the junket into small cubes and spoon into a serving dish or into individual bowls. Pour the fruit salad, with the syrup, over the junket and serve.

Toffee Apples

A variety of fruits, such as bananas and pineapple, can be prepared and cooked in this way.

INGREDIENTS

Serves 4
4 firm eating apples
115g/4oz plain flour
about 120ml/4fl oz/¹/₂ cup water
1 egg, beaten
vegetable oil, for deep frying, plus
   30ml/2 tbsp for the toffee
115g/4oz sugar

1 Peel and core each apple and cut into eight pieces. Dust each piece of apple with a little of the flour.

2 Sift the remaining flour into a mixing bowl, then slowly add the cold water and stir well to make a smooth batter. Add the beaten egg and blend well.

3 Heat the oil for deep frying in a wok. Dip the apple pieces in the batter and deep fry for about 3 minutes or until golden. Remove and drain. Drain off the oil.

4 Heat the remaining oil in the wok, add the sugar and stir continuously until the sugar has caramelized. Quickly add the apple pieces and blend well so that each piece of apple is thoroughly coated with the toffee. Dip the apple pieces in cold water to harden before serving.

JAPAN

Pork and Vegetable Soup

INGREDIENTS

Serves 4

50g/2oz gobo (optional)
5ml/1 tsp rice vinegar
½ black konnyaku, 125g/4oz
10ml/2 tsp oil
200g/7oz pork belly, cut into thin
  3–4cm/1½–1in long strips
115g/4oz daikon, peeled and
  thinly sliced
50g/2oz carrot, thinly sliced
1 medium potato, thinly sliced
4 shiitake mushrooms, stems removed
  and thinly sliced
800ml/27fl oz/3½ cups kombu and
  bonito stock or instant dashi
15ml/1 tbsp sake or dry white wine
45ml/3 tbsp red or white miso paste

For the garnish

2 scallions, thinly sliced
seven-spice flavouring (shichimi)

1 Scrub the skin off the gobo, if using, with a vegetable brush. Slice the vegetable into fine shavings. Soak the prepared gobo for 5 minutes in plenty of water with the vinegar added to remove any bitter taste, then drain.

2 Put the piece of konnyaku in a small pan and add enough water just to cover it. Bring to the boil over a medium heat, then drain and allow to cool. This removes any bitter taste.

3 Using your hands, tear the konnyaku into 2cm/1in lumps. Do not use a knife, as a smooth cut surface will not absorb any flavour.

4 Heat the oil in a deep saucepan and quickly stir-fry the pork. Add all the gobo, konnyaku, daikon, carrot, potato and shiitake mushrooms, then stir-fry for one minute. Pour in the stock and sake or wine.

5 Bring the soup to the boil, then skim it and simmer for 10 minutes, until the vegetables have softened.

6 Ladle a little of the soup into a small bowl and dissolve the miso paste in it. Pour the mixture back into the saucepan and bring to the boil once more. Do not continue to boil or the flavour will be lost. Remove from the heat, then pour into serving bowls. Sprinkle with the scallions and seven-spice flavouring, and serve immediately.

Fish Ball Soup

Tsumire means, quite literally, sardine balls and these are added to this delicious *Tsumire-jiru* soup to impart their robust fish flavour. This is a warming and nutritious dish for winter.

INGREDIENTS

Serves 4
20g/³/₄oz fresh root ginger
800g/1³/₄lb fresh sardines, gutted and
    heads removed
30ml/2 tbsp white miso paste
15ml/1 tbsp sake or dry white wine
7.5ml/¹/₂ tbsp sugar
1 egg
30ml/2 tbsp cornflour
150g/5oz shimeji mushrooms or 6
    shiitake mushrooms
1 leek or large spring onion

For the soup
100ml/3¹/₂fl oz/generous ¹/₃ cup sake
    or dry white wine
1.2 litres/2 pints/5 cups instant dashi
    (stock)
60ml/4 tbsp white miso paste

1 First make the fish balls. Grate the ginger and squeeze it well to yield 5ml/1 tsp ginger juice.

2 Rinse the sardines under cold running water, then cut in half along the backbone. Remove all the bones. To skin a boned sardine, lay it skin side down on a board, then run a sharp knife slowly along the skin from tail to head.

3 Coarsely chop the sardines and process with the ginger juice, miso, sake or wine, sugar and egg to a thick paste in a food processor or blender. Transfer to a bowl and mix in the cornflour well.

4 Trim the shimeji mushrooms and separate each stem or remove the stems from the shiitake mushrooms and shred them. Cut the leek or spring onion into 4cm/1¹/₂in long strips.

5 Bring the ingredients for the soup to the boil. Use two wet spoons to shape small portions of the sardine mixture into bite-sized balls and drop them into the soup. Add the mushrooms and leeks or spring onions.

6 Simmer until the sardine balls float to the surface. Serve immediately, in four deep bowls.

Rolled Sushi with Mixed Filling

INGREDIENTS

Makes 32 pieces

For the filling

4 large dried shiitake mushrooms
1 small carrot, quartered lengthways
1 chikuwa fish cake or 4 crab sticks, cut
  into strips as for the carrot
¹/₂ cucumber, quartered lengthways,
  seeds removed
4 sheets yaki-nori seaweed, for rolling
soy sauce and gari (ginger pickles),
  to serve

For the seasoning

37.5ml/7¹/₂ tsp soy sauce
15ml/1 tbsp each of mirin, sake or dry
  white wine and sugar

For the Rolled Omelette

2 size 1 eggs
10ml/2 tsp sugar
pinch of salt

For the rice

320g/11¹/₂oz/1¹/₂ cups Japanese rice,
  cooked as for Shaped Sushi, using
  Mixed Vinegar (below)

For the Mixed Vinegar

40ml/8 tsp rice vinegar
22.5ml/4¹/₂ tsp sugar
3ml/²/₃ tsp salt

1 Soak the shiitake in 200ml/
7fl oz/scant 1 cup water for
30 minutes; drain, reserving the stock,
and remove their stems. Pour the stock
into a saucepan, add the seasoning
ingredients and simmer the carrots,
mushrooms and chikuwa or crab sticks
for 4–5 minutes. Remove the carrots
and chikuwa or crab sticks. Simmer the
shiitake until all the liquid has
evaporated, then thinly slice them.
Make the Rolled Omelette.

2 Place a bamboo mat (*makisu*) on a
chopping board. Lay a sheet of
nori, shiny side down, lengthways.

3 Spread a quarter of the prepared,
dressed rice over the nori using
your fingers, leaving a 1cm/¹/₂in space
at the top and bottom.

4 Place a quarter of each of the filling
ingredients across the middle of the
layer of rice.

5 Carefully hold the nearest edge of
the nori and the mat, then roll up
the nori using the mat as a guide to
make a neat tube of rice with the filling
ingredients in the middle. Roll the rice
tightly to ensure that the grains stick
together and to keep the filling in
place. Roll the sushi off the mat and
make three more rolls in the same way.

6 Using a wet knife, cut each roll
into eight pieces and stand them
upright on a platter. Serve soy sauce
and gari with the sushi.

COOK'S TIP

When cutting sushi, use a large cook's
knife and rinse it with cold water. To
prevent the rice from sticking to the
knife, wipe the blade and rinse it under cold
water between cuts - or at least after every
few cuts.

Tofu-wrapped Sushi

This is another popular picnic dish, particularly with children who like its slightly sweet flavour. The tofu should be prepared while the rice is cooking (or beforehand) as the rice has to be warm so that it can be packed into the tofu. Wasabi is not used for this *Inari-sushi*.

INGREDIENTS

Makes 12
6 sheets fried tofu (*aburage*)
200ml/7fl oz/scant 1 cup kombu and
 bonito stock or instant dashi
45ml/3 tbsp sugar
37.5ml/7¹/₂ tsp soy sauce
30ml/2 tbsp sake or dry white wine
30ml/2 tbsp mirin
dash of rice vinegar
gari (ginger pickles), to garnish

For the rice
240g/8¹/₂oz/1¹/₈ cups Japanese rice
15ml/1 tbsp sake

For the sushi vinegar
30ml/2 tbsp rice vinegar
15ml/1 tbsp sugar
2.5ml/¹/₂ tsp salt

1 Lay a sheet of fried tofu on a board. Using a chopstick as a rolling pin, roll the tofu, this will ensure that it opens easily when boiled. Bring a large saucepan of water to the boil and blanch the tofu to remove excess fat, then drain and squeeze it. Cut the sheets of tofu in half widthways, then carefully open out with a knife to make 12 small sacks or pockets.

2 Bring the stock, sugar, soy sauce, sake or wine, mirin and rice vinegar to the boil. Add the tofu, cover with folded foil and simmer until the liquid has virtually evaporated, pressing the foil down occasionally to squeeze the soup from the tofu and prevent the packets from filling. Drain and cool. Heat the ingredients for the sushi vinegar and leave to cool.

3 Cook the rice, replacing 15ml/ 1 tbsp of the measured cooking water with the sake. Add the sushi vinegar to the rice and stir well with a spatula. Divide the warm rice between the tofu and fold the tofu to enclose the rice in neat parcels. Arrange on plates with the folded sides underneath and serve garnished with gari.

Yakitori Chicken

Yakitori are Japanese-style chicken kebabs. They are easy to eat and ideal for barbecues or parties.

INGREDIENTS

Serves 4
6 boneless chicken thighs (with skin)
bunch of spring onions
seven flavour spice (*shichimi*), to serve
(optional)

For the yakitori sauce
150ml/¼ pint/⅔ cup soy sauce
90g/3½oz/½ cup sugar
25ml/5 tsp sake or dry white wine
15ml/1 tbsp plain flour

1 To make the sauce, stir the soy sauce, sugar and sake or wine into the flour in a small saucepan and bring to the boil, stirring. Reduce the heat and simmer for 10 minutes, until the sauce is reduced by one-third. Then set aside.

2 Cut each chicken thigh into six chunks and cut the spring onions into 3cm/1¼in long pieces.

3 Thread the chicken and spring onions alternately on to 12 bamboo skewers. Grill under a medium heat or on the barbecue, brushing generously several times with the sauce. Allow 5–10 minutes, until the chicken is cooked but still moist.

4 Serve with a little extra yakitori sauce, offering seven flavour spice with the kebabs if possible.

Chicken Cakes with Teriyaki Sauce

These small chicken cakes, about the size of small meatballs, are known as *Tsukune*. Here, they are cooked with a glaze and garnished with spring onions.

INGREDIENTS

Serves 4
For the chicken cakes
400g/14oz minced chicken
1 size 4 egg
60ml/4 tbsp grated onion
7.5ml/1½ tsp sugar
7.5ml/1½ tsp soy sauce
cornflour, for coating
15ml/1 tbsp oil
½ bunch spring onions, finely
shredded, to garnish

For the teriyaki sauce
30ml/2 tbsp sake or dry white wine
30ml/2 tbsp sugar
30ml/2 tbsp mirin
30ml/2 tbsp soy sauce

1 Mix the minced chicken with the egg, grated onion, sugar and soy sauce until the ingredients are thoroughly combined and well bound together. This process takes about 3 minutes, until the mixture is quite sticky, which gives a good texture. Shape the mixture into 12 small, flat round cakes and dust them lightly all over with cornflour.

2 Soak the spring onions in cold water for 5 minutes and drain well.

3 Heat the oil in a frying pan. Place the chicken cakes in the pan in a single layer, and cook over a moderate heat for 3 minutes. Turn the cakes and cook for 3 minutes on the second side.

4 Mix the ingredients for the sauce and pour it into the pan. Turn the chicken cakes occasionally until they are evenly glazed. Move or gently shake the pan constantly to prevent the sauce from burning.

5 Arrange the chicken cakes on a plate and top with the spring onions. Serve immediately.

--- COOK'S TIP ---

To make *Tsukune Chicken*, a grilled version of this recipe, make smaller chicken cakes. Cook them under a moderately hot grill, brushing with the Teriyaki Sauce.

Simmered Beef with Potatoes

Another typical example of Japanese home cooking, known as *Nikujaga*, this would be thought of as one of mother's special dishes.

INGREDIENTS

Serves 4

4 medium potatoes, peeled
300g/11oz beef topside, thinly sliced
30ml/2 tbsp frozen peas
15ml/1 tbsp oil
1 large mild onion, cut into wedges
200ml/7fl oz/scant 1 cup instant dashi (stock) or water
30ml/2 tbsp sugar
22.5ml/4½ tsp sake or dry white wine
22.5ml/4½ tsp mirin
22.5ml/4½ tsp soy sauce

1 Cut each potato into thirds or quarters and soak them in cold water for 5 minutes. Drain well.

2 Cut the beef into 3–4cm/ 1¼–1½in long strips. Pour hot water over the frozen peas and leave until thawed, then drain.

3 Heat the oil in a deep frying pan or saucepan. Remove from the heat and add the beef. Replace the pan on the heat and fry the beef for 1 minute. Add the onion and potatoes, and fry for a further 2 minutes.

4 Fold a sheet of foil in half so that it is just smaller than the diameter of the frying pan. Pour in the stock or water and bring to the boil. Skim the broth carefully. When the soup clears, cover the pan with the foil and simmer for 3–4 minutes. Stir in the sugar and sake or wine, cover and simmer for a further 4–5 minutes.

5 Add the mirin and 15ml/3 tsp soy sauce, re-cover the pan and simmer for 6–7 minutes.

6 Finally, stir in the remaining soy sauce and simmer, uncovered, until only a little soup remains. Shake the pan gently occasionally to prevent the ingredients from burning. Serve the beef and potatoes in a large bowl, sprinkled with the peas.

Japanese-style Hamburgers

This recipe makes soft and moist hamburgers that are delicious with rice, especially with the mooli topping which adds its own refreshing flavour.

INGREDIENTS

Serves 4

30ml/2 tbsp oil, plus extra for greasing hands
1 small onion, finely chopped
500g/1¼lb minced beef
50g/2oz/1 cup fresh white breadcrumbs
1 egg
5ml/1 tsp salt
black pepper
115g/4oz shiitake mushrooms, stems discarded and sliced
200g/7oz mooli (daikon radish), finely grated and drained in a sieve
4 shiso leaves, finely shredded (optional)
30ml/1½ tbsp soy sauce

1 Heat 15ml/1 tbsp oil in a frying pan and fry the onion gently until soft but not browned. Leave to cool.

2 Put the minced beef in a large bowl with the fried onion, breadcrumbs and egg. Season with the salt and pepper. Knead well by hand until the ingredients are thoroughly combined and the mixture becomes sticky. It is important to keep the meat soft and juicy for this recipe. Divide the mixture into four.

3 Put a little oil on your hands. Take a portion of the mixture and throw it from one hand to the other five or six times to remove any air. Then shape the mixture into a 2cm/¾in thick burger. Repeat with the remaining mixture.

4 Heat the remaining oil in a frying pan and add the burgers. Fry over a high heat until browned on one side, then turn over. Place the shiitake mushrooms in the pan, next to the burgers, cover and cook over a low heat for 3–4 minutes or until cooked through, stirring the mushrooms occasionally.

5 Serve the burgers topped with the mooli, shiitake mushrooms and shiso leaves (if used). Pour 7.5ml/1½ tsp soy sauce over each burger just before it is served.

Fried Pork in a Ginger Marinade

Ginger – *shoga* – is a popular spice in Japanese cooking. Plain cooked rice complements this recipe very well.

INGREDIENTS

Serves 4
400g/14oz pork loin, cut into slices
   1cm/¹/₂ in thick
2 tomatoes
punnet of cress
mixed salad leaves, for serving
7.5ml/1¹/₂ tsp oil, for cooking

For the marinade
20g/³/₄oz fresh root ginger
60ml/4 tbsp soy sauce
15ml/1 tbsp sake or dry white wine

1 To prepare the marinade, grate the ginger and squeeze it well over a dish to yield 5ml/1 tsp ginger juice. Mix in the soy sauce and sake or wine. Place the pork slices in a shallow dish, pour over the marinade and turn them to coat well. Set aside for about 15 minutes.

2 Meanwhile cut the tomatoes into four wedges. Cut the cress off its roots, wash and drain it. Chill the prepared ingredients and salad leaves.

3 Heat the oil in a frying pan. Place the pork in the pan, in a single layer and add the marinade. Fry over a medium-high heat, turning the pork once, until golden on both sides.

4 Arrange the pork on a plate with the salad leaves, tomatoes and cress. Pour cooking juices from the pan over the pork and serve immediately.

Deep Fried Pork Strips with Shredded Cabbage

Deep-fried pork is very tasty when served with soft green cabbage and a fruity sauce, known as *Tonkatsu*. This dish is enjoyed throughout Japan.

INGREDIENTS

Serves 4
4 boneless pork loin steaks (115g/4oz each)
7.5ml/1½ tsp salt
black pepper
plain flour, for coating
2 eggs, very lightly beaten
50g/2oz fresh white breadcrumbs
½ soft green cabbage, finely shredded
oil, for deep frying

For the sauce
100ml/3½fl oz/generous ⅓ cup brown sauce (select a fruity brand)
45ml/3 tbsp tomato ketchup
15ml/1 tbsp sugar

1 Snip any fat on the pork steaks to ensure the meat remains flat when frying. Then beat the pork with a meat mallet or rolling pin to tenderize it. Season with the salt and black pepper, and dust the pork lightly with flour.

COOK'S TIP

Commercial Japanese *Tonkatsu* sauce is available ready prepared and it may be substituted for the ingredients given above.

2 Dip the steaks into the egg first and then coat them with the breadcrumbs. Press the breadcrumbs on to the steaks with your fingers to ensure they stick well. Chill for about 10 minutes to allow the coating time to set slightly.

3 Meanwhile, soak the shredded cabbage in cold water for about 5 minutes. Drain well and chill. Mix the ingredients for the sauce, stirring until the sugar has dissolved.

4 Slowly heat the oil for deep frying to 165–170°C/330–340°F. Deep fry two steaks at a time for about 6 minutes, turning them until they are crisp and golden. Skim any floating breadcrumbs from the oil occasionally to prevent them from burning. Drain the steaks well and keep hot.

5 Cut the steaks into 2cm/¾in strips and place on a plate. Arrange the cabbage beside the pork and pour the sauce over. Serve immediately.

Sliced Raw Salmon

Sliced fresh fish is known as *Sashimi*. This recipe introduces the cutting technique known as *hira zukuri*. Salmon is a good choice for those who have not tried sashimi before as most people are familiar with smoked salmon which is uncooked.

INGREDIENTS

Serves 4

2 fresh salmon fillets, skinned and any bones removed (about 400g/14oz total weight)

For the garnish

50g/2oz/¼ cup mooli (daikon radish)
wasabi paste
shiso leaf
soy sauce, to serve

1 Put the salmon fillets in a freezer for 10 minutes to make them easier to cut, then lay them skinned side up with the thick end to your right and away from you. Use a long sharp knife and tilt it to the left. Slice carefully towards you, starting the cut from the point of the knife, then slide the slice away from the fillet, to the right. Always slice from the far side towards you.

2 Finely shred the mooli, place in a bowl of cold water and leave for 5 minutes, then drain well.

3 Place three slices on a plate, then overlap another two slices on them diagonally. You can arrange fewer or more slices per portion, but an odd number looks better.

4 Garnish with the mooli, wasabi and shiso leaf, then serve immediately.

Brill Cured in Seaweed

The fish for this *Sashimi* is cut very fine by a technique called *sogi giri*, then flavoured with kombu. Begin a day in advance as the fish is cured overnight for this dish known as brill *Kobujime*. A small snapper, filleted, can be used instead of brill.

INGREDIENTS

Serves 4

200g/7oz brill fillets, skinned
4 sheets kombu seaweed (18 x 15cm/ 7 x 6in each)
165g/5½oz broccoli
salt

For the vinegar dressing

120ml/4fl oz/½ cup kombu and bonito stock
100ml/3½ fl oz/generous ⅓ cup rice vinegar
30ml/2 tbsp soy sauce
7.5ml/1½ tsp sugar

1 Remove any stray bones from the brill and lay it skinned side up. Slice the fish into 4 x 4cm/1½ x 1½in pieces, as thin as a credit card, slicing the knife towards you, and sprinkle lightly with salt.

2 Clean the kombu seaweed by wiping it with a damp dish towel.

3 Lay the brill on a sheet of kombu in a single layer – do not pile up the slices. Then place another sheet of kombu on top. Repeat with the remaining kombu and brill.

4 Wrap tightly in clear film and place in a large shallow dish or tin. Put a book on top as a weight and place in the fridge overnight.

5 Cut the broccoli into small florets, discarding excess stems, then boil them until tender and drain. Refresh in cold water for 1 minute, then drain.

6 Place the ingredients for the vinegar dressing in a saucepan and bring to the boil. Remove the pan from the heat and leave the dressing to cool, then chill well. Discard the kombu wrapping from the brill.

7 Pile the brill into pyramid shapes in four small bowls or shallow plates. Place a small arrangement of broccoli on each portion and pour chilled sauce over just before serving the brill.

Teriyaki Trout

Teriyaki sauce is very useful, not only for fish but also for meat.

INGREDIENTS

Serves 4
4 trout fillets

For the marinade
75ml/5 tbsp soy sauce
75ml/5 tbsp sake or dry white wine
75ml/5 tbsp mirin

COOK'S TIP

To make a teriyaki barbecue sauce, heat the marinade until boiling, then reduce it until it thickens. When you grill the fish or meat, brush it with the sauce several times.

1 Lay the trout fillets in a shallow dish in a single layer. Mix the ingredients for the marinade and pour the marinade over the fish. Cover and marinate in the fridge for 5–6 hours, turning occasionally.

2 Thread two trout fillets neatly together on two metal skewers. Repeat with the remaining two fillets. You could cut the fillets in half if they are too big.

3 Grill the trout on a barbecue, over a high heat. Keep the fish about 10cm/4in away from the flame and brush it with the marinade several times. Grill each side until shiny and the trout is cooked through. Alternatively, cook the trout under a conventional grill.

4 Slide the trout off the skewers while it is hot. Serve hot or cold with any remaining marinade.

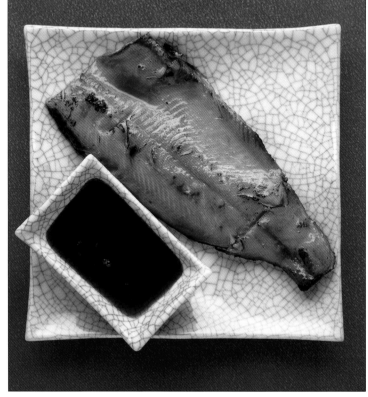

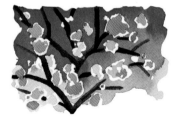

Grilled Tuna Kebabs

It is difficult to buy tuna fresh enough for *Sashimi*, so try this recipe. Choose a fatty portion of tuna steak. This oily, pinkish part of the tuna is better for grilling and has a good texture.

INGREDIENTS

Serves 4
200g/7oz tuna steak
bunch of spring onions
1 lime, quartered

For the marinade
10ml/2 tsp mirin
45ml/3 tbsp soy sauce

1 Cut the tuna into 24 cubes, each about 2cm/³⁄₄in. Mix the mirin and soy sauce, pour this over the tuna and leave to marinate for 30 minutes. Cut the spring onions into lengths, about 2.5cm/1in each.

COOK'S TIP

Soaking bamboo skewers in water for at least 30 minutes before using them helps to prevent them from catching fire under a hot grill or on the barbecue. Drain the skewers just before threading the food on them and cook the kebabs immediately after threading them.

2 Thread the tuna and the spring onions alternately on to eight bamboo skewers.

3 Preheat the grill to the hottest setting and grill the tuna, turning the skewers frequently to avoid burning them. Brush the tuna with the marinade several times during cooking. Grill until the tuna is lightly cooked but still moist inside.

4 Serve the kebabs immediately, with lime wedges.

Fried Swordfish

This is a light and tasty cold dish that is suitable for serving on a hot summer's day.

INGREDIENTS

Serves 4
4 swordfish steaks, boned, skin left on
   (about 600g/1lb 5oz total weight)
15ml/1 tbsp soy sauce
7.5ml/1½ tsp rice vinegar
bunch of spring onions
4 asparagus spears, trimmed
30ml/2 tbsp oil, for cooking

For the marinade
45ml/3 tbsp soy sauce
45ml/3 tbsp rice vinegar
30ml/2 tbsp sake or dry white wine
15ml/1 tbsp sugar
15ml/1 tbsp instant dashi (stock) or
   water
7.5ml/1½ tsp sesame oil

1 Cut the swordfish steaks into 4cm/1½in chunks and place in a dish. Pour the 15ml/1 tbsp soy sauce and 7.5ml/1½ tsp rice vinegar over the fish, then set aside for 5 minutes. Meanwhile, cut the spring onions into 3cm/1¼in lengths and the asparagus into 4cm/1½in lengths.

2 Mix the ingredients for the marinade in a dish. Heat three-quarters of the oil in a frying pan. Wipe the swordfish with paper towel and fry over a moderate heat for about 1–2 minutes on each side, or until cooked. Remove the fish from the frying pan and place it in the marinade.

3 Clean the frying pan and heat the remaining oil in it. Fry the spring onions over a moderate heat until browned, then add them to the fish. Fry the asparagus in the oil remaining in the pan over a low heat for 3–4 minutes, then add to the fish.

4 Leave the fish and vegetables to marinate for 10–20 minutes, turning the pieces occasionally. Serve the cold fish with the marinade on a large, deep plate.

Prawn and Avocado with Wasabi

This dish is a perfect starter for entertaining as it can be made easily; however, the whole dish must be made just before serving to prevent the avocado from discolouring and to preserve the flavour of the wasabi, which will be lost if allowed to stand for any length of time.

INGREDIENTS

Serves 4
2 avocados, halved, stoned and skinned
200g/7oz cooked king prawns, shelled,
   or 8 raw tiger prawns, heads removed

For the wasabi dressing
20ml/4 tsp usukuchi soy sauce
30ml/2 tbsp rice vinegar
10ml/2 tsp wasabi paste

1 Mix the ingredients for the wasabi dressing.

2 Cut each half of the avocados into 2cm/¾in cubes.

3 If using raw prawns, remove the black intestinal vein from the back with a toothpick. Cook them in salted simmering water for 1 minute, until they turn orange. Remove their shells and tails. Cut the prawns into pieces measuring about 2.5cm/1in long.

4 Put the prawns and the avocados in a bowl, and toss well with the dressing, then serve promptly.

Mooli with Sesame Miso Sauce

This simple vegetable dish makes a good starter for a dinner party.

INGREDIENTS

Serves 4

1 medium mooli (daikon radish), about 800g/1³/₄lb
15ml/1 tbsp rice, washed
1 sheet kombu seaweed (20 x 10cm/ 8 x 4in)
punnet of cress, to garnish
salt

For the sesame miso sauce

75g/3oz/generous ¹/₃ cup red miso paste
75g/3oz/generous ¹/₃ cup white miso paste
60ml/4 tbsp mirin
30ml/2 tbsp sugar
20ml/4 tsp ground white sesame seeds

1 Slice the mooli into 2cm/³/₄in thick slices, then peel off the skin. Wrap the rice in a piece of muslin or cheesecloth and tie it with string, allowing room for the rice to expand during cooking. The bundle of rice should look like a commercial dried bouquet garni.

2 Place the mooli in a saucepan and fill with water. Add the rice bag and a little salt, bring to the boil, then simmer for 15 minutes. Gently drain the mooli and discard the rice.

— COOK'S TIP —

The small bag of uncooked rice is added to the cooking water to keep the mooli white during cooking and remove any bitterness from the vegetable.

3 Place the seaweed in a large shallow pan, lay the mooli on top and fill with water. Bring to the boil, then simmer for 20 minutes.

4 Meanwhile, make the sauce. Mix the red and white miso pastes well in a saucepan. Add the mirin and sugar, then simmer for 5–6 minutes, stirring continuously. Remove from the heat and add the sesame seeds.

5 Arrange the mooli and seaweed in a large dish with their hot cooking stock. Sprinkle cress over the top. Serve the mooli on small plates with the sesame miso sauce poured over and garnished with some of the cress. The seaweed is used only to flavour the mooli, it is not eaten.

Rice Omelette

Rice omelettes are a great
favourite with Japanese children,
who usually top them with
tomato ketchup.

INGREDIENTS

Serves 4
115g/4oz skinned boneless chicken
   thigh, cut into 1cm/¹/₂in cubes
35ml/7 tsp butter
1 small onion, chopped
30g/1¹/₄oz/¹/₄ cup carrot, chopped
2 shiitake or closed cup mushrooms,
   stems removed and chopped
15ml/1 tbsp finely chopped parsley
380g/13 oz/2¹/₄ cups freshly boiled rice
30ml/2 tbsp tomato ketchup
6 size 1 eggs
60ml/4 tbsp milk
3ml/²/₃ tsp salt plus extra to season and
   black or white pepper

For the garnish
tomato ketchup
parsley sprigs

1 Season the chicken with salt and
pepper. Melt 7.5ml/1¹/₂ tsp butter
in a frying pan. Fry the onion for
1 minute, then add the chicken and fry
until the chicken is white and cooked.
Add the carrots and mushrooms, stir-
fry until soft over a moderate heat,
then add the parsley. Set this mixture
aside and clean the frying pan.

2 Melt 7.5ml/1¹/₂ tsp butter in the
frying pan, add the rice and stir
well. Mix in the fried ingredients,
tomato ketchup and pepper. Stir well,
adding salt to taste if necessary. Keep
the mixture warm.

3 Beat the eggs lightly, add the milk,
3ml/²/₃ tsp salt and pepper.

4 Melt 5ml/1 tsp butter in an
omelette pan over a moderate heat.
Pour in a quarter of the egg mixture
and stir it briefly with a fork, then
leave to set for 1 minute. Top with a
quarter of the rice mixture.

5 Fold the omelette over the rice and
slide it to the edge of the pan to
shape it into a curve. Do not cook the
omelette too much.

6 Invert the omelette on to a
warmed plate, cover with a paper
towel and press neatly into a
rectangular shape. Cook another three
omelettes from the remaining
ingredients. Serve immediately with
tomato ketchup on top, garnished
with parsley.

Winter Tofu and Vegetables

This dish is brought bubbling hot to the table with a pot of dip to accompany the freshly cooked tofu and vegetables.

INGREDIENTS

Serves 4

1 sheet kombu seaweed (20 x 10cm/ 8 x 4in)
2 packets Japanese silken tofu (each 10 x 8 x 3cm/4 x 3¼ x 1¼in), about 600g/1lb 5oz
2 leeks
4 shiitake mushrooms, stems removed and cross cut in top
spring onions, chopped, to garnish

For the dip

200ml/7fl oz/scant 1 cup soy sauce
generous 15ml/1 tbsp mirin
100ml/3½fl oz/generous ⅓ cup bonito flakes

1 Half fill a large flameproof casserole or saucepan with cold water and soak the kombu seaweed in it for 30 minutes.

2 Cut the tofu into 4cm/1½in cubes. Slice the leek diagonally into 2cm/¾in thick slices.

3 To make the dip, bring the soy sauce and mirin to the boil, then add the bonito flakes. Remove from the heat and leave until all the flakes have sunk to the bottom of the pan, then strain the sauce and pour it into a small heatproof basin.

4 Stand the basin in the middle of the pan placing it on an upturned saucer, if necessary, so that it is well above the level of the water. This keeps the dip hot. Bring the water to the boil. Add the mushrooms and leeks, and cook over a moderate heat until softened – about 5 minutes. Then gently add the tofu. When the tofu starts floating, it is ready to eat. If the tofu won't all fit in the pan, it can be added during the meal.

5 Take the pan to the table and spoon the dip into four small bowls. Sprinkle the spring onions into the dip. Diners help themselves to tofu and vegetables from the pan and eat them with the dip. The kombu seaweed is used only to flavour the dish, it is not eaten.

Koya-tofu and Shiitake Stew

Koya-tofu takes its name from Mount Koya where tofu was frozen in the winter snows, then thawed. It is famous for being part of the diet of the Buddhist monks of the Koya temple. The process of freezing and thawing produces its characteristic texture.

INGREDIENTS

Serves 4

2 pieces dried Koya-tofu, 15g/^{1}/$_2$oz each
8 dried shiitake mushrooms

For the soup

400ml/14fl oz/1^2/$_3$ cups kombu and bonito stock or instant dashi
22.5ml/4^1/$_2$ tsp sake
30ml/2 tbsp mirin
2ml/^{1}/$_3$ tsp salt
15ml/1 tbsp usukuchi soy sauce

1 Cut a piece of foil just smaller than the saucepan.

2 Soak the dried Koya-tofu in tepid water for 30 minutes, then gently press out the water by hand. Soak the dried shiitake mushrooms in cold water for 20 minutes. Put a small saucer or plate on top to keep the mushrooms submerged. Drain the mushrooms and remove their stems.

3 Bring the stock to the boil and add the seasoning ingredients for the soup. Add the Koya-tofu, cover with a piece of folded foil on the surface of the liquid and simmer for 5–6 minutes.

4 Remove the foil. Add the drained shiitake mushrooms and simmer for a further 12–13 minutes. Leave the ingredients to cool in the soup.

5 To serve, cut the Koya-tofu into four pieces. Arrange these in a shallow bowl with the shiitake mushrooms. Serve warm or cold, but not chilled.

Salmon Sealed with Egg

Tamago-toji, meaning egg cover, is the Japanese title for this type of dish which can be made from various ingredients. Canned pink salmon is used here for a very delicate flavour. Fried beancurd can be used instead of salmon.

INGREDIENTS

Serves 4

1 x 400g/14oz can pink salmon, drained, bones and skin removed
10 mangetouts, trimmed
2 large mild onions, sliced
40ml/8 tsp sugar
30ml/2 tbsp soy sauce
4 size 4 eggs, beaten

1 Flake the salmon. Boil the mangetouts for 2–3 minutes, drain and slice finely.

2 Put the onions in a frying pan, add 200ml/7fl oz/scant 1 cup water and bring to the boil. Cook for 5 minutes over a moderate heat, then add the sugar and soy sauce. Cook for a further 5 minutes.

3 Add the salmon and cook for 2–3 minutes or until the soup has virtually evaporated. Pour the egg over to cover the surface. Sprinkle in the mangetouts and cover the pan. Cook for 1 minute over a moderate heat, until just set. Do not overcook or the eggs will curdle and separate. Spoon on to a plate from the pan and serve immediately.

Japanese Savoury Custard

INGREDIENTS

Serves 4

3 size 3 eggs
3ml/²⁄₃ tsp salt
5ml/1 tsp usukuchi soy sauce
3ml/²⁄₃ tsp sugar
400ml/14fl oz/1²⁄₃ cups kombu and bonito stock
50g/2oz chicken breast fillet, thinly sliced
4 shiitake mushrooms, stems removed and sliced
4 medium prawns, shelled and thawed if frozen
10ml/2 tsp sake or dry white wine
10ml/2 tsp soy sauce
mitsuba leaves or cress to garnish

1 Break the eggs into a bowl. To avoid introducing too much air, do not beat the eggs, but stir them using a pair of chopsticks and a cutting action.

2 Stir the salt, usukuchi soy sauce and sugar into the cold stock, then add the egg. Strain the mixture through a fine sieve into another bowl.

3 Season the chicken, shiitake mushrooms and prawns with the sake or wine and soy sauce, then divide them equally between four custard cups or individual soufflé dishes. Pour the egg mixture over.

4 Place in a steamer over a saucepan or wok of boiling water and cover. Steam over a medium-high heat for 2–3 minutes, then remove the lid from the steamer and lay a dish towel over the top. Replace the lid and cook over a low heat for 18–20 minutes, or until set.

5 Insert a bamboo skewer to check if the mixture is cooked: if a little clear liquid comes out, it is cooked. Garnish with mitsuba leaves or cress. If you have lids for the cups, put them on and serve immediately. Provide spoons with which to eat the custard.

Individual Noodle Casseroles

Traditionally these individual casseroles are cooked in earthenware pots. *Nabe* means pot and *yaki* means to heat, providing the Japanese title of *Nabeyaki Udon* for this recipe.

INGREDIENTS

Serves 4
115g/4oz boneless chicken thigh
2.5ml/¹/₂ tsp salt
2.5ml/¹/₂ tsp sake or dry white wine
2.5ml/¹/₂ tsp soy sauce
1 leek
115g/4oz whole spinach, trimmed
300g/11oz dried udon noodles or
 500g/1¹/₄lb fresh
4 shiitake mushrooms, stems removed
4 size 4 eggs
seven flavour spice (*shichimi*), to serve
 (optional)

For the soup

1.4 litres/2¹/₃ pints/6 cups kombu and
 bonito stock or instant dashi
22.5ml/4¹/₂ tsp soy sauce
7ml/1¹/₃ tsp salt
15ml/1 tbsp mirin

1 Cut the chicken into small chunks and sprinkle with the salt, sake or wine and soy sauce. Cut the leek diagonally into 4.5cm/1³/₄in slices.

2 Boil the spinach for 1–2 minutes, then drain and soak in cold water for 1 minute. Drain, squeeze lightly, then cut into 4cm/1¹/₂in lengths.

3 Boil dried udon according to the packet instruction, allowing 3 minutes less than the suggested cooking time. If using fresh udon, place them in boiling water, disentangle the noodles well and then drain them.

4 Bring the ingredients for the soup to the boil in a saucepan and add the chicken and leek. Skim the broth, then cook for 5 minutes. Divide the udon noodles between four individual flameproof casseroles. Pour the soup, chicken and leeks into the casseroles. Place over a moderate heat, then add the shiitake mushrooms.

5 Gently break an egg into each casserole. Cover and simmer for 2 minutes. Divide the spinach between the casseroles and simmer for 1 minute.

6 Serve immediately, standing the hot casseroles on plates or table mats. Sprinkle seven flavour spice over the casseroles if you like.

---— COOK'S TIP ———

Assorted tempura could be served in these casseroles instead of chicken and egg.

Chilled Noodles

This classic Japanese dish of cold noodles is known as *somen*. The noodles are surprisingly refreshing when eaten with the accompanying ingredients and a delicately flavoured dip. The noodles are served with ice to ensure that they remain chilled until they are eaten.

INGREDIENTS

Serves 4

oil, for cooking
2 size 4 eggs, beaten with a pinch of salt
1 sheet yaki-nori seaweed, finely shredded
1/2 bunch spring onions, thinly sliced
wasabi paste
400g/14oz dried somen noodles
ice cubes, for serving

For the dip

1 litre/1³/₄ pints/4 cups kombu and bonito stock or instant dashi
200ml/7fl oz/scant 1 cup soy sauce
15ml/1 tbsp mirin

1 Prepare the dip in advance so that it has time to cool and chill: bring the ingredients to the boil, then leave to cool and chill thoroughly.

2 Heat a little oil in a frying pan. Pour in half the egg, tilting the pan to coat the base evenly. Leave the egg to set, then turn it over and cook the second side briefly. Turn the omelette out on to a board. Cook the remaining egg in the same way.

3 Leave the omelettes to cool and then shred them finely. Place the shredded omelette, nori, spring onions and wasabi in four small bowls.

4 Boil the somen noodles according to the packet instructions and drain. Rinse the noodles in or under cold running water, stirring with chopsticks, then drain well.

5 Place the noodles on a large plate and add some ice cubes on top to keep them cool.

6 Pour the cold dip into four small bowls. Noodles and selected accompaniments are dipped into the chilled dip before they are eaten.

--- COOK'S TIP ---

Use scissors to finely shred the nori. Stir the noodles gently with chopsticks when rinsing them, as they are tender once cooked and easily damaged.

Chicken and Egg with Rice

Oyako-don, the Japanese title for this dish means parent (*oya*), child (*ko*) and bowl (*don*); it is so called because it uses both chicken meat and egg. It is a classic dish which is eaten throughout the year.

Ingredients

Serves 4
300g/11oz boneless chicken thighs
1 large mild onion, thinly sliced
200ml/7fl oz/scant 1 cup kombu and
　bonito stock or instant dashi
22.5ml/4¹⁄₂ tsp sugar
60ml/4 tbsp soy sauce
30ml/2 tbsp mirin
1kg/2¹⁄₄lb/7 cups freshly boiled rice
4–6 size 1 eggs, beaten
60ml/4 tbsp frozen peas, thawed
¹⁄₂ sheet yaki-nori seaweed, shredded,
　to garnish

1 Slice the chicken diagonally, then cut it into 3cm/1¹⁄₄ in lengths.

2 Place the onion, stock, sugar, soy sauce and mirin in a saucepan and bring to the boil. Add the chicken and cook over a moderate heat for about 5 minutes, or until the chicken is cooked. Skim any scum off the sauce.

3 Ladle a quarter of the mixture into a frying pan and bring to the boil.

4 Spoon a quarter of the rice into an individual serving bowl.

5 Pour a quarter of the egg over the mixture in the frying pan and sprinkle with a quarter of the peas. Cover and cook over a moderate heat until the egg is set to your taste.

6 Slide the cooked mixture on to the rice. Prepare the remaining three portions in the same way. Serve hot, sprinkled with the yaki-nori seaweed.

Steak Bowl

This appetizing dish looks very good at a dinner party and it is also very easy to prepare, leaving the cook time to relax.

Ingredients

Serves 4
1 large mild onion
1 red pepper, seeded
30ml/2 tbsp oil
30ml/2 tbsp butter
400g/14oz sirloin steak, trimmed of
　excess fat
60ml/4 tbsp tomato ketchup
30ml/2 tbsp Worcestershire sauce
30ml/2 tbsp chopped parsley
1kg/2¹⁄₄lb/7 cups freshly boiled rice
salt and black pepper

For the garnish
bunch of watercress
a few red peppercorns (optional)

1 Cut the onion and red pepper into 7–8mm/¹⁄₃in slices.

2 Heat 15ml/1 tbsp oil in a frying pan and cook the onion until golden on both sides, adding salt and pepper, then set aside.

3 Heat 15ml/1 tbsp oil and 15ml/1 tbsp butter. Cook the steak over a high heat until browned on both sides, then cut it into bite-size pieces and set aside. For well-done steak, cook it over a moderate heat for 1–2 minutes each side.

4 For the sauce, mix the tomato ketchup, Worcestershire sauce and 30ml/2 tbsp water in the pan in which the steak was cooked. Stir over a moderate heat for 1 minute, mixing in the meat residue.

5 Mix the remaining butter and the chopped parsley into the hot rice. Divide between four serving bowls. Top the rice with the red pepper, onion and steak, and pour over the sauce. Garnish with watercress and red peppercorns (if using) and serve.

Mixed Rice

This recipe makes a very good party dish, and you can add a variety of ingredients to create your own special version.

INGREDIENTS

Serves 4
6 dried shiitake mushrooms
2 sheets fried tofu (*aburage*), each
   13 x 6cm/5 x 2$\frac{1}{2}$in
6 mangetouts
1 carrot, cut into matchstick strips
115g/4oz chicken fillet, diced
30ml/2 tbsp sugar
37.5ml/7$\frac{1}{2}$ tsp soy sauce
1kg/2$\frac{1}{4}$lb/7 cups freshly boiled rice
salt

1 Soak the dried shiitake mushrooms in 800ml/27fl oz/3$\frac{1}{2}$ cups water for 30 minutes. Place a small plate or saucer on top of the mushrooms to keep them submerged.

2 Put the fried tofu into a strainer and pour over hot water from a kettle to remove excess fat. Squeeze the tofu and cut it in half lengthways, then slice it into 5mm/$\frac{1}{4}$in wide strips.

3 Boil the mangetouts, drain and refresh in cold water and then drain well. Shred the mangetouts finely.

4 Drain the shiitake mushrooms, reserving the soaking water, remove their stems and finely slice the caps. Pour the soaking water into a saucepan. Add the tofu, carrot, chicken and shiitake mushrooms.

5 Bring to the boil, then skim the broth and simmer for 1–2 minutes. Add the sugar and cook for 1 minute, then add the soy sauce and salt. Simmer until most of the liquid has evaporated, leaving only a small amount of concentrated broth.

6 Mix in the hot rice, sprinkle the mangetouts over and serve the mixed rice at once.

Rice Balls

Picnics are very popular in Japan, where eating outdoors is considered to be great fun. Various cooked meals are taken on picnics, including rice balls, or *onigiri*. You can put anything you like in the rice, so you could invent your own onigiri.

INGREDIENTS

Serves 4 (8 rice balls)
15ml/1 tbsp salt
1kg/2¼lb/7 cups freshly boiled
   Japanese rice
4 umeboshi (plum pickles)
1 salmon steak, grilled
½ sheet yaki-nori seaweed
15ml/1 tbsp white or black sesame
   seeds

1 Put the salt in a bowl. Spoon an eighth of the rice into a small rice bowl. Make a hole in the middle and put in one umeboshi. Cover with rice.

2 Wet the palms of both hands with cold water, put a finger into the salt bowl and then rub the salt evenly on to your palms.

3 Empty the rice and umeboshi from the bowl on to one hand. Use both hands to shape the rice into a triangular shape, using firm but not heavy pressure. Make another three rice triangles in the same way.

4 Flake the salmon, discarding the skin and bones. Mix the fish into the remaining rice, then shape it into triangles as before.

5 Cut the yaki-nori into four even strips and wrap a strip around each of the umeboshi rice balls. Sprinkle sesame seeds on the salmon rice balls.

COOK'S TIP

Always use hot rice to make the balls, then allow them to cool completely and wrap each one in foil or clear film.

Green Tea Cake

Baking cakes for desserts takes on a new twist when using Japanese ingredients. For example, glacé aduki beans are used in the same way as marrons glacés and the cake remains moist and light.

INGREDIENTS

Makes a 18 x 7.5 x 10cm/7 x 3 x 4in loaf tin

115g/4oz/1 cup plain flour
15g/¹/₂oz green tea powder
2.5ml/¹/₂ tsp baking powder
3 size 3 eggs
75g/3oz/¹/₃ cup granulated sugar
75g/3oz/¹/₃ cup ama-natto (glacé Japanese aduki beans)
65g/2¹/₂oz/5 tbsp lightly salted butter, melted
whipped cream, to serve (optional)

1 Preheat the oven to 180°C/350°F/Gas 4. Line and grease a loaf tin. Sift the flour, green tea powder and baking powder together and set aside.

2 In a large heatproof bowl, whisk the eggs and sugar over a saucepan of hot water until pale and thick.

3 Sprinkle the sifted flour over the mixture. Before the flour sinks into the mixture, add the Japanese glacé aduki beans, then fold in the ingredients gently using a spatula. Fold the mixture over from the bottom once or twice. Do not mix too hard. Fold in the melted butter.

4 Pour the mixture into the tin and smooth the top. Bake in the lower part of the oven for 35–40 minutes or until a warm metal skewer inserted into the centre of the cake comes out free of sticky mixture. Turn out the cake on to a wire rack and remove the lining paper while it is hot. Leave to cool. Slice and serve with whipped cream, if you like.

Rice Cakes with Strawberries

Whereas traditionally an ingredient such as aduki bean paste would have been the sole accompaniment for these rice cakes, in this fairly modern dessert, fresh fruit is also served.

INGREDIENTS

Makes 5

100g/3¾oz/scant ½ cup shiratama-ko powder
15ml/1 tbsp granulated sugar
cornflour, for coating
10 strawberries
115g/4oz/scant ½ cup canned *neri-an* (Japanese soft aduki bean paste), cut into 5 pieces

1 In a microwaveproof bowl, mix the shiratama-ko powder and sugar. Gradually add 200ml/7fl oz/scant 1 cup water, then knead well to make a thick paste.

2 Cover and cook in a microwave for 1½–2 minutes (600 or 500W). Alternatively, steam the mixture in a bowl over a saucepan of simmering water for 10–15 minutes.

3 Lightly dust a chopping board with cornflour. Turn out the mixture on to it and divide it into five pieces. Roll out a portion of mixture into a small oval shape.

4 Put a strawberry and a piece of *neri-an* in the middle. Fold the rice cake in half and serve decorated with a strawberry. Make a further four rice cakes. Eat the rice cakes on the day they are prepared – if left for any longer they will harden.

Sweet Aduki Bean Soup with Rice Cakes

This is another well-known classic Japanese dessert – *Zenzai* is a really sweet aduki bean soup and is served with rice cakes. Ready-to-eat rice cakes (*mochi*) can be found in most Japanese supermarkets.

INGREDIENTS

Serves 4

165g/5¹⁄₂oz/scant 1 cup dried aduki
    beans
185–200g/6¹⁄₂–7oz/about 1 cup
    granulated sugar
pinch of salt
4 ready-to-eat rice cakes (*mochi*)

1 Wash the aduki beans in cold running water, then drain them and place in a large saucepan. Add 1 litre/1³⁄₄ pints/4 cups water and bring to the boil. Drain the beans and replace them in the pan. Add 1.2 litres/2 pints/5 cups water and bring to the boil, then add a further 100ml/3¹⁄₂fl oz/generous ¹⁄₃ cup water and bring it to the boil again. Simmer for 30 minutes until the beans are softened. Skim the broth constantly to ensure that it does not have a bitter taste.

2 When the beans are soft enough to be mashed between your fingers, add half the sugar and simmer for a further 20 minutes. Then add the remaining sugar and the salt, and stir until dissolved.

3 Grill both sides of the rice cakes until softened. Add the rice cakes to the soup and bring to the boil. Serve immediately in four deep bowls. Japanese green tea goes well with this dessert.

Caramelized Sweet Potatoes

Caramelized sweet potatoes are delicious served hot or cold.

INGREDIENTS

Serves 4

500g/1¹⁄₄lb sweet potato
oil, for deep frying
115g/4oz/generous ¹⁄₂ cup granulated
    sugar
15ml/1 tbsp golden syrup or Japanese
    syrup (*mizu-ame*)
black sesame seeds, to decorate

1 Thickly peel the potatoes and cut them into bite-size narrow pieces, then soak them in cold water for 5 minutes.

2 Slowly heat the oil for deep frying to 170°C/340°F. Wipe the potatoes well on paper towels and deep fry them slowly until golden. Drain the potatoes well.

3 In a large frying pan, heat the sugar and 45ml/3 tbsp water until caramelized. Add the syrup and mix.

4 Add the potatoes to the caramel and turn them to coat them thoroughly. Remove from the heat and sprinkle with the sesame seeds.

INDONESIA

Spiced Vegetable Soup with Chicken and Prawns

INGREDIENTS

Serves 6–8
1 onion, ½ cut in two, ½ sliced
2 garlic cloves, crushed
1 fresh red or green chilli, seeded
    and sliced
1cm/½in cube *terasi*
3 macadamia nuts or 6 almonds
1cm/½in *lengkuas*, peeled and sliced, or
    5ml/1 tsp *lengkuas* powder
5ml/1 tsp sugar
oil for frying
225g/8oz boned, skinned chicken
    breast, cut in 1cm/½in cubes
300ml/½ pint/1¼ cups coconut milk
1.2 litres/2 pints/5 cups chicken stock
1 aubergine, diced
225g/8oz French beans, chopped
small wedge of crisp white
    cabbage, shredded
1 red pepper, seeded and finely sliced
115g/4oz cooked, peeled prawns
salt and freshly ground black pepper

1 Grind the onion quarters, garlic, chilli, *terasi*, nuts, *lengkuas* and sugar to a paste in a food processor or with a pestle and mortar.

2 Heat a wok, add the oil and then fry the paste, without browning, until it gives off a rich aroma. Add the sliced onion and chicken cubes and cook for 3–4 minutes. Stir in the coconut milk and stock. Bring to the boil and simmer for a few minutes.

3 Add the diced aubergine to the soup, with the beans, and cook for only a few minutes, until the beans are almost cooked.

4 A few minutes before serving, stir the cabbage, red pepper and prawns into the soup. The vegetables should be cooked so that they are still crunchy and the prawns merely heated through. Taste the soup and adjust the seasoning if necessary.

Spiced Beef Satés

INGREDIENTS

Makes 18 skewers
450g/1lb rump steak, cut in 1cm/½in
    slices or strips
5ml/1 tsp coriander seeds, dry-fried
    and ground
2.5ml/½ tsp cumin seeds, dry-fried
    and ground
5ml/1 tsp tamarind pulp
1 small onion
2 garlic cloves
15ml/1 tbsp brown sugar
15ml/1 tbsp dark soy sauce
salt

To serve
cucumber chunks
lemon or lime wedges
Sambal Kecap

1 Mix the meat and spices in a non-metallic bowl. Soak the tamarind pulp in 75ml/3fl oz/⅓ cup water.

2 Strain the tamarind and reserve the juice. Put the onion, garlic, tamarind juice, sugar and soy sauce in a food processor and blend well. Alternatively, pound the onion and garlic in a mortar with a pestle, and add the remaining ingredients.

3 Pour the marinade over the meat and spices in the bowl and toss well together. Leave for at least 1 hour. Meanwhile, soak some bamboo skewers in water to prevent them from burning whilst cooking.

4 Preheat the grill. Thread 5 or 6 pieces of meat on to each of the skewers and sprinkle the meat with salt. Place under the hot grill, or even better, over a charcoal barbecue, and cook, turning frequently, until tender. Baste with the marinade throughout the cooking, turning the skewers over from time to time.

5 Serve on a platter garnished with cucumber chunks and wedges of lemon or lime to squeeze over the *satés*. Put the Sambal Kecap in a small bowl and serve alongside.

Vegetable Broth with Minced Beef

INGREDIENTS

Serves 6

30ml/2 tbsp groundnut oil
115g/4oz finely minced beef
1 large onion, grated or finely chopped
1 garlic clove, crushed
1–2 fresh chillies, seeded and chopped
1cm/½in cube *terasi*, prepared
3 macadamia nuts or 6 almonds,
   finely ground
1 carrot, finely grated
5ml/1 tsp brown sugar
1 litre/1¾ pints/4 cups chicken stock
50g/2oz dried shrimps, soaked in warm
   water for 10 minutes
225g/8oz spinach, rinsed and
   finely shredded
8 baby sweetcorn, sliced, or 200g/7oz
   canned sweetcorn kernels
1 large tomato, chopped
juice of ½ lemon
salt

1 Heat the oil in a saucepan. Add the beef, onion and garlic and cook, stirring, until the meat changes colour.

2 Add the chillies, *terasi*, nuts, carrot, sugar and salt to taste.

3 Add the stock and bring gently to the boil. Reduce the heat to a simmer and then add the soaked shrimps, with their soaking liquid. Simmer for about 10 minutes.

4 A few minutes before serving, add the spinach, sweetcorn, tomato and lemon juice. Simmer for a minute or two, to heat through. Do not overcook at this stage because this will spoil the appearance and the taste of the *sayur*.

——————— COOK'S TIP ———————

To make this broth, *Sayur Menir,* very hot and spicy, add the seeds from the chillies.

Omelettes with Spicy Meat Filling

INGREDIENTS

Serves 4
For the filling
1cm/½in cube *terasi*
3 garlic cloves, crushed
4 macadamia nuts or 8 almonds
1cm/½in fresh *lengkuas*, peeled and
   sliced, or 5ml/1 tsp *lengkuas*
   powder (optional)
5ml/1 tsp ground coriander
2.5ml/½ tsp ground turmeric
5ml/1 tsp salt
30ml/2 tbsp oil
225g/8oz minced beef
2 spring onions, chopped
½ celery stick, finely chopped
30–45ml/2–3 tbsp coconut milk

For the omelettes
oil for frying
4 eggs, beaten with 60ml/4 tbsp water
salt and freshly ground black pepper
salad and celery leaves, to serve

1 Grind the *terasi* to a paste, in a food processor or with a pestle and mortar, with the garlic, nuts and fresh *lengkuas*, if using. Add the coriander, turmeric, *lengkuas* powder, (if using), and the salt.

2 Heat the oil and fry the mixture for 1–2 minutes. Stir in the beef and cook until it changes colour. Continue to cook for 2–3 minutes. Stir in the spring onions, celery and coconut milk. Cover and cook gently for 5 minutes.

3 Meanwhile, prepare the omelettes. Heat a little oil in an omelette or frying pan. Season the eggs and use to make four thin omelettes in the usual way. When each omelette is almost cooked, spoon a quarter of the filling on top and roll up. Keep warm while making the remaining omelettes.

4 Cut the rolled omelettes in half and arrange on a serving dish. Serve garnished with a few salad and celery leaves.

Peanut Fritters

You can buy rice powder and rice flour in any Asian shop. For this recipe, *Rempeyak Kacang*, it is best to use the rice flour which is ideal as it has a slightly more grainy texture. Peanut fritters are easy and quick to prepare. They go well with Festive Rice and make a good addition to a buffet.

INGREDIENTS

Makes 15–20
50g/2oz rice flour
2.5ml/½ tsp baking powder
1 garlic clove, crushed
2.5ml/½ tsp ground coriander
2 pinches ground cumin
2.5ml/½ tsp ground turmeric
50g/2oz peanuts, lightly crushed
about 150ml/¼ pint/⅔ cup water, or
   coconut milk or a mixture
oil for shallow-frying
salt
coriander leaves, to garnish

1 Put the rice flour, salt to taste and baking powder into a bowl. Add the garlic, coriander, cumin, turmeric and peanuts. Gradually stir in the water or coconut milk, to make a smooth, slightly runny batter.

2 Heat a little oil in a frying pan. Use a dessertspoon to spoon the batter into the pan and cook several fritters at a time. When the tops are no longer runny and the undersides are lacy and golden brown, turn them over with a spatula and cook the other sides until crisp and brown.

3 Lift out and drain on kitchen paper. Either use immediately or cool and store in an airtight tin.

4 To reheat the fritters, arrange in a single layer on a large baking sheet. Bake at 180°C/350°F/Gas 4 for about 10 minutes. Garnish with coriander.

> —————— COOK'S TIP ——————
>
> You can use either salted or unsalted peanuts in this recipe, but remember to adjust the seasoning accordingly.

Prawn Crackers

In Indonesia one can find a wide range of *kroepoek* (the 'oe' spelling betrays the Dutch influence). They can be made from rice, wheat, corn or cassava and so have differing flavours – rather like our crisps. You may use the tiny Chinese-style prawn crackers which are more readily available from oriental stores and some large supermarkets.

INGREDIENTS

oil for deep-frying
225g/8oz packet prawn crackers, or
   ½ x 500g/1¼lb packet large
   Indonesian prawn crackers

1 Heat the oil in a deep-frying pan to 190°C/375°F, or when a cube of day-old bread browns in 30 seconds.

2 Fry just one of the large *kroepoek* at a time, especially if they are being cooked whole. Cook 8–10 small crackers at a time.

3 As soon as they have expanded and become very puffy, remove them immediately from the oil with a slotted spoon. Do not allow them to colour. Drain the crackers on kitchen paper. They can be cooked a few hours in advance and any leftovers can be kept in an airtight container.

Spicy Meat Fritters

INGREDIENTS

Makes 30

450g/1lb potatoes, boiled and drained
450g/1lb lean minced beef
1 onion, quartered
1 bunch spring onions, chopped
3 garlic cloves, crushed
5ml/1 tsp ground nutmeg
15ml/1 tbsp coriander seeds, dry-fried
and ground
10ml/2 tsp cumin seeds, dry-fried
and ground
4 eggs, beaten
oil for shallow-frying
salt and freshly ground black pepper

1 While the potatoes are still warm, mash them in the pan until they are well broken up. Add to the minced beef and mix well together.

2 Finely chop the onion, spring onions and garlic. Add to the meat with the ground nutmeg, coriander and cumin. Stir in enough beaten egg to give a soft consistency which can be formed into fritters. Season to taste.

3 Heat the oil in a large frying pan. Using a dessertspoon, scoop out 6–8 oval-shaped fritters and drop them into the hot oil. Allow to set, so that they keep their shape (this will take about 3 minutes) and then turn over and cook for a further minute.

4 Drain well on kitchen paper and keep warm while cooking the remaining fritters.

Barbecued Pork Spareribs

INGREDIENTS

Serves 4

1kg/2¼ lb pork spareribs
1 onion
2 garlic cloves
2.5cm/1in fresh root ginger
75ml/3fl oz/⅓ cup dark soy sauce
1–2 fresh red chillies, seeded
and chopped
5ml/1 tsp tamarind pulp, soaked in
75ml/3fl oz/⅓ cup water
15–30ml/1–2 tbsp dark brown sugar
30ml/2 tbsp groundnut oil
salt and freshly ground black pepper

1 Wipe the pork ribs and place them in a wok, wide frying pan or large flameproof casserole.

2 Finely chop the onion, crush the garlic and peel and slice the ginger. Blend the soy sauce, onion, garlic, ginger and chopped chillies together to a paste in a food processor or with a pestle and mortar. Strain the tamarind and reserve the juice. Add the tamarind juice, brown sugar, oil and seasoning to taste to the onion mixture and mix well together.

3 Pour the sauce over the ribs and toss well to coat. Bring to the boil and then simmer, uncovered and stirring frequently, for 30 minutes. Add extra water if necessary.

4 Put the ribs on a rack in a roasting tin, place under a preheated grill, on a barbecue or in the oven at 200°C/400°F/Gas 6 and continue cooking until the ribs are tender, about 20 minutes, depending on the thickness of the ribs. Baste the ribs with the sauce and turn them over from time to time.

Rendang

INGREDIENTS

Serves 6–8

1kg/2¼ lb prime beef in one piece
2 onions or 5–6 shallots, sliced
4 garlic cloves, crushed
2.5cm/1in fresh *lengkuas*, peeled and
    sliced, or 5ml/1 tsp *lengkuas* powder
2.5cm/1in fresh root ginger, peeled
    and sliced
4–6 fresh red chillies, seeded and sliced
1 lemon grass stem, lower part, sliced
2.5cm/1in fresh turmeric, peeled and
    sliced, or 5ml/1 tsp ground turmeric
5ml/1 tsp coriander seeds, dry-fried
    and ground
5ml/1 tsp cumin seeds, dry-fried
    and ground
2 lime leaves
5ml/1 tsp tamarind pulp, soaked in
    60ml/4 tbsp warm water
2 x 400ml/14fl oz cans coconut milk
300ml/½ pint/1¼ cups water
30ml/2 tbsp dark soy sauce
8 small new potatoes, scrubbed
salt
Deep-fried Onions, to garnish

1 Cut the meat in long strips and
then into pieces of even size and
place in a bowl.

2 Grind the onions or shallots, garlic,
lengkuas or *lengkuas* powder, ginger,
chillies, sliced lemon grass and turmeric
to a fine paste in a food processor or
with a pestle and mortar.

3 Add the paste to the meat with the
coriander and cumin and mix well.
Tear the lime leaves and add them to
the mixture. Cover and leave in a cool
place to marinate while you prepare
the other ingredients.

4 Strain the tamarind and reserve
the juice. Pour the coconut milk,
water and the tamarind juice into a
wok or flameproof casserole and stir in
the spiced meat and soy sauce. Add
seasoning as desired.

5 Stir until the liquid comes to the
boil and then reduce the heat and
simmer gently, half-covered, for about
1½–2 hours or until the meat is tender
and the liquid reduced.

6 Add the potatoes 20–25 minutes
before the end of the cooking
time. They will absorb some of the
sauce, so add a little more water to
compensate for this, if you prefer the
Rendang to be rather moister than it
would be in Indonesia.

7 Adjust the seasoning and transfer
to a serving bowl. Serve garnished
with the crisp Deep-fried Onions.

COOK'S TIP

This is even better cooked a day or two in
advance, to allow the flavours to mellow.
Stop at the end of step 5 and add the potatoes when you reheat.

Beef and Aubergine Curry

INGREDIENTS

Serves 6

120ml/4fl oz/½ cup sunflower oil
2 onions, thinly sliced
2.5cm/1in fresh root ginger, sliced and
  cut in matchsticks
1 garlic clove, crushed
2 fresh red chillies, seeded and very
  finely sliced
2.5cm/1in fresh turmeric, peeled and
  crushed, or 5ml/1 tsp
  ground turmeric
1 lemon grass stem, lower part sliced
  finely, top bruised
675g/1½ lb braising steak, cut in even-
  size strips
400ml/14fl oz can coconut milk
300ml/½ pint/1¼ cups water
1 aubergine, sliced and patted dry
5ml/1 tsp tamarind pulp, soaked in
  60ml/4 tbsp warm water
salt and freshly ground black pepper
finely sliced chilli, (optional) and Deep-
  fried Onions, to garnish
boiled rice, to serve

1 Heat half the oil and fry the onions, ginger and garlic until they give off a rich aroma. Add the chillies, turmeric and the lower part of the lemon grass. Push to one side and then turn up the heat and add the steak, stirring until the meat changes colour.

— COOK'S TIP —

If you want to make this curry, *Gulai Terung Dengan Daging,* ahead, prepare to the end of step 2 and finish later.

2 Add the coconut milk, water, lemon grass top and seasoning to taste. Cover and simmer gently for 1½ hours, or until the meat is tender.

3 Towards the end of the cooking time heat the remaining oil in a frying pan. Fry the aubergine slices until brown on both sides.

4 Add the browned aubergine slices to the beef curry and cook for a further 15 minutes. Stir gently from time to time. Strain the tamarind and stir the juice into the curry. Taste and adjust the seasoning. Put into a warm serving dish. Garnish with the sliced chilli, if using, and Deep-fried Onions, and serve with boiled rice.

Balinese Spiced Duck

There is a delightful hotel on the beach at Sanur which cooks this delicious duck dish perfectly.

INGREDIENTS

Serves 4

8 duck portions, fat trimmed
  and reserved
50g/2oz desiccated coconut
175ml/6fl oz/³⁄₄ cup coconut milk
salt and freshly ground black pepper
Deep-fried Onions and salad leaves or
  fresh herb sprigs, to garnish

For the spice paste
1 small onion or 4–6 shallots, sliced
2 garlic cloves, sliced
2.5cm/½in fresh root ginger, peeled
  and sliced
1cm/½in fresh *lengkuas*, peeled
  and sliced
2.5cm/1in fresh turmeric or 2.5ml/
  ½ tsp ground turmeric
1–2 red chillies, seeded and sliced
4 macadamia nuts or 8 almonds
5ml/1 tsp coriander seeds, dry-fried

1 Place the duck fat trimmings in a heated frying pan, without oil, and allow the fat to render. Reserve the fat.

2 Dry-fry the desiccated coconut in a preheated pan until crisp and brown in colour.

3 To make the spice paste, blend the onion or shallots, garlic, ginger, *lengkuas*, fresh or ground turmeric, chillies, nuts and coriander seeds to a paste in a food processor or with a pestle and mortar.

4 Spread the spice paste over the duck portions and leave to marinate in a cool place for 3–4 hours. Preheat the oven to 160°C/325°F/ Gas 3. Shake off the spice paste and transfer the duck breasts to an oiled roasting tin. Cover with a double layer of foil and cook the duck in the oven for 2 hours.

5 Turn the oven temperature up to 190°C/375°F/Gas 5. Heat the reserved duck fat in a pan, add the spice paste and fry for 1–2 minutes. Stir in the coconut milk and simmer for 2 minutes. Discard the duck juices then cover the duck with the spice mixture and sprinkle with the toasted coconut. Cook in the oven for 20–30 minutes.

6 Arrange the duck on a warm serving platter and sprinkle with the Deep-fried Onions. Season to taste and serve with the salad leaves or fresh herb sprigs of your choice.

Duck with Chinese Mushrooms and Ginger

Ducks are often seen, comically herded in single file, along the water channels between the rice paddies throughout the country. The substantial Chinese population in Indonesia is particularly fond of duck and the delicious ingredients in this recipe give it an oriental flavour.

INGREDIENTS

Serves 4
2.5kg/5½lb duck
5ml/1 tsp sugar
50ml/2fl oz/¼ cup light soy sauce
2 garlic cloves, crushed
8 dried Chinese mushrooms, soaked in
  350ml/12fl oz/1½ cups warm water
  for 15 minutes
1 onion, sliced
5cm/2in fresh root ginger, sliced and
  cut in matchsticks
200g/7oz baby sweetcorn
½ bunch spring onions, white bulbs left
  whole, green tops sliced
15–30ml/1–2 tbsp cornflour, mixed to
  a paste with 60ml/4 tbsp water
salt and freshly ground black pepper
boiled rice, to serve

1 Cut the duck along the breast, open it up and cut along each side of the backbone. Use the backbone, wings and giblets to make a stock, to use later in the recipe. Any trimmings of fat can be rendered in a frying pan, to use later in the recipe. Cut each leg and each breast in half. Place in a bowl, rub with the sugar and then pour over the soy sauce and garlic.

2 Drain the mushrooms, reserving the soaking liquid. Trim and discard the stalks.

3 Fry the onion and ginger in the duck fat, in a frying pan, until they give off a good aroma. Push to one side. Lift the duck pieces out of the soy sauce and fry them until browned. Add the mushrooms and reserved liquid.

4 Add 600ml/1 pint/2½ cups of the duck stock or water to the browned duck pieces. Season, cover and cook over a gentle heat for about 1 hour, until the duck is tender.

5 Add the sweetcorn and the white part of the spring onions and cook for a further 10 minutes. Remove from the heat and add the cornflour paste. Return to the heat and bring to the boil, stirring. Cook for 1 minute until glossy. Serve, scattered with the spring onion tops, with boiled rice.

VARIATION

Replace the corn with chopped celery and slices of drained, canned water chestnuts.

Aromatic Chicken from Madura

Magadip is best cooked ahead so that the flavours permeate the chicken flesh making it even more delicious. A cool cucumber salad is a good accompaniment.

INGREDIENTS

Serves 4

1.5kg/3–3½lb chicken, cut in quarters, or 4 chicken quarters
5ml/1 tsp sugar
30ml/2 tbsp coriander seeds
10ml/2 tsp cumin seeds
6 whole cloves
2.5ml/½ tsp ground nutmeg
2.5ml/½ tsp ground turmeric
1 small onion
2.5cm/1in fresh root ginger, peeled and sliced
300ml/½ pint/1¼ cups chicken stock or water
salt and freshly ground black pepper
boiled rice and Deep-fried Onions, to serve

1 Cut each chicken quarter in half to obtain eight pieces. Place in a flameproof casserole, sprinkle with sugar and salt and toss together. This helps release the juices in the chicken. Use the backbone and any remaining carcass to make chicken stock for use later in the recipe, if you like.

COOK'S TIP

Add a large piece of bruised ginger and a small onion to the chicken stock to ensure a good flavour.

2 Dry-fry the coriander, cumin and whole cloves until the spices give off a good aroma. Add the nutmeg and turmeric and heat briefly. Grind in a food processor or a pestle and mortar.

3 If using a processor, process the onion and ginger until finely chopped. Otherwise, finely chop the onion and ginger and pound to a paste with a pestle and mortar. Add the spices and stock or water and mix well.

4 Pour over the chicken in the flameproof casserole. Cover with a lid and cook over a gentle heat until the chicken pieces are really tender, about 45–50 minutes.

5 Serve portions of the chicken, with the sauce, on boiled rice, scattered with crisp Deep-fried Onions.

Chicken Cooked in Coconut Milk

Traditionally, the chicken pieces would be part-cooked by frying, but I think that roasting in the oven is a better option. *Ayam Opor* is an unusual recipe in that the sauce is white as it does not contain chillies or turmeric, unlike many other Indonesian dishes. The dish is served with crisp Deep-fried Onions.

INGREDIENTS

Serves 4

1.5kg/3–3½ lb chicken or
    4 chicken quarters
4 garlic cloves
1 onion, sliced
4 macadamia nuts or 8 almonds
15ml/1 tbsp coriander seeds, dry-fried,
    or 5ml/1 tsp ground coriander
45ml/3 tbsp oil
2.5cm/1in fresh *lengkuas*, peeled
    and bruised
2 lemon grass stems, fleshy part bruised
3 lime leaves
2 bay leaves
5ml/1 tsp sugar
600ml/1 pint/2½ cups coconut milk
salt
boiled rice and Deep-fried Onions,
    to serve

1 Preheat the oven to 190°C/375°F/ Gas 5. Cut the chicken into four or eight pieces. Season with salt. Put in an oiled roasting tin and cook in the oven for 25–30 minutes. Meanwhile prepare the sauce.

2 Grind the garlic, onion, nuts and coriander to a fine paste in a food processor or with a pestle and mortar. Heat the oil and fry the paste to bring out the flavour. Do not allow it to brown.

3 Add the part-cooked chicken pieces to a wok together with the *lengkuas*, lemon grass, lime and bay leaves, sugar, coconut milk and salt to taste. Mix well to coat in the sauce.

4 Bring to the boil and then reduce the heat and simmer gently for 30–40 minutes, uncovered, until the chicken is tender and the coconut sauce is reduced and thickened. Stir the mixture occasionally during cooking.

5 Just before serving remove the bruised *lengkuas* and lemon grass. Serve with boiled rice sprinkled with crisp Deep-fried Onions.

Prawns with Chayote in Turmeric Sauce

This delicious, attractively coloured dish is called *Gule Udang Dengan Labu Kuning*.

INGREDIENTS

Serves 4
1–2 chayotes or 2–3 courgettes
2 fresh red chillies, seeded
1 onion, quartered
5mm/¼in fresh *lengkuas*, peeled
1 lemon grass stem, lower 5cm/2in sliced, top bruised
2.5cm/1in fresh turmeric, peeled
200ml/7fl oz/scant 1 cup water
lemon juice
400ml/14fl oz can coconut milk
450g/1lb cooked, peeled prawns
salt
red chilli shreds, to garnish (optional)
boiled rice, to serve

1 Peel the chayotes, remove the seeds and cut into strips. If using courgettes, cut into 5cm/2in strips.

2 Grind the fresh red chillies, onion, sliced *lengkuas*, sliced lemon grass and the fresh turmeric to a paste in a food processor or with a pestle and mortar. Add the water to the paste mixture, with a squeeze of lemon juice and salt to taste.

3 Pour into a pan. Add the top of the lemon grass stem. Bring to the boil and cook for 1–2 minutes. Add the chayote or courgette pieces and cook for 2 minutes. Stir in the coconut milk. Taste and adjust the seasoning.

4 Stir in the prawns and cook gently for 2–3 minutes. Remove the lemon grass stem. Garnish with shreds of chilli, if using, and serve with rice.

Doedoeh of Fish

Haddock or cod fillet may be substituted in this recipe.

INGREDIENTS

Serves 6–8
1kg/2¼lb fresh mackerel fillets, skinned
30ml/2 tbsp tamarind pulp, soaked in 200ml/7fl oz/scant 1 cup water
1 onion
1cm/½in fresh *lengkuas*
2 garlic cloves
1–2 fresh red chillies, seeded, or 5ml/ 1 tsp chilli powder
5ml/1 tsp ground coriander
5ml/1 tsp ground turmeric
2.5ml/½ tsp ground fennel seeds
15ml/1 tbsp dark brown sugar
90–105ml/6–7 tbsp oil
200ml/7fl oz/scant 1 cup coconut cream
salt and freshly ground black pepper
fresh chilli shreds, to garnish

1 Rinse the fish fillets in cold water and dry them well on kitchen paper. Put into a shallow dish and sprinkle with a little salt. Strain the tamarind and pour the juice over the fish fillets. Leave for 30 minutes.

2 Quarter the onion, peel and slice the *lengkuas* and peel the garlic. Grind the onion, *lengkuas*, garlic and chillies or chilli powder to a paste in a food processor or with a pestle and mortar. Add the ground coriander, turmeric, fennel seeds and sugar.

3 Heat half of the oil in a frying pan. Drain the fish fillets and fry for 5 minutes, or until cooked. Set aside.

4 Wipe out the pan and heat the remaining oil. Fry the spice paste, stirring all the time, until it gives off a spicy aroma. Do not let it brown. Add the coconut cream and simmer gently for a few minutes. Add the fish fillets and gently heat through.

5 Taste for seasoning and serve scattered with shredded chilli.

Chilli Crabs

It is possible to find variations on *Kepitang Pedas* all over Asia. It will be memorable whether you eat in simple surroundings or in a sophisticated restaurant.

INGREDIENTS

Serves 4

2 cooked crabs, about 675g/1½lb
1cm/½in cube *terasi*
2 garlic cloves
2 fresh red chillies, seeded, or 5ml/
  1 tsp chopped chilli from a jar
1cm/½in fresh root ginger, peeled
  and sliced
60ml/4 tbsp sunflower oil
300ml/½ pint/1¼ cups tomato ketchup
15ml/1 tbsp dark brown sugar
150ml/¼ pint/⅔ cup warm water
4 spring onions, chopped, to garnish
cucumber chunks and hot toast,
  to serve (optional)

1 Remove the large claws of one crab and turn on to its back, with the head facing away from you. Use your thumbs to push the body up from the main shell. Discard the stomach sac and "dead men's fingers", i.e. lungs and any green matter. Leave the creamy brown meat in the shell and cut the shell in half, with a cleaver or strong knife. Cut the body section in half and crack the claws with a sharp blow from a hammer or cleaver. Avoid splintering the claws. Repeat with the other crab.

2 Grind the *terasi*, garlic, chillies and ginger to a paste in a food processor or with a pestle and mortar.

3 Heat a wok and add the oil. Fry the spice paste, stirring it all the time, without browning.

4 Stir in the tomato ketchup, sugar and water and mix the sauce well. When just boiling, add all the crab pieces and toss in the sauce until well-coated and hot. Serve in a large bowl, sprinkled with the spring onions. Place in the centre of the table for everyone to help themselves. Accompany this finger-licking dish with cool cucumber chunks and hot toast for mopping up the sauce, if you like.

Boemboe Bali of Fish

The island of Bali has wonderful fish, surrounded as it is by sparkling blue sea. This simple fish "curry" is packed with many of the characteristic flavours associated with Indonesia.

INGREDIENTS

Serves 4–6

675g/1½lb cod or haddock fillet
1cm/½in cube *terasi*
2 red or white onions
2.5cm/1in fresh root ginger, peeled
   and sliced
1cm/½in fresh *lengkuas*, peeled and
   sliced, or 5ml/1 tsp *lengkuas* powder
2 garlic cloves
1–2 fresh red chillies, seeded, or
   10ml/2 tsp Chilli Sambal, or
   5–10ml/1–2 tsp chilli powder
90ml/6 tbsp sunflower oil
15ml/1 tbsp dark soy sauce
5ml/1 tsp tamarind pulp, soaked in
   30ml/2 tbsp warm water
250ml/8fl oz/1 cup water
celery leaves or chopped fresh chilli,
   to garnish
boiled rice, to serve

1 Skin the fish, remove any bones and then cut the flesh into bite-size pieces. Pat dry with kitchen paper and set aside.

2 Grind the *terasi*, onions, ginger, *lengkuas*, garlic and fresh chillies, if using, to a paste in a food processor or with a pestle and mortar. Stir in the Chilli Sambal or chilli powder and *lengkuas* powder, if using.

3 Heat 30ml/2 tbsp of the oil and fry the spice mixture, stirring, until it gives off a rich aroma. Add the soy sauce. Strain the tamarind and add the juice and water. Cook for 2–3 minutes.

— VARIATION —

Substitute 450g/1lb cooked tiger prawns. Add them 3 minutes before the end.
---

4 In a separate pan, fry the fish in the remaining oil for 2–3 minutes. Turn once only so that the pieces stay whole. Lift out with a draining spoon and put into the sauce.

5 Cook the fish in the sauce for a further 3 minutes and serve with boiled rice. Garnish the dish with feathery celery leaves or a little chopped fresh chilli, if liked.

Spicy Fish

If you make *Ikan Kecap* a day ahead, put it straight on to a serving dish after cooking and then pour over the sauce, cover and chill until required.

INGREDIENTS

Serves 3–4

450g/1lb fish fillets, such as mackerel,
  cod or haddock
30ml/2 tbsp plain flour
groundnut oil for frying
1 onion, roughly chopped
1 small garlic clove, crushed
4cm/1½in fresh root ginger, peeled
  and grated
1–2 fresh red chillies, seeded and sliced
1cm/½in cube *terasi,* prepared
60ml/4 tbsp water
juice of ½ lemon
15ml/1 tbsp brown sugar
30ml/2 tbsp dark soy sauce
salt
roughly torn lettuce leaves, to serve

1 Rinse the fish fillets under cold water and dry well on absorbent kitchen paper. Cut into serving portions and remove any bones.

2 Season the flour with salt and use it to dust the fish. Heat the oil in a frying pan and fry the fish on both sides for 3–4 minutes, or until cooked. Lift on to a plate and set aside.

3 Rinse out and dry the pan. Heat a little more oil and fry the onion, garlic, ginger and chillies just to bring out the flavour. Do not brown.

4 Blend the *terasi* with a little water, to make a paste. Add it to the onion mixture, with a little extra water if necessary. Cook for 2 minutes and then stir in the lemon juice, brown sugar and soy sauce.

5 Pour over the fish and serve, hot or cold, with roughly torn lettuce.

COOK'S TIP

For a buffet dish cut the fish into bite-size pieces or serving portions.

Squid from Madura

This squid dish, *Cumi Cumi Madura,* is popular in Indonesia. It is quite usual to be invited into the restaurant kitchen and given a warm welcome.

INGREDIENTS

Serves 2–3

450g/1lb cleaned and drained squid,
  body cut in strips, tentacles left whole
3 garlic cloves
1.5ml/¼ tsp ground nutmeg
1 bunch of spring onions
60ml/4 tbsp sunflower oil
250ml/8fl oz/1 cup water
15ml/1 tbsp dark soy sauce
salt and freshly ground black pepper
1 lime, cut in wedges (optional)
boiled rice, to serve

1 Squeeze out the little central "bone" from each tentacle. Heat a wok, toss in all the squid and stir-fry for 1 minute. Remove the squid.

2 Crush the garlic with the nutmeg and some salt and pepper. Trim the roots from the spring onions, cut the white part into small pieces, slice the green part and then set aside.

3 Heat the wok, add the oil and fry the white part of the spring onions. Stir in the garlic paste and the squid.

4 Rinse out the garlic paste container with the water and soy sauce and add to the pan. Half-cover and simmer for 4–5 minutes. Add the spring onion tops, toss lightly and serve at once, with lime, if using, and rice.

Sambal Kecap

This can be served as a dip for *satés* instead of the usual peanut sauce and is particularly good with beef and chicken *satés* and deep-fried chicken.

INGREDIENTS

Makes about 150ml/¼ pint/⅔ cup
1 fresh red chilli, seeded and
  chopped finely
2 garlic cloves, crushed
60ml/4 tbsp dark soy sauce
20ml/4 tsp lemon juice, or
  15–25ml/1–1½ tbsp prepared
  tamarind juice
30ml/2 tbsp hot water
30ml/2 tbsp Deep-fried Onions

1 Mix the chilli, garlic, soy sauce, lemon or tamarind juice and hot water together in a bowl.

2 Stir in the Deep-fried Onions, if using, and leave to stand for 30 minutes before serving.

Deep-fried Onions

Known as *Bawang Goreng,* these are a traditional garnish and accompaniment to many Indonesian dishes. Oriental stores sell them ready-prepared, but it is simple to make them at home, using fresh onions, or for an even faster way, use an 75g/3oz packet of quick-dried onions, which you can fry in about 250ml/8fl oz/1 cup of sunflower oil. This gives you 115g/4oz of fried onion flakes. The small red onions that can be bought in Asian shops are excellent when deep-fried as they contain less water than most European varieties.

INGREDIENTS

Makes 450g/1lb
450g/1lb onions
oil for deep-frying

1 Peel and slice the onions as evenly and finely as possible.

2 Spread out thinly on kitchen paper, in an airy place, and leave to dry for 30 minutes–2 hours.

3 Heat the oil in deep-fryer or wok to 190°C/375°F. Fry the onions in batches, until crisp and golden, turning all the time. Drain well on kitchen paper and cool. Deep-fried Onions may be stored in an airtight container.

--- COOK'S TIP ---

Garlic can be prepared and cooked in the same way, or some can be fried with the last batch of onions. Deep-fried Garlic gives an added dimension in flavour as a garnish for many dishes.

Festive Rice

Nasi Kuning is served at special events – weddings, birthdays or farewell parties.

INGREDIENTS

Serves 8

450g/1lb Thai fragrant rice
60ml/4 tbsp oil
2 garlic cloves, crushed
2 onions, finely sliced
5cm/2in fresh turmeric, peeled and crushed
750ml/1¼ pints/3 cups water
400ml/14fl oz can coconut milk
1–2 lemon grass stems, bruised
1–2 *pandan* leaves (optional)
salt

For the accompaniments

omelette strips
2 fresh red chillies, shredded
cucumber chunks
tomato wedges
Deep-fried Onions
Coconut and Peanut Relish (optional)
Prawn Crackers

1 Wash the rice in several changes of water. Drain well.

2 Heat the oil in a wok and gently fry the crushed garlic, the finely sliced onions and the crushed fresh turmeric for a few minutes until soft but not browned.

COOK'S TIP

It is the custom to shape the rice into a cone (to represent a volcano) and then surround with the accompaniments. Shape with oiled hands or use a conical sieve.

3 Add the rice and and stir well so that each grain is thoroughly coated. Pour in the water and coconut milk and add the lemon grass, *pandan* leaves, if using, and salt.

4 Bring to the boil, stirring well. Cover and cook gently for about 15–20 minutes, until all of the liquid has been absorbed.

5 Remove from the heat. Cover with a dish towel, put on the lid and leave to stand in a warm place, for 15 minutes. Remove the lemon grass and *pandan* leaves.

6 Turn on to a serving platter and garnish with the accompaniments.

Nasi Goreng

One of the most familiar and well-known Indonesian dishes. This is a marvellous way to use up leftover rice, chicken and meats such as pork. It is important that the rice is quite cold and the grains separate before adding the other ingredients, so it's best to cook the rice the day before.

INGREDIENTS

Serves 4–6

350g/12oz dry weight long-grain rice, such as basmati, cooked and allowed to become completely cold
2 eggs
30ml/2 tbsp water
105ml/7 tbsp oil
225g/8oz pork fillet or fillet of beef
115g/4oz cooked, peeled prawns
175g–225g/6–8oz cooked chicken, chopped
2–3 fresh red chillies, seeded and sliced
1cm/½in cube *terasi*
2 garlic cloves, crushed
1 onion, sliced
30ml/2 tbsp dark soy sauce or 45–60ml/3–4 tbsp tomato ketchup
salt and freshly ground black pepper
celery leaves, Deep-fried Onions and coriander sprigs, to garnish

1 Once the rice is cooked and cooled, fork it through to separate the grains and keep it in a covered pan or dish until required.

2 Beat the eggs with seasoning and the water and make two or three omelettes in a frying pan, with a minimum of oil. Roll up each omelette and cut in strips when cold. Set aside.

3 Cut the pork or beef into neat strips and put the meat, prawns and chicken pieces in separate bowls. Shred one of the chillies and reserve it.

4 Put the *terasi*, with the remaining chilli, garlic and onion, in a food processor and grind to a fine paste. Alternatively, pound together using a pestle and mortar.

5 Fry the paste in the remaining hot oil, without browning, until it gives off a rich, spicy aroma. Add the pork or beef, tossing the meat all the time, to seal in the juices. Cook for 2 minutes, stirring constantly. Add the prawns, cook for 2 minutes and then stir in the chicken, cold rice, dark soy sauce or ketchup and seasoning to taste. Stir all the time to keep the rice light and fluffy and prevent it from sticking.

6 Turn on to a hot platter and garnish with the omelette strips, celery leaves, onions, reserved shredded chilli and the coriander sprigs.

Spiced Cauliflower Braise

A delicious vegetable stew, known as *Sambal Kol Kembang,* which combines coconut milk with spices and is perfect as a vegetarian main course or as part of a buffet.

INGREDIENTS

Serves 4

1 cauliflower
2 medium or 1 large tomato(es)
1 onion, chopped
2 garlic cloves, crushed
1 fresh green chilli, seeded
2.5ml/½ tsp ground turmeric
1cm/½ in cube *terasi*
30ml/2 tbsp sunflower oil
400ml/14fl oz coconut milk
250ml/8fl oz/1 cup water
5ml/1 tsp sugar
5ml/1 tsp tamarind pulp, soaked in
    45ml/3 tbsp warm water
salt

1 Trim the stalk from the cauliflower and divide into tiny florets. Skin the tomato(es) if liked. Chop the flesh into 1–2.5cm/½–1in pieces.

2 Grind the chopped onion, garlic, green chilli, ground turmeric and *terasi* together to a paste in a food processor or with a pestle and mortar. Heat the sunflower oil in a wok or large frying pan and fry the spice paste to bring out the aromatic flavours, without allowing it to brown.

3 Add the cauliflower florets and toss well to coat in the spices. Stir in the coconut milk, water, sugar and salt to taste. Simmer for 5 minutes. Strain the tamarind and reserve the juice.

4 Add the tamarind juice and chopped tomatoes to the pan then cook for 2–3 minutes only. Taste and check the seasoning and serve.

Spicy Scrambled Eggs

This is a lovely way to liven up scrambled eggs. When making *Orak Arik,* prepare all the ingredients ahead so that the vegetables retain all their crunch and colour.

INGREDIENTS

Serves 4

30ml/2 tbsp sunflower oil
1 onion, finely sliced
225g/8oz Chinese leaves, finely sliced
    or cut in diamonds
200g/7oz can sweetcorn kernels
1 small fresh red chilli, seeded and
    finely sliced (optional)
30ml/2 tbsp water
2 eggs, beaten
salt and freshly ground black pepper
Deep-fried Onions, to garnish

1 Heat a wok, add the oil and fry the onion, until soft but not browned.

2 Add the Chinese leaves and toss well together. Add the sweetcorn, chilli and water. Cover with a lid and cook for 2 minutes.

3 Remove the lid and stir in the beaten eggs and seasoning. Stir constantly until the eggs are creamy and just set. Serve on warmed plates, scattered with crisp Deep-fried Onions.

Cooked Vegetable Gado-Gado

Instead of putting everything on a large platter, you can serve individual servings of this salad. It is a perfect recipe for lunchtime or informal gatherings.

INGREDIENTS

Serves 6

225g/8oz waxy potatoes, cooked
450g/1lb mixed cabbage, spinach and
    beansprouts, in equal proportions,
    rinsed and shredded
½ cucumber, cut in wedges, salted and
    set aside for 15 minutes
2–3 eggs, hard-boiled and shelled
115g/4oz fresh bean curd
oil for frying
6–8 large Prawn Crackers
lemon juice
Deep-fried Onions, to garnish
Peanut Sauce, to serve

1 Cube the potatoes and set aside. Bring a large pan of salted water to the boil. Plunge one type of raw vegetable at a time into the pan for just a few seconds to blanch. Lift out the vegetables with a large draining spoon or sieve and run under very cold water. Or plunge them into iced water and leave for 2 minutes. Drain thoroughly. Blanch all the vegetables, except the cucumber, in this way.

2 Rinse the cucumber pieces and drain them well. Cut the eggs in quarters. Cut the bean curd into cubes.

3 Fry the bean curd in hot oil in a wok until crisp on both sides. Lift out and drain on kitchen paper.

4 Add more oil to the pan and then deep-fry the Prawn Crackers one or two at a time. Reserve them on a tray lined with kitchen paper.

5 Arrange all the cooked vegetables attractively on a platter, with the cucumber, hard-boiled eggs and bean curd. Scatter with the lemon juice and Deep-fried Onions at the last minute.

6 Serve with the prepared Peanut Sauce and hand round the fried Prawn Crackers separately.

Stir-fried Greens

Quail's eggs look very attractive in *Chah Kang Kung*, but you can substitute some baby sweetcorn, halved at an angle.

INGREDIENTS

Serves 4

2 bunches spinach or chard or 1 head Chinese leaves or 450g/1lb curly kale
3 garlic cloves, crushed
5cm/2in fresh root ginger, peeled and cut in matchsticks
45–60ml/3–4 tbsp groundnut oil
115g/4oz boneless, skinless chicken breast, or pork fillet, or a mixture of both, very finely sliced
12 quail's eggs, hard-boiled and shelled
1 fresh red chilli, seeded and shredded
30–45ml/2–3 tbsp oyster sauce
15ml/1 tbsp brown sugar
10ml/2 tsp cornflour, mixed with 50ml/2fl oz/¼ cup cold water
salt

— COOK'S TIP —

As with all stir-fries, don't start cooking until you have prepared all the ingredients and arranged them to hand. Cut everything into small, even-size pieces so the food can be cooked very quickly and all the colours and flavours preserved.

1 Wash the chosen leaves well and shake them dry. Strip the tender leaves from the stems and tear them into pieces. Discard the lower, tougher part of the stems and slice the remainder evenly.

2 Fry the garlic and ginger in the hot oil, without browning, for a minute. Add the chicken and/or pork and keep stirring it in the wok until the meat changes colour. When the meat looks cooked, add the sliced stems first and cook them quickly; then add the torn leaves, quail's eggs and chilli. Spoon in the oyster sauce and a little boiling water, if necessary. Cover and cook for 1–2 minutes only.

3 Remove the cover, stir and add sugar and salt to taste. Stir in the cornflour and water mixture and toss thoroughly. Cook until the mixture is well coated in a glossy sauce.

4 Serve immediately, while still very hot and the colours are bright and positively jewel-like.

Black Glutinous Rice Pudding

This very unusual rice pudding, *Bubor Pulot Hitam,* which uses bruised fresh root ginger, is quite delicious. When cooked, black rice still retains its husk and has a nutty texture. Serve in small bowls, with a little coconut cream poured over each helping.

INGREDIENTS

Serves 6

115g/4oz black glutinous rice
475ml/16fl oz/2 cups water
1cm/½ in fresh root ginger, peeled
 and bruised
50g/2oz dark brown sugar
50g/2oz caster sugar
300ml/½ pint/1¼ cups coconut milk
 or cream, to serve

1 Put the rice in a sieve and rinse well under cold running water. Drain and put in a large pan, with the water. Bring to the boil and stir to prevent the rice from settling on the base of the pan. Cover and cook for about 30 minutes.

2 Add the ginger and both the brown and caster sugar. Cook for a further 15 minutes, adding a little more water if necessary, until the rice is cooked and porridge-like. Remove the ginger and serve warm, in bowls, topped with coconut milk or cream.

Deep-fried Bananas

Known as *Pisang Goreng,* these delicious deep-fried bananas should be cooked at the last minute, so that the outer crust of batter is crisp in texture and the banana is soft and warm inside.

INGREDIENTS

Serves 8

115g/4oz self-raising flour
40g/1½oz rice flour
2.5ml/½ tsp salt
200ml/7fl oz /scant 1 cup water
finely grated lime rind (optional)
8 small bananas
oil for deep-frying
sugar and 1 lime, cut in wedges,
 to serve

1 Sift both the flours and the salt together into a bowl. Add just enough water to make a smooth, coating batter. Mix well, then add the lime rind, if using.

2 Peel the bananas and dip them into the batter two or three times.

3 Heat the oil to 190°C/375°F or when a cube of day-old bread browns in 30 seconds. Deep-fry the battered bananas until crisp and golden. Drain and serve hot, dredged with sugar and with the lime wedges to squeeze over the bananas.

Pancakes Filled with Sweet Coconut

Traditionally, the pale green colour in the batter for *Dadar Gulung* was obtained from the juice squeezed from *pandan* leaves – a real labour of love. Green food colouring can be used as the modern alternative to this lengthy process.

INGREDIENTS

Makes 12–15 pancakes
175g/6oz dark brown sugar
450ml/15fl oz/scant 2 cups water
1 *pandan* leaf, stripped through with a
 fork and tied into a knot
175g/6oz desiccated coconut
oil for frying
salt

For the pancake batter
225g/8oz plain flour, sifted
2 eggs, beaten
2 drops of edible green food colouring
few drops of vanilla essence
450ml/15fl oz/scant 2 cups water
45ml/3 tbsp groundnut oil

1 Dissolve the sugar in the water with the *pandan* leaf, in a pan over gentle heat, stirring all the time. Increase the heat and allow to boil gently for 3–4 minutes, until the mixture just becomes syrupy. Do not let it caramelize.

2 Put the coconut into a wok with a pinch of salt. Pour over the prepared sugar syrup and cook over a very gentle heat, stirring from time to time, until the mixture becomes almost dry; this will take 5–10 minutes. Set aside until required.

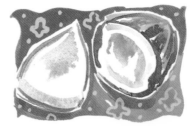

3 To make the batter, blend together the flour, eggs, food colouring, vanilla essence, water and oil either by hand or in a food processor.

4 Brush an 18cm/7in frying pan with oil and cook 12–15 pancakes. Keep the pancakes warm. Fill each pancake with a generous spoonful of the coconut mixture, roll up and serve them immediately.

Steamed Coconut Custard

Srikaya is a very popular dessert that pops up all over South-east Asia, rather as crème caramel is found all over Europe or, indeed, wherever Europeans have settled.

INGREDIENTS

Serves 8

400ml/14fl oz can coconut milk
75ml/5 tbsp water
25g/1oz sugar
3 eggs, beaten
25g/1oz cellophane noodles, soaked in
    warm water for 5 minutes
4 ripe bananas or plantains, peeled and
    cut in small pieces
salt
vanilla ice cream, to serve (optional)

1 Stir the coconut milk, water and sugar into the beaten eggs and whisk well together.

2 Strain into a 1.75 litre/3 pint/ 7½ cup heatproof soufflé dish.

3 Drain the noodles well and cut them into small pieces with scissors. Stir the noodles into the coconut milk mixture, together with the chopped bananas or plantains. Stir in a pinch of salt.

4 Cover the dish with foil and place in a steamer for about 1 hour, or until set. Test by inserting a thin, small knife or skewer into the centre. Serve hot or cold, on its own or topped with vanilla ice cream.

THAILAND

Ginger, Chicken and Coconut Soup

This aromatic soup is rich with coconut milk and intensely flavoured with galangal, lemon grass and kaffir lime leaves.

INGREDIENTS

Serves 4–6
750ml/1¼ pints/3 cups coconut milk
475ml/16fl oz/2 cups chicken stock
4 stalks lemon grass, bruised
  and chopped
2.5cm/1in piece galangal, thinly sliced
10 black peppercorns, crushed
10 kaffir lime leaves, torn
300g/11oz boneless chicken, cut
  into thin strips
115g/4oz button mushrooms
50g/2oz baby sweetcorn
60ml/4 tbsp lime juice
45ml/3 tbsp fish sauce
2 red chillies, chopped, to garnish
chopped spring onions, to garnish
coriander leaves, to garnish

1 Bring the coconut milk and chicken stock to the boil. Add the lemon grass, galangal, peppercorns and half the kaffir lime leaves, reduce the heat and simmer gently for 10 minutes.

2 Strain the stock into a clean pan. Return to the heat, then add the chicken, button mushrooms and baby sweetcorn. Cook for about 5–7 minutes or until the chicken is cooked.

3 Stir in the lime juice, fish sauce to taste and the rest of the lime leaves. Serve hot, garnished with red chillies, spring onions and coriander.

Hot And Sour Prawn Soup with Lemon Grass

This is a classic Thai seafood soup – *Tom Yam Goong* – and is probably the most popular and well known soup from Thailand.

INGREDIENTS

Serves 4–6
450g/1lb king prawns
1 litre/1¾ pints/4 cups chicken stock
  or water
3 stalks lemon grass
10 kaffir lime leaves, torn in half
225g/8oz can straw mushrooms,
  drained
45ml/3 tbsp fish sauce
50ml/2fl oz/¼ cup lime juice
30ml/2 tbsp chopped spring onion
15ml/1 tbsp coriander leaves
4 red chillies, seeded and chopped
2 spring onions, finely chopped

1 Shell and devein the prawns and set aside. Rinse the prawn shells and place in a large saucepan with the stock or water and bring to the boil.

2 Bruise the lemon grass stalks with the blunt edge of a chopping knife and add them to the stock together with half of the lime leaves. Simmer gently for 5–6 minutes, until the stalks change colour and the stock is fragrant.

3 Strain the stock and return to the saucepan and reheat. Add the mushrooms and prawns, then cook until the prawns turn pink.

4 Stir in the fish sauce, lime juice, spring onions, coriander, red chillies and the rest of the lime leaves. Taste and adjust the seasoning. It should be sour, salty, spicy and hot.

Rice Cakes with Spicy Dipping Sauce

Rice cakes are a classic Thai appetizer. They are easy to make and can be kept in an airtight box almost indefinitely.

INGREDIENTS

Serves 4–6
175g/6oz/1 cup jasmine rice
350ml/12fl oz/1½ cups water
oil for frying and greasing

For the spicy dipping sauce
6–8 dried chillies
2.5ml/½ tsp salt
2 shallots, chopped
2 garlic cloves, chopped
4 coriander roots
10 white peppercorns
250ml/8fl oz/1 cup coconut milk
5ml/1 tsp shrimp paste
115g/4oz minced pork
115g/4oz cherry tomatoes, chopped
15ml/1 tbsp fish sauce
15ml/1 tbsp palm sugar
30ml/2 tbsp tamarind juice
30 ml/2 tbsp coarsely chopped
   roasted peanuts
2 spring onions, finely chopped

1 Stem the chillies and remove most of the seeds. Soak the chillies in warm water for 20 minutes. Drain and transfer to a mortar.

2 Add the salt and grind with a pestle until the chillies are crushed. Add the shallots, garlic, coriander roots and peppercorns. Pound together until you have a coarse paste.

3 Pour the coconut milk into a saucepan and boil until it begins to separate. Add the pounded chilli paste. Cook for 2–3 minutes until it is fragrant. Stir in the shrimp paste. Cook for another minute.

4 Add the pork, stirring to break up any lumps. Cook for about 5–10 minutes. Add the tomatoes, fish sauce, palm sugar and tamarind juice. Simmer until the sauce thickens.

5 Stir in the chopped peanuts and spring onions. Remove from the heat and leave to cool.

6 Wash the rice in several changes of water. Put in a saucepan, add the water and cover with a tight-fitting lid. Bring to the boil, reduce the heat and simmer gently for about 15 minutes.

7 Remove the lid and fluff up the rice. Turn out on to a lightly greased tray and press down with the back of a large spoon. Leave to dry out overnight in a very low oven until it is completely dry and firm.

8 Remove the rice from the tray and break into bite-size pieces. Heat the oil in a wok or deep-fat fryer.

9 Deep fry the rice cakes in batches for about 1 minute, until they puff up, taking care not to brown them too much. Remove and drain. Serve accompanied with the dipping sauce.

Fish Cakes with Cucumber Relish

These wonderful small fish cakes are a very familiar and popular appetizer. They are usually accompanied with Thai beer.

INGREDIENTS

Makes about 12
300g/11oz white fish fillet, such as cod,
   cut into chunks
30ml/2 tbsp red curry paste
1 egg
30ml/2 tbsp fish sauce
5ml/1 tsp granulated sugar
30ml/2 tbsp cornflour
3 kaffir lime leaves, shredded
15ml/1 tbsp chopped coriander
50g/2oz green beans, finely sliced
oil for frying
Chinese mustard cress, to garnish

For the cucumber relish
60ml/4 tbsp Thai coconut or
   rice vinegar
60ml/4 tbsp water
50g/2oz sugar
1 head pickled garlic
1 cucumber, quartered and sliced
4 shallots, finely sliced
15ml/1 tbsp finely chopped root ginger

1 To make the cucumber relish, bring the vinegar, water and sugar to the boil. Stir until the sugar dissolves, then remove from the heat and cool.

2 Combine the rest of the relish ingredients together in a bowl and pour over the vinegar mixture.

3 Combine the fish, curry paste and egg in a food processor and process well. Transfer the mixture to a bowl, add the rest of the ingredients, except for the oil and garnish, and mix well.

4 Mould and shape the mixture into cakes about 5cm/2in in diameter and 5mm/¼in thick.

5 Heat the oil in a wok or deep-fat fryer. Fry the fish cakes, a few at a time, for about 4–5 minutes or until golden brown. Remove and drain on kitchen paper. Garnish with Chinese mustard cress and serve with the cucumber relish.

Pork Satay

Originating in Indonesia, satay are skewers of meat marinated with spices and grilled quickly over charcoal. It's street food at its best, prepared by vendors with portable grills who set up stalls at every street corner and market place. You can make satay with chicken, beef or lamb. Serve with Satay Sauce and Cucumber Relish.

INGREDIENTS

Makes about 20
450g/1lb lean pork
5ml/1 tsp grated root ginger
1 stalk lemon grass, finely chopped
3 garlic cloves, finely chopped
15ml/1 tbsp medium curry paste
5ml/1 tsp ground cumin
5ml/1 tsp ground turmeric
60ml/4 tbsp coconut cream
30ml/2 tbsp fish sauce
5ml/1 tsp granulated sugar
20 wooden satay skewers
oil for cooking

For the satay sauce
250 ml/8fl oz/1 cup coconut milk
30ml/2 tbsp red curry paste
75g/3oz crunchy peanut butter
120ml/4fl oz/½ cup chicken stock
45ml/3 tbsp brown sugar
30ml/2 tbsp tamarind juice
15ml/1 tbsp fish sauce
2.5ml/1 tsp salt

1 Cut the pork thinly into 5cm/2in strips. Mix together the ginger, lemon grass, garlic, medium curry paste, cumin, turmeric, coconut cream, fish sauce and sugar.

2 Pour over the pork and leave to marinate for about 2 hours.

3 Meanwhile, make the sauce. Heat the coconut milk over a medium heat, then add the red curry paste, peanut butter, chicken stock and sugar.

4 Cook and stir until smooth, about 5–6 minutes. Add the tamarind juice, fish sauce and salt to taste.

5 Thread the meat on to skewers. Brush with oil and grill over charcoal or under a preheated grill for 3–4 minutes on each side, turning occasionally, until cooked and golden brown. Serve with the satay sauce.

Chicken and Sticky Rice Balls

These balls can either be steamed or deep fried. The fried versions are crunchy and are excellent for serving at drinks parties.

INGREDIENTS

Makes about 30
450g/1lb minced chicken
1 egg
15ml/1 tsp tapioca flour
4 spring onions, finely chopped
30ml/2 tbsp chopped coriander
30ml/2 tbsp fish sauce
pinch of granulated sugar
freshly ground black pepper
225g/8oz cooked sticky rice
banana leaves
oil for brushing
1 small carrot, shredded, to garnish
1 red pepper, cut into strips, to garnish
snipped chives, to garnish
sweet chilli sauce, to serve

1 In a mixing bowl, combine the minced chicken, egg, tapioca flour, spring onions and coriander. Mix well and season with fish sauce, sugar and freshly ground black pepper.

2 Spread the cooked sticky rice on a plate or flat tray.

3 Place a teaspoonful of the chicken mixture on the bed of rice. With damp hands, roll and shape the mixture in the rice to make a ball about the size of a walnut. Repeat with the rest of the chicken mixture.

--- COOK'S TIP ---

Sticky rice, also known as glutinous rice, has a very high gluten content. It is so called because the grains stick together when it is cooked. It can be eaten both as a savoury and as a sweet dish.

4 Line a bamboo steamer with banana leaves and lightly brush them with oil. Place the chicken balls on the leaves, spacing well apart to prevent them sticking together. Steam over a high heat for about 10 minutes or until cooked.

5 Remove and arrange on serving plates. Garnish with shredded carrots, red pepper and chives. Serve with sweet chilli sauce to dip in.

Green Beef Curry with Thai Aubergine

This is a very quick curry so be
sure to use good quality meat.

INGREDIENTS

Serves 4–6
15ml/1 tbsp vegetable oil
45ml/3 tbsp green curry paste
600ml/1 pint/2½ cups coconut milk
450g/1lb beef sirloin
4 kaffir lime leaves, torn
15–30ml/1–2 tbsp fish sauce
5ml/1 tsp palm sugar
150g/5oz small Thai aubergines, halved
a small handful of Thai basil
2 green chillies, to garnish

For the green curry paste
15 hot green chillies
2 stalks lemon grass, chopped
3 shallots, sliced
2 garlic cloves
15ml/1 tbsp chopped galangal
4 kaffir lime leaves, chopped
2.5ml/½ tsp grated kaffir lime rind
5ml/1 tsp chopped coriander root
6 black peppercorns
5ml/1 tsp coriander seeds, roasted
5ml/1 tsp cumin seeds, roasted
15ml/1 tbsp sugar
5ml/1 tsp salt
5ml/1 tsp shrimp paste (optional)

1 Make the green curry paste.
Combine all the ingredients, except
for the oil. Pound in a pestle and
mortar or process in a food processor
until smooth. Add the oil a little at a
time and blend well between each
addition. Keep in a glass jar in the
fridge until required.

2 Heat the oil in a large saucepan or
wok. Add 45ml/3 tbsp curry paste
and fry until fragrant.

3 Stir in half the coconut milk, a
little at a time. Cook for about 5–6
minutes, until an oily sheen appears.

4 Cut the beef into long thin slices
and add to the saucepan with the
kaffir lime leaves, fish sauce, sugar and
aubergines. Cook for 2–3 minutes, then
stir in the remaining coconut milk.

5 Bring back to a simmer and cook
until the meat and aubergines are
tender. Stir in the Thai basil just before
serving. Finely shred the green chillies
and use to garnish the curry.

Steamed Eggs with Beef and Spring Onions

This is a very delicate dish. You can add less liquid for a firmer custard, but cooked this way it is soft and silky. Other types of meat or seafood can be used instead of beef.

INGREDIENTS

Serves 4–6

115g/4oz sirloin or rump steak
5ml/1 tsp grated fresh root ginger
15ml/1 tbsp fish sauce
freshly ground black pepper
3 eggs
120ml/4fl oz/½ cup chicken stock
   or water
30ml/2 tbsp chopped spring onion
15ml/1 tbsp vegetable oil
2 garlic cloves, finely sliced

1 Finely chop the beef and place in a large bowl. Add the ginger, fish sauce and freshly ground black pepper.

2 Beat the eggs together with the stock. Stir the mixture into the beef, add the spring onions and beat together until well-blended. Try to avoid making too many bubbles.

3 Pour the mixture into a heatproof dish or individual ramekins.

4 Place in a steamer and steam over a gentle heat for 10–15 minutes or until the custard is set.

5 Meanwhile, heat the oil in a frying pan. Add the garlic and stir to break up any clumps and fry until golden – about 2 minutes.

6 To serve, pour the garlic and oil over the egg custards. Allow to cool slightly before serving.

COOK'S TIP

The Japanese make a similar version of this recipe called *Chewan Mushi*, using spinach, prawns and shiitake mushrooms.

Sweet and Sour Pork, Thai-style

Sweet and sour is traditionally a
Chinese creation but the Thais
do it very well. This version has
an altogether fresher and cleaner
flavour and it makes a good one-
dish meal when served over rice.

INGREDIENTS

Serves 4

350g/12oz lean pork
30ml/2 tbsp vegetable oil
4 garlic cloves, finely sliced
1 small red onion, sliced
30ml/2 tbsp fish sauce
15ml/1 tbsp granulated sugar
1 red pepper, seeded and diced
½ cucumber, seeded and sliced
2 plum tomatoes, cut into wedges
115g/4oz pineapple, cut into
 small chunks
freshly ground black pepper
2 spring onions, cut into short lengths
coriander leaves, to garnish
spring onions, shredded, to garnish

1 Slice the pork into thin strips. Heat
the oil in a wok or large frying pan.

2 Add the garlic and fry until golden,
then add the pork and stir-fry for
about 4–5 minutes. Add the onion.

3 Season with fish sauce, sugar and
freshly ground black pepper. Stir
and cook for 3–4 minutes, or until the
pork is cooked.

4 Add the rest of the vegetables, the
pineapple and spring onions. You
may need to add a few tablespoons of
water. Continue to stir-fry for another
3–4 minutes. Serve hot garnished with
coriander leaves and spring onion.

Burmese-style Pork Curry

Burmese-style curries use pork instead of chicken or beef and water rather than coconut milk. The flavours of this delicious dish improve when it is reheated.

INGREDIENTS

Serves 4–6

2.5cm/1in piece fresh root ginger, crushed
8 dried red chillies, soaked in warm water for 20 minutes
2 stalks lemon grass, finely chopped
15ml/1 tbsp chopped galangal
15ml/1 tbsp shrimp paste
30ml/2 tbsp brown sugar
675g/1½lb pork with some of its fat
600ml/1 pint/2½ cups water
10ml/2 tsp ground turmeric
5ml/1 tsp dark soy sauce
4 shallots, finely chopped
15ml/1 tbsp chopped garlic
45ml/3 tbsp tamarind juice
5ml/1 tsp sugar
15ml/1 tbsp fish sauce
green beans, to serve
red chillies, to garnish

1 In a mortar, pound the ginger, chillies, lemon grass and galangal into a coarse paste with a pestle, then add the shrimp paste and brown sugar to produce a dark, grainy purée.

2 Cut the pork into large chunks and place in a large heavy-based saucepan. Add the curry purée and stir to coat the meat thoroughly.

3 Cook over a low heat, stirring occasionally, until the meat has changed colour and rendered some of its fat and the curry paste is fragrant.

4 Stir in the water, turmeric and soy sauce. Simmer gently for about 40 minutes, until the meat is tender.

5 Add the shallots, garlic, tamarind juice, sugar and fish sauce. Serve with freshly cooked green beans, and garnish with chillies.

Savoury Pork Ribs with Snake Beans

This is a rich and pungent dish. If snake beans are hard to find, you can substitute fine green or runner beans.

INGREDIENTS

Serves 4–6

675g/1½lb pork spare ribs or belly of pork
30ml/2 tbsp vegetable oil
120ml/4fl oz/½ cup water
15ml/1 tbsp palm sugar
15ml/1 tbsp fish sauce
150g/5oz snake beans, cut into 5cm/2in lengths
2 kaffir lime leaves, finely sliced
2 red chillies, finely sliced, to garnish

For the chilli paste

3 dried red chillies, seeded and soaked
4 shallots, chopped
4 garlic cloves, chopped
5ml/1 tsp chopped galangal
1 stalk lemon grass, chopped
6 black peppercorns
5ml/1 tsp shrimp paste
30ml/2 tbsp dried shrimp, rinsed

1 Put all the ingredients for the chilli paste in a mortar and grind together with a pestle until it forms a thick paste.

2 Slice and chop the spare ribs (or belly pork) into 4cm/1½in lengths.

3 Heat the oil in a wok or frying pan. Add the pork and fry for about 5 minutes, until lightly browned.

4 Stir in the chilli paste and continue to cook for another 5 minutes, stirring constantly to stop the paste from sticking to the pan.

5 Add the water, cover and simmer for 7–10 minutes or until the spare ribs are tender. Season with palm sugar and fish sauce.

6 Mix in the snake beans and kaffir lime leaves and fry until the beans are cooked. Serve garnished with sliced red chillies.

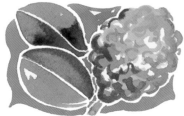

Chicken Livers, Thai-style

Chicken liver is a good source of iron and is a popular meat, especially in the north-east of Thailand. Serve this dish as a starter with salad, or as part of a main course with jasmine rice.

INGREDIENTS

Serves 4–6
45ml/3 tbsp vegetable oil
450g/1lb chicken livers, trimmed
4 shallots, chopped
2 garlic cloves, chopped
15ml/1 tbsp roasted ground rice
45ml/3 tbsp fish sauce
45ml/3 tbsp lime juice
5ml/1 tsp sugar
2 stalks lemon grass, bruised
  and finely chopped
30ml/2 tbsp chopped coriander
10–12 mint leaves, to garnish
2 red chillies, chopped, to garnish

1 Heat the oil in a wok or large frying pan. Add the livers and fry over a medium-high heat for about 4 minutes, until the liver is golden brown and cooked, but still pink inside.

2 Move the liver to one side of the pan and add the shallots and garlic. Fry for about 1–2 minutes.

3 Add the roasted ground rice, fish sauce, lime juice, sugar, lemon grass and coriander. Stir to combine. Remove from the heat and serve garnished with mint leaves and chillies.

Barbecued Chicken

Barbecued chicken is served almost everywhere in Thailand, from portable roadside stalls to sports stadiums and beaches.

INGREDIENTS

Serves 4–6
1 chicken, about 1.5kg/3–3½ lb, cut
  into 8–10 pieces
2 limes, cut into wedges, to garnish
2 red chillies, finely sliced, to garnish

For the marinade
2 stalks lemon grass, chopped
2.5cm/1in piece fresh root ginger
6 garlic cloves
4 shallots
½ bunch coriander roots
15ml/1 tbsp palm sugar
120ml/4fl oz/½ cup coconut milk
30ml/2 tbsp fish sauce
30ml/2 tbsp soy sauce

1 To make the marinade, put all the ingredients into a food processor and process until smooth.

2 Put the chicken pieces in a dish and pour over the marinade. Leave in a cool place to marinate for at least 4 hours or overnight.

3 Barbecue the chicken over glowing coals, or place on a rack over a baking tray and bake at 200°C/400°F/ Gas 6 for about 20–30 minutes or until the chicken is cooked and golden brown. Turn the pieces occasionally and brush with the marinade.

4 Garnish with lime wedges and finely sliced red chillies.

Cashew Chicken

In this Chinese-inspired dish, tender pieces of chicken are stir-fried with cashew nuts, red chillies and a touch of garlic, for a delicious combination.

INGREDIENTS

Serves 4–6

450g/1lb boneless chicken breasts
30ml/2 tbsp vegetable oil
2 garlic cloves, sliced
4 dried red chillies, chopped
1 red pepper, seeded and cut into
    2cm/³⁄₄in dice
30ml/2 tbsp oyster sauce
15ml/1 tbsp soy sauce
pinch of granulated sugar
1 bunch spring onions, cut into
    5cm/2in lengths
175g/6oz cashew nuts, roasted
coriander leaves, to garnish

1 Remove and discard the skin from the chicken breasts. With a sharp knife, cut the chicken into bite-size pieces and set aside.

2 Heat the oil in a wok and swirl it around. Add the garlic and dried chillies and fry until golden.

3 Add the chicken and stir-fry until it changes colour, then add the red pepper. If necessary, add a little water.

4 Stir in the oyster sauce, soy sauce and sugar. Add the spring onions and cashew nuts. Stir-fry for about another 1–2 minutes. Serve garnished with coriander leaves.

Stir-fried Chicken with Basil and Chillies

This quick and easy chicken dish is an excellent introduction to Thai cuisine. Deep frying the basil adds another dimension to this dish. Thai basil, which is sometimes known as Holy basil, has a unique, pungent flavour that is both spicy and sharp. The dull leaves have serrated edges.

INGREDIENTS

Serves 4–6
45ml/3 tbsp vegetable oil
4 garlic cloves, sliced
2–4 red chillies, seeded and chopped
450g/1lb chicken, cut into
  bite-size pieces
30–45ml/2–3 tbsp fish sauce
10ml/2 tsp dark soy sauce
5ml/1 tsp sugar
10–12 Thai basil leaves
2 red chillies, finely sliced, to garnish
20 Thai basil leaves, deep fried
  (optional)

1 Heat the oil in a wok or large frying pan and swirl it around.

2 Add the garlic and chillies and stir-fry until golden.

3 Add the chicken and stir-fry until it changes colour.

— COOK'S TIP —

To deep fry Thai basil leaves, make sure that the leaves are completely dry. Deep fry in hot oil for about 30–40 seconds, lift out and drain on kitchen paper.

4 Season with fish sauce, soy sauce and sugar. Continue to stir-fry for 3-4 minutes or until the chicken is cooked. Stir in the fresh Thai basil leaves. Garnish with sliced chillies and the deep fried basil, if using.

Baked Fish in Banana Leaves

Fish that is prepared in this way is particularly succulent and flavourful. Fillets are used here rather than whole fish – easier for those who don't like to mess about with bones. It is a great dish for outdoor barbecues.

INGREDIENTS

Serves 4

250ml/8fl oz/1 cup coconut milk
30ml/2 tbsp red curry paste
45ml/3 tbsp fish sauce
30ml/2 tbsp caster sugar
5 kaffir lime leaves, torn
4 x 175g/6oz fish fillets, such
   as snapper
175g/6oz mixed vegetables, such as
   carrots or leeks, finely shredded
4 banana leaves
30ml/2 tbsp shredded spring onions,
   to garnish
2 red chillies, finely sliced, to garnish

1 Combine the coconut milk, curry paste, fish sauce, sugar and kaffir lime leaves in a shallow dish.

2 Marinate the fish in this mixture for about 15–30 minutes. Preheat the oven to 200°C/400°F/Gas 6.

3 Mix the vegetables together and lay a portion on top of a banana leaf. Place a piece of fish on top with a little of its marinade.

4 Wrap the fish up by turning in the sides and ends of the leaf and secure with cocktail sticks. Repeat with the rest of the leaves and fish.

5 Bake in the hot oven for 20–25 minutes or until the fish is cooked. Alternatively, cook under the grill or on the barbeque. Just before serving, garnish the fish with a sprinkling of spring onions and sliced red chillies.

Stir-fried Scallops with Asparagus

Asparagus is extremely popular among the Chinese Thai. The combination of garlic and black pepper gives this dish its spiciness. You can substitute the scallops with prawns or other firm fish.

INGREDIENTS

Serves 4–6

60ml/4 tbsp vegetable oil
1 bunch asparagus, cut into 5cm/2in
   lengths
4 garlic cloves, finely chopped
2 shallots, finely chopped
450g/1lb scallops, cleaned
30ml/2 tbsp fish sauce
2.5ml/½ tsp coarsely ground
   black pepper
120ml/4fl oz/½ cup coconut milk
coriander leaves, to garnish

1 Heat half the oil in a wok or large frying pan. Add the asparagus and stir-fry for about 2 minutes. Transfer the asparagus to a plate and set aside.

2 Add the rest of the oil, garlic and shallots to the same wok and fry until fragrant. Add the scallops and cook for another 1–2 minutes.

3 Return the asparagus to the wok. Add the fish sauce, black pepper and coconut milk.

4 Stir and cook for another 3–4 minutes or until the scallops and asparagus are cooked. Garnish with the coriander leaves.

Satay Prawns

An enticing and tasty dish. Serve with greens and jasmine rice.

INGREDIENTS

Serves 4–6

450g/1lb king prawns, shelled, tail ends
   left intact and deveined
½ bunch coriander leaves, to garnish
4 red chillies, finely sliced, to garnish
spring onions, cut diagonally, to garnish

For the peanut sauce

45ml/3 tbsp vegetable oil
15ml/1 tbsp chopped garlic
1 small onion, chopped
3–4 red chillies, crushed and chopped
3 kaffir lime leaves, torn
1 stalk lemon grass, bruised
   and chopped
5ml/1 tsp medium curry paste
250ml/8fl oz/1 cup coconut milk
1.5cm/½in cinnamon stick
75g/3oz crunchy peanut butter
45ml/3 tbsp tamarind juice
30ml/2 tbsp fish sauce
30ml/2 tbsp palm sugar
juice of ½ lemon

1 To make the sauce, heat half the oil in a wok or large frying pan and add the garlic and onion. Cook until it softens, about 3–4 minutes.

2 Add the chillies, kaffir lime leaves, lemon grass and curry paste. Cook for a further 2–3 minutes.

--- COOK'S TIP ---

Curry paste has a far superior, authentic flavour to powdered varieties. Once opened, they should be kept in the fridge and used within 2 months.

3 Stir in the coconut milk, cinnamon stick, peanut butter, tamarind juice, fish sauce, palm sugar and lemon juice.

4 Reduce the heat and simmer gently for 15–20 minutes until the sauce thickens, stirring occasionally to ensure the sauce doesn't stick to the bottom of the wok or frying pan.

5 Heat the rest of the oil in a wok or large frying pan. Add the prawns and stir-fry for about 3–4 minutes or until the prawns turn pink and are slightly firm to the touch.

6 Mix the prawns with the sauce. Serve garnished with coriander leaves, red chillies and spring onions.

Sweet and Sour Fish

When fish is cooked in this way the skin becomes crispy on the outside, while the flesh remains moist and juicy inside. The sweet and sour sauce, with its colourful cherry tomatoes, complements the fish beautifully.

INGREDIENTS

Serves 4–6

1 large or 2 medium-size fish such as
   snapper or mullet, heads removed
20ml/4 tsp cornflour
120ml/4fl oz/½ cup vegetable oil
15ml/1 tbsp chopped garlic
15ml/1 tbsp chopped root ginger
30ml/2 tbsp chopped shallots
225g/8oz cherry tomatoes
30ml/2 tbsp red wine vinegar
30ml/2 tbsp granulated sugar
30ml/2 tbsp tomato ketchup
15ml/1 tbsp fish sauce
45ml/3 tbsp water
salt and freshly ground black pepper
coriander leaves, to garnish
shredded spring onions, to garnish

1 Thoroughly rinse and clean the fish. Score the skin diagonally on both sides of the fish.

2 Coat the fish lightly on both sides with 15ml/1 tbsp cornflour. Shake off any excess.

3 Heat the oil in a wok or large frying pan and slide the fish into the wok. Reduce the heat to medium and fry the fish until crisp and brown, about 6–7 minutes on both sides.

4 Remove the fish with a fish slice and place on a large platter.

5 Pour off all but 30ml/2 tbsp of the oil and add the garlic, ginger and shallots. Fry until golden.

6 Add the cherry tomatoes and cook until they burst open. Stir in the vinegar, sugar, tomato ketchup and fish sauce. Simmer gently for 1–2 minutes and adjust the seasoning.

7 Blend the remaining 5ml/1 tsp cornflour with the water. Stir into the sauce and heat until it thickens. Pour the sauce over the fish and garnish with coriander leaves and shredded spring onions.

Pineapple Curry with Prawns and Mussels

The delicate sweet and sour flavour of this curry comes from the pineapple and although it seems an odd combination, it is rather delicious. Use the freshest shellfish that you can find.

INGREDIENTS

Serves 4–6
600ml/1 pint/2½ cups coconut milk
30ml/2 tbsp red curry paste
30ml/2 tbsp fish sauce
15ml/1 tbsp granulated sugar
225g/8oz king prawns, shelled
   and deveined
450g/1lb mussels, cleaned and
   beards removed
175g/6oz fresh pineapple, finely
   crushed or chopped
5 kaffir lime leaves, torn
2 red chillies, chopped, to garnish
coriander leaves, to garnish

1 In a large saucepan, bring half the coconut milk to the boil and heat, stirring, until it separates.

2 Add the red curry paste and cook until fragrant. Add the fish sauce and sugar and continue to cook for a few moments.

3 Stir in the rest of the coconut milk and bring back to the boil. Add the king prawns, mussels, pineapple and kaffir lime leaves.

4 Reheat until boiling and then simmer for 3–5 minutes, until the prawns are cooked and the mussels have opened. Remove any mussels that have not opened and discard. Serve garnished with chopped red chillies and coriander leaves.

Curried Prawns in Coconut Milk

A curry-like dish where the prawns are cooked in a spicy coconut gravy.

INGREDIENTS

Serves 4–6
600ml/1 pint/2½ cups coconut milk
30ml/2 tbsp yellow curry paste (see
   Cook's Tip)
15ml/1 tbsp fish sauce
2.5ml/½ tsp salt
5ml/1 tsp granulated sugar
450g/1lb king prawns, shelled, tails left
   intact and deveined
225g/8oz cherry tomatoes
juice of ½ lime, to serve
2 red chillies, cut into strips, to garnish
coriander leaves, to garnish

1 Put half the coconut milk into a pan or wok and bring to the boil.

2 Add the yellow curry paste to the coconut milk, stir until it disperses, then simmer for about 10 minutes.

3 Add the fish sauce, salt, sugar and remaining coconut milk. Simmer for another 5 minutes.

4 Add the prawns and cherry tomatoes. Simmer very gently for about 5 minutes until the prawns are pink and tender.

5 Serve sprinkled with lime juice and garnish with chillies and coriander.

--- COOK'S TIP ---

To make yellow curry paste, process together 6–8 yellow chillies, 1 chopped lemon grass stalk, 4 peeled shallots, 4 garlic cloves, 15ml/1 tbsp peeled chopped fresh root ginger, 5ml/1 tsp coriander seeds, 5ml/1 tsp mustard powder, 5ml/1 tsp salt, 2.5ml/½ tsp ground cinnamon, 15ml/1 tbsp light brown sugar and 30ml/2 tbsp oil in a blender or food procesor. When a paste has formed, transfer to a glass jar and keep in the fridge.

Water Spinach with Brown Bean Sauce

Water spinach, often known as Siamese watercress, is a green vegetable with arrowhead-shaped leaves. If you can't find it, use spinach, watercress, pak choy or even broccoli, and adjust the cooking time accordingly. There are excellent variations to this recipe using black bean sauce, shrimp paste or fermented bean curd instead of brown bean sauce.

INGREDIENTS

Serves 4–6

1 bunch water spinach, about
  1kg/2¼lb in weight
45ml/3 tbsp vegetable oil
15ml/1 tbsp chopped garlic
15ml/1 tbsp brown bean sauce
30ml/2 tbsp fish sauce
15ml/1 tbsp granulated sugar
freshly black ground pepper

1 Trim and discard the bottom coarse, woody end of the water spinach. Cut the remaining part into 5cm/2in lengths, keeping the leaves separate from the stems.

2 Heat the oil in a wok or large frying pan. When it starts to smoke, add the chopped garlic and toss for 10 seconds.

3 Add the stem part of the water spinach, let it sizzle and cook for 1 minute, then add the leafy parts.

4 Stir in the brown bean sauce, fish sauce, sugar and pepper. Toss and turn over the spinach until it begins to wilt, about 3–4 minutes. Transfer to a serving dish and serve immediately.

Mixed Vegetables in Coconut Milk

A most delicious way of cooking vegetables. If you don't like highly spiced food, use fewer red chilli peppers.

INGREDIENTS

Serves 4–6

450g/1lb mixed vegetables, such as
  aubergines, baby sweetcorn, carrots,
  snake beans and patty pan squash
8 red chillies, seeded
2 stalks lemon grass, chopped
4 kaffir lime leaves, torn
30ml/2 tbsp vegetable oil
250ml/8fl oz/1 cup coconut milk
30ml/2 tbsp fish sauce
salt
15–20 Thai basil leaves, to garnish

1 Cut the vegetables into similar size shapes using a sharp knife.

2 Put the red chillies, lemon grass and kaffir lime leaves in a mortar and grind together with a pestle.

3 Heat the oil in a wok or large deep frying pan. Add the chilli mixture and fry for 2–3 minutes.

4 Stir in the coconut milk and bring to the boil. Add the vegetables and cook for about 5 minutes or until they are tender. Season with the fish sauce and salt, and garnish with basil leaves.

Cabbage Salad

A simple and delicious way of using cabbage. Other vegetables such as broccoli, cauliflower, beansprouts and Chinese cabbage can also be prepared this way.

INGREDIENTS

Serves 4–6

30ml/2 tbsp fish sauce
grated rind of 1 lime
30ml/2 tbsp lime juice
120ml/4fl oz/½ cup coconut milk
30ml/2 tbsp vegetable oil
2 large red chillies, seeded and finely
　　cut into strips
6 garlic cloves, finely sliced
6 shallots, finely sliced
1 small cabbage, shredded
30ml/2 tbsp coarsely chopped roasted
　　peanuts, to serve

1 Make the dressing by combining the fish sauce, lime rind and juice and coconut milk. Set aside.

2 Heat the oil in a wok or frying pan. Stir-fry the chillies, garlic and shallots, until the shallots are brown and crisp. Remove and set aside.

3 Blanch the cabbage in boiling salted water for about 2–3 minutes, drain and put into a bowl.

4 Stir the dressing into the cabbage, toss and mix well. Transfer the salad into a serving dish. Sprinkle with the fried shallot mixture and the chopped roasted peanuts.

Bamboo Shoot Salad

This salad, which has a hot and sharp flavour, originated in north-east Thailand. Use fresh young bamboo shoots when you can find them, otherwise substitute canned bamboo shoots.

INGREDIENTS

Serves 4

400g/14oz can whole bamboo shoots
25g/1oz glutinous rice
30ml/2 tbsp chopped shallots
15ml/1 tbsp chopped garlic
45ml/3 tbsp chopped spring onions
30ml/2 tbsp fish sauce
30ml/2 tbsp lime juice
5ml/1 tsp granulated sugar
2.5ml/½ tsp dried flaked chillies
20–25 small mint leaves
15ml/1 tbsp toasted sesame seeds

3 Tip the rice into a bowl, add the shallots, garlic, spring onions, fish sauce, lime juice, granulated sugar, chillies and half the mint leaves.

4 Mix thoroughly, then pour over the bamboo shoots and toss together. Serve sprinkled with sesame seeds and the remaining mint leaves.

1 Rinse and drain the bamboo shoots, finely slice and set aside.

2 Dry roast the rice in a frying pan until it is golden brown. Remove and grind to fine crumbs with a pestle and mortar.

Jasmine Rice

A naturally aromatic, long grain white rice, jasmine rice is the staple of most Thai meals. If you eat rice regularly, you might want to invest in an electric rice cooker.

INGREDIENTS

Serves 4–6
450g/1lb/2 cups jasmine rice
750ml/1¼ pint/3 cups cold water

> ——— COOK'S TIP ———
>
> An electric rice cooker cooks the rice and keeps it warm. Different sizes and models of rice cookers are available. The top of the range is a non-stick version, which is expensive, but well worth the money

1 Rinse the rice thoroughly at least three times in cold water until the water runs clear.

2 Put the rice in a heavy-based saucepan and add the water. Bring the rice to a vigorous boil, uncovered, over a high heat.

3 Stir and reduce the heat to low. Cover and simmer for up to 20 minutes, or until all the water has been absorbed. Remove from the heat and leave to stand for 10 minutes.

4 Remove the lid and stir the rice gently with a rice paddle or a pair of wooden chopsticks, to fluff up and separate the grains.

Fried Jasmine Rice with Prawns and Thai Basil

Thai basil (*bai grapao*), also known as Holy basil, has a unique, pungent flavour that is both spicy and sharp. It can be found in most Oriental food markets.

INGREDIENTS

Serves 4–6
45ml/3 tbsp vegetable oil
1 egg, beaten
1 onion, chopped
15ml/1 tbsp chopped garlic
15ml/1 tbsp shrimp paste
1kg/2¼lb/4 cups cooked jasmine rice
350g/12oz cooked shelled prawns
50g/2oz thawed frozen peas
oyster sauce, to taste
2 spring onions, chopped
15–20 Thai basil leaves, roughly snipped, plus an extra sprig, to garnish

1 Heat 15ml/1 tbsp of the oil in a wok or frying pan. Add the beaten egg and swirl it around the pan to set like a thin pancake.

2 Cook until golden, slide out on to a board, roll up and cut into thin strips. Set aside.

3 Heat the remaining oil in the wok, add the onion and garlic and fry for 2–3 minutes. Stir in the shrimp paste and mix well.

4 Add the rice prawns and peas and toss and stir together, until everything is heated through.

5 Season with oyster sauce to taste, taking great care as the shrimp paste is salty. Add the spring onions and basil leaves. Transfer to a serving dish and serve topped with the strips of egg pancake. Garnish with a sprig of basil.

Coconut Rice

This rich dish is usually served with a tangy papaya salad.

INGREDIENTS

Serves 4–6

450g/1lb/2 cups jasmine rice
250ml/8fl oz/1 cup water
475ml/16fl oz/2 cups coconut milk
2.5ml/½ tsp salt
30ml/2 tbsp granulated sugar
fresh shredded coconut, to garnish
(optional)

1 Wash the rice in several changes of cold water until it runs clear. Place the water, coconut milk, salt and sugar in a heavy-bottomed saucepan.

2 Add the rice, cover and bring to the boil. Reduce the heat to low and simmer for about 15–20 minutes or until the rice is tender to the bite and cooked through.

3 Turn off the heat and allow the rice to rest in the saucepan for a further 5–10 minutes.

4 Fluff up the rice with chopsticks before serving.

Pineapple Fried Rice

When buying a pineapple, look for a sweet-smelling fruit with an even brownish/yellow skin. To test for ripeness, tap the base – a dull sound indicates that the fruit is ripe. The flesh should also give slightly when pressed.

INGREDIENTS

Serves 4–6

1 pineapple
30ml/2 tbsp vegetable oil
1 small onion, finely chopped
2 green chillies, seeded and chopped
225g/8oz lean pork, cut into
    small dice
115g/4oz cooked shelled prawns
675–900g/1½–2 lb/3–4 cups cooked
    cold rice
50g/2oz roasted cashew nuts
2 spring onions, chopped
30ml/2 tbsp fish sauce
15ml/1 tbsp soy sauce
10–12 mint leaves, to garnish
2 red chillies, sliced, to garnish
1 green chilli, sliced, to garnish

1 Cut the pineapple in half lengthways and remove the flesh from both halves by cutting round inside the skin. Reserve the skin shells. You need 115g/4oz of fruit, chopped finely (keep the rest for a dessert).

— COOK'S TIP —

This dish is ideal to prepare for a special occasion meal. Served in the pineapple skin shells, it is sure to be the talking point of the dinner.

2 Heat the oil in a wok or large frying pan. Add the onion and chillies and fry for about 3–5 minutes until softened. Add the pork and cook until it is brown on all sides.

3 Stir in the prawns and rice and toss well together. Continue to stir-fry until the rice is thoroughly heated.

4 Add the chopped pineapple, cashew nuts and spring onions. Season with fish sauce and soy sauce.

5 Spoon into the pineapple skin shells. Garnish with shredded mint leaves and red and green chillies.

Crispy Fried Rice Vermicelli

Mee Krob is usually served at celebration meals. It is a crisp tangle of fried rice vermicelli, which is tossed in a piquant garlic, sweet and sour sauce.

INGREDIENTS

Serves 4–6
oil for frying
175g/6oz rice vermicelli
15ml/1 tbsp chopped garlic
4–6 dried chillies, seeded and chopped
30ml/2 tbsp chopped shallot
15ml/1 tbsp dried shrimps, rinsed
115g/4oz minced pork
115g/4oz uncooked shelled prawns, chopped
30ml/2 tbsp brown bean sauce
30ml/2 tbsp rice wine vinegar
45ml/3 tbsp fish sauce
75g/3 tbsp palm sugar
30ml/2 tbsp tamarind or lime juice
115g/4oz beansprouts

For the garnish
2 spring onions, shredded
30ml/2 tbsp fresh coriander leaves
2 heads pickled garlic (optional)
2-egg omelette, rolled and sliced
2 red chillies, chopped

1 Heat the oil in a wok. Break the rice vermicelli apart into small handfuls about 7.5cm/3in long. Deep fry in the hot oil until they puff up. Remove and drain on kitchen paper.

2 Leave 30ml/2 tbsp of the hot oil in the wok, add the garlic, chillies, shallots and shrimps. Fry until fragrant.

3 Add the minced pork and stir-fry for about 3–4 minutes, until it is no longer pink. Add the prawns and fry for a further 2 minutes. Remove the mixture and set aside.

4 To the same wok, add the brown bean sauce, vinegar, fish sauce and palm sugar. Bring to a gentle boil, stir to dissolve the sugar and cook until thick and syrupy.

5 Add the tamarind or lime juice and adjust the seasoning. It should be sweet, sour and salty.

6 Reduce the heat. Add the pork and prawn mixture and the beansprouts to the sauce; stir to mix.

7 Add the rice noodles and toss gently to coat them with the sauce without breaking the noodles too much. Transfer the noodles to a platter. Garnish with spring onions, coriander leaves, pickled garlic, omelette strips and red chillies.

Thai Fried Noodles

Phat Thai has a fascinating flavour and texture. It is made with rice noodles and is considered one of the national dishes of Thailand.

INGREDIENTS

Serves 4–6

350g/12oz rice noodles
45ml/3 tbsp vegetable oil
15ml/1 tbsp chopped garlic
16 uncooked king prawns, shelled, tails
   left intact and deveined
2 eggs, lightly beaten
15ml/1 tbsp dried shrimps, rinsed
30ml/2 tbsp pickled white radish
50g/2oz fried bean curd, cut into
   small slivers
2.5ml/½ tsp dried chilli flakes
115g/4oz garlic chives, cut into
   5cm/2in lengths
225g/8oz beansprouts
50g/2oz roasted peanuts, coarsely
   ground
5ml/1 tsp granulated sugar
15ml/1 tbsp dark soy sauce
30ml/2 tbsp fish sauce
30ml/2 tbsp tamarind juice
30ml/2 tbsp coriander leaves,
   to garnish
1 kaffir lime, to garnish

1 Soak the noodles in warm water for 20–30 minutes, then drain.

2 Heat 15ml/1 tbsp of the oil in a wok or large frying pan. Add the garlic and fry until golden. Stir in the prawns and cook for about 1–2 minutes until pink, tossing from time to time. Remove and set aside.

3 Heat another 15ml/1 tbsp of oil in the wok. Add the eggs and tilt the wok to spread them into a thin sheet. Stir to scramble and break the egg into small pieces. Remove from the wok and set aside with the prawns.

4 Heat the remaining oil in the same wok. Add the dried shrimps, pickled radish, bean curd and dried chillies. Stir briefly. Add the soaked noodles and stir-fry for 5 minutes.

5 Add the garlic chives, half the beansprouts and half the peanuts. Season with the granulated sugar, soy sauce, fish sauce and tamarind juice. Mix well and cook until the noodles are heated through.

6 Return the prawn and egg mixture to the wok and mix with the noodles. Serve garnished with the rest of the beansprouts, peanuts, coriander leaves and lime wedges.

INDIA

Spicy Pepper Soup

This is a highly soothing broth for winter evenings, also known as *Mulla-ga-tani*. Serve with the whole spices, or strain and reheat if you prefer. The lemon juice may be adjusted to taste, but this dish should be distinctly sour.

INGREDIENTS

Serves 4

30ml/2 tbsp vegetable oil
2.5ml/½ tsp freshly ground
  black pepper
5ml/1 tsp cumin seeds
2.5 ml/½ tsp mustard seeds
1.5ml/¼ tsp asafoetida
2 whole dried red chillies
4–6 curry leaves
2.5ml/½ tsp ground turmeric
2 garlic cloves, crushed
300ml/½ pint/1¼ cups tomato juice
juice of 2 lemons
120ml/4fl oz/½ cup water
salt, to taste
coriander leaves, chopped, to garnish

COOK'S TIP

Don't be put off by the unpleasant smell of asafoetida as it disappears when cooked. Used in small quantities, as here, asafoetida adds an oniony flavour to foods.

VARIATION

For a slightly more bitter flavour, use lime juice instead of lemon juice. Add 5ml/ 1 tsp tamarind paste for extra sourness.

1 In a heavy-based saucepan, heat the oil and fry the pepper, cumin and mustard seeds, asafoetida, chillies, curry leaves, turmeric and garlic until the chillies are nearly black and the garlic is golden brown.

2 Lower the heat and add the tomato juice, lemon juice, water and salt. Bring the soup to the boil, then lower the heat and simmer gently for about 10 minutes. Pour the soup into bowls, garnish with the chopped coriander and serve immediately.

Vegetable Samosas

A selection of highly spiced vegetables in a pastry casing makes these samosas a delicious snack at any time of the day.

INGREDIENTS

Makes 28
14 sheets of filo pastry, thawed and
   wrapped in a damp dish towel
oil for brushing the pastries

For the filling
3 large potatoes, boiled and
   coarsely mashed
75g/3oz/¾ cup frozen peas, thawed
50g/2oz/⅓ cup canned
   sweetcorn, drained
5ml/1 tsp ground coriander
5ml/1 tsp ground cumin
5ml/1 tsp dry mango powder (*amchur*)
1 small onion, finely chopped
2 green chillies, finely chopped
30ml/2 tbsp coriander leaves, chopped
30ml/2 tbsp mint leaves, chopped
juice of 1 lemon
salt, to taste

1 Preheat the oven to 200°C/400°F/
Gas 6. Cut each sheet of filo pastry
in half lengthways and fold
each piece in half lengthways to give
28 thin strips. Lightly brush with oil.

COOK'S TIP

Work with one or two sheets of filo pastry at a time and keep the rest covered with a damp dish towel to prevent it drying out.

2 Toss all the filling ingredients
together in a large mixing bowl
until they are well blended. Adjust
the seasoning with salt and lemon
juice if necessary.

3 Using one strip of the pastry at a
time, place 15ml/1 tbsp of the
filling mixture at one end of the strip
and diagonally fold the pastry up to
form a triangle shape. Brush the
samosas with oil and bake in the oven
for 10–15 minutes, until golden brown.

Ginger Chicken Wings

INGREDIENTS

Serves 4

10–12 chicken wings, skinned
175ml/6fl oz/³/₄ cup natural low
  fat yogurt
7.5ml/1½ tsp ginger pulp
5ml/1 tsp salt
5ml/1 tsp Tabasco sauce
15ml/1 tbsp tomato ketchup
5ml/1 tsp garlic pulp
15ml/1 tbsp lemon juice
15ml/1 tbsp fresh coriander leaves
15ml/1 tbsp oil
2 medium onions, sliced
15ml/1 tbsp shredded root ginger

1 Place the chicken wings in a glass or china bowl. Pour the yogurt into a separate bowl along with the ginger pulp, salt, Tabasco sauce, tomato ketchup, garlic pulp, lemon juice and half the fresh coriander leaves. Whisk everything together, then pour the mixture over the chicken wings and stir gently to coat the chicken.

2 Heat the oil in a wok or heavy-based frying pan and fry the onions until soft.

3 Pour in the chicken wings and cook over a medium heat, stirring occasionally, for 10–15 minutes.

4 Add the remaining coriander and the shredded ginger and serve hot.

COOK'S TIP

You can substitute drumsticks or other chicken portions for the wings in this recipe, but remember to increase the cooking time.

Glazed Garlic Prawns

It is best to peel the prawns for this dish as it helps them to absorb maximum flavour. Serve with salad as a starter or with rice and accompaniments for a more substantial meal.

INGREDIENTS

Serves 4
15ml/1 tbsp oil
3 garlic cloves, roughly chopped
3 tomatoes, chopped
2.5ml/½ tsp salt
5ml/1 tsp crushed red chillies
5ml/1 tsp lemon juice
15ml/1 tbsp mango chutney
1 fresh green chilli, chopped
15–20 cooked king prawns, peeled
fresh coriander sprigs, to garnish

1 In a medium heavy-based saucepan, heat the oil and add the garlic, cooking gently for a few minutes.

------ COOK'S TIP ------

Use a skewer or the point of a knife to remove the black intestinal vein running down the back of the prawns.

2 Lower the heat and add the chopped tomatoes to the saucepan along with the salt, crushed red chillies, lemon juice, mango chutney and fresh green chilli.

3 Finally, add the prawns, turn up the heat and stir-fry these quickly, until heated through.

4 Transfer the prawns to a serving dish. Serve garnished with fresh coriander sprigs.

Balti Keema with Curry Leaves and Chillies

Minced lamb is cooked in its own juices with a few spices and herbs, but no other liquid.

INGREDIENTS

Serves 4
10ml/2 tsp oil
2 medium onions, chopped
10 curry leaves
6 green chillies
350g/12oz lean minced lamb
5ml/1 tsp garlic pulp
5ml/1 tsp ginger pulp
5ml/1 tsp chilli powder
1.5ml/¼ tsp ground turmeric
5ml/1 tsp salt
2 tomatoes, peeled and quartered
15ml/1 tbsp chopped fresh coriander

1 Heat the oil in a wok or heavy-based frying pan and fry the onions together with the curry leaves and 3 of the whole green chillies.

COOK'S TIP

This curry also makes a terrific brunch if served with fried eggs.

2 Put the lamb into a bowl and blend thoroughly with the garlic, ginger, chilli powder, turmeric and salt.

3 Add the lamb to the onions and stir-fry for 7–10 minutes.

4 Add the tomatoes, coriander and chillies and stir-fry for 2 minutes.

Creamy Lamb Korma

Cutting the lamb into strips for this lovely dish makes it easier and quicker to cook.

INGREDIENTS

Serves 4

2 green chillies
120ml/4fl oz/½ cup natural low
   fat yogurt
50ml/2fl oz/¼ cup coconut milk
15ml/1 tbsp ground almonds
5ml/1 tsp salt
5ml/1 tsp garlic pulp
5ml/1 tsp ginger pulp
5ml/1 tsp garam masala
1.5ml/¼ tsp ground cardamom
large pinch of ground cinnamon
15ml/1 tbsp chopped fresh mint
15ml/1 tbsp oil
2 medium onions, diced
1 bay leaf
4 black peppercorns
225g/8oz lean lamb, cut into strips
150ml/¼ pint/⅔ cup water
fresh mint leaves, to garnish

1 Finely chop the chillies. Whisk the yogurt with the chillies, coconut milk, ground almonds, salt, garlic, ginger, garam masala, cardamom, cinnamon and mint.

2 Heat the oil in a wok or heavy-based frying pan and fry the onions with the bay leaf and peppercorns for about 5 mintues.

3 When the onions are soft and golden brown, add the lamb and stir-fry for about 2 minutes.

4 Pour in the yogurt mixture and water, lower the heat, cover and cook for about 15 minutes or until the lamb is cooked through, stirring occasionally. Stir-fry for a further 2 minutes. Serve garnished with fresh mint leaves.

COOK'S TIP

Pea and Mushroom Pilau goes very well with this korma.

Beef Madras

Madras curries originate from southern India and are aromatic, robust and pungent in flavour. This recipe uses stewing beef, but you can replace it with lean lamb if you prefer.

INGREDIENTS

Serves 4
900g/2lb lean stewing beef
15ml/1 tbsp oil
1 large onion, finely chopped
4 cloves
4 green cardamom pods
2 green chillies, finely chopped
2.5cm/1in piece root ginger, finely chopped
2 garlic cloves, crushed
2 dried red chillies
15ml/1 tbsp curry paste
10ml/2 tsp ground coriander
5ml/1 tsp ground cumin
2.5ml/½ tsp salt
150ml/¼ pint/⅔ cup beef stock
fresh coriander, to garnish
rice, to serve

1 Remove any visible fat from the beef and cut the meat into 2.5cm/1in cubes.

2 Heat the oil in a large heavy-based frying pan and stir-fry the onion, cloves and cardamom pods for about 5 minutes. Add the fresh green chillies, ginger, garlic and dried red chillies and fry for a further 2 minutes.

3 Add the curry paste and fry for about 2 minutes. Add the beef and fry for 5–8 minutes until all the meat pieces are lightly browned.

4 Add the coriander, cumin, salt and stock. Cover and simmer gently for 1–1½ hours or until the meat is tender. Serve with rice and garnish with fresh coriander.

— COOK'S TIP —

When whole cardamom pods are used as a flavouring, they are not meant to be eaten. In India, they are left on the side of the plate, along with any bones.

Balti Beef

INGREDIENTS

Serves 4

1 red pepper
1 green pepper
15ml/1 tbsp oil
5ml/1 tsp cumin seeds
2.5ml/½ tsp fennel seeds
1 onion, cut into thick wedges
1 garlic clove, crushed
2.5cm/1in piece root ginger,
   finely chopped
1 red chilli, finely chopped
15ml/1 tbsp curry paste
2.5ml/½ tsp salt
675g/1½lb lean rump or fillet steak,
   cut into thick strips
naan bread, to serve

1 Cut the red and green peppers into 2.5cm/1in chunks.

2 Heat the oil in a non-stick wok or frying pan and fry the cumin and fennel seeds for about 2 minutes or until they begin to splutter. Add the onion, garlic, ginger and chilli and fry for a further 5 minutes.

3 Add the curry paste and salt and fry for a further 3–4 minutes.

4 Add the peppers and stir-fry for about 5 minutes. Stir in the beef strips and continue to fry for 10–12 minutes or until the meat is tender. Serve with warm naan bread.

Chicken Tikka Masala

Tender chicken pieces are cooked
in a creamy, spicy tomato sauce
and served on naan bread.

INGREDIENTS

Serves 4
675g/1½lb chicken breasts, skinned
90ml/6 tbsp tikka paste
120ml/4fl oz/½ cup natural low
  fat yogurt
15ml/1 tbsp oil
1 onion, chopped
1 garlic clove, crushed
1 green chilli, seeded and chopped
2.5cm/1in piece root ginger, grated
15ml/1 tbsp tomato purée
250ml/8fl oz/1 cup water
a little melted butter
15ml/1 tbsp lemon juice
fresh coriander sprigs, natural low
  fat yogurt and toasted cumin seeds,
  to garnish
naan bread, to serve

—————— COOK'S TIP ——————

Soak the wooden skewers in cold water
before using to prevent them from burning
while under the grill.

1 Remove any visible fat from the
chicken and cut the meat into
2.5cm/1in cubes. Put 45ml/3 tbsp of
the tikka paste and 60ml/4 tbsp of the
yogurt into a bowl. Add the chicken
and leave to marinate for 20 minutes.

2 For the tikka sauce, heat the oil
in a heavy-based pan and fry the
onion, garlic, chilli and ginger for
5 minutes. Add the remaining tikka
paste and fry for 2 minutes. Add the
tomato purée and water, bring to the
boil and simmer for 15 minutes.

3 Meanwhile, thread the chicken
pieces on to wooden kebab
skewers. Preheat the grill.

4 Brush the chicken pieces lightly
with melted butter and grill under
a medium heat for 15 minutes, turning
the skewers occasionally.

5 Put the tikka sauce into a food
processor or blender and process
until smooth. Return to the pan.

6 Add the remaining yogurt and
lemon juice, remove the grilled
chicken pieces from the skewers and
add to the saucepan, then simmer for
5 minutes. Garnish with fresh
coriander, yogurt and toasted cumin
seeds and serve on naan bread.

Tandoori Chicken

A most popular Indian/Pakistani chicken dish which is cooked in a clay oven called a *tandoor*, this is extremely popular in the West and appears on the majority of restaurant menus. Although the authentic tandoori flavour is very difficult to achieve in conventional ovens, this version still makes a very tasty dish.

INGREDIENTS

Serves 4

4 chicken quarters, skinned
175ml/6fl oz/¾ cup natural low fat yogurt
5ml/1 tsp garam masala
5ml/1 tsp ginger pulp
5ml/1 tsp garlic pulp
7.5ml/1½ tsp chilli powder
1.5ml/¼ tsp ground turmeric
5ml/1 tsp ground coriander
15ml/1 tbsp lemon juice
5ml/1 tsp salt
few drops of red food colouring
15ml/1 tbsp oil
mixed salad leaves and lime wedges, to garnish

1 Rinse and pat dry the chicken quarters. Make two deep slits in the flesh of each piece, place in a dish and set aside.

COOK'S TIP

The traditional bright red colour is derived from food colouring. This is only optional and may be omitted if you wish.

2 Mix together the yogurt, garam masala, ginger, garlic, chilli powder, turmeric, coriander, lemon juice, salt, red food colouring and oil, and beat so that all the ingredients are well combined.

3 Cover the chicken quarters with the spice mixture and leave to marinate for about 3 hours.

4 Preheat the oven to 240°C/475°F/ Gas 9. Transfer the chicken pieces to an ovenproof dish.

5 Bake the chicken in the oven for 20–25 minutes or until the chicken is cooked right through and evenly browned on top.

6 Remove from the oven, transfer to a serving dish and garnish with the salad leaves and lime wedges.

Chicken Jalfrezi

A Jalfrezi curry is a stir-fried dish cooked with onions, ginger and garlic in a rich pepper sauce.

INGREDIENTS

Serves 4

675g/1½lb chicken breasts, skinned
15ml/1 tbsp oil
5ml/1 tsp cumin seeds
1 onion, finely chopped
1 green pepper, seeded and
  finely chopped
1 red pepper, seeded and
  finely chopped
1 garlic clove, crushed
2cm/¾in piece root ginger,
  finely chopped
15ml/1 tbsp curry paste
1.5ml/¼ tsp chilli powder
5ml/1 tsp ground coriander
5ml/1 tsp ground cumin
2.5ml/½ tsp salt
400g/14oz can chopped tomatoes
30ml/2 tbsp chopped fresh coriander
fresh coriander sprig, to garnish
plain rice, to serve

1 Remove any visible fat from the chicken and cut the meat into 2.5cm/1in cubes.

2 Heat the oil in a wok or heavy-based frying pan and fry the cumin seeds for 2 minutes until they splutter. Add the onion, peppers, garlic and ginger and fry for 6–8 minutes.

3 Add the curry paste and fry for about 2 minutes. Stir in the chilli powder, ground coriander, cumin and salt and add 15ml/1 tbsp water; fry for a further 2 minutes.

4 Add the chicken cubes and fry for about 5 minutes. Add the canned tomatoes and chopped fresh coriander. Cover the wok or frying pan with a lid and cook for about 15 minutes or until the chicken cubes are tender. Garnish with a sprig of fresh coriander and serve with rice.

Balti Chicken Curry

Tender pieces of chicken are
lightly cooked with fresh
vegetables and aromatic spices
in the traditional Balti style.

INGREDIENTS

Serves 4

675g/1½lb chicken breasts, skinned
15ml/1 tbsp oil
2.5ml/½ tsp cumin seeds
2.5ml/½ tsp fennel seeds
1 onion, thickly sliced
2 garlic cloves, crushed
2.5cm/1in piece root ginger, finely
   chopped
15ml/1 tbsp curry paste
225g/8oz broccoli, broken into florets
4 tomatoes, cut into thick wedges
5ml/1 tsp garam masala
30ml/2 tbsp chopped fresh coriander
naan bread, to serve

1 Remove any visible fat from the
chicken and cut the meat into
2.5cm/1in cubes.

2 Heat the oil in a wok or heavy-
based frying pan and fry the cumin
and fennel seeds for 2 minutes until
the seeds begin to splutter. Add the
onion, garlic and ginger and cook
for 5–7 minutes. Stir in the curry paste
and cook for a further 2–3 minutes.

3 Add the broccoli florets and fry for
about 5 minutes. Add the chicken
cubes and fry for 5–8 minutes.

4 Add the tomato wedges to the
wok with the garam masala and
the chopped fresh coriander. Cook the
curry for a further 5–10 minutes or
until the chicken cubes are tender.
Serve with naan bread.

Balti Chicken in a Thick Creamy Coconut Sauce

If you like the flavour of
coconut, you will really love
this aromatic curry.

INGREDIENTS

Serves 4

15ml/1 tbsp ground almonds
15ml/1 tbsp desiccated coconut
75ml/3fl oz/¹⁄₃ cup coconut milk
175g/6oz/²⁄₃ cup low fat fromage frais
7.5ml/1½ tsp ground coriander
5ml/1 tsp chilli powder
5ml/1 tsp garlic pulp
7.5ml/1½ tsp ginger pulp
5ml/1 tsp salt
15ml/1 tbsp oil
225g/8oz boneless chicken, skinned
  and cubed
3 green cardamom pods
1 bay leaf
1 dried red chilli, crushed
30ml/2 tbsp chopped fresh coriander

1 Using a heavy-based saucepan,
dry-roast the ground almonds and
desiccated coconut until they turn just
a shade darker. Transfer the nut mixture
to a mixing bowl.

2 Add the coconut milk, fromage
frais, ground coriander, chilli
powder, garlic, ginger and salt to the
mixing bowl.

3 Heat the oil in a wok or heavy-
based frying pan and add the
chicken cubes, cardamoms and bay
leaf. Stir-fry for about 2 minutes to
seal the chicken but not cook it.

4 Pour in the coconut milk mixture
and blend everything together.
Lower the heat, add the chilli and
fresh coriander, cover and cook for
10–12 minutes, stirring occasionally.
Uncover, then stir and cook for a
further 2 minutes before serving,
making sure the chicken is cooked.

Chicken Biryani

Biryanis originated in Persia and are traditionally made with a combination of meat and rice. They are often served at dinner parties and on festive occasions.

INGREDIENTS

Serves 4

275g/10oz/1½ cups basmati rice
30ml/2 tbsp oil
1 onion, thinly sliced
2 garlic cloves, crushed
1 green chilli, finely chopped
2.5cm/1in piece root ginger, finely chopped
675g/1½lb chicken breast fillets, skinned and cut into 2.5cm/1in cubes
45ml/3 tbsp curry paste
1.5ml/¼ tsp salt
1.5ml/¼ tsp garam masala
3 tomatoes, cut into thin wedges
1.5ml/¼ tsp ground turmeric
2 bay leaves
4 green cardamom pods
4 cloves
1.5ml/¼ tsp saffron strands

1 Wash the rice in several changes of cold water. Put into a large bowl, cover with plenty of water and leave to soak for 30 minutes.

2 Meanwhile, heat the oil in a large heavy-based frying pan and fry the onion for about 5–7 minutes until lightly browned. Add the garlic, chilli and ginger and fry for about 2 minutes.

3 Add the chicken and fry for about 5 minutes, stirring occasionally.

4 Add the curry paste, salt and garam masala to the chicken mixture and cook for 5 minutes. Gently stir in the tomato wedges and continue cooking for another 3–4 minutes, then remove from the heat and set aside.

5 Preheat the oven to 190°C/375°F/ Gas 5. Bring a large saucepan of water to the boil. Drain the rice and add it to the pan with the turmeric. Cook for about 10 minutes, or until the rice is almost tender. Drain the rice and toss together with the bay leaves, cardamoms, cloves and saffron.

6 Layer the rice and chicken in a shallow, ovenproof dish until all the mixture has been used, finishing off with a layer of rice. Cover and bake in the oven for 15–20 minutes or until the chicken is tender.

Prawn Curry

A rich flavoursome curry made with prawns and a delicious blend of aromatic spices.

INGREDIENTS

Serves 4

675g/1½lb uncooked tiger prawns
4 dried red chillies
25g/1oz/½ cup desiccated coconut
5ml/1 tsp black mustard seeds
1 large onion, chopped
30ml/2 tbsp oil
4 bay leaves
2.5cm/1in piece root ginger, finely
  chopped
2 garlic cloves, crushed
15ml/1 tbsp ground coriander
5ml/1 tsp chilli powder
5ml/1 tsp salt
4 tomatoes, finely chopped
plain rice, to serve

1 Peel the prawns and discard the shells. Run a sharp knife along the centre back of each prawn to make a shallow cut and carefully remove the thin black intestinal vein.

—————— COOK'S TIP ——————

Serve extra tiger prawns unpeeled, on the edge of each plate, for an attractive garnish. Cook them with the peeled prawns.

2 Put the dried red chillies, coconut, mustard seeds and onion in a large heavy-based frying pan and dry-fry for 8–10 minutes or until the spices begin to brown but not burn. Put into a food processor or blender and process to a coarse paste.

3 Heat the oil in the frying pan and fry the bay leaves for 1 minute. Add the chopped ginger and the garlic and fry for 2–3 minutes.

4 Add the coriander, chilli powder, salt and the coconut paste and fry gently for 5 minutes.

5 Stir in the chopped tomatoes and about 175ml/6fl oz/¾ cup water and simmer gently for 5–6 minutes or until the sauce has thickened.

6 Add the prawns and cook for about 4–5 minutes or until they turn pink and the edges are curling slightly. Serve with plain boiled rice.

Green Fish Curry

This dish combines all the flavours of the East.

INGREDIENTS

Serves 4

1.5ml/¼ tsp ground turmeric
30ml/2 tbsp lime juice
pinch of salt
4 cod fillets, skinned and cut into
  5cm/2in chunks
1 onion, chopped
1 green chilli, roughly chopped
1 garlic clove, crushed
25g/1oz/¼ cup cashew nuts
2.5ml/½ tsp fennel seeds
30ml/2 tbsp desiccated coconut
30ml/2 tbsp oil
1.5ml/¼ tsp cumin seeds
1.5ml/¼ tsp ground coriander
1.5ml/¼ tsp ground cumin
1.5ml/¼ tsp salt
150ml/¼ pint/⅔ cup water
175ml/6fl oz/¾ cup natural low fat
  yogurt
45ml/3 tbsp finely chopped fresh
  coriander
fresh coriander sprig, to garnish
Pea and Mushroom Pilau, to serve

1 Mix together the turmeric, lime juice and salt and rub over the fish. Cover and marinate for 15 minutes.

2 Meanwhile, process the onion, chilli, garlic, cashew nuts, fennel seeds and coconut to a paste. Spoon the paste into a bowl and set aside.

3 Heat the oil in a large heavy-based frying pan and fry the cumin seeds for 2 minutes or until they begin to splutter. Add the paste and fry for 5 minutes, then stir in the ground coriander, cumin, salt and water and cook for about 2–3 minutes.

4 Add the yogurt and the chopped fresh coriander. Simmer gently for 5 minutes. Add the fish fillets and gently stir in. Cover and cook gently for 10 minutes until the fish is tender. Serve with Pea and Mushroom Pilau, garnished with a coriander sprig.

Stir-fried Vegetables with Monkfish

Monkfish is a rather expensive fish, but ideal to use in stir-fry recipes as it is quite tough and does not break easily.

INGREDIENTS

Serves 4
30ml/2 tbsp oil
2 medium onions, sliced
5ml/1 tsp garlic pulp
5ml/1 tsp ground cumin
5ml/1 tsp ground coriander
5ml/1 tsp chilli powder
175g/6oz monkfish, cut into cubes
30ml/2 tbsp fresh fenugreek leaves
2 tomatoes, seeded and sliced
1 courgette, sliced
salt
15ml/1 tbsp lime juice

1 Heat the oil in a wok or heavy-based frying pan and fry the onions over a low heat until soft.

2 Meanwhile mix together the garlic, cumin, coriander and chilli powder. Add this spice mixture to the onions and stir-fry for about 1 minute.

3 Add the fish and continue to stir-fry for 3–5 minutes until the fish is well cooked through.

4 Add the fenugreek, tomatoes and courgette, followed by salt to taste, and stir-fry for a further 2 minutes. Sprinkle with lime juice before serving.

COOK'S TIP

Try to use monkfish for this recipe, but if it is not available, either cod or prawns make a suitable substitute.

Vegetable Kashmiri

This is a wonderful vegetable curry, in which fresh mixed vegetables are cooked in a spicy aromatic yogurt sauce.

INGREDIENTS

Serves 4

10ml/2 tsp cumin seeds
8 black peppercorns
2 green cardamom pods, seeds only
5cm/2in cinnamon stick
2.5ml/½ tsp grated nutmeg
30ml/2 tbsp oil
1 green chilli, chopped
2.5cm/1in piece root ginger, grated
5ml/1 tsp chilli powder
2.5ml/½ tsp salt
2 large potatoes, cut into 2.5cm/
  1in chunks
225g/8oz cauliflower, broken
  into florets
225g/8oz okra, trimmed and
  thickly sliced
150ml/¼ pint/⅔ cup natural low
  fat yogurt
150ml/¼ pint/⅔ cup vegetable stock
toasted flaked almonds (optional) and
  fresh coriander sprigs, to garnish

1 Grind the cumin seeds, peppercorns, cardamom seeds, cinnamon stick and nutmeg to a fine powder using a coffee blender or a pestle and mortar.

2 Heat the oil in a large heavy-based saucepan and fry the chilli powder and ginger for 2 minutes, stirring all the time.

3 Add the chilli powder, salt and ground spice mixture and fry for about 2–3 minutes, stirring all the time to prevent the spices from sticking.

—————— COOK'S TIP ——————

Instead of the vegetable mixture used here, try cooking other ones of your choice in this lovely yogurt sauce.

4 Stir in the potatoes, cover and cook for 10 minutes over a low heat, stirring from time to time.

5 Add the cauliflower and okra and cook for 5 minutes.

6 Add the yogurt and stock. Bring to the boil, then reduce the heat. Cover and simmer for 20 minutes, or until all the vegetables are tender. Garnish with toasted almonds, if using, and coriander sprigs.

Aloo Saag

Spinach, potatoes and traditional
Indian spices are the main
ingredients in this simple but
authentic curry.

INGREDIENTS

Serves 4

450g/1lb spinach
15ml/1 tbsp oil
5ml/1 tsp black mustard seeds
1 onion, thinly sliced
2 garlic cloves, crushed
2.5cm/1in piece root ginger,
   finely chopped
675g/1½lb potatoes, cut into
   2.5cm/1in chunks
5ml/1 tsp chilli powder
5ml/1 tsp salt
120ml/4fl oz/½ cup water

--------- COOK'S TIP ---------

To make certain that the spinach is
completely dry, put it in a clean dish towel,
roll up tightly and squeeze gently to
remove any excess liquid. Use a waxy
variety of potato for this dish so that the
pieces do not break up during cooking.

1 Wash and trim the spinach, then
blanch it in a saucepan of boiling
water for about 3–4 minutes.

2 Drain the spinach thoroughly and
set aside. When it is cool enough
to handle, use your hands to squeeze
out any remaining liquid (see Cook's
Tip) and set aside.

3 Heat the oil in a large heavy-based
saucepan and fry the mustard seeds
for 2 minutes or until they splutter.

4 Add the sliced onion, garlic cloves
and chopped ginger to the mustard
seeds and fry for 5 minutes, stirring.

5 Add the potato chunks, chilli
powder, salt and water and stir-fry
for a further 8 minutes.

6 Add the drained spinach. Cover
the pan with a lid and simmer for
10–15 minutes or until the potatoes
are tender. Serve hot.

Balti Stir-fried Vegetables with Cashew Nuts

This quick and versatile stir-fry will accommodate most other combinations of vegetables – you do not have to use the selection suggested here.

INGREDIENTS

Serves 4
2 medium carrots
1 medium red pepper, seeded
1 medium green pepper, seeded
2 courgettes
115g/4oz green beans
1 medium bunch spring onions
15ml/1 tbsp oil
4–6 curry leaves
2.5ml/½ tsp cumin seeds
4 dried red chillies
10–12 cashew nuts
5ml/1 tsp salt
30ml/2 tbsp lemon juice
fresh mint leaves, to garnish

1 Prepare the vegetables: cut the carrots, peppers and courgettes into matchsticks, halve the beans and chop the spring onions. Set aside.

2 Heat the oil in a wok or heavy-based frying pan and fry the curry leaves, cumin seeds and dried chillies for about 1 minute.

3 Add the vegetables and nuts and stir them around gently. Add the salt and lemon juice. Continue to stir and cook for about 3–5 minutes.

4 Transfer the vegetables to a serving dish, garnish with fresh mint leaves and serve immediately.

COOK'S TIP

If you are short of time, substitute frozen mixed vegetables for the carrots, peppers, courgettes and green beans; they work equally well in this dish.

Tarka Dhal

Tarka Dhal is probably the most popular of Indian lentil dishes and is found today in most Indian/Pakistani restaurants.

INGREDIENTS

Serves 4
115g/4oz/¼ cup *masoor dhal*
50g/2oz/¼ cup *moong dhal*
600ml/1 pint/2½ cups water
5ml/1 tsp ginger pulp
5ml/1 tsp garlic pulp
1.5ml/¼ tsp ground turmeric
2 fresh green chillies, chopped
7.5ml/1½ tsp salt

For the *tarka*
30ml/2 tbsp oil
1 onion, sliced
1.5ml/¼ tsp mixed mustard and
   onion seeds
4 dried red chillies
1 tomato, sliced

For the garnish
15ml/1 tbsp chopped fresh coriander
1–2 fresh green chillies, seeded
   and sliced
15ml/1 tbsp chopped fresh mint

1 Boil the two lentils in the water with the ginger and garlic pulp, turmeric and chopped green chillies for 15–20 minutes until soft.

2 Mash the lentil mixture with a fork or pound with a rolling pin until the consistency of a creamy chicken soup.

3 If the lentil mixture looks too dry, add a little more water. Season with the salt. To prepare the *tarka*, heat the oil in a heavy-based frying pan and fry the onion with the mustard and onion seeds, dried red chillies and tomato for 2 minutes.

4 Pour the *tarka* over the mashed lentils and garnish with fresh coriander, green chillies and mint.

--- COOK'S TIP ---

Dried red chillies are available in many different sizes. If the ones you have are large, or if you want a less spicy flavour, reduce the quantity specified to 1–2.

Mung Beans with Potatoes

Mung beans are one of the quicker-cooking pulses which do not require soaking and are very easy and convenient to use. In this recipe they are cooked with potatoes and Indian spices to give a tasty nutritious dish.

INGREDIENTS

Serves 4

175g/6oz/1 cup mung beans
750ml/1¼ pints/3 cups water
225g/8oz potatoes, cut into
   2cm/¾in chunks
30ml/2 tbsp oil
2.5ml/½ tsp cumin seeds
1 green chilli, finely chopped
1 garlic clove, crushed
2.5cm/1in piece root ginger,
   finely chopped
1.5ml/¼ tsp ground turmeric
2.5ml/½ tsp chilli powder
5ml/1 tsp salt
5ml/1 tsp sugar
4 curry leaves
5 tomatoes, skinned and
   finely chopped
15ml/1 tbsp tomato purée
curry leaves, to garnish
plain rice, to serve

1 Wash the beans. Bring to the boil in the water, cover and simmer until soft, about 30 minutes. Drain. Par-boil the potatoes for 10 minutes in another saucepan, then drain well.

2 Heat the oil in a heavy-based pan and fry the cumin seeds until they splutter. Add the chilli, garlic and ginger and fry for 3–4 minutes.

3 Add the turmeric, chilli powder, salt and sugar and cook for 2 minutes, stirring to prevent the mixture from sticking to the saucepan.

4 Add the 4 curry leaves, chopped tomatoes and tomato purée and simmer for about 5 minutes until the sauce thickens. Add the tomato sauce and the potatoes to the mung beans and mix well together. Garnish with the extra curry leaves and serve with plain boiled rice.

Madras Sambal

There are many variations of this popular dish but it is regularly cooked in one form or another in almost every south-Indian home. You can use any combination of vegetables that are in season.

INGREDIENTS

Serves 4

225g/8oz/1 cup *toovar dhal* or red split lentils
600ml/1 pint/2½ cups water
2.5ml/½ tsp ground turmeric
2 large potatoes, cut into 2.5cm/ 1in chunks
30ml/2 tbsp oil
2.5ml/½ tsp black mustard seeds
1.5ml/¼ tsp fenugreek seeds
4 curry leaves
1 onion, thinly sliced
115g/4oz French beans, cut into 2.5cm/1in lengths
5ml/1 tsp salt
2.5ml/½ tsp chilli powder
15ml/1 tbsp lemon juice
toasted coconut, to garnish
Tomato and Onion Chutney, to serve

1 Wash the *toovar dhal* or lentils in several changes of water. Place in a heavy-based saucepan with the water and the turmeric. Bring to the boil, cover and simmer for 30–35 minutes until the lentils are soft.

2 Par-boil the potatoes in a large pan of boiling water for 10 minutes. Drain well and set aside.

3 Heat the oil in a large frying pan and fry the mustard and fenugreek seeds and curry leaves for 2–3 minutes until the seeds begin to splutter. Add the sliced onion and the French beans and stir-fry for 7–8 minutes. Add the par-boiled potatoes and cook for a further 2 minutes.

4 Stir in the lentils with the salt, chilli powder and lemon juice and simmer for 2 minutes. Garnish with toasted coconut and serve with freshly made Tomato and Onion Chutney.

Pea and Mushroom Pilau

It is best to use button mushrooms and petits pois for this delectable rice dish as they make the pilau look truly attractive and appetizing.

INGREDIENTS

Serves 6
450g/1lb/2¼ cups basmati rice
15ml/1 tbsp oil
2.5ml/½ tsp cumin seeds
2 black cardamom pods
2 cinnamon sticks
3 garlic cloves, sliced
5ml/1 tsp salt
1 medium tomato, sliced
50g/2oz/⅔ cup button mushrooms
75g/3oz/generous ⅓ cup petits pois
750ml/1¼ pints/3 cups water

1 Wash the rice well and leave it to soak in water for 30 minutes.

2 In a medium heavy-based saucepan, heat the oil and add the spices, garlic and salt.

3 Add the tomato and mushrooms and stir-fry for 2–3 minutes.

4 Drain the rice and add it to the pan with the peas. Stir gently, making sure that you do not break up the grains of rice.

5 Add the water and bring to the boil. Lower the heat, cover and continue to cook for 15–20 minutes.

— COOK'S TIP —

Petits pois are small green peas, picked when very young. The tender, sweet peas inside are ideal for this delicately flavoured rice dish. However, if you can't find petit pois, garden peas can be used instead.

Basmati Rice with Potato

Rice is eaten at all meals in Indian and Pakistani homes. There are several ways of cooking rice and mostly whole spices are used. Always choose a good-quality basmati rice.

INGREDIENTS

Serves 4
300g/11oz/1½ cups basmati rice
15ml/1 tbsp oil
1 small cinnamon stick
1 bay leaf
1.5ml/¼ tsp black cumin seeds
3 green cardamom pods
1 medium onion, sliced
5ml/1 tsp ginger pulp
5ml/1 tsp garlic pulp
1.5ml/¼ tsp ground turmeric
7.5ml/1½ tsp salt
1 large potato, roughly diced
475ml/16fl oz/2 cups water
15ml/1 tbsp chopped fresh coriander

1 Wash the rice well and leave it to soak in water for 30 minutes. Heat the oil in a heavy-based saucepan, add the cinnamon, bay leaf, black cumin seeds, cardamoms and onion and cook for about 2 minutes.

—————— COOK'S TIP ——————

Serve the rice and potato mixture using a slotted spoon and handle it gently to avoid breaking the delicate grains of rice.

2 Add the ginger, garlic, turmeric, salt and potato and cook for 1 minute.

3 Drain the rice and add to the potato and spices in the pan.

4 Stir to mix, then pour in the water followed by the coriander. Cover the pan with a lid and cook for 15–20 minutes. Remove from the heat and leave to stand, still covered, for 5–10 minutes before serving.

Tomato and Onion Chutney

Chutneys are served with most meat dishes in Indian cuisine.

INGREDIENTS

Serves 4

8 tomatoes
1 medium onion, chopped
45ml/3 tbsp brown sugar
5ml/1 tsp garam masala
5ml/1 tsp ginger powder
175ml/6fl oz/³/₄ cup malt vinegar
5ml/1 tsp salt
15ml/1 tbsp clear honey
natural low fat yogurt, sliced green
    chilli and fresh mint leaves, to garnish

──────── COOK'S TIP ────────

This chutney will keep for about 2 weeks
in a covered jar in the refrigerator.

1 Wash the tomatoes and cut them into quarters.

2 Place them with the onion in a heavy-based saucepan.

3 Add the sugar, garam masala, ginger, vinegar, salt and honey, half-cover the pan with a lid and cook over a low heat for about 20 minutes.

4 Mash the tomatoes with a fork to break them up, then continue to cook on a slightly higher heat until the chutney thickens. Serve chilled, garnished with yogurt, sliced chilli and mint leaves.

Sweet-and-sour Raita

Raitas are traditionally served with most Indian meals as accompaniments which are cooling to the palate. They go particularly well with biryanis.

INGREDIENTS

Serves 4

475ml/16fl oz/2 cups natural low
   fat yogurt
5ml/1 tsp salt
5ml/1 tsp sugar
30ml/2 tbsp honey
7.5ml/1½ tsp mint sauce
30ml/2 tbsp roughly chopped
   fresh coriander
1 green chilli, seeded and
   finely chopped
1 medium onion, diced
50ml/2fl oz/¼ cup water

1 Pour the yogurt into a bowl and whisk it well. Add the salt, sugar, honey and mint sauce.

2 Taste to check the sweetness and add more honey, if desired.

3 Reserve a little chopped coriander for the garnish and add the rest to the yogurt mixture, with the chilli, onion and water.

4 Whisk once again and pour into a serving bowl. Garnish with the reserved coriander and place in the refrigerator until ready to serve.

_____ COOK'S TIP _____

A 5–10cm/2–4in piece of peeled, seeded and grated cucumber can also be added to raita. Alternatively, cut it into small dice.

Ground Rice Pudding

This delicious and light ground rice pudding is the perfect end to a spicy meal. It can be served either hot or cold.

INGREDIENTS

Serves 4–6

50g/2oz/½ cup coarsely ground rice
4 green cardamom pods, crushed
900ml/1½ pints/3¾ cups semi-skimmed milk
90ml/6 tbsp sugar
15ml/1 tbsp rose water
15ml/1 tbsp crushed pistachio nuts, to garnish

1 Place the ground rice in a saucepan with the cardamoms. Add 600ml/1 pint/2½ cups milk and bring to the boil over a medium heat, stirring occasionally.

2 Add the remaining milk and cook over a medium heat for about 10 minutes or until the rice mixture thickens to a creamy consistency.

3 Stir in the sugar and rose water and continue to cook for a further 2 minutes. Serve garnished with the pistachio nuts.

COOK'S TIP

Rose water is a distillation of scented rose petals which has the intense fragrance and flavour of roses. It is a popular flavouring in Indian cooking. Use it cautiously, adding just enough to suit your taste.

Vermicelli

Indian vermicelli, made from wheat, is much finer than Italian vermicelli and is readily available from Asian stores.

INGREDIENTS

Serves 4

115g/4oz/1 cup vermicelli
1.2 litres/2 pints/5 cups water
2.5ml/½ tsp saffron strands
15ml/1 tbsp sugar
60ml/4 tbsp low fat fromage frais, to serve (optional)

For the garnish

15ml/1 tbsp shredded fresh or desiccated coconut
15ml/1 tbsp flaked almonds
15ml/1 tbsp chopped pistachio nuts
15ml/1 tbsp sugar

1 Crush the vermicelli in your hands and place in a saucepan. Pour in the water, add the saffron and bring to the boil. Boil for about 5 minutes.

2 Stir in the sugar and continue cooking until the water has evaporated. Strain through a sieve, if necessary, to remove any excess liquid.

3 Place the vermicelli in a serving dish and garnish with the coconut, almonds, pistachio nuts and sugar. Serve with fromage frais, if wished.

—————— COOK'S TIP ——————

You can use a variety of fruits instead of nuts to garnish this dessert. Try a few soft fruits such as blackberries, raspberries or strawberries, or add some chopped dried apricots or sultanas.

MIDDLE EAST

Beef and Herb Soup with Yogurt

This classic Iranian soup, *Aashe Maste*, is almost a meal in itself. It is full of invigorating herbs, and is a popular cold weather dish.

INGREDIENTS

Serves 6
2 large onions
30ml/2 tbsp oil
15ml/1 tbsp ground turmeric
100g/3½ oz/½ cup yellow split peas
1.2 litres/2 pints/5 cups water
225g/8oz minced beef
200g/7oz/1 cup rice
45ml/3 tbsp each fresh chopped
     parsley, coriander and chives
15g/½ oz/1 tbsp butter
1 large garlic clove, finely chopped
60ml/4 tbsp chopped mint
2–3 saffron strands dissolved in
     15ml/1 tbsp boiling water (optional)
salt and freshly ground black pepper
yogurt and naan bread, to serve

1 Chop one of the onions then heat the oil in a large saucepan and fry the onion until golden brown. Add the turmeric, split peas and water, bring to the boil, then reduce the heat and simmer for 20 minutes.

—— COOK'S TIP ——

Fresh spinach is also delicious in this soup. Add 50g/2oz finely chopped spinach leaves to the soup with the parsley, coriander and chives.

2 Grate the other onion into a bowl, add the minced beef and seasoning and mix well. Using your hands, form the mixture into small balls, about the size of walnuts. Carefully add to the pan and simmer for 10 minutes.

3 Add the rice, then stir in the parsley, coriander, and chives and simmer for about 30 minutes, until the rice is tender, stirring frequently.

4 Melt the butter in a small pan and gently fry the garlic. Add the mint, stir briefly and sprinkle over the soup with the saffron, if using.

5 Spoon the soup into warmed serving dishes and serve with yogurt and naan bread.

Spinach and Lemon Soup with Meatballs

Aarshe Saak is almost standard fare in many parts of the Middle East. In Greece it is normally made without the meatballs and is called Avgolemono.

INGREDIENTS

Serves 6

2 large onions
45ml/3 tbsp oil
15ml/1 tbsp ground turmeric
100g/3½oz/½ cup yellow split peas
1.2 litres/2 pints/5 cups water
225g/8oz minced lamb
450g/1lb spinach, chopped
50g/2oz/½ cup rice flour
juice of 2 lemons
1–2 garlic cloves, very
   finely chopped
30ml/2 tbsp chopped fresh mint
4 eggs, beaten
salt and freshly ground black pepper

1 Chop one of the onions, heat 30ml/2 tbsp of the oil in a large frying pan and fry the onion until golden. Add the turmeric, split peas and water and bring to the boil. Reduce the heat and simmer for 20 minutes.

2 Grate the other onion. Put it into a bowl, add the minced lamb and seasoning and mix well. Using your hands, form the mixture into small balls, about the size of walnuts. Carefully add to the pan and simmer for 10 minutes, then add the chopped spinach, cover and simmer for 20 minutes.

3 Mix the flour with about 250ml/ 8fl oz/1 cup cold water to make a smooth paste, then slowly add to the pan, stirring all the time to prevent lumps. Stir in the lemon juice, season with salt and pepper and cook over a gentle heat for 20 minutes.

4 Meanwhile, heat the remaining oil in a small pan and fry the garlic briefly until golden. Stir in the mint and remove the pan from the heat.

5 Remove the soup from the heat and stir in the beaten eggs. Sprinkle the garlic and mint garnish over the soup and serve.

COOK'S TIP

If preferred, use less lemon juice to begin with and then add more to taste once the soup is cooked.

Böreks

In Turkey, little stuffed pasties are very popular. They are easy to make and are ideal for starters, parties or finger canapés.

INGREDIENTS

Makes 35–40
225g/8oz feta cheese, grated
225g/8oz mozzarella, grated
2 eggs, beaten
45ml/3 tbsp chopped fresh parsley
45ml/3 tbsp snipped fresh chives
45ml/3 tbsp chopped fresh mint
pinch of nutmeg
225g/8oz filo pastry
45–60ml/3–4 tbsp melted butter
freshly ground black pepper

1 Preheat the oven to 180°C/350°F/ Gas 4. In a bowl, blend the feta and mozzarella cheeses with the beaten eggs. Add the chopped herbs, season with black pepper and nutmeg, and stir well to mix.

2 Cut the sheets of pastry into four rectangular strips approximately 7.5cm/3in wide. Cover all but one or two strips of the pastry with a damp cloth to prevent them from drying out.

3 Brush one strip of pastry at a time with a little melted butter.

4 Place 5ml/1 tsp of filling at the bottom edge. Fold one corner over the filling to make a triangle shape. Continue folding the pastry over itself until you get to the end of the strip. Keep making triangles until all the mixture is used up.

5 Place the *böreks* on a greased baking tray and bake in the oven for about 30 minutes until golden brown and crisp. Serve warm or cold.

--- COOK'S TIP ---

A mixture of almost any cheeses can be used but avoid cream cheeses.

Baked Eggs with Herbs and Vegetables

Eggs, baked or fried as omelettes with vegetables and herbs and sometimes meat, too, are popular throughout the Middle East. This particular dish, *Kuku Sabzi*, comes from Persia and is a traditional New Year favourite.

INGREDIENTS

Serves 4–6

2–3 saffron strands
8 eggs
2 leeks
115g/4oz fresh spinach
½ iceberg lettuce
4 spring onions
45ml/3 tbsp chopped fresh parsley
45ml/3 tbsp snipped fresh chives
45ml/3 tbsp chopped fresh coriander
1 garlic clove, crushed
30ml/2 tbsp chopped walnuts
   (optional)
25g/1oz/2 tbsp butter
salt and freshly ground black pepper
yogurt and pitta bread, to serve

1 Preheat the oven to 180°C/350°F/ Gas 4. Soak the saffron strands in 15ml/1 tbsp boiling water.

COOK'S TIP

To bring out their flavour, lightly toast the walnuts in a moderate oven, or under a hot grill before chopping.

2 Beat the eggs in a large bowl. Chop the leeks, spinach, lettuce and spring onions finely and add to the eggs together with the chopped herbs, garlic, and walnuts, if using. Season with salt and pepper, add the saffron water and stir thoroughly to mix.

3 Melt the butter in a large ovenproof dish and pour in the vegetable and egg mixture.

4 Bake in the oven for 35–40 minutes until the egg mixture is set and the top is golden. Serve hot or cold, cut into wedges, with yogurt and pitta bread.

Falafel

These tasty deep fried patties are one of the national dishes of Egypt. They make an excellent starter or else can be served as a buffet dish.

INGREDIENTS

Serves 6
450g/1lb/2½ cups dried white beans
2 red onions, chopped
2 large garlic cloves, crushed
45ml/3 tbsp finely chopped fresh parsley
5ml/1 tsp ground coriander
5ml/1 tsp ground cumin
7.5ml/1½ tsp baking powder
oil, for deep frying
salt and freshly ground black pepper
tomato salad, to serve

1 Soak the white beans overnight in water. Remove the skins and process in a blender or food processor. Add the chopped onions, garlic, parsley, coriander, cumin, baking powder and seasoning and blend again to make a very smooth paste. Allow the mixture to stand at room temperature for at least 30 minutes.

2 Take walnut-sized pieces of mixture and flatten into small patties. Set aside again for about 15 minutes.

3 Heat the oil until it's very hot and then fry the patties in batches until golden brown. Drain on kitchen paper and then serve with a tomato salad.

Houmus

This popular Middle Eastern dip is widely available in supermarkets, but nothing compares with the delicious home-made variety.

INGREDIENTS

Serves 4–6
175g/6oz/1 cup cooked chick-peas
120ml/4fl oz/½ cup tahini paste
3 garlic cloves
juice of 2 lemons
45–60ml/3–4 tbsp water
salt and freshly ground black pepper
fresh radishes, to serve

For the garnish
15ml/1 tbsp olive oil
15ml/1 tbsp finely chopped fresh parsley
2.5ml/½ tsp paprika
4 black olives

1 Place the chick-peas, tahini paste, garlic, lemon juice, seasoning and a little of the water in a blender or food processor. Process until smooth adding a little more water, if necessary.

2 Alternatively if you don't have a blender or food processor, mix the ingredients together in a small bowl until smooth in consistency.

3 Spoon the mixture into a shallow dish. Make a dent in the middle and pour the olive oil into it. Garnish with parsley, paprika and olives and serve with the radishes.

COOK'S TIP

Canned chick-peas can be used for houmus. Drain and rinse under cold water before processing.

Persian Kebabs

Kebabs are eaten throughout the Middle East and almost always cooked over a wood or charcoal fire. There are many variations; this particular recipe, *Kabab Bahrg*, comes from Iran and many restaurants serve only this dish.

INGREDIENTS

Serves 4
450g/1lb lean lamb or beef fillet
2–3 saffron strands
1 large onion, grated
4–6 tomatoes, halved
15ml/1 tbsp butter, melted
salt and freshly ground black pepper
45ml/3 tbsp *sumac*, to garnish
   (optional)
rice, to serve

1 Place the meat on a chopping board. Using a sharp knife remove any excess fat from the meat and cut the meat into strips, approximately 1cm/½in thick and 4cm/1½in long.

2 Soak the saffron in 15ml/1 tbsp boiling water, pour into a small bowl and mix with the grated onion. Add to the meat and stir a few times so that the meat is coated thoroughly. Cover loosely with clear film and leave to marinate overnight in the fridge.

3 Season the meat with salt and pepper and then thread on to flat skewers, aligning the strips in neat rows. Thread the tomatoes on to two separate skewers.

4 Grill the kebabs and tomatoes over hot charcoal for 10–12 minutes, basting with butter and turning occasionally. Serve with rice, sprinkled with *sumac*, if you like.

Shish Kebab

INGREDIENTS

Serves 4
450g/1lb boned leg of lamb, cubed
1 large green pepper, seeded and cut
   into squares
1 large yellow pepper, seeded and cut
   into squares
8 baby onions, halved
225g/8oz button mushrooms
4 tomatoes, halved
15ml/1 tbsp melted butter
bulgur wheat, to serve

For the marinade
45ml/3 tbsp olive oil
juice of 1 lemon
2 garlic cloves, crushed
1 large onion, grated
15ml/1 tbsp fresh oregano
salt and freshly ground black pepper

1 First make the marinade: blend together the oil, lemon juice, garlic, onion, oregano and seasoning. Place the meat in a shallow dish and pour over the marinade.

2 Cover with clear film and leave to marinate overnight in the fridge.

3 Thread the cubes of lamb on to skewers, alternating with pieces of green and yellow pepper, onions and mushrooms. Thread the tomatoes on to separate skewers. Grill the kebabs and tomatoes over hot charcoal for 10–12 minutes basting with butter. Serve with bulgur wheat.

Tangy Beef and Herb Khoresh

Lamb, beef or poultry stews combined with vegetables, fruit, herbs and spices, are called *khoresh* in Farsi and are among the most loved of Persian dishes. Like this beef stew, *Khoreshe Gormeh Sabzi*, they are mildly spiced and are ideal for a simple but delicious dinner party.

INGREDIENTS

Serves 4
45ml/3 tbsp oil
1 large onion, chopped
450g/1lb lean stewing beef, cubed
15ml/1 tbsp fenugreek leaf
10ml/2 tsp ground turmeric
2.5ml/½ tsp ground cinnamon
600ml/1 pint/2½ cups water
25g/1oz fresh parsley, chopped
25g/1oz fresh chives, snipped
425g/15oz can red kidney beans
juice of 1 lemon
salt and freshly ground black pepper
rice, to serve

1 Heat 30ml/2 tbsp of the oil in a large saucepan or flameproof casserole and fry the onion for about 3–4 minutes until lightly golden. Add the beef and fry for a further 5–10 minutes until browned, stirring so that the meat browns on all sides.

2 Add the fenugreek, turmeric and cinnamon and cook for about 1 minute, stirring, then add the water and bring to the boil. Cover and simmer over a low heat for 45 minutes, stirring occasionally.

3 Heat the remaining oil in a small frying pan and fry the parsley and chives over a moderate heat for 2–3 minutes, stirring frequently.

4 Drain the kidney beans and stir them into the beef with the herbs and lemon juice. Season with salt and pepper. Simmer the stew for a further 30–35 minutes, until the meat is tender. Serve on a bed of rice.

Sautéed Lamb with Yogurt

In the Middle East meat is normally stewed or barbecued. Here's a delicious exception from Turkey where the lamb is pan-fried instead.

INGREDIENTS

Serves 4

450g/1lb lean lamb, preferably boned leg, cubed
40g/1½oz/3 tbsp butter
4 tomatoes, skinned and chopped
4 thick slices of bread, crusts removed
250ml/8fl oz/1 cup Greek yogurt
2 garlic cloves, crushed
salt and freshly ground black pepper
paprika and mint leaves, to garnish

For the marinade
120ml/4fl oz/½ cup Greek yogurt
1 large onion, grated

1 First make the marinade: blend together the yogurt, onion and a little seasoning in a large bowl. Add the cubed lamb, cover loosely with clear film and leave to marinate in a cool place for at least 1 hour.

2 Melt half the butter in a frying pan and fry the meat for 5–10 minutes, until tender but still moist. Transfer to a plate with a slotted spoon and keep warm while cooking the tomatoes.

3 Melt the remaining butter in the same pan and fry the tomatoes for 4–5 minutes until soft. Meanwhile, toast the bread and arrange in the bottom of a shallow serving dish.

4 Season the tomatoes and then spread over the toasted bread in an even layer.

5 Blend the yogurt and garlic and season with salt and pepper. Spoon over the tomatoes.

6 Arrange the meat in a layer on top. Sprinkle with paprika and mint leaves and serve at once.

Stuffed Spring Chickens

This dish is widely found in the Lebanon and Syria. The stuffing is a delicious blend of meat, nuts and rice and makes a great dinner party dish.

INGREDIENTS

Serves 6–8
2 x 1kg/2¼lb chickens
15ml/1 tbsp butter
yogurt and salad, to serve

For the stuffing
45ml/3 tbsp oil
1 onion, chopped
450g/1lb minced lamb
75g/3oz/¾ cup almonds, chopped
75g/3oz/¾ cup pine nuts
350g/12oz/2 cups cooked rice
salt and freshly ground black pepper

1 Preheat the oven to 180°C/350°F/ Gas 4. Remove the giblets, if necessary, from the chickens and rinse the body cavities in cold water.

2 Heat the oil in a large frying pan and sauté the onion until slightly softened. Add the minced lamb and cook over a moderate heat for 4–8 minutes until well browned, stirring frequently. Set aside.

3 Heat a small pan over a moderate heat and dry fry the almonds and pine nuts for 2–3 minutes until golden, shaking the pan frequently.

4 Mix together the meat mixture, almonds, pine nuts and cooked rice. Season with salt and pepper, and then spoon the mixture into the body cavities of the chickens. Rub the chickens all over with the butter.

5 Place the chickens in a large roasting dish, cover with foil and bake in the oven for 45–60 minutes. After about 30 minutes, remove the foil and baste the chickens with the pan juices. Continue cooking without the foil until the chickens are cooked through and the meat juices run clear. Serve the chickens, cut into portions, with yogurt and a salad.

Chicken and Aubergine Khoresh

In Persian or Farsi this dish is known as *Khoreshe Bademjun*, *khoresh* meaning stew and *bademjun* meaning aubergines. It is often served on festive occasions and is believed to have been a favourite of kings.

INGREDIENTS

Serves 4
30ml/2 tbsp oil
1 whole chicken or 4 large
  chicken pieces
1 large onion, chopped
2 garlic cloves, crushed
400g/14oz can chopped tomatoes
250ml/8fl oz/1 cup water
3 aubergines, sliced
3 peppers, preferably red, green and
  yellow, seeded and sliced
30ml/2 tbsp lemon juice
15ml/1 tbsp ground cinnamon
salt and freshly ground black pepper
Persian rice, to serve

1 Heat 15ml/1 tbsp of the oil in a large saucepan or flameproof casserole and fry the chicken or chicken pieces on both sides for about 10 minutes. Add the onion and fry for a further 4–5 minutes, until the onion is golden brown.

2 Add the garlic, the chopped tomatoes and their liquid, water and seasoning. Bring to the boil, then reduce the heat and simmer slowly, covered, for 10 minutes.

3 Meanwhile, heat the remaining oil and fry the aubergines in batches until lightly golden. Transfer to a plate with a slotted spoon. Add the peppers to the pan and fry for a few minutes until slightly softened.

4 Place the aubergines over the chicken or chicken pieces and then add the peppers. Sprinkle over the lemon juice and cinnamon, then cover and continue cooking over a low heat for about 45 minutes, or until the chicken is cooked.

5 Transfer the chicken to a serving plate and spoon the aubergines and peppers around the edge. Reheat the sauce if necessary, adjust the seasoning and pour over the chicken. Serve the *khoresh* with Persian rice.

Chicken Kebabs

Chicken kebabs are prepared in very much the same way all over the Middle East and are a great favourite everywhere. They are ideal for barbecues on hot summer evenings.

INGREDIENTS

Serves 6–8
2 young chickens
1 large onion, grated
2 garlic cloves, crushed
120ml/4fl oz/½ cup olive oil
juice of 1 lemon
5ml/1 tsp paprika
2–3 saffron strands, soaked in
   15ml/1 tbsp boiling water
salt and freshly ground black pepper
naan or pitta bread, to serve

1 Cut the chicken into small pieces, removing the bone if preferred, and place in a shallow bowl. Mix the onion, garlic, olive oil, lemon juice, paprika and saffron, and season with salt and pepper.

2 Pour the marinade over the chicken, turning the chicken so that all the pieces are covered evenly. Cover the bowl loosely with clear film and leave in a cool place to marinate for at least 2 hours.

3 Thread the chicken on to long, preferably metal, skewers. If barbecuing, once the coals are ready, cook for 10–15 minutes, turning occasionally. Or, if you prefer, cook under a moderately hot grill for about 10–15 minutes, turning occasionally.

4 Serve with naan or pitta bread. Or you could remove boneless chicken from the skewers and serve it in pitta bread as a sandwich accompanied by a garlicky yogurt sauce.

Baked Poussins

This dish is ideal for dinner parties. It is very easy to make and very tasty too. Allow ample time to make this recipe, however. The poussins should be allowed to marinate to make them extra delicious.

INGREDIENTS

Serves 4
475ml/16fl oz/2 cups yogurt
60ml/4 tbsp olive oil
1 large onion, grated
2 garlic cloves, crushed
2.5ml/½ tsp paprika
2–3 saffron strands, soaked in
   15ml/1 tbsp boiling water
juice of 1 lemon
4 poussins, halved
salt and freshly ground black pepper
cos lettuce salad, to serve

1 Blend together the yogurt, olive oil, onion, garlic, paprika, saffron and lemon juice, and season with salt and pepper.

2 Place the poussin halves in a shallow dish, pour over the marinade and then cover and allow to marinate overnight in a cool place or for at least 4 hours in the fridge.

3 Preheat the oven to 180°C/350°F/ Gas 4. Arrange the poussins in a greased ovenproof dish and bake in the oven for 30–45 minutes, basting frequently until cooked. Serve with cos lettuce salad.

--- COOK'S TIP ---

The poussins can also be barbecued, for an authentic and even more delicious taste.

Prawns in Tomato Sauce

Prawns are popular everywhere in the Middle East. This delicious recipe is an easy way of making the most of them.

INGREDIENTS

Serves 4
30ml/2 tbsp oil
2 onions, finely chopped
2–3 garlic cloves, crushed
5–6 tomatoes, peeled and chopped
30ml/2 tbsp tomato purée
120ml/4fl oz/¹/₂ cup fish stock
  or water
2.5ml/¹/₂ tsp ground cumin
2.5ml/¹/₂ tsp ground cinnamon
450g/1lb raw, peeled Mediterranean
  prawns
juice of 1 lemon
salt and freshly ground black pepper
fresh parsley, to garnish
rice, to serve

1 Heat the oil in a large frying pan or saucepan and fry the onions for 3–4 minutes until golden. Add the garlic, fry for about 1 minute, and then stir in the tomatoes.

2 Blend the tomato purée with the stock or water and stir into the pan with the cumin, cinnamon and seasoning. Simmer, covered, over a low heat for 15 minutes, stirring occasionally. Do not allow to boil.

3 Add the prawns and lemon juice and simmer the sauce for a further 10–15 minutes over a low to moderate heat until the prawns are cooked and the stock is reduced by about half.

4 Serve with plain rice or in a decorative ring of Persian Rice, garnished with parsley.

Swordfish Kebabs

Fish is most delicious when cooked over hot charcoal.

INGREDIENTS

Serves 4–6
900g/2lb swordfish steaks
45ml/3 tbsp olive oil
juice of ¹/₂ lemon
1 garlic clove, crushed
5ml/1 tsp paprika
3 tomatoes, quartered
2 onions, cut into wedges
salt and freshly ground black pepper
salad and pitta bread, to serve

—— COOK'S TIP ——

Almost any type of firm white fish can be used for this recipe.

1 Cut the fish into large cubes and place in a dish.

2 Blend together the oil, lemon juice, garlic, paprika and seasoning in a small mixing bowl and pour over the fish. Cover loosely with clear film and leave to marinate in a cool place for up to 2 hours.

3 Thread the fish cubes on to skewers alternating with pieces of tomato and onion.

4 Grill the kebabs over hot charcoal for 5–10 minutes, basting frequently with the remaining marinade and turning occasionally. Serve with salad and pitta bread.

Tahini Baked Fish

This simple dish is a great favourite in many Arab countries, particularly Egypt, the Lebanon and Syria.

INGREDIENTS

Serves 6

6 cod or haddock fillets
juice of 2 lemons
60ml/4 tbsp olive oil
2 large onions, chopped
250ml/8fl oz/1 cup tahini paste
1 garlic clove, crushed
45–60ml/3–4 tbsp water
salt and freshly ground black pepper
rice and salad, to serve

1 Preheat the oven to 180°C/350°F/ Gas 4. Arrange the fish fillets in a shallow ovenproof dish, pour over 15ml/1 tbsp each of the lemon juice and olive oil and bake in the oven for 20 minutes.

2 Meanwhile heat the remaining oil in a large frying pan and fry the onions for 6–8 minutes until well browned and almost crisp.

3 Put the tahini paste, garlic and seasoning in a small bowl and slowly beat in the remaining lemon juice and water, a little at a time, until the sauce is light and creamy.

4 Sprinkle the onions over the fish, pour over the tahini sauce and bake for a further 15 minutes, until the fish is cooked through and the sauce is bubbling. Serve the fish at once with rice and a salad.

Baked Fish with Nuts

This speciality comes from Egypt and is as delicious as it is unusual.

INGREDIENTS

Serves 4

45ml/3 tbsp oil
4 small red mullet
1 large onion, finely chopped
75g/3oz/¾ cup hazelnuts, chopped
75g/3oz/¾ cup pine nuts
3–4 tomatoes, sliced
45–60ml/3–4 tbsp finely chopped
    fresh parsley
250ml/8fl oz/1 cup fish stock
salt and freshly ground black pepper
parsley sprigs, to garnish
new potatoes or rice, and vegetables or
    salad, to serve

1 Preheat the oven to 190°C/375°F/ Gas 5. Heat 30ml/2 tbsp of the oil in a frying pan and fry the fish, two at a time, until crisp on both sides.

2 Heat the remaining oil in a large saucepan or flameproof casserole and fry the onion for 3–4 minutes until golden. Add the chopped hazelnuts and pine nuts and stir fry for a few minutes.

3 Stir in the tomatoes, cook for a few minutes and then add the parsley, seasoning and stock and simmer for 10–15 minutes, stirring occasionally.

--- COOK'S TIP ---

Other small whole fish, such as snapper or trout, can be used for this recipe if mullet is unavailable.

4 Place the fish in an ovenproof dish and spoon the sauce over. Bake in the oven for 20 minutes or until the fish is cooked through and flakes easily if pierced with a fork.

5 Serve the fish at once accompanied by new potatoes or rice, and vegetables or salad.

Aubergine Bake

Aubergines are extremely popular all over the Middle East. This particular dish, *Kuku Bademjan*, comes from Iran.

INGREDIENTS

Serves 4

60ml/4 tbsp oil
1 onion, finely chopped
3–4 garlic cloves, crushed
4 aubergines, cut into quarters
6 eggs
2–3 saffron strands, soaked in 15ml/ 1 tbsp boiling water
5ml/1 tsp paprika
salt and freshly ground black pepper
chopped fresh parsley, to garnish
bread and salad, to serve

1 Preheat the oven to 180°C/350°F/ Gas 4. Heat 30ml/2 tbsp of the oil in a frying pan and fry the onion until golden. Add the garlic, fry for about 2 minutes and then add the aubergines and cook for 10–12 minutes until soft and golden brown. Cool and then chop the aubergines.

2 Beat the eggs in a large bowl and stir in the aubergine mixture, saffron water, paprika and seasoning. Place the remaining oil in a deep ovenproof dish. Heat in the oven for a few minutes, then add the egg and aubergine mixture. Bake for 30–40 minutes until set. Garnish with parsley and serve with bread and salad.

Turkish-style Vegetable Casserole

INGREDIENTS

Serves 4

60ml/4 tbsp olive oil
1 large onion, chopped
2 aubergines, cut into small cubes
4 courgettes, cut into small chunks
4–5 okra, soaked in vinegar for 30 minutes, cut into short lengths
1 green pepper, seeded and chopped
1 red or yellow pepper, seeded and chopped
115g/4oz/1 cup fresh or frozen peas
115g/4oz French beans
450g/1lb new potatoes, cubed
2.5ml/½ tsp ground cinnamon
2.5ml/½ tsp ground cumin
5ml/1 tsp paprika
4–5 tomatoes, skinned
400g/14oz can chopped tomatoes
30ml/2 tbsp chopped fresh parsley
3–4 garlic cloves, crushed
350ml/12fl oz/1½ cups vegetable stock
salt and freshly ground black pepper
black olives, to garnish

1 Preheat the oven to 190°C/375°F/ Gas 5. Heat 45ml/3 tbsp of the oil in a heavy-based pan and fry the onion until golden. Add the aubergines, sauté for about 3 minutes and then add the courgettes, okra, green and red pepper, peas, beans and potatoes, together with the spices and seasoning. Cook for a further 3 minutes, stirring all the time. Transfer to a shallow ovenproof dish.

2 Chop and seed the fresh tomatoes and mix with the canned tomatoes, parsley, garlic and the remaining olive oil in a bowl.

3 Pour the stock over the vegetables and then spoon over the tomato mixture. Cover and cook in the oven for 45–60 minutes. Serve, garnished with black olives.

Baked Stuffed Aubergines

The name of this famous Turkish *mezze* dish, *Imam Bayaldi*, literally means, "the Imam fainted" – perhaps with pleasure at the deliciousness of the dish.

INGREDIENTS

Serves 6

3 aubergines
60ml/4 tbsp olive oil
1 large onion, chopped
1 small red pepper, seeded and diced
1 small green pepper, seeded and diced
3 garlic cloves, crushed
5–6 tomatoes, skinned and chopped
30ml/2 tbsp chopped fresh parsley
about 250ml/8fl oz/1 cup
    boiling water
15ml/1 tbsp lemon juice
salt and freshly ground black pepper
chopped fresh parsley, to garnish
bread, salad and yogurt dip, to serve

COOK'S TIP

This flavourful dish can be made in advance and is ideal for a buffet table.

1 Preheat the oven to 190°C/375°F/ Gas 5. Cut the aubergines in half lengthways and scoop out the flesh, reserving the shells.

2 Heat 30ml/2 tbsp of the olive oil and fry the onion and peppers for 5–6 minutes until both are slightly softened but not too tender.

3 Add the garlic and continue to cook for a further 2 minutes then stir in the tomatoes, parsley and aubergine flesh. Season and then stir well and fry over a moderate heat for 2–3 minutes.

4 Heat the remaining oil in a separate pan and fry the aubergine shells, two at a time, on both sides.

5 Stuff the shells with the sautéed vegetables. Arrange the aubergines closely together in an ovenproof dish and pour enough boiling water around the aubergines to come halfway up their sides.

6 Cover with foil and bake in the oven for 45–60 minutes until the aubergines are tender and most of the liquid has been absorbed.

7 Place a half aubergine on each serving plate and sprinkle with a little lemon juice. Serve the aubergines hot or cold, garnished with parsley and accompanied by bread, salad and a yogurt dip.

Spinach Pie

This Turkish dish, *Fatayer*, makes a healthy vegetarian dish.

INGREDIENTS

Serves 6

900g/2lb fresh spinach, chopped
25g/1oz/2 tbsp butter or margarine
2 onions, chopped
2 garlic cloves, crushed
275g/10oz feta, crumbled
115g/4oz/¾ cup pine nuts
5 eggs, beaten
2 saffron strands, soaked in 10ml/
  2 tbsp boiling water
5ml/1 tsp paprika
1.5ml/¼ tsp ground cumin
1.5ml/¼ tsp ground cinnamon
14 sheets filo pastry
about 60ml/4 tbsp olive oil
salt and freshly ground black pepper
lettuce, to serve

1 Place the spinach in a large colander, sprinkle with a little salt, rub into the leaves and leave for 30 minutes to drain the excess liquid.

2 Preheat the oven to 180°C/350°F/ Gas 4. Melt the butter or margarine in a large pan and fry the onions until golden. Add the garlic, cheese and nuts. Remove from the heat and stir in the eggs, spinach, saffron and spices. Season with salt and pepper and mix well.

----- COOK'S TIP -----

Cheddar, Parmesan or any hard cheese can be added to this dish as well as the feta.

3 Grease a large rectangular baking dish. Take seven of the sheets of filo and brush one side with a little olive oil. Place on the bottom of the dish, overlapping the sides.

4 Spoon all of the spinach mixture over the pastry and carefully dribble 30ml/2 tbsp of the remaining olive oil over the top.

5 Fold the overlapping pastry over the filling. Cut the remaining pastry sheets to the dish size and brush each one with more olive oil. Arrange on top of the filling.

6 Brush with water to prevent curling and then bake in the oven for about 30 minutes, until the pastry is golden brown. Serve with the lettuce.

Turkish Salad

This classic salad is a wonderful combination of textures and flavours. The saltiness of the cheese is perfectly balanced by the refreshing salad vegetables.

INGREDIENTS

Serves 4
1 cos lettuce heart
1 green pepper
1 red pepper
½ cucumber
4 tomatoes
1 red onion
225g/8oz feta cheese, crumbled
black olives, to garnish

For the dressing
45ml/3 tbsp olive oil
45ml/3 tbsp lemon juice
1 garlic clove, crushed
15ml/1 tbsp chopped fresh parsley
15ml/1 tbsp chopped fresh mint
salt and freshly ground black pepper

1 Chop the lettuce into bite-size pieces. Seed the peppers, remove the cores and cut the flesh into thin strips. Chop the cucumber and slice or chop the tomatoes. Cut the onion in half, then slice finely.

2 Place the chopped lettuce, peppers, cucumber, tomatoes and onion in a large bowl. Scatter the feta over the top and toss together lightly.

3 To make the dressing: blend together the olive oil, lemon juice and garlic in a small bowl. Stir in the parsley and mint and season with salt and pepper to taste.

4 Pour the dressing over the salad, toss lightly and serve garnished with a handful of black olives.

Persian Salad

This very simple salad can be served with pretty well any Persian dish – don't add the dressing until just before you are ready to serve.

INGREDIENTS

Serves 4
4 tomatoes
½ cucumber
1 onion
1 cos lettuce heart

For the dressing
30ml/2 tbsp olive oil
juice of 1 lemon
1 garlic clove, crushed
salt and freshly ground black pepper

1 Cut the tomatoes and cucumber into small cubes. Finely chop the onion and tear the lettuce into pieces.

2 Place the tomatoes, cucumber, onion and lettuce in a large salad bowl and mix lightly together.

3 To make the dressing, pour the olive oil into a small bowl. Add the lemon juice, garlic and seasoning and blend together well. Pour over the salad and toss lightly to mix. Sprinkle with black pepper and serve with meat or rice dishes.

Tabbouleh

This classic Lebanese salad has become very popular in other countries. It makes an ideal substitute for a rice dish on a buffet table and is excellent served with cold sliced lamb.

INGREDIENTS

Serves 4
175g/6oz/1 cup fine
  bulgur wheat
juice of 1 lemon
45ml/3 tbsp olive oil
40g/1½oz fresh parsley, finely
  chopped
45ml/3 tbsp fresh mint, chopped
4–5 spring onions, chopped
1 green pepper, seeded and sliced
salt and freshly ground black pepper
2 large tomatoes, diced, and black

1 Put the bulgur wheat in a bowl. Add enough cold water to cover the wheat and let it stand for at least 30 minutes and up to 2 hours.

2 Drain and squeeze with your hands to remove excess water. The bulgur wheat will swell to double the size. Spread on kitchen paper to dry the bulgur wheat completely.

3 Place the bulgur wheat in a large bowl, add the lemon juice, the oil and a little salt and pepper. Allow to stand for 1–2 hours if possible, in order for the flavours to develop.

4 Add the chopped parsley, mint, spring onions and pepper and mix well. Garnish with diced tomatoes and olives and serve.

Yogurt with Cucumber

INGREDIENTS

Serves 4–6
½ cucumber
1 small onion
2 garlic cloves
10g/¼oz fresh parsley
475ml/16fl oz/2 cups natural
  yogurt
1.5ml/¼ tsp paprika
salt and white pepper
mint leaves, to garnish

1 Finely chop the cucumber and onion, crush the garlic and finely chop the parsley.

--- COOK'S TIP ---

It's not traditional, but other herbs, such as mint or chives, would be equally good in this dish.

2 Lightly beat the yogurt and then add the cucumber, onion, garlic and parsley and season with salt and pepper to taste.

3 Sprinkle with a little paprika and chill for at least 1 hour. Garnish with mint leaves and serve with warm pitta bread or as an accompaniment to meat, poultry and rice dishes.

Sweet Rice

In Iran, sweet rice, *Shirin Polo*, is always served at wedding banquets and on other traditional special occasions.

INGREDIENTS

Serves 8–10

3 oranges
90ml/6 tbsp sugar
45ml/3 tbsp melted butter
5–6 carrots, cut into julienne strips
50g/2oz/½ cup mixed chopped
   pistachios, almonds and pine nuts
675g/1½lb/3½ cups basmati rice,
   soaked in salted water for 2 hours
2–3 saffron strands, soaked in
   15ml/1 tbsp boiling water
salt

— COOK'S TIP —

Take care to cook this rice over a very low heat as it can burn easily owing to the sugar in the carrots.

1 Cut the peel from the oranges in wide strips using a potato peeler, and cut the peel into thin shreds.

2 Place the strips of peel in a saucepan with enough water to cover and bring to the boil. Simmer for a few minutes, drain and repeat this process until you have removed the bitter flavour of the peel.

3 Place the peel back in the pan with 45ml/3 tbsp of the sugar and 60ml/4 tbsp water. Bring to the boil and then simmer until the water is reduced by half. Set aside.

4 Heat 15ml/1 tbsp of the butter in a pan and fry the carrots for 2–3 minutes. Add the remaining sugar and 60ml/4 tbsp water and simmer for 10 minutes until almost evaporated.

5 Stir the carrots and half of the nuts into the orange peel and set aside. Drain the rice, boil in salted water for 5 minutes, then reduce the heat and simmer very gently for 10 minutes until half cooked. Drain and rinse.

6 Heat 15ml/1 tbsp of the remaining butter in the pan and add 45ml/3 tbsp water. Fork a little of the rice into the pan and spoon on some of the orange mixture. Make layers until all the mixture has been used.

7 Cook gently for 10 minutes. Pour over the remaining butter and cover with a clean dish towel. Secure the lid and steam for 30–45 minutes. Serve garnished with the remaining nuts and the saffron water.

Rice with Fresh Herbs

INGREDIENTS

Serves 4

350g/12oz/scant 2 cups basmati
   rice, soaked in salted water for
   2 hours
30ml/2 tbsp finely chopped
   fresh parsley
30ml/2 tbsp finely chopped
   fresh coriander
30ml/2 tbsp finely snipped
   fresh chives
15ml/1 tbsp finely chopped fresh dill
3–4 spring onions, finely chopped
60ml/4 tbsp butter
5ml/1 tsp ground cinnamon
2–3 saffron strands, soaked in
   15ml/1 tbsp boiling water
salt

1 Drain the rice, and then boil in salted water for 5 minutes, reduce the heat and simmer for 10 minutes.

2 Stir in the herbs and spring onions and mix well with a fork. Simmer for a few minutes more, then drain but do not rinse. Wash and dry the pan.

3 Heat half of the butter in the pan, add 15ml/1 tbsp water, then stir in the rice. Cook over a very low heat for 10 minutes, then test to see if it is half cooked. Add the remaining butter, the cinnamon and saffron water and cover the pan with a clean dish towel. Secure with a tight-fitting lid, and steam over a very low heat for 30–40 minutes.

Persian Melon

Called *Paludeh Garmac*, this is a typical Persian dessert, using delicious, sweet fresh fruits flavoured with rose-water and a hint of aromatic mint.

INGREDIENTS

Serves 4

2 small melons
225g/8oz/1 cup strawberries, sliced
3 peaches, peeled and cut into
   small cubes
1 bunch of seedless grapes (green or red)
30ml/2 tbsp caster sugar
15ml/1 tbsp rose-water
15ml/1 tbsp lemon juice
crushed ice (optional)
4 sprigs of mint, to decorate

1 Carefully cut the melons in half and remove the seeds. Scoop out the flesh with a melon baller, making sure not to damage the skin. Reserve the melon shells. Alternatively, if you don't have a melon baller, scoop out the flesh using a large spoon and cut into bite-size pieces.

2 Reserve four strawberries and slice the others. Place in a bowl with the melon balls, the peaches, grapes, sugar, rose-water and lemon juice.

3 Pile the fruit into the melon shells and chill in the fridge for 2 hours.

4 To serve, sprinkle with crushed ice, decorating each melon with a whole strawberry and a sprig of mint.

COOK'S TIP

To peel peaches, cover with boiling water and leave to stand for a couple of minutes. Cool under cold water before peeling.

Oranges in Syrup

This is a favourite classic dessert. It is light and simple-to-make, refreshing and delicious.

INGREDIENTS

Serves 4

4 oranges
600ml/1 pint/2½ cups water
350g/12oz/1½ cups sugar
30ml/2 tbsp lemon juice
30ml/2 tbsp orange blossom water or rose-water
50g/2oz/½ cup pistachio nuts, shelled and chopped

COOK'S TIP

A perfect dessert to serve after a heavy main course dish. Almonds could be substituted for the pistachio nuts, if you like.

1 Peel the oranges with a potato peeler down to the pith.

2 Cut the orange peel into fine strips and boil in water several times to remove the bitterness. Drain and set aside until required.

3 Place the water, sugar and lemon juice in a saucepan. Bring to the boil and then add the orange peel and simmer until the syrup thickens. Add the orange blossom or rose-water, stir and leave to cool.

4 Completely peel the pith from the oranges and cut them into thick slices. Arrange in a shallow serving dish and pour over the syrup. Chill for about 1–2 hours and then decorate with pistachio nuts and serve.

Baklava

This is queen of all pastries with its exotic flavours and is usually served for the Persian New Year on 21st March, celebrating the first day of spring.

INGREDIENTS

Serves 6–8

350g/12oz/3¾ cups ground
  pistachio nuts
150g/5oz/1¼ cups icing sugar
15ml/1 tbsp ground cardamom
150g/5oz/⅔ cup unsalted butter,
  melted
450g/1lb filo pastry

For the syrup

450g/1lb/2 cups granulated
  sugar
300ml/½ pint/1¼ cups water
30ml/2 tbsp rose-water

1 First make the syrup: place the sugar and water in a saucepan, bring to the boil and then simmer for 10 minutes until syrupy. Stir in the rose-water and leave to cool.

2 Mix together the nuts, icing sugar and cardamom. Preheat the oven to 160°C/325°F/Gas 3 and brush a large rectangular baking tin with a little melted butter.

3 Taking one sheet of filo pastry at a time, and keeping the remainder covered with a damp cloth, brush with melted butter and lay on the bottom of the tin. Continue until you have six buttered layers in the tin. Spread half of the nut mixture over, pressing down with a spoon.

4 Take another six sheets of filo pastry, brush with butter and lay over the nut mixture. Sprinkle over the remaining nuts and top with a final layer of six filo sheets brushed again with butter. Cut the pastry diagonally into small lozenge shapes using a sharp knife. Pour the remaining melted butter over the top.

5 Bake for 20 minutes then increase the heat to 200°C/400°F/Gas 6 and bake for 15 minutes until light golden in colour and puffed.

6 Remove from the oven and drizzle about three quarters of the syrup over the pastry, reserving the remainder for serving. Arrange the baklava lozenges on a large glass dish and serve with extra syrup.

Omm Ali

Here's an Egyptian version of
bread and butter pudding.

INGREDIENTS

Serves 4
10–12 sheets filo pastry
600ml/1 pint/2½ cups milk
250ml/8fl oz/1 cup double cream
1 egg, beaten
30ml/2 tbsp rose-water
50g/2oz/½ cup each chopped
  pistachio nuts, almonds and hazelnuts
115g/4oz/⅔ cup raisins
15ml/1 tbsp ground cinnamon
single cream, to serve

1 Preheat the oven to 160°C/325°F/
Gas 3. Bake the filo pastry, on a
baking sheet, for 15–20 minutes until
crisp. Remove from the oven and raise
the temperature to 200°C/400°F/Gas 6.

2 Scald the milk and cream by
pouring into a pan and heating
very gently until hot but not boiling.
Slowly add the beaten egg and the
rose-water. Cook over a very low heat,
until the mixture begins to thicken,
stirring all the time.

3 Crumble the pastry using your
hands and then spread in layers
with the nuts and raisins into the base
of a shallow baking dish.

4 Pour the custard mixture over the
nut and pastry base and bake in the
oven for 20 minutes until golden.
Sprinkle with cinnamon and serve with
single cream.

MOROCCO

Harira

INGREDIENTS

Serves 6

75g/3oz/½ cup chick-peas, soaked
   overnight
15g/½oz/1 tbsp butter
225g/8oz lamb, cut into cubes
1 onion, chopped
450g/1lb tomatoes, peeled
   and chopped
a few celery leaves, chopped
30ml/2 tbsp chopped fresh parsley
15ml/1 tbsp chopped fresh coriander
2.5ml/½ tsp ground ginger
2.5ml/½ tsp ground turmeric
5ml/1 tsp ground cinnamon
75g/3oz/scant ½ cup green lentils
75g/3oz vermicelli or soup pasta
2 egg yolks
juice of ½–1 lemon
salt and freshly ground black pepper
fresh coriander, to garnish
lemon wedges, to serve

1 Drain the chick-peas, rinse under cold water and set aside. Melt the butter in a large flameproof casserole or saucepan and fry the lamb and onion for 2–3 minutes, stirring, until the lamb is just browned.

2 Add the tomatoes, celery leaves, herbs and spices and season well with black pepper. Cook for about 1 minute and then stir in 1.75 litres/3 pints/7½ cups water and add the lentils and chick-peas.

3 Slowly bring to the boil and skim the surface to remove the surplus froth. Boil rapidly for 10 minutes, then reduce the heat and simmer very gently for about 2 hours or until the chick-peas are very tender. Season with salt and a little more pepper if necessary.

4 Add the vermicelli or soup pasta and cook for 5–6 minutes until it is just cooked through. If the soup is very thick at this stage, add a little more water.

5 Beat the egg yolks with the lemon juice and stir into the simmering soup. Immediately remove the soup from the heat and stir until thickened. Pour into warmed serving bowls and garnish with fresh coriander. Serve with lemon wedges.

--- COOK'S TIP ---

If you have forgotten to soak the chick-peas, place them in a pan with about four times their volume of cold water. Bring very slowly to the boil, and then cover and remove from the heat. Allow to stand for 45 minutes. They can then be drained and used as described in the recipe.

Chick-pea and Parsley Soup

INGREDIENTS

Serves 6

225g/8oz/1⅓ cups chick-peas, soaked
   overnight
1 small onion
1 bunch fresh parsley (about 40g/1½ oz)
30ml/2 tbsp olive and sunflower
   oil, mixed
1.2 litres/2 pints/5 cups chicken stock
juice of ½ lemon
salt and freshly ground black pepper
lemon wedges and finely pared strips of
   rind, to garnish
fresh crusty bread, to serve

1 Drain the chick-peas and rinse under cold water. Cook them in boiling water for 1–1½ hours until tender. Drain and peel (see Cook's Tip).

2 Place the onion and parsley in a food processor or blender and process until finely chopped.

3 Heat the olive and sunflower oils in a saucepan or flameproof casserole and fry the onion mixture for about 4 minutes over a low heat until the onion is slightly softened.

4 Add the chick-peas, cook gently for 1–2 minutes and add the stock. Season well with salt and pepper. Bring the soup to the boil, then cover and simmer for 20 minutes until the chick-peas are very tender.

5 Allow the soup to cool a little and then part-purée in a food processor or blender, or by mashing the chick-peas fairly roughly with a fork, so that the soup is thick but still quite chunky.

COOK'S TIP

Chick-peas, particularly canned ones, blend better in soups and other dishes if the outer skin is rubbed away with your fingers. Although this will take you some time, the final result is much better, so it is well worth doing.

6 Return the soup to a clean pan, add the lemon juice and adjust the seasoning if necessary. Heat gently and then serve garnished with lemon wedges and finely pared rind, and accompanied by fresh crusty bread.

Olives with Moroccan Marinades

INGREDIENTS

Serves 6–8
225g/8oz/1⅓ cups green or tan olives
  (unpitted) for each marinade

For the Moroccan marinade
45ml/3 tbsp chopped fresh coriander
45ml/3 tbsp chopped fresh flat
  leaf parsley
1 garlic clove, finely chopped
good pinch of cayenne pepper
good pinch of ground cumin
30–45ml/2–3 tbsp olive oil
30–45ml/2–3 tbsp lemon juice

For the spicy herb marinade
60ml/4 tbsp chopped fresh coriander
60ml/4 tbsp chopped fresh flat
  leaf parsley
1 garlic clove, finely chopped
5ml/1 tsp grated fresh root ginger
1 red chilli, seeded and finely sliced
¼ preserved lemon, cut into thin strips

1 Crack the olives, hard enough to break the flesh, but taking care not to crack the stone. Place in a bowl of cold water and leave overnight to remove the excess brine. Drain thoroughly and place in a jar.

2 Blend the ingredients for the Moroccan marinade and pour over half the olives, adding more olive oil and lemon juice to cover, if necessary.

3 To make the spicy herb marinade, mix together the coriander, parsley, garlic, ginger, chilli and preserved lemon. Add the remaining olives. Store the olives in the fridge for at least 1 week, shaking the jars occasionally.

Byesar

The Arab dish Byesar is similar to Middle Eastern hummus, but uses broad beans instead of chick-peas. In Morocco, it is eaten by dipping bread into ground spices and then scooping up the purée.

INGREDIENTS

Serves 4–6
115g/4oz dried broad beans, soaked
2 garlic cloves, peeled
5ml/1 tsp cumin seeds
about 60ml/4 tbsp olive oil
salt
mint sprigs, to garnish
extra cumin, cayenne pepper and
  bread, to serve

1 Put the dried broad beans in a pan with the whole garlic cloves and cumin seeds and add enough water just to cover. Bring to the boil, then reduce the heat and simmer until the beans are tender. Drain, cool and then slip off the outer skin of each bean.

2 Purée the beans in a blender or food processor, adding sufficient olive oil and water to give a smooth soft dip. Season to taste with plenty of salt. Garnish with sprigs of mint and serve with extra cumin seeds, cayenne pepper and bread.

Sizzling Prawns

For a really tasty starter, fry prawns in a blend of Moroccan spices. It couldn't be simpler.

INGREDIENTS

Serves 4

450g/1lb raw king prawns in their shells
30ml/2 tbsp olive oil
25–40g/1–1½oz/2–3 tbsp butter
2 garlic cloves, crushed
5ml/1 tsp ground cumin
2.5ml/½ tsp ground ginger
10ml/2 tsp paprika
1.5ml/¼ tsp cayenne pepper
lemon wedges and fresh coriander sprigs, to garnish

1 Pull the heads off the prawns and then peel away the shells, legs and tails. Using a sharp knife, cut along the back of each prawn and pull away and discard the dark thread.

2 Heat the olive oil and butter in a frying pan. When the butter begins to sizzle, add the garlic and cook for about 30 seconds.

3 Add the cumin, ginger, paprika and cayenne pepper. Cook briefly, stirring for a few seconds, and then add the prawns. Cook for 2–3 minutes over a high heat, until they turn pink, stirring frequently.

4 Transfer the prawns to four warmed serving dishes and pour the butter and spicy mixture over. Garnish with lemon wedges and coriander and serve immediately.

Grilled Keftas

INGREDIENTS

Makes 12–14

675g/1½lb lamb
1 onion, quartered
3–4 fresh parsley sprigs
2–3 fresh coriander sprigs
1–2 fresh mint sprigs
2.5ml/½ tsp ground cumin
2.5ml/½ tsp mixed spice
5ml/1 tsp paprika
salt and freshly ground black pepper
fresh crusty bread, to serve

For the mint dressing

30ml/2 tbsp finely chopped fresh mint
90ml/6 tbsp natural yogurt

1 Roughly chop the lamb, place in a food processor and process until smooth. Transfer to a plate.

2 Add the onion, parsley, coriander and mint to the processor and process until finely chopped. Add the lamb together with the spices and seasoning and process again until very smooth. Transfer to a bowl and chill for about 1 hour.

3 Make the dressing. Blend the chopped fresh mint with the yogurt and chill until required.

4 Mould the meat into small sausage shapes and skewer with wooden or metal kebab sticks. Preheat a grill or barbecue.

5 Cook the keftas for 5–6 minutes, turning once. Serve immediately with the mint dressing. Fresh crusty bread makes a good accompaniment.

Chakcouka

This is a Moroccan version of a dish from neighbouring Tunisia. Include one or two red or orange peppers as you need the sweetness of the riper fruit.

INGREDIENTS

Serves 4
45ml/3 tbsp olive oil
1 Spanish onion, finely sliced
1 garlic clove, crushed
4 peppers, cored, seeded and sliced
4–5 tomatoes, peeled and chopped
250ml/8fl oz/1 cup puréed canned
    tomatoes or tomato juice
25ml/1½ tbsp chopped fresh parsley
5ml/1 tsp paprika (optional)
a little lemon juice (optional)
4 eggs
45ml/3 tbsp single cream
salt and freshly ground black pepper

1 Preheat the oven to 180°C/350°F/ Gas 4. Heat the oil in a frying pan and gently fry the onion and garlic for about 5 minutes until softened, stirring occasionally.

2 Add the sliced peppers to the pan and fry over a gentle heat for about 10 minutes, stirring occasionally, until softened slightly.

3 Add the chopped tomatoes, the puréed tomatoes or juice, 15ml/ 1 tbsp of the parsley, the paprika, if using, and seasoning and stir well. Cook over a gentle heat for a further 10 minutes until the peppers are fairly soft. Season to taste, and sharpen with lemon juice, if liked.

4 Spoon the mixture into four ovenproof dishes, preferably earthenware. Make a well in the centre and break an egg into each hole. Spoon some of the cream over each egg yolk and sprinkle with a little black pepper or paprika, as liked.

5 Bake for about 15 minutes until the white of the egg is set. Sprinkle with the remaining chopped parsley before serving.

Roasted Aubergines

Aubergines are a favourite Moroccan vegetable. They are often eaten fried or, as here, roasted with spices in a hot oven.

INGREDIENTS

Serves 4
1 large or 2 small aubergines
salt
ground cumin, paprika and cayenne
    pepper, or lemon wedges and mint
    leaves, to serve

For the paprika oil
10ml/2 tsp paprika
60ml/4 tbsp water
60ml/4 tbsp sunflower oil

1 Slice the aubergines lengthways, place in a colander, sprinkle with salt and set aside on a plate for about 30 minutes. Meanwhile, make the paprika oil. Place the paprika, water and oil in a pan, bring to the boil and simmer for 10 minutes. Carefully pour the oil from the surface into a heatproof container, discarding the sediment. Preheat the oven to 190°C/375°F/ Gas 5. Rinse the aubergines and pat dry with kitchen paper.

2 Brush each side of the aubergines generously with the paprika oil and place on a baking tray. Bake for 15–20 minutes until lightly golden.

3 Blend together equal proportions of cumin and paprika and season with cayenne pepper. Serve the aubergine slices warm with the spice mixture, or simply serve with salt and a sprinkling of mint leaves plus lemon wedges for squeezing.

Moroccan Rabbit

The subtle spices make the perfect accompaniments to rabbit.

INGREDIENTS

Serves 4
675g/1½lb prepared rabbit pieces
pinch of saffron
1 garlic clove, crushed
pinch of ground turmeric
5ml/1 tsp paprika
good pinch of ground cumin
1 onion, grated
25g/1oz/2 tbsp butter
15ml/1 tbsp finely chopped fresh
  coriander
50g/2oz/scant ½ cup raisins
5ml/1 tsp garam masala or mixed spice
salt and freshly ground black pepper
30ml/2 tbsp flaked almonds, toasted,
  to garnish

1 Preheat the oven to 180°C/350°F/Gas 4 and place the rabbit pieces in a casserole.

2 Blend together the saffron and 30ml/2 tbsp boiling water and stir to dissolve. Add the garlic, turmeric, paprika, cumin and salt and pepper and rub this mixture into the rabbit pieces.

3 Add the onion, half the butter, the coriander and 600ml/1 pint/2½ cups boiling water. Cover and cook in the oven for 50 minutes, then transfer the rabbit pieces to a shallow heatproof dish and rub with the remaining butter.

4 Increase the oven temperature to 190°C/375°F/Gas 5. Cook the rabbit pieces for 8–10 minutes until browned and place on a serving plate.

5 Meanwhile, pour the sauce into a small saucepan, add the raisins and garam masala or mixed spice and simmer until reduced by about half. Pour the sauce over the rabbit and garnish with the flaked almonds.

Moroccan-style Roast Lamb

Lamb is by far the most favoured meat of Morocco, where whole or half lambs are still cooked over open fires. In this oven-roasted variation of *M'choui* the meat is cooked in a very hot oven to start and then finished in a cooler oven until it is so tender that it falls from the bone.

INGREDIENTS

Serves 6
1.5kg/3–3½lb leg of lamb
40g/1½oz/3 tbsp butter
2 garlic cloves, crushed
2.5ml/½ tsp cumin seeds
1.5ml/¼ tsp paprika
pinch of cayenne pepper
salt
fresh coriander, to garnish
bread or roast potatoes, to serve

1 Trim the lamb of excess fat and make several shallow diagonal cuts over the meat.

2 Blend together the butter, garlic, cumin, paprika, cayenne pepper and salt and spread over the surface of the lamb, pressing the mixture into the slits. Set aside for at least 2 hours or overnight.

3 Preheat the oven to 220°C/425°F/Gas 7. Place the meat in a large roasting tin and cook for 15 minutes. (Be warned: the butter will burn, but the resulting flavour is delicious.) Reduce the oven temperature to 180°C/350°F/Gas 4 and continue cooking for 1½–2 hours, until the meat is well cooked and very tender, basting several times with the meat juices.

4 Place the cooked meat on a serving plate and serve immediately. In Morocco, it is customary to pull the meat away from the bone using a fork; however, it may be carved if you prefer. Garnish with fresh coriander and serve Moroccan-style with bread, or with roast potatoes.

Beef Tagine with Sweet Potatoes

This warming dish is eaten during the winter in Morocco, where, especially in the mountains, the weather can be surprisingly cold. Tagines, by definition, are cooked on the hob (or, more often in Morocco, over coals). However, this works well cooked in the oven.

INGREDIENTS

Serves 4
675–900g/1½–2lb braising or
  stewing beef
30ml/2 tbsp sunflower oil
good pinch of ground turmeric
1 large onion, chopped
1 red or green chilli, seeded
  and chopped
7.5ml/1½ tsp paprika
good pinch of cayenne pepper
2.5ml/½ tsp ground cumin
450g/1lb sweet potatoes
15ml/1 tbsp chopped fresh parsley
15ml/1 tbsp chopped fresh coriander
15g/½oz/1 tbsp butter
salt and freshly ground black pepper

1 Trim the meat and cut into 2cm/¾in cubes. Heat the oil in a flameproof casserole and fry the meat, together with the turmeric and seasoning, over a medium heat for 3–4 minutes until evenly brown, stirring frequently.

2 Cover the pan tightly and cook for 15 minutes over a fairly gentle heat, without lifting the lid. Preheat the oven to 180°C/350°F/Gas 4.

3 Add the onion, chilli, paprika, cayenne pepper and cumin to the pan together with just enough water to cover the meat. Cover tightly and cook in the oven for 1–1½ hours until the meat is very tender, checking occasionally and adding a little extra water to keep the stew fairly moist.

4 Meanwhile, peel the sweet potatoes and slice them straight into a bowl of salted water (sweet potatoes discolour very quickly). Transfer to a pan, bring to the boil and then simmer for 2–3 minutes until just tender. Drain.

5 Stir the herbs into the meat, adding a little extra water if the stew appears dry. Arrange the potato slices over the meat and dot with the butter. Cover and cook in the oven for a further 10 minutes or until the potatoes feel very tender. Increase the oven temperature to 200°C/400°F/Gas 6 or heat the grill.

6 Remove the lid of the casserole and cook in the oven or under the grill for a further 5–10 minutes until the potatoes are golden.

Grilled Spatchcocked Poussins

These little chickens can be cooked under the grill, but taste best if cooked, Moroccan-style, over charcoal.

INGREDIENTS

Serves 4
2 large or 4 small poussins
green salad, to serve

For the marinade
150ml/¼ pint/⅔ cup olive oil
1 onion, grated
1 garlic clove, crushed
15ml/1 tbsp chopped fresh mint
15ml/1 tbsp chopped fresh flat
   leaf parsley
15ml/1 tbsp chopped fresh coriander
5–10ml/1–2 tsp ground cumin
5ml/1 tsp paprika
pinch of cayenne pepper

1 Tuck the wings of each poussin under the body and remove the wishbone. Turn the birds over and cut along each side of the backbone with poultry shears and remove.

2 Push down on each bird to break the breast bone. Keeping the bird flat, push a skewer through the wings and breast. Push another skewer through the thighs.

3 Blend together all the marinade ingredients and spread over both sides of the poussins. Place in a large shallow dish, cover with clear film and marinate for at least 4 hours or overnight.

4 Prepare a barbecue or preheat the grill. Barbecue the poussins for about 25–35 minutes, turning occasionally and brushing with the marinade. If grilling, cook under a medium grill about 7.5cm/3in from the heat for 25–35 minutes or until cooked through, turning and basting occasionally.

5 When ready to serve, cut the birds in half. Serve with a green salad.

Chicken Kdra with Chick-peas and Almonds

A *kdra* is a type of tagine that is traditionally cooked with *smen*, a strong Moroccan butter, and a lot of onions. The almonds in this recipe are precooked until soft, adding an interesting texture and flavour to the chicken.

INGREDIENTS

Serves 4
75g/3oz/½ cup blanched almonds
75g/3oz /½ cup chick-peas, soaked overnight
4 part-boned chicken breasts, skinned
50g/2oz/4 tbsp butter
2.5ml/½ tsp saffron
2 Spanish onions, finely sliced
900ml/1½ pints/3¾ cups chicken stock
1 small cinnamon stick
60ml/4 tbsp chopped fresh flat leaf parsley, plus extra to garnish
lemon juice, to taste
salt and freshly ground black pepper

1 Place the almonds in a pan of water and simmer for 1½–2 hours until fairly soft, then drain. Cook the chick-peas for 1–1½ hours until soft. Drain the chick-peas, then place in a bowl of cold water and rub with your fingers to remove the skins. Discard the skins and drain.

2 Place the chicken pieces in a pan, together with the butter, half of the saffron, salt and plenty of black pepper. Heat gently, stirring, until the butter has melted.

3 Add the onions and stock, bring to the boil and then add the chick-peas and cinnamon stick. Cover and cook very gently for 45–60 minutes until the chicken is completely tender.

4 Transfer the chicken to a serving plate and keep warm. Bring the sauce to the boil and simmer until well reduced, stirring frequently. Add the almonds, parsley and remaining saffron and cook for a further 2–3 minutes. Sharpen the sauce with a little lemon juice, then pour over the chicken and serve, garnished with extra parsley.

Chicken with Tomatoes and Honey

INGREDIENTS

Serves 4
30ml/2 tbsp sunflower oil
25g/1oz/2 tbsp butter
4 chicken quarters or 1 whole chicken, quartered
1 onion, grated or very finely chopped
1 garlic clove, crushed
5ml/1 tsp ground cinnamon
good pinch of ground ginger
1.5kg/3–3½lb tomatoes, peeled, cored and roughly chopped
30ml/2 tbsp clear honey
50g/2oz/⅓ cup blanched almonds
15ml/1 tbsp sesame seeds
salt and freshly ground black pepper
fresh crusty bread, to serve

1 Heat the oil and butter in a large casserole. Add the chicken pieces and cook over a medium heat for about 3 minutes until the chicken is lightly browned.

2 Add the onion, garlic, cinnamon, ginger, tomatoes and seasoning, and heat gently until the tomatoes begin to bubble.

3 Lower the heat, cover and simmer very gently for 1 hour, stirring and turning the chicken occasionally, until it is completely cooked through.

4 Transfer the chicken pieces to a plate and then increase the heat and cook the tomatoes until the sauce is reduced to a thick purée, stirring frequently. Stir in the honey, cook for a minute and then return the chicken to the pan and cook for 2–3 minutes to heat through. Dry fry the almonds and sesame seeds or toast under the grill until golden.

5 Transfer the chicken and sauce to a warmed serving dish and sprinkle with the almonds and sesame seeds. Serve with fresh crusty bread.

Sea Bream with Artichokes and Courgettes

INGREDIENTS

Serves 4

1 or 2 whole sea bream or sea bass,
    about 1.5kg/3–3½ lb, cleaned and
    scaled, with the head and tail left on
2 onions
2–3 courgettes
4 tomatoes
45ml/3 tbsp olive oil
5ml/1 tsp fresh thyme
400g/14oz can artichoke hearts
lemon wedges and finely pared rind,
    black olives and fresh coriander
    leaves, to garnish

For the *charmoula*

1 onion, chopped
2 garlic cloves, halved
½ bunch fresh parsley
3–4 fresh coriander sprigs
pinch of paprika
45ml/3 tbsp olive oil
30ml/2 tbsp white wine vinegar
15ml/1 tbsp lemon juice
salt and freshly ground black pepper

1 First make the *charmoula*. Place the ingredients in a food processor with 45ml/3 tbsp water and process until the onion is finely chopped and the ingredients are well combined. Alternatively, chop the onion, garlic and herbs finely and blend with the other ingredients and the water.

2 Make three or four slashes on both sides of the fish. Place in a bowl and spread with the *charmoula* marinade, pressing into both sides of the fish. Set aside for 2–3 hours, turning the fish occasionally.

3 Slice the onions. Top and tail the courgettes and cut into julienne strips. Peel the tomatoes, discard the seeds and chop roughly.

4 Preheat the oven to 220°C/425°F/ Gas 7. Place the onions, courgettes and tomatoes in a shallow ovenproof dish. Sprinkle with the olive oil, salt and thyme and roast in the oven for 15–20 minutes, until softened and slightly charred, stirring occasionally.

5 Reduce the oven temperature to 180°C/350°F/Gas 4. Add the artichokes to the dish and place the fish, together with the marinade, on top of the vegetables. Pour over 150ml/¼ pint/⅔ cup water and cover with foil.

6 Bake for 30–35 minutes or until the fish is tender. (It will depend on whether you are cooking 1 large or 2 smaller fish.) For the last 5 minutes of cooking, remove the foil to allow the skin to brown lightly. Alternatively, place under a hot grill for 2–3 minutes.

7 Arrange the fish on a large, warmed serving platter and spoon the vegetables around the sides. Garnish with lemon wedges and finely pared strips of rind, black olives and fresh coriander leaves before serving.

Fish Boulettes in Hot Tomato Sauce

This is an unusual and tasty dish that needs scarcely any preparation and produces very little washing up, as it is all cooked in one pan. It serves four people as a main course, but also makes a great starter for eight.

INGREDIENTS

Serves 4

675g/1½lb cod, haddock or
   sea bass fillets
pinch of saffron
½ bunch flat leaf parsley
1 egg
25g/1oz/½ cup white breadcrumbs
25ml/1½ tbsp olive oil
15ml/1 tbsp lemon juice
salt and freshly ground black pepper
fresh flat leaf parsley and lemon
   wedges, to garnish

For the sauce

1 onion, very finely chopped
2 garlic cloves, crushed
6 tomatoes, peeled, seeded and
   chopped
1 green or red chilli, seeded and
   finely sliced
90ml/6 tbsp olive oil
150ml/¼ pint/⅔ cup water
15ml/1 tbsp lemon juice

1 Skin the fish and, if necessary, remove any bones. Cut the fish into large chunks and place in a blender or a food processor.

2 Dissolve the saffron in 30ml/2 tbsp boiling water and pour into the blender or food processor with the parsley, egg, breadcrumbs, olive oil and lemon juice. Season well with salt and pepper and process for 10–20 seconds until the fish is finely chopped and all the ingredients are combined.

3 Mould the mixture into small balls about the size of walnuts and place them in a single layer on a plate.

4 To make the sauce, place the onion, garlic, tomatoes, chilli, olive oil and water in a saucepan. Bring to the boil and then simmer, partially covered, for 10–15 minutes until the sauce is slightly reduced.

5 Add the lemon juice and then place the fish balls in the simmering sauce. Cover and simmer very gently for 12–15 minutes until the fish balls are cooked through, turning them over occasionally.

6 Serve the fish balls and sauce immediately, garnished with flat leaf parsley and lemon wedges.

Monkfish Couscous

Since fish needs very little cooking, it is quickest and easiest to cook the couscous using this simple method. However, if you prefer to steam couscous, steam it over the onions and peppers.

INGREDIENTS

Serves 4

675g/1½lb monkfish
30ml/2 tbsp olive oil
1 onion, very thinly sliced into rings
25g/1oz/3 tbsp raisins
40g/1½ oz/¼ cup cashew nuts
1 small red pepper, cored, seeded and sliced
1 small yellow pepper, cored, seeded and sliced
4 tomatoes, peeled, seeded and sliced
350ml/12fl oz/1½ cups fish stock
15ml/1 tbsp chopped fresh parsley
salt and freshly ground black pepper

For the couscous

275g/10oz/1⅔ cups couscous
525ml/18fl oz/2¼ cups boiling vegetable stock or water

1 Bone and skin the monkfish, if necessary, and cut into bite-size chunks using a sharp knife.

2 Heat half the oil in a saucepan or flameproof casserole and fry about a quarter of the onion rings for 5–6 minutes until they are a dark golden brown. Transfer to a plate lined with kitchen paper.

3 Add the raisins and stir-fry for 30–60 seconds until they begin to plump up. Add to the plate with the onion rings. Add the cashew nuts to the pan and stir-fry for 30–60 seconds until golden. Place on the plate with the onion and raisins and set aside.

4 Heat the remaining oil in the pan and add the remaining onion rings. Cook for 4–5 minutes until golden, and then add the pepper slices. Cook over a fairly high heat for 6–8 minutes until the peppers are soft, stirring occasionally. Add the tomatoes and fish stock, reduce the heat and simmer for 10 minutes.

5 Meanwhile, prepare the couscous. Place in a bowl, pour over the boiling stock or water and stir once or twice. Set aside for 10 minutes so that the couscous can absorb the liquid, then fluff up with a fork. Cover and keep warm. Alternatively, prepare according to the instructions on the packet.

6 Add the fish to the peppers and onion, partially cover and simmer for 6–8 minutes until the fish is tender, stirring gently occasionally. Season to taste with salt and pepper.

7 Pile the couscous on to a large serving plate and make a hollow in the middle. Pour over the monkfish and peppers with all the sauce. Sprinkle with the parsley and the reserved onion rings, raisins and cashew nuts and serve.

Sea Bass and Fennel Tagine

This is a delicious tagine where the fish is flavoured with *charmoula*, a favourite blend of herbs and spices used especially in fish dishes.

INGREDIENTS

Serves 4

675g/1½lb sea bass, monkfish or
  cod fillets
225g/8oz raw Mediterranean prawns
30ml/2 tbsp olive oil
1 onion, chopped
1 fennel bulb, sliced
225g/8oz small new potatoes, halved
475ml/16fl oz/2 cups fish stock
lemon wedges, to serve (optional)

For the *charmoula*
2 garlic cloves, crushed
20ml/4 tsp ground cumin
20ml/4 tsp paprika
pinch of chilli powder or
  cayenne pepper
30ml/2 tbsp chopped fresh parsley
30ml/2 tbsp chopped fresh coriander
45ml/3 tbsp white vinegar
15ml/1 tbsp lemon juice

1 First make the *charmoula* by blending the crushed garlic, spices, herbs, vinegar and lemon juice together in a bowl.

2 Skin the fish if necessary and remove any bones, then cut into large bite-size chunks. Top and tail the prawns and pull away the shell. Using a sharp knife, cut along the back of each prawn and pull away and discard the dark thread.

3 Place the fish and prawns in two separate shallow dishes, add half the *charmoula* marinade to each dish and stir well to coat evenly. Cover with clear film and set aside in a cool place for 30 minutes–2 hours.

4 Heat the oil in a large flameproof casserole and fry the onion for 2 minutes. Add the sliced fennel and continue cooking over a gentle heat for 5–6 minutes until the onion and fennel are flecked with brown. Add the potatoes and fish stock and cook for a further 10–15 minutes until the potatoes are tender.

5 Add the marinated fish, stir gently and cook for 4 minutes, then add the prawns and all the remaining marinade and cook for a further 5–6 minutes until the fish is tender and the prawns are pink.

6 Serve in bowls, with lemon wedges for squeezing if you wish.

Pumpkin Couscous

Pumpkin is a very popular Moroccan ingredient and this is another traditional couscous, with echoes of the very early vegetable couscous dishes made by the Berbers.

Ingredients

Serves 4–6
75g/3oz/½ cup chick-peas, soaked
  overnight
675g/1½lb lean lamb, cut into
  bite-size pieces
2 Spanish onions, sliced
pinch of saffron
1.5ml/¼ tsp ground ginger
2.5ml/½ tsp ground turmeric
5ml/1 tsp ground black pepper
450g/1lb carrots
675g/1½lb pumpkin
75g/3oz/⅔ cup raisins
400g/14oz/2 cups couscous
salt
fresh parsley, to garnish

1 Drain the chick-peas and cook in plenty of boiling water for 1–1½ hours until tender. Place in a bowl of cold water and remove the skins by rubbing with your fingers. The skins will float to the surface. Discard the skins and drain.

2 Place the lamb, onions, saffron, ginger, turmeric, pepper, salt and 1.2 litres/2 pints/5 cups water in a *couscousier* or large saucepan. Slowly bring to the boil, then cover and simmer for about 1 hour until the meat is tender.

3 Meanwhile, prepare the vegetables. Peel or scrape the carrots and cut into 6cm/2½in pieces. Cut the pumpkin into 2.5cm/1in cubes, discarding the skin, seeds and pith.

4 Stir the carrots, pumpkin and raisins into the meat mixture, cover the pan and simmer for a further 30–35 minutes until the vegetables and meat are completely tender.

5 Prepare the couscous according to the instructions on the packet.

6 Spoon the couscous on to a large warmed serving plate, making a well in the centre. Spoon the stew and the gravy into the centre, arranging some of the pieces of carrot down the sides of the couscous, or alternatively stir the stew into the couscous. Extra gravy can be poured into a separate jug. Garnish with parsley and serve.

Seven-vegetable Couscous

Seven is a magical number in Morocco and there are many recipes for this glorious celebration couscous. The vegetables here are carrots, parsnips, turnips, onions, courgettes, tomatoes and French beans. You could substitute different vegetables if you wish.

INGREDIENTS

Serves 6

30ml/2 tbsp sunflower or olive oil
450g/1lb lean lamb, cut into
  bite-size pieces
2 chicken breast quarters, halved
2 onions, chopped
350g/12oz carrots, cut into chunks
225g/8oz parsnips, cut into chunks
115g/4oz turnips, cut into cubes
6 tomatoes, peeled and chopped
900ml/1½ pints/3¾ cups chicken stock
good pinch of ginger
1 cinnamon stick
400g/14oz can chick-peas, drained
400g/14oz/2 cups couscous
2 small courgettes, cut into
  julienne strips
115g/4oz French beans, trimmed and
  halved if necessary
50g/2oz/⅓ cup raisins
a little harissa or Tabasco sauce
salt and freshly ground black pepper

1 Heat half the oil in a large saucepan or flameproof casserole and fry the lamb, in batches if necessary, until evenly browned, stirring frequently. Transfer to a plate with a slotted spoon. Add the chicken pieces and cook until evenly browned. Transfer to the plate with the lamb.

2 Heat the remaining oil and add the onions. Fry over a gentle heat for 2–3 minutes, stirring occasionally, then add the carrots, parsnips and turnips. Stir well, cover with a lid and "sweat" over a gentle heat for 5–6 minutes, stirring once or twice.

3 Add the tomatoes, lamb, chicken and stock. Season with salt and black pepper and add the ginger and cinnamon. Bring to the boil and simmer gently for 35–45 minutes until the meat is nearly tender.

4 Skin the chick-peas by placing them in a bowl of cold water and rubbing them between your fingers. The skins will rise to the surface. Discard the skins and drain. Prepare the couscous according to the instructions on the packet.

5 Add the skinned chick-peas, courgettes, beans and raisins to the meat mixture, stir gently and continue cooking for 10–15 minutes until the vegetables and meat are tender. Pile the couscous on to a large serving platter, making a slight well in the centre.

6 Transfer the chicken to a plate and remove the skin and bone, if you wish. Spoon 3–4 large spoonfuls of stock into a separate saucepan. Stir the chicken back into the stew, add harissa or Tabasco sauce to the separate stock and heat both gently. Spoon the stew over the couscous. Serve the harissa sauce in a separate bowl.

Spinach and Chick-pea Pancakes

In this Moroccan-style dish spinach and courgettes are combined with chick-peas and wrapped in light pancakes.

INGREDIENTS

Serves 4–6
15ml/1 tbsp olive oil
1 large onion, chopped
250g/9oz fresh spinach
400g/14oz can chick-peas, drained
2 courgettes, grated
30ml/2 tbsp chopped fresh coriander
2 eggs, beaten
salt and freshly ground black pepper
fresh coriander leaves, to garnish

For the pancake batter
150g/5oz/1¼ cups plain flour
1 egg
about 350ml/12fl oz/1½ cups milk
15ml/1 tbsp sunflower or olive oil
butter or oil, for greasing

For the sauce
25g/1oz/2 tbsp butter
30ml/2 tbsp plain flour
about 300ml/½ pint/1¼ cups milk

1 First make the pancakes. Blend together the flour, a little salt, the egg, milk and 75ml/5 tbsp water to make a fairly thin batter. Stir in the oil.

2 Heat a large griddle, grease lightly and fry the pancakes on one side only, to make eight large pancakes. Set aside while preparing the filling.

3 Heat the oil in a small frying pan and fry the onion for 4–5 minutes until soft, stirring occasionally. Wash the spinach, place in a pan and cook until wilted, shaking the pan occasionally. Chop the spinach roughly.

4 Skin the chick-peas: place them in a bowl of cold water and rub them until the skins float to the surface. Mash the skinned chick-peas roughly with a fork. Add the onion, grated courgettes, spinach and coriander. Stir in the beaten eggs, season and mix well.

5 Place the pancakes, cooked side up, on a work surface and place spoonfuls of filling down the centre. Fold one half of each pancake over the filling and roll up. Place in a large buttered ovenproof dish and preheat the oven to 180°C/350°F/Gas 4.

6 Melt the butter for the sauce in a small saucepan, stir in the flour and then gradually add the milk to make a smooth sauce. Season with salt and pepper and pour over the pancakes.

7 Bake in the oven for about 15 minutes until golden and serve garnished with coriander leaves.

Schlada

This is the Moroccan cousin of gazpacho – indeed the word gazpacho is Arabic in origin, meaning soaked bread. The Spaniards learned of gazpacho from the Moors, who made it with garlic, bread, olive oil and lemon juice. Tomatoes and peppers were introduced later, after Columbus returned from America with these new world fruits, and this version of the dish in turn made its way back to North Africa.

INGREDIENTS

Serves 4
3 green peppers, quartered
4 large tomatoes
2 garlic cloves, finely chopped
30ml/2 tbsp olive oil
30ml/2 tbsp lemon juice
good pinch of paprika
pinch of ground cumin
¼ preserved lemon
salt and freshly ground black pepper
fresh coriander and flat leaf parsley,
    to garnish

1 Grill the peppers skin side up until the skins are blackened, place in a plastic bag and tie the ends. Leave for about 10 minutes until the peppers are cool enough to handle and peel away the skins.

2 Cut the peppers into small pieces, discarding the seeds and core, and place in a serving dish.

3 Peel the tomatoes by placing in boiling water for 1 minute, then plunging into cold water. Peel off the skins, then quarter them, discarding the core and seeds. Chop roughly and add to the peppers. Scatter the chopped garlic on top and chill for 1 hour.

4 Blend together the olive oil, lemon juice, paprika and cumin and pour over the salad. Season with salt and pepper.

5 Rinse the preserved lemon in cold water and remove the flesh and pith. Cut the peel into slivers and sprinkle over the salad. Garnish with coriander and flat leaf parsley.

Okra and Tomato Tagine

A spicy vegetarian dish that is delicious served either with other vegetable dishes or as a side dish to accompany a meat tagine.

INGREDIENTS

Serves 4
350g/12oz okra
5–6 tomatoes
2 small onions
2 garlic cloves, crushed
1 green chilli, seeded
5ml/1 tsp paprika
small handful of fresh coriander
30ml/2 tbsp sunflower oil
juice of 1 lemon

1 Trim the okra and then cut into 1cm/½in lengths. Peel and seed the tomatoes and chop roughly.

2 Roughly chop one of the onions and place in a food processor or blender with the garlic, chilli, paprika, coriander and 60ml/4 tbsp water. Blend to a paste.

3 Thinly slice the second onion and fry in the oil for 5–6 minutes until golden brown. Transfer to a plate with a slotted spoon.

4 Reduce the heat and pour in the onion and coriander mixture. Cook for 1–2 minutes, stirring frequently, and then add the okra, tomatoes, lemon juice and about 120ml/4fl oz/½ cup water. Stir well to mix, cover tightly and simmer over a low heat for about 15 minutes until the okra is tender.

5 Transfer to a serving dish, sprinkle with the fried onion rings and serve immediately.

Tagine of Onions

This is a typically sweet dish, flavoured with ground cinnamon, that is much appreciated in Morocco. A Moroccan cook might add three or four times the amount of cinnamon and twice the amount of sugar, but if you're unsure about such sweet flavours with onions, follow this recipe, which uses less than the normal Moroccan quantities.

INGREDIENTS

Serves 4
675g/1½lb Spanish or red onions
90ml/6 tbsp olive or sunflower oil or a mixture of both
pinch of saffron
2.5ml/½ tsp ground ginger
5ml/1 tsp ground black pepper
5ml/1 tsp ground cinnamon
15ml/1 tbsp sugar

2 Blend together the olive or sunflower oil, saffron, ginger, black pepper, cinnamon and sugar and pour over the onions. Stir gently to mix and then set aside for 2 hours.

1 Slice the onions very thinly and place in a shallow dish.

3 Preheat the oven to 160°C/325°F/ Gas 3 and pour the onions and the marinade into an ovenproof dish or casserole.

4 Fold a piece of foil into three and place over the top of the dish or casserole, securing with a lid.

5 Cook in the oven for 45 minutes or until the onions are very soft. Increase the oven temperature to 200°C/400°F/Gas 6, remove the lid and foil and cook for 5–10 minutes more until the onions are lightly glazed. Serve with grilled meats.

Marrakesh Pizza

In Morocco, cooks tend to place flavourings inside rather than on top of the bread. The result is surprising – and very delicious.

INGREDIENTS

Makes 4 pizzas

5ml/1 tsp sugar
10ml/2 tsp dried yeast
450g/1lb/4 cups white flour (or a mixture of white and wholemeal flour, according to preference)
10ml/2 tsp salt
melted butter, for brushing
rocket salad and black olives, to serve

For the filling

1 small onion, very finely chopped
2 tomatoes, peeled, seeded and chopped
25ml/1½ tbsp chopped fresh parsley
25ml/1½ tbsp chopped fresh coriander
5ml/1 tsp paprika
5ml/1 tsp ground cumin
50g/2oz vegetable suet, finely chopped
40g/1½ oz Cheddar cheese, grated

1 First prepare the yeast. Place 150ml/¼ pint/⅔ cup warm water in a small bowl or jug, stir in the sugar and then sprinkle with the yeast. Stir once or twice, then set aside in a warm place for about 10 minutes until the yeast is frothy.

2 Meanwhile, make the filling. Mix together the onion, tomatoes, parsley, coriander, paprika, cumin, suet and cheese, then season with salt and set aside.

3 In a large bowl, mix together the flour and 10ml/2 tsp salt. Add the yeast mixture and enough warm water to make a fairly soft dough (about 250ml/8fl oz/1 cup). Knead the mixture into a ball and then knead on a floured work surface for 10–12 minutes until the dough is firm and elastic.

4 Break the dough into four pieces and roll each into a rectangle, measuring 20 x 30cm/8 x 12in. Spread the filling down the centre of each rectangle, then fold into three, to make a rectangle 20 x 10cm/8 x 4in.

5 Roll out the dough again, until it is the same size as before and again fold into three to make a smaller rectangle. (The filling will be squeezed out in places, but don't worry – just push it back inside the dough.)

6 Place the pizzas on a buttered baking sheet, cover with oiled clear film and leave in a warm place for about 1 hour until slightly risen.

7 Heat a griddle and brush with butter. Prick the pizzas with a fork five or six times on both sides and then fry for about 8 minutes on each side until crisp and golden. Serve immediately, with a little melted butter if liked, and accompanied by rocket salad and black olives.

Holiday Bread

This bread is often made on special occasions – not just holidays, but for birthdays, weddings, or for one of the many religious festivals.

INGREDIENTS

Makes 2 loaves
375g/12oz/3 cups strong white flour
115g/4oz/1 cup corn meal
10ml/2 tsp salt
150ml/¼ pint/⅔ cup warm milk and
    water mixed
25ml/1½ tbsp pumpkin seeds
25ml/1½ tbsp sunflower seeds
15ml/1 tbsp sesame seeds

For the yeast starter
150ml/¼ pint/⅔ cup warm water
5ml/1 tsp sugar
10ml/2 tsp dried yeast

1 First prepare the yeast. Place the warm water in a small bowl or jug, stir in the sugar and then sprinkle with the yeast. Stir once or twice, then set aside in a warm place for about 10 minutes until the yeast is frothy.

2 In a large bowl, mix together the flour, corn meal and salt. Add the yeast mixture and enough of the warm milk and water mixture to make a fairly soft dough. Knead the mixture into a ball and then knead on a floured work surface for about 5 minutes.

3 Add the seeds and knead into the dough. Continue kneading for about 5–6 minutes until the dough is firm and elastic.

4 Break the dough into two pieces and shape into balls, flattening to make a frisbee shape. Place on floured baking trays and press down with your hand to make round breads about 13–15cm/5–6in in diameter.

5 Cover with oiled clear film or a damp cloth and set aside for 1–1½ hours in a warm place until risen. The bread is ready to bake when it springs back if gently pressed with a finger.

6 Preheat the oven to 200°C/400°F/ Gas 6 and bake the breads in the oven for 12 minutes. Reduce the oven temperature to 150°C/300°F/Gas 2 and continue cooking for 20–30 minutes until the loaves are golden and sound hollow if tapped.

Moroccan Serpent Cake

This is perhaps the most famous of all Moroccan pastries, filled with lightly fragrant almond paste.

INGREDIENTS

Serves 8

8 sheets of filo pastry
50g/2oz/4 tbsp butter, melted
1 egg, beaten
5ml/1 tsp ground cinnamon
icing sugar, for dusting

For the almond paste
about 50g/2oz/4 tbsp butter, melted
225g/8oz/2 cups ground almonds
2.5ml/¹⁄₂ tsp almond essence
50g/2oz/¹⁄₂ cup icing sugar
egg yolk, beaten
15ml/1 tbsp rose water or orange
   flower water (optional)

1 First make the almond paste. Blend the melted butter with the ground almonds and almond essence. Add the sugar, egg yolk and rose or orange flower water, if using, mix well and knead until soft and pliable. Chill for about 10 minutes.

2 Break the almond paste into 10 even-size balls and roll them into 10cm/4in "sausages". Chill again.

3 Preheat the oven to 180°C/350°F/ Gas 4. Place two sheets of filo pastry on the work surface so that they overlap to form an 18 x 56cm/7 x 22in rectangle. Brush the overlapping pastry to secure and then brush all over with butter. Cover with another two sheets of filo and brush again with butter.

4 Place five "sausages" of almond paste along the lower edge of the filo sheet and roll up the pastry tightly, tucking in the ends. Shape the roll into a loose coil. Repeat with the remaining filo and almond paste, so that you have two coils.

5 Brush a large baking sheet with butter and place the coils together to make a "snake".

6 Beat together the egg and half of the cinnamon. Brush over the pastry snake and then bake in the oven for 20–25 minutes until golden brown. Carefully invert the snake on to another baking sheet and return to the oven for 5–10 minutes until golden.

7 Place on a serving plate. Dust with icing sugar and then sprinkle with the remaining cinnamon. Serve warm.

Apricots stuffed with Almond Paste

Almonds, whether whole, flaked or ground, are a favourite Moroccan ingredient. They have a delightful affinity with apricots and this is a popular – and delicious – dessert.

INGREDIENTS

Serves 6

75g/3oz/scant ½ cup caster sugar
30ml/2 tbsp lemon juice
115g/4oz/1 cup ground almonds
50g/2oz/½ cup icing sugar or caster sugar
a little orange flower water (optional)
25g/1oz/2 tbsp melted butter
2.5ml/½ tsp almond essence
900g/2lb fresh apricots
fresh mint sprigs, to decorate

1 Preheat the oven to 180°C/350°F/ Gas 4. Place the sugar, lemon juice and 300ml/½ pint/1¼ cups water in a small saucepan and bring to the boil, stirring occasionally until the sugar has dissolved. Simmer gently for 5–10 minutes to make a thin sugar syrup.

2 Blend together the ground almonds, icing sugar, orange flower water, if using, butter and almond essence to make a smooth paste.

3 Wash the apricots and then make a slit in the flesh and ease out the stone. Take small pieces of the almond paste, roll into balls and press one into each of the apricots.

4 Arrange the stuffed apricots in a shallow ovenproof dish and carefully pour the sugar syrup around them. Cover with foil and bake in the oven for 25–30 minutes.

5 Serve the apricots with a little of the syrup, if liked, and decorated with sprigs of mint.

Fragrant Rice

Rice puddings are very popular all over Morocco, served either sprinkled with nuts and honey or wrapped in a variety of pastries.

INGREDIENTS

Serves 4

75g/3oz/½ cup short-grain rice
about 900ml/1½ pints/3¾ cups milk
30ml/2 tbsp ground rice
50g/2oz/¼ cup caster sugar
40g/1½oz/⅓ cup ground almonds
5ml/1 tsp vanilla essence
2.5ml/½ tsp almond essence
a little orange flower water (optional)
30ml/2 tbsp chopped dates
30ml/2 tbsp pistachio nuts, finely
    chopped
30ml/2 tbsp flaked almonds, toasted

1 Place the rice in a saucepan with 750ml/1¼ pints/3 cups of the milk and gradually heat until simmering. Cook, uncovered, over a very low heat for 30–40 minutes, until the rice is completely tender, stirring frequently and adding more milk if necessary.

COOK'S TIP

Orange flower water is used in surprisingly large quantities in Moroccan sweets and pastries. However, unless you are partial to the strongly perfumed flavour, add it very sparingly, taste, then add more as required.

2 Blend the ground rice with the remaining milk and stir into the rice pudding. Slowly bring back to the boil and cook for 1 minute. Stir in the sugar, ground almonds, vanilla and almond essence and orange flower water, if using, and cook until the pudding is thick and creamy. Pour into serving bowls and sprinkle with the chopped dates, pistachios and almonds.

Orange and Date Salad

This is simplicity itself, yet is wonderfully fresh-tasting and essentially Moroccan.

INGREDIENTS

Serves 4–6

6 oranges
15-30ml/1-2 tbsp orange flower water
    or rose water (optional)
lemon juice (optional)
115g/4oz/⅔ cup stoned dates
50g/2oz/⅓ cup pistachio nuts
icing sugar, to taste
a few toasted almonds

COOK'S TIP

Use fresh dates, if you can, although dried dates are delicious in this salad, too.

1 Peel the oranges with a sharp knife, removing all the pith, and cut into segments, catching the juice in a bowl. Place in a serving dish.

2 Stir in the juice from the bowl together with a little orange flower or rose water, if using, and sharpen with lemon juice, if liked.

3 Chop the dates and pistachio nuts and sprinkle over the salad with a little icing sugar. Chill for 1 hour.

4 Just before serving, sprinkle over the toasted almonds and a little extra icing sugar and serve.

Figs and Pears in Honey

A stunningly simple dessert which uses two Moroccan favourites – fresh figs and pears.

INGREDIENTS

Serves 4
1 lemon
90ml/6 tbsp clear honey
1 cinnamon stick
1 cardamom pod
2 pears
8 fresh figs, halved

1 Pare the rind from the lemon using a zester or vegetable peeler and cut into very thin strips.

2 Place the lemon rind, honey, cinnamon stick, cardamom pod and 350ml/12fl oz/1½ cups water in a pan and boil, uncovered, for about 10 minutes until reduced by about half.

3 Cut the pears into eighths, discarding the core. Leave the peel on or discard as preferred. Place in the syrup, add the figs and simmer for about 5 minutes until the fruit is tender.

4 Transfer the fruit to a serving bowl. Continue cooking the liquid until syrupy, then discard the cinnamon stick and pour over the figs and pears.

Moroccan-style Cherry Batter Pudding

In France, a batter pudding called clafouti is thickened with flour and eggs. This is a Moroccan version, where ground rice and almonds are used to thicken a more Arab-type milk mixture.

INGREDIENTS

Serves 4
450g/1lb cherries or other fruit
  (see Cook's Tip)
600ml/1 pint/2½ cups skimmed or
  semi-skimmed milk
45ml/3 tbsp ground rice
30–45ml/2–3 tbsp caster sugar
75g/3oz/³⁄₄ cup flaked almonds
30ml/2 tbsp orange flower water or
  rose water, to taste

1 Preheat the oven to 190°C/375°F/ Gas 5. Stone the cherries or prepare other fruit appropriately.

2 Bring the milk to the boil. Blend the ground rice with 30–45ml/ 2–3 tbsp cold water, beating well to remove lumps. Pour the milk over the blended rice and then pour back into the pan and simmer over a low heat for 5 minutes until the mixture thickens, stirring all the time.

--------- COOK'S TIP ---------

Cherries taste delicious in this clafouti but if out of season, almost any fruit, such as apricots, peaches, plums or greengages, can be used. Remove the stones from the fruit and, for apples or pears, peel if liked.

3 Add the sugar and flaked almonds and cook gently for a further 5 minutes, then stir in the orange flower or rose water and simmer for about 2 minutes more.

4 Butter a shallow ovenproof dish and pour in the almond milk mixture. Arrange the fruit on top and bake for about 25–30 minutes until the fruit has softened. Dust with icing sugar and serve.

ITALY

Tuscan Bean Soup

INGREDIENTS

Serves 3–4

45ml/3 tbsp extra virgin olive oil
1 onion, roughly chopped
2 leeks, roughly chopped
1 large potato, peeled and diced
2 garlic cloves, finely chopped
1.2 litres/2 pints/5 cups vegetable
  stock
400g/14oz can cannellini beans,
  drained, liquid reserved
175g/6oz Savoy cabbage, shredded
45ml/3 tbsp chopped flat leaf parsley
30ml/2 tbsp chopped fresh oregano
75g/3oz/1 cup Parmesan cheese
salt and freshly ground black pepper

For the garlic toasts

30–45ml/2–3 tbsp extra virgin
  olive oil
6 thick slices country bread
1 garlic clove, peeled and bruised

3 Stir in the cabbage and beans, and half the herbs. Season, and cook for 10 minutes more. Spoon about one-third of the soup into a food processor or blender and process until fairly smooth. Return to the soup in the pan, taste for seasoning and heat through for 5 minutes.

4 For the garlic toasts, drizzle a little oil over the slices of bread, then rub both sides of each slice with the garlic. Toast until browned on both sides. Ladle the soup into bowls. Sprinkle with the remaining herbs and shavings of Parmesan, drizzle with olive oil and serve with the toasts.

1 Heat the oil in a large saucepan and gently cook the onion, leeks, potato and garlic for 4–5 minutes.

2 Pour the stock and the reserved liquid from the beans into the saucepan. Cover with a lid and allow to simmer for 15 minutes.

Clam and Pasta Soup

This soup is a play on the pasta dish *spaghetti alle vongole*.

INGREDIENTS

Serves 4

30ml/2 tbsp olive oil
1 large onion, finely chopped
2 garlic cloves, crushed
400g/14oz can chopped tomatoes
15ml/1 tbsp sun-dried tomato paste
5ml/1 tsp granulated sugar
5ml/1 tsp dried mixed herbs
about 750ml/1¼ pints/3 cups fish or
   vegetable stock
150ml/¼ pint/⅔ cup red wine
50g/2oz/½ cup small pasta shapes
150g/5oz jar or can clams in juice
30ml/2 tbsp finely chopped flat leaf
   parsley, plus extra leaves to garnish
salt and freshly ground black pepper

3 Add the pasta and continue simmering, uncovered, for 10–12 minutes or until *al dente*. Stir occasionally, to prevent the pasta shapes from sticking together.

4 Add the clams and their juice and heat through for 3–4 minutes, adding more stock if required. Do not allow to boil or the clams will be tough. Remove from the heat, stir in the parsley and taste the soup for seasoning. Serve hot, sprinkled with fresh black pepper and parsley leaves.

1 Heat the oil in a large saucepan. Cook the onion gently for 5 minutes, stirring, until softened.

2 Add the garlic, tomatoes, tomato paste, sugar, herbs, stock and wine, with salt and pepper to taste. Bring to the boil. Lower the heat, half cover the pan and simmer for 10 minutes, stirring occasionally.

Marinated Vegetable Antipasto

INGREDIENTS

Serves 4

For the peppers
3 red peppers
3 yellow peppers
4 garlic cloves, sliced
handful fresh basil, plus extra to garnish
extra virgin olive oil
salt

For the mushrooms
450g/1lb open cap mushrooms
60ml/4 tbsp extra virgin olive oil
1 large garlic clove, crushed
15ml/1 tbsp chopped fresh rosemary
250ml/8fl oz/1 cup dry white wine
fresh rosemary sprigs, to garnish
salt and freshly ground black pepper

For the olives
1 dried red chilli, crushed
grated rind of 1 lemon
120ml/4fl oz/½ cup extra virgin
　olive oil
225g/8oz/1⅓ cups black olives
30ml/2 tbsp chopped flat leaf parsley
1 lemon wedge, to serve

1 Place the peppers under a hot grill. Turn occasionally until they are blackened and blistered all over. Remove from the heat and place in a plastic bag. When cool, remove the skin, halve the peppers and remove the seeds. Cut the flesh into strips lengthways and place in a bowl with the sliced garlic and basil leaves. Add salt to taste, cover with olive oil and marinate for 3–4 hours before serving, tossing occasionally. Garnish with basil leaves to serve.

2 Slice the mushrooms and place in a bowl. Heat the oil in a pan and add the garlic and rosemary. Pour in the wine. Bring to the boil, then lower the heat and simmer for 3 minutes. Add seasoning to taste.

3 Pour the mixture over the mushrooms. Mix well, then leave aside until cool, stirring occasionally. Cover and marinate overnight. Serve at room temperature, garnished with fresh rosemary sprigs.

4 Prepare the olives. Place the chilli and lemon rind in a small pan with the olive oil. Heat gently for about 3 minutes. Add the olives and heat for 1 minute more. Tip into a bowl and leave to cool. Marinate overnight. Sprinkle with parsley and serve with the lemon wedge.

Pan-fried Chicken Liver Salad

INGREDIENTS

Serves 4

75g / 3oz fresh baby spinach leaves
75g / 3oz lollo rosso leaves
75ml / 5 tbsp olive oil
15ml / 1 tbsp butter
225g / 8oz chicken livers, trimmed
45ml / 3 tbsp vin santo
50−75g / 2−3oz Parmesan cheese
salt and freshly ground black pepper

1 Wash and dry the spinach and lollo rosso. Tear the leaves into a large bowl, season with salt and pepper to taste and toss gently to mix.

2 Heat 30ml/2 tbsp of the oil with the butter in a large heavy-based frying pan. Slice the chicken livers and add to the pan when the butter is foaming. Toss over a medium to high heat for 5 minutes or until the livers are browned on the outside but still pink in the centre. Remove the frying pan from the heat.

3 Remove the chicken livers from the pan with a slotted spoon, drain them on kitchen paper, then place on top of the spinach.

4 Return the pan to a medium heat, add the remaining oil and the vin santo and stir until sizzling.

5 Pour the hot dressing over the spinach and livers and toss to coat. Put the salad in a serving bowl and sprinkle over shavings of Parmesan cheese. Serve at once.

Three-cheese Lasagne

The cheese makes this lasagne quite expensive, so reserve it for a special occasion.

INGREDIENTS

Serves 6–8
30ml/2 tbsp olive oil
1 onion, finely chopped
1 carrot, finely chopped
1 celery stick, finely chopped
1 garlic clove, crushed
675g/1½lb minced beef
400g/14oz can chopped tomatoes
300ml/½pint/1¼ cups beef stock
300ml/½ pint/1¼ cups red wine
30ml/2 tbsp sun-dried tomato paste
10ml/2 tsp dried oregano
9 sheets no-precook lasagne
3 x 150g/5oz packets mozzarella cheese, thinly sliced
450g/1lb/2 cups ricotta cheese
115g/4oz Parmesan cheese, grated
salt and freshly ground black pepper

1 Heat the oil and cook the onion, carrot, celery and garlic gently for 10 minutes, until softened.

2 Add the beef and cook until it changes colour, stirring constantly and breaking up the meat.

3 Add the tomatoes, stock, wine, tomato paste, oregano and salt and pepper and bring to the boil, stirring. Cover, lower the heat and simmer gently for 1 hour.

4 Preheat the oven to 190°C/375°F/Gas 5. Season to taste, then ladle one-third of the meat sauce into a 23 x 33cm/9 x 13in baking dish and cover with 3 sheets of lasagne. Arrange one-third of the mozzarella over the top, dot with one-third of the ricotta, then sprinkle with one-third of the Parmesan.

5 Repeat these layers twice, then bake for 40 minutes. Leave to cool for 10 minutes before serving.

Tortiglioni with Spicy Sausage Sauce

INGREDIENTS

Serves 4
30ml/2 tbsp olive oil
1 onion, finely chopped
1 celery stick, finely chopped
2 large garlic cloves, crushed
1 fresh red chilli, seeded and chopped
450g/1lb ripe plum tomatoes, peeled and finely chopped
30ml/2 tbsp tomato purée
150ml/¼ pint/⅔ cup red wine
5ml/1 tsp sugar
300g/11oz dried tortiglioni
175g/6oz spicy salami
salt and freshly ground black pepper
30ml/2 tbsp chopped fresh parsley, to garnish
grated Parmesan cheese, to serve

1 Heat the oil, then add the onion, celery, garlic and chilli and cook gently for about 10 minutes, stirring frequently, until softened.

2 Add the tomatoes, tomato purée, wine, sugar and seasoning. Bring to the boil, stirring. Lower the heat, cover and simmer gently for 20 minutes, stirring occasionally. Add a little water from time to time if the sauce becomes too thick.

3 Add the pasta to a pan of rapidly boiling salted water and simmer, uncovered, for 10–12 minutes.

4 Chop the salami into bite-size chunks and add to the sauce. Heat through and season to taste.

5 Drain the pasta, tip it into a large bowl, then pour the sauce over and toss to mix. Scatter over the parsley and grated Parmesan.

Tagliatelle with Bolognese Sauce

INGREDIENTS

Serves 4

30ml/2 tbsp olive oil
1 onion, finely chopped
1 carrot, finely chopped
1 celery stick, finely chopped
1 garlic clove, crushed
350g/12oz minced beef
150ml/¼ pint/⅔ cup red wine
250ml/8fl oz/1 cup milk
400g/14oz can chopped tomatoes
15ml/1 tbsp sun-dried tomato paste
350g/12oz dried tagliatelle
salt and freshly ground black pepper
shredded fresh basil, to garnish
grated Parmesan cheese, to serve

3 Pour in the wine. Stir frequently until it has evaporated, then add the milk and continue cooking and stirring until this has evaporated, too.

4 Stir in the tomatoes and tomato paste, with salt and pepper to taste. Simmer the sauce uncovered, over the lowest possible heat for at least 45 minutes.

5 Cook the tagliatelle in a pan of rapidly boiling salted water for 8–10 minutes or until *al dente*. Drain and tip into a warmed bowl. Pour over the sauce and toss to combine. Garnish with basil and serve at once, with Parmesan cheese on the side.

--- COOK'S TIP ---

Don't skimp on the cooking time – it is essential for a full-flavoured Bolognese sauce. Some Italian cooks insist on cooking the sauce for 3–4 hours, so the longer you can leave it the better.

1 Heat the oil in a large pan. Add the onion, carrot, celery and garlic and cook gently, stirring often, for 10 minutes until softened. Do not allow the vegetables to colour.

2 Add the minced beef to the pan with the vegetables and cook over a medium heat until the meat changes colour, stirring constantly and breaking up any lumps with a wooden spoon.

Penne alla Carbonara

INGREDIENTS

Serves 3–4

300g/11oz dried penne
30ml/2 tbsp olive oil
1 small onion, finely chopped
175g/6oz pancetta rashers, any rinds
    removed, cut into bite-size strips
1–2 garlic cloves, crushed
5 egg yolks
175ml/6fl oz/¾ cup double cream
115g/4oz/1⅓ cups grated Parmesan
    cheese, plus extra to serve
salt and freshly ground black pepper

1 Cook the penne in a large pan of rapidly boiling salted water for about 10 minutes, or until *al dente*.

2 Meanwhile, heat the oil in a large flameproof casserole. Add the onion and cook for about 5 minutes, stirring, until softened. Add the pancetta and garlic. Cook over a medium heat until the pancetta is cooked but not crisp. Remove the pan from the heat and set aside.

3 Put the egg yolks in a jug and add the cream and Parmesan cheese. Grind in plenty of black pepper. Beat well to mix.

4 Drain the penne and tip into the casserole. Toss over a medium heat, stirring so the pancetta mixture blends evenly with the pasta.

5 Remove from the heat, pour in the egg yolk mixture and toss well to combine. Spoon into a large shallow serving dish, grind a little black pepper over and sprinkle with some of the extra Parmesan. Serve the rest of the Parmesan separately.

— COOK'S TIP —

Don't return the pan to the heat after adding the egg yolks as they will scramble and give the pasta a curdled appearance.

Spinach and Ricotta Gnocchi

The mixture for these tasty herb dumplings needs to be handled carefully to keep the dumplings light. Serve with sage butter and Parmesan.

INGREDIENTS

Serves 4

6 garlic cloves, unpeeled
25g/1oz mixed fresh herbs, such as parsley, basil, thyme, coriander and chives, finely chopped
225g/8oz fresh spinach leaves
250g/9oz/generous 1 cup ricotta cheese
1 egg yolk
50g/2oz/⅔ cup grated Parmesan cheese
75g/3oz/⅔ cup plain flour
50g/2oz/¼ cup butter
30ml/2 tbsp fresh sage, chopped
salt

2 Mix the ricotta with the egg yolk, spinach, herbs and garlic. Mix in half the Parmesan and the flour.

3 Using floured hands, break off pieces of the spinach mixture, slightly smaller than a walnut, and roll them into small dumplings.

4 Cook the gnocchi in boiling salted water. They will rise to the top of the pan when cooked.

5 The gnocchi should be light and fluffy all the way through. If not, simmer for a further minute. Drain well. Meanwhile, melt the butter in a frying pan and add the sage. Simmer gently for 1 minute. Add the gnocchi to the frying pan and toss in the butter over a gentle heat for 1 minute. Serve sprinkled with the remaining Parmesan cheese.

1 Cook the garlic cloves in boiling water for 4 minutes. Drain and pop out of the skins. Place in a food processor with the herbs and blend to a purée, or mash the garlic with a fork, add the herbs and mix well. Place the spinach in a large pan with just the water that clings to the leaves and cook gently until wilted. Leave the spinach leaves to cool, then squeeze out as much liquid as possible. Chop the leaves finely.

Pasta all' arrabbiata

This is a speciality of Lazio – the word *arrabbiata* means rabid or angry, and describes the heat that comes from the chilli. This quick version of the dish is made with bottled sugocasa, or crushed Italian tomatoes.

INGREDIENTS

Serves 4

500g/1lb sugocasa
2 garlic cloves, crushed
150ml/¼ pint ⅔ dry white wine
15ml/1 tbsp sun-dried tomato purée
1 fresh red chilli
300g/11oz penne or tortiglioni
60ml/4 tbsp chopped flat leaf parsley
salt and freshly ground black pepper
freshly grated Pecorino cheese,
    to serve

1 Put the sugocasa, garlic, wine, tomato purée and whole chilli in a saucepan and bring to the boil. Cover and simmer gently.

2 Drop the penne or tortiglioni pasta into a large saucepan of rapidly boiling salted water and simmer for 10–12 minutes or until the pasta is *al dente*.

3 Remove the chilli from the sauce and add half the chopped fresh parsley. Taste for seasoning. If you prefer a hotter taste, chop some or all of the chilli and return it to the sauce.

4 Drain the pasta and tip into a warmed large bowl. Pour the sauce over the pasta and toss to mix. Serve at once, sprinkled with grated Pecorino and the remaining parsley.

Saffron Risotto

This classic risotto makes a delicious first course, or a light supper dish in its own right.

INGREDIENTS

Serves 4
about 1.2 litres/2 pints/5 cups beef or
   chicken stock
good pinch of saffron threads or
   1 sachet of saffron powder
75g/3oz/6 tbsp butter
1 onion, finely chopped
275g/10oz/1½ cups risotto rice
75g/3oz/1 cup grated Parmesan
   cheese
salt and freshly ground black pepper

1 Bring the stock to the boil, then reduce to a low simmer. Ladle a little stock into a small bowl. Add the saffron threads or powder and leave to infuse.

2 Melt 50g/2oz/4 tbsp of the butter in a large saucepan until foaming. Add the onion and cook gently for about 3 minutes, stirring frequently, until softened.

3 Add the rice. Stir until the grains start to swell and burst, then add a few ladlefuls of the stock and the saffron liquid, and season to taste. Stir over a low heat until the stock is absorbed. Add the remaining stock, allowing the rice to absorb the liquid before adding more, and stirring constantly. After 20–25 minutes, the rice should be *al dente* and the risotto golden yellow, moist and creamy.

4 Gently stir in about two-thirds of the grated Parmesan and the remaining butter. Heat through until the butter has melted, then taste for seasoning. Transfer the risotto to a warmed serving bowl or platter and serve hot, with the remaining grated Parmesan sprinkled on top.

Polenta Elisa

INGREDIENTS

Serves 4
250ml/8fl oz/1 cup milk
225g/8oz/2 cups pre-cooked polenta
115g/4oz/1 cup grated Gruyère
   cheese
115g/4oz/1 cup torta di Dolcelatte
   cheese, crumbled
50g/2oz/¼ cup butter
2 garlic cloves, roughly chopped
a few fresh sage leaves, chopped
salt and freshly ground black pepper
prosciutto, to serve

1 Preheat the oven to 200°C/ 400°F/Gas 6. Lightly butter a 20–25cm/8–10in baking dish.

2 Bring the milk and 750ml/ 1¼ pints/3 cups water to the boil in a large saucepan, add 5ml/1 tsp salt, then tip in the polenta. Cook for about 8 minutes or according to the instructions on the packet.

3 Spoon half the polenta into the baking dish. Cover with half the grated Gruyère and Dolcelatte. Spoon the remaining polenta evenly over the top and sprinkle with the remaining cheeses.

4 Melt the butter in a saucepan until foaming, add the garlic and sage, and fry until the butter browns.

5 Drizzle the butter mixture over the polenta and cheese and grind black pepper liberally over the top. Bake for 5 minutes. Serve hot, with slices of prosciutto.

Pizza Margherita

The Margherita is named after the nineteenth century Queen of Italy, and is one of the most popular of all pizzas.

INGREDIENTS

Serves 4

450g/1lb peeled plum tomatoes, fresh or canned
1 quantity pizza dough, rolled out
350g/12oz/1¾ cups mozzarella cheese, diced
10–12 fresh basil leaves, torn
60ml/4 tbsp freshly grated Parmesan cheese (optional)
salt and freshly ground black pepper
45ml/3 tbsp olive oil

1 Preheat the oven to 250°C/ 475°F/Gas 9 for at least 20 minutes before baking. Strain the tomatoes through the medium holes of a food mill placed over a bowl, scraping in all the tomato pulp.

2 Spread the puréed tomatoes over the prepared pizza dough, leaving the rim uncovered.

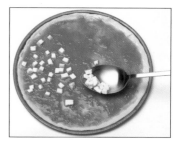

3 Sprinkle mozzarella cheese over the pizza base. Dot with the torn pieces of basil and sprinkle with the Parmesan, if using. Season with salt and freshly ground black pepper and drizzle with olive oil. Immediately place the pizzas in the oven. Bake for about 15–20 minutes, or until the crust is golden brown and the cheeses are melted and bubbling.

Pizza Napoletana

If you ask for a pizza in the Neapolitan manner anywhere in Italy other than Naples, you will be given this pizza with anchovies.

INGREDIENTS

Serves 4

450g/1lb peeled tomatoes, fresh or canned
1 quantity pizza dough, rolled out
40g/1½oz/3 tbsp anchovy fillets in oil, drained and cut into strips
350g/12oz/1¾ cups mozzarella cheese, diced
5ml/1 tsp oregano leaves, fresh or dried
45ml/3 tbsp olive oil
salt and freshly ground black pepper

1 Preheat the oven to 250°C/ 475°F/Gas 9 for at least 20 minutes before baking. Strain the tomatoes through the medium holes of a food mill placed over a bowl, scraping in all the tomato pulp.

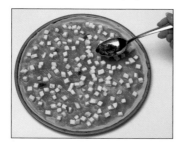

2 Spread the puréed tomatoes over the prepared pizza dough, leaving the rim uncovered. Dot evenly with the anchovy strips and the diced mozzarella cheese.

3 Sprinkle the pizza with oregano, salt and freshly ground black pepper and drizzle with olive oil. Immediately place the pizza in the preheated oven. Bake for about 15–20 minutes, or until the crust is golden brown and the cheese is melted and bubbling.

Pizza Quattro Stagioni

INGREDIENTS

Serves 4

450g/1lb peeled plum tomatoes,
  fresh or canned
75ml/5 tbsp olive oil
115g/4oz/1 cup mushrooms
1 garlic clove, finely chopped
1 quantity pizza dough, rolled out
350g/12oz/1¾ cups mozzarella
  cheese, diced
4 thin slices of ham, cut into 5cm/
  2in squares
32 black olives, stoned and halved
8 artichoke hearts preserved in oil,
  drained and cut in half
5ml/1 tsp oregano leaves
salt and freshly ground black pepper

1 Preheat the oven to 250°C/
475°F/Gas 9 for at least 20
minutes before baking the pizza.
Strain the tomatoes through the
medium holes of a food mill placed
over a bowl, scraping in all the pulp.

2 Heat 30ml/2 tbsp of the olive oil
in a frying pan. Thinly slice the
mushrooms and sauté lightly. Stir in
the garlic and cook gently. Set aside.

3 Spread the puréed tomato over
the prepared pizza dough, leaving
the rim uncovered. Sprinkle evenly
with the diced mozzarella cheese.
Spread the mushrooms over one
quarter of the pizza.

4 Arrange the ham on another
quarter, and the olives and
artichoke hearts on the two
remaining quarters. Sprinkle with
oregano, then season and drizzle over
the remaining olive oil. Immediately
place the pizza in the oven. Bake
for about 15–20 minutes, or until
the crust is golden brown and the
topping is melted and bubbling.

Ricotta and Fontina Pizza

INGREDIENTS

Makes 4 x 25cm/10in thin crust pizza

For the pizza dough
2.5ml/½ tsp active dried yeast
pinch of granulated sugar
450g/1lb/4 cups strong white flour
5ml/1 tsp salt
30ml/2 tbsp olive oil

For the tomato sauce
400g/14oz can chopped tomatoes
150ml/¼ pint/⅔ cup passata
1 large garlic clove, finely chopped
5ml/1 tsp dried oregano
1 bay leaf
10ml/2 tsp malt vinegar
salt and freshly ground black pepper

For the topping
30ml/2 tbsp olive oil
1 garlic clove, finely chopped
350g/12oz/4 cups mushrooms, sliced
30ml/2 tbsp chopped fresh oregano,
  plus whole leaves, to garnish
250g/9oz/1 cup ricotta cheese
225g/8oz/scant 1 cup Fontina cheese
salt and freshly ground black pepper

1 Make the dough. Put 300ml/ ½ pint/1¼ cups warm water in a measuring jug. Add the yeast and sugar and leave for 5–10 minutes until frothy. Sift the flour and salt into a bowl and make a well in the centre. Gradually pour in the yeast mixture and the olive oil. Mix to a smooth dough. Knead on a lightly floured surface for 10 minutes until smooth, springy and elastic. Place the dough in a floured bowl, cover and leave to rise in a warm place for 1½ hours.

2 Meanwhile, make the tomato sauce. Place all the ingredients in a saucepan, cover and bring to the boil. Lower the heat, remove the lid and simmer gently for about 20 minutes, stirring occasionally, until the mixture is reduced.

3 Make the pizza topping. Heat the oil in a frying pan. Add the garlic and mushrooms, with salt and pepper to taste. Cook, stirring, for about 5 minutes or until the mushrooms are tender and golden. Set aside.

4 Preheat the oven to 220°C/ 425°F/Gas 7. Brush four baking sheets with oil. Knead the dough for 2 minutes, then divide into four equal pieces. Roll out each piece to a 25cm/10in round and place each on a prepared baking sheet.

5 Spoon the tomato sauce over each dough round and brush the edges with olive oil. Add the mushrooms, oregano and slices of the cheese. Bake for 15 minutes until golden. Sprinkle with oregano leaves.

Monkfish with Tomato and Olive Sauce

INGREDIENTS

Serves 4

450g/1lb fresh mussels, scrubbed
2 garlic cloves, roughly chopped
300ml/½ pint/1¼ cups dry white
   wine
30ml/2tbsp olive oil
15g/½oz/1 tbsp butter
900g/2lb monkfish fillets, skinned
   and cut into large chunks
1 onion, finely chopped
500g/1¼lb jar sugocasa or passata
15ml/1 tbsp sun-dried tomato paste
115g/4oz/1 cup stoned black olives
salt and freshly ground black pepper
a few fresh basil sprigs, plus extra
   fresh basil leaves, to garnish

1 Put the mussels in a casserole with some basil leaves, the garlic and the wine. Cover and bring to the boil. Lower the heat and simmer for 5 minutes. Remove the mussels, discarding any that fail to open. Strain the cooking liquid and reserve.

2 Heat the oil and butter until foaming, add the monkfish pieces and sauté over a medium heat until they just change colour. Remove.

3 Add the onion to the juices in the casserole and cook gently for about 5 minutes, stirring frequently, until softened. Add the sugocasa or passata, the reserved cooking liquid from the mussels and the tomato paste. Season with salt and pepper to taste. Bring to the boil, stirring, then lower the heat, cover and simmer for 20 minutes, stirring occasionally.

4 Pull off and discard the top shells from the mussels. Add the monkfish pieces to the tomato sauce and cook for 5 minutes. Stir in the olives and remaining basil, then taste for seasoning. Place the mussels in their half shells on top of the sauce, cover the pan and heat the mussels through for 1–2 minutes. Serve at once, garnished with fresh basil.

Char-grilled Squid

INGREDIENTS

Serves 2

2 whole prepared squid, with
  tentacles
75ml/5 tbsp olive oil
30ml/2 tbsp balsamic vinegar
2 fresh red chillies, finely chopped
60ml/4 tbsp dry white wine
salt and freshly ground black pepper
hot cooked risotto rice, to serve
sprigs of fresh parsley, to garnish

3 Cut the squid bodies into diagonal strips. Pile the hot risotto rice in the centre of heated soup plates and top with the strips of squid, arranging them criss-cross fashion. Keep hot.

4 Add the chopped tentacles and chillies to the pan and toss over a medium heat for 2 minutes. Stir in the wine, then drizzle over the squid and rice. Garnish with the sprigs of fresh parsley and serve at once.

1 Make a lengthways cut down the body of each squid, then open out the body flat. Score the flesh on both sides of the bodies in a criss-cross pattern with the tip of a sharp knife. Chop the tentacles. Place all the squid in a china or glass dish. Whisk the oil and vinegar in a small bowl. Add salt and pepper to taste and pour over the squid. Cover and leave to marinate for about 1 hour.

2 Heat a ridged cast-iron pan until hot. Add the body of one of the squid. Cook over a medium heat for 2–3 minutes, pressing the squid with a fish slice to keep it flat. Repeat on the other side. Cook the other squid body in the same way.

Beef Stew with Tomatoes, Wine and Peas

INGREDIENTS

Serves 4

30ml/2 tbsp plain flour
10ml/2 tsp chopped fresh thyme or
    5ml/1 tsp dried thyme
1kg/2¼lb braising or stewing steak,
    cut into large cubes
45ml/3 tbsp olive oil
1 medium onion, roughly chopped
450g/1lb jar sugocasa or passata
250ml/8fl oz/1 cup beef stock
250ml/8fl oz/1 cup red wine
2 garlic cloves, crushed
30ml/2 tbsp tomato purée
275g/10oz/2 cups shelled fresh peas
5ml/1 tsp sugar
salt and freshly ground black pepper
fresh thyme, to garnish

3 Add the onion to the pan, scraping the base of the pan to mix in any sediment. Cook for 3 minutes, stirring until softened, then stir in the sugocasa or passata, stock, wine, garlic and tomato purée. Bring to the boil, stirring. Return the beef to the pan and stir well to coat with the sauce. Cover and cook in the oven for 1½ hours.

4 Stir in the peas and the sugar. Return the casserole to the oven and cook for 30 minutes more, or until the beef is tender. Taste for seasoning. Garnish with fresh thyme before serving.

1 Preheat the oven to 160°C/ 325°F/Gas 3. Put the flour in a shallow dish and season with the thyme and salt and pepper. Add the beef cubes and coat evenly.

2 Heat the oil in a large flameproof casserole. Add the beef and brown on all sides over a medium to high heat. Remove with a slotted spoon and drain on paper towels.

Veal Cutlets with Lemon

INGREDIENTS

Serves 4
4 veal cutlets
30–45ml/2–3 tbsp plain flour
50g/2oz/¼ cup butter
60ml/4 tbsp olive oil
60ml/4 tbsp Italian dry white
  vermouth or dry white wine
45ml/3 tbsp lemon juice
salt and freshly ground black pepper
lemon wedges and fresh parsley, to
  garnish

1 Put each veal cutlet between two sheets of clear film and pound until very thin.

2 Cut the pounded cutlets in half or quarters, if you like, and coat them in the flour, seasoned with salt and pepper.

3 Melt the butter with half the oil in a large, heavy frying pan until sizzling. Add as many cutlets as the pan will hold. Fry over a medium to high heat for 1–2 minutes on each side until lightly coloured. Remove with a fish slice and keep hot. Add the remaining oil and cook the remaining cutlets in the same way.

4 Remove the pan from the heat and add the vermouth or wine and the lemon juice. Stir vigorously to mix with the pan juices, then return the pan to the heat and return all the veal to the pan. Spoon the sauce over the veal. Shake the pan over a medium heat until all of the cutlets are coated in the sauce and heated through.

5 Serve at once, garnished with lemon wedges and parsley. Lightly cooked green beans and peperonata would make a delicious accompaniment.

Chicken with Parma Ham and Cheese

The Italian name for this dish, *Valdostana,* is derived from Val d'Aosta, home of Fontina cheese.

INGREDIENTS

Serves 4
2 thin slices Parma ham
2 thin slices Fontina cheese
4 part-boned chicken breasts
4 fresh basil sprigs
30ml/2 tbsp olive oil
15g/½oz/1 tbsp butter
120ml/4fl oz/½ cup dry white wine
salt and freshly ground black pepper

COOK'S TIP

There is nothing quite like the buttery texture and nutty flavour of Fontina cheese, and it also has superb melting qualities, but you could also use a Swiss or French mountain cheese, such as Gruyère or Emmental. Ask for the cheese to be sliced thinly on the machine slicer, as you may find it difficult to slice it thinly yourself.

1 Preheat the oven to 200°C/400°F/Gas 6. Lightly oil a baking dish. Cut the Parma ham and Fontina slices in half crossways. Skin the chicken breasts, open out the slit in the centre of each one, and fill each cavity with half a ham slice and a sprig of fresh basil.

2 Heat the oil and butter in a wide heavy-based frying pan until foaming. Cook the chicken breasts over a medium heat for 1–2 minutes on each side until they change colour. Transfer to the baking dish. Add the wine to the pan juices, stir until sizzling, then pour over the chicken and season to taste.

3 Top each chicken breast with a slice of Fontina. Bake for 20 minutes or until the chicken is tender. Serve hot, with salad leaves.

Devilled Chicken

INGREDIENTS

Serves 4
120ml/4fl oz/½ cup olive oil
finely grated rind and juice of
 1 large lemon
2 garlic cloves, finely chopped
10ml/2 tsp finely chopped or
 crumbled dried red chillies
12 skinless, boneless chicken thighs,
 each cut into 3 or 4 pieces
salt and freshly ground black pepper
flat leaf parsley leaves, to garnish
lemon wedges, to serve

1 For the marinade, mix the oil, lemon rind and juice, garlic and chillies in a shallow glass dish. Season to taste. Whisk, then add the chicken, turning to coat. Cover and marinate in the fridge for at least 4 hours.

2 Preheat the grill and thread the chicken pieces on to eight oiled metal skewers. Cook under a hot grill for 6–8 minutes, turning frequently, until tender. Garnish with parsley and serve hot, with lemon wedges.

Radicchio and Chicory Gratin

Vegetables like radicchio and chicory take on a different flavour when cooked in this way. The creamy béchamel combines wonderfully with the bitter leaves.

INGREDIENTS

Serves 4

2 heads radicchio, quartered lengthways
2 heads chicory, quartered lengthways
25g/1oz/½ cup drained sun-dried tomatoes in oil, chopped roughly
25g/1oz/2 tbsp butter
15g/½oz/1 tbsp plain flour
250ml/8fl oz/1 cup milk
pinch grated nutmeg
50g/2oz/½ cup grated Emmental cheese
salt and freshly ground black pepper
chopped fresh parsley, to garnish

1 Preheat the oven to 180°C/ 350°F/Gas 4. Grease a 1.2 litre/ 2 pint/ 5 cup baking dish. Trim the radicchio and chicory and discard any damaged or wilted leaves. Quarter them lengthways and arrange in the baking dish. Scatter over the sun-dried tomatoes and brush the leaves liberally with the oil from the jar. Sprinkle with salt and pepper and cover with foil. Bake for 15 minutes, then remove the foil and bake for 10 minutes more.

2 Make the sauce. Place the butter in a small saucepan and melt over a moderate heat. When the butter is foaming, add the flour and cook for 1 minute, stirring. Remove from the heat and gradually add the milk, whisking all the time. Return to the heat and bring to the boil, and simmer for 2–3 minutes to thicken. Season to taste and add the nutmeg.

3 Pour the sauce over the vegetables and sprinkle with the grated cheese. Bake for about 20 minutes until golden. Serve immediately, garnished with parsley.

COOK'S TIP

In Italy radicchio and chicory are often grilled on an outside barbecue. To do this, simply prepare the vegetables as above and brush with olive oil. Place cut-side down on the grill for about 10 minutes, until browned. Turn and grill for about 5 minutes more, until the other side is browned.

Stuffed Aubergines

This typical Ligurian dish is spiked with paprika and allspice, a legacy from the days when spices from the East came into northern Italy via the port of Genoa.

INGREDIENTS

Serves 4

2 aubergines, about 225g/8oz each, stalks removed
275g/10oz potatoes, peeled and diced
30ml/2 tbsp olive oil
1 small onion, finely chopped
1 garlic clove, finely chopped
good pinch each of ground allspice and paprika
1 egg, beaten
40g/1½oz/½ cup grated Parmesan cheese
15ml/1 tbsp fresh white breadcrumbs
salt and freshly ground black pepper
fresh mint sprigs, to garnish
salad leaves, to serve

1 Bring a large saucepan of salted water to the boil. Add the whole aubergines and cook for 5 minutes, turning frequently. Remove and set aside. Add the potatoes to the pan and cook for 20 minutes until soft. Cut the aubergines in half lengthways and scoop out the flesh, leaving 5mm/¼in of the shell intact. Select a baking dish that will hold the aubergine shells snugly in a single layer. Brush it lightly with oil. Put the shells in the baking dish and chop the aubergine flesh roughly.

2 Heat the oil in a frying pan, and cook the onion until softened. Add the aubergine flesh and the garlic. Cook, stirring, for 6 minutes. Tip into a bowl. Preheat the oven to 190°C/375°F/Gas 5.

3 Drain and mash the potatoes. Add to the aubergine mixture with the spices and beaten egg. Set aside 15ml/1 tbsp of the Parmesan and add the rest to the aubergine mixture. Season to taste.

4 Spoon the mixture into the aubergine shells in the dish. Mix the breadcrumbs with the reserved Parmesan cheese and sprinkle the mixture over the aubergines. Bake for 40–45 minutes until the topping is crisp. Garnish with fresh mint sprigs and serve with salad leaves.

Fennel, Orange and Rocket Salad

This light and refreshing salad is ideal to serve alongside spicy or rich foods.

INGREDIENTS

Serves 4
2 oranges
1 fennel bulb
115g/4oz rocket leaves
50g/2oz/⅓ cup black olives

For the dressing
30ml/2 tbsp extra virgin olive oil
15ml/1 tbsp balsamic vinegar
1 small garlic clove, crushed
salt and freshly ground black pepper

1 With a vegetable peeler, cut strips of rind from the oranges, leaving the pith behind, and cut into thin julienne strips. Cook in boiling water for a few minutes. Drain. Peel the oranges, removing all the white pith. Slice them into thin rounds and discard any seeds.

2 Cut the fennel bulb in half lengthways and slice across the bulb as thinly as possible, preferably in a food processor fitted with a slicing disc or using a mandoline.

3 Combine the oranges and fennel in a serving bowl and toss with the rocket leaves.

4 Mix together the oil, vinegar, garlic and seasoning. Pour over the salad, toss together well and leave to stand for a few minutes. Sprinkle with the black olives and julienne strips of orange.

Aubergine, Lemon and Caper Salad

This cooked vegetable relish is a classic Sicilian dish. Serve as an accompaniment to cold meats, with pasta or simply on its own with some good crusty bread. Make sure the aubergine is cooked until it is soft.

INGREDIENTS

Serves 4
1 large aubergine, about 675g/1½lb
60ml/4 tbsp olive oil
grated rind and juice of 1 lemon
30ml/2 tbsp capers, rinsed
12 stoned green olives
30ml/2 tbsp chopped fresh flat
  leaf parsley
salt and freshly ground black pepper

1 Cut the aubergine into 2.5cm/ 1in cubes. Heat the olive oil in a large frying pan and cook the aubergine cubes over a medium heat for about 10 minutes, tossing regularly, until golden and softened. You may need to do this in two batches. Drain on paper towels and sprinkle with a little salt.

2 Place the aubergine cubes in a large serving bowl, toss with the lemon rind and juice, capers, olives and chopped parsley and season well with salt and pepper. Serve the salad at room temperature.

Italian Olive Bread

INGREDIENTS

Makes 1 loaf
340g/12oz/3 cups strong plain flour
2.5ml/½ tsp salt
5ml/1 tsp easy-blend dry yeast
5ml/1 tsp dried thyme
45ml/3 tbsp olive oil
4 black olives, stoned and chopped
3 sun-dried tomatoes in oil, chopped
crushed rock salt

1 Place the flour and salt in a bowl
and sprinkle over the yeast and
thyme. Make a well in the centre and
pour in 200ml/7fl oz of warm water
and 30ml/2 tbsp olive oil.

2 Mix to a dough and knead on
a floured surface for 10 minutes,
until elastic (or use a food processor
or a mixer with a dough attachment).

3 Place the dough in a large oiled
plastic bag. Seal and leave in a
warm place for about 2 hours, or
until the dough has doubled in size.

4 Turn out the dough on a floured
surface and knead lightly. Flatten
with your hands. Sprinkle over the
olives and tomatoes and knead in until
well distributed. Shape the dough into
a long oval and place on a greased
baking sheet. Cover and leave to rise
in a warm place for 45 minutes.
Preheat the oven to 190°C/375°F/
Gas 5.

5 When risen, press your finger
several times into the dough,
drizzle over the remaining oil and
sprinkle with the rock salt. Bake in
the oven for 35–40 minutes, until
the loaf is golden and sounds hollow
when tapped on the bottom.

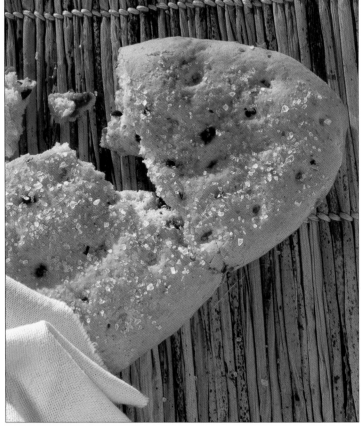

Focaccia with Onions

INGREDIENTS

Serves 6–8

1lb/450g plain flour
1 sachet easy-blend yeast
5ml/1 tsp salt
pinch of sugar
75ml/5 tbsp olive oil
1 onion, sliced thinly and cut into
   short lengths
2.5ml/½ tsp fresh thyme leaves
coarse sea salt

1 Place the flour, yeast, salt and sugar in a bowl. Make a well in the centre and pour in 250ml/8fl oz lukewarm water and 15ml/1 tbsp oil. Mix to a dough and knead until smooth and elastic.

2 Place the dough in a large oiled bowl, cover with clear film and leave in a warm place until doubled in size. Turn out the dough on to a floured surface and knead lightly for 3–4 minutes.

3 After punching the dough down, knead it on a lightly floured surface for 3–4 minutes. Brush a large shallow baking pan with 1 tbsp of the oil. Place the dough in the pan, and use your fingers to press it into an even layer, about 2cm/1in thick. Cover the dough with a cloth, and leave to rise in a warm place for 30 minutes. Meanwhile, preheat the oven to 200°C/400°F/Gas 6.

4 While the focaccia is rising, heat 45ml/3 tbsp of the oil in a medium frying pan. Add the onion and cook over low heat until soft. Stir in the thyme leaves.

5 Just before baking, use your fingers to press rows of light indentations into the surface of the focaccia. Brush with the remaining oil.

6 Spread the onion evenly over the top, and sprinkle lightly with coarse salt. Bake in the oven for 25 minutes or until just golden. Cut into squares or wedges and serve as an accompaniment to a meal, or alone, warm or at room temperature.

Chocolate Bread

In Italy it is the custom to serve this dessert bread with mascarpone or Gorgonzola cheese and a glass of red wine.

INGREDIENTS

Makes 2 loaves
450g/1lb/4 cups strong plain flour
2.5ml/½ tsp salt
30ml/2 tbsp butter
30ml/2 tbsp caster sugar
10ml/2 tsp easy-blend dried yeast
30ml/2 tbsp cocoa powder
75g/3oz/½ cup plain chocolate chips
melted butter, for brushing

1 Sift the flour and salt into a large bowl, cut in the butter with a knife, then stir in the sugar, yeast and cocoa powder.

2 Gradually add 300ml/½ pint/ 1¼ cups of tepid water to the flour mixture, and gather the dough together with your hands.

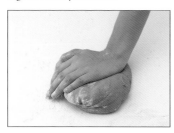

3 Turn the dough out on to a lightly floured surface and knead for about 10 minutes until the dough is smooth and elastic.

4 Cut the dough in half and knead half the chocolate chips into each piece of dough until they are evenly distributed. Shape into rounds, place on lightly oiled baking sheets and cover with oiled clear film. Leave to rise in a warm place for 1–2 hours until the dough has doubled in bulk.

5 Preheat the oven to 220°C/ 425°F/Gas 7. Bake the loaves for 10 minutes, then reduce the oven temperature to 190°C/ 375°F/Gas 5 and bake for a further 15–20 minutes.

6 Place the loaves on a wire rack and brush with butter. Cover with a tea towel and leave to cool.

Spicy Fruit Cake from Siena

This flat cake has a wonderful spicy flavour. *Panforte* is very rich, so should be cut into small wedges to serve – offer a glass of sparkling wine to go with it.

INGREDIENTS

Serves 12–14
butter, for greasing
175g/6oz/1 cup hazelnuts,
  roughly chopped
75g/3oz/½ cup whole almonds,
  roughly chopped
225g/8oz/1⅓ cups mixed candied
  fruits, diced
1.5ml/¼ tsp ground coriander
4ml/¾ tsp ground cinnamon
1.5ml/¼ tsp ground cloves
1.5ml/¼ tsp grated nutmeg
50g/2oz/½ cup plain flour
115g/4oz/⅓ cup honey
115g/4oz/generous 1 cup
  granulated sugar
icing sugar, for dusting

2 In a small heavy saucepan, stir together the honey and sugar and bring to the boil. Cook the mixture until it reaches 138°C/280°F on a sugar thermometer or when a small bit forms a hard ball when pressed between fingertips in iced water. Take care when doing this as the mixture will be extemely hot; use a teaspoon to remove a little mixture out of the pan for testing.

3 At this stage, pour the sugar syrup into the dry ingredients and stir until evenly coated. Pour into the prepared tin. Dip a spoon into water and use the back of the spoon to press the mixture into the tin. Bake in the preheated oven for 1 hour.

4 The cake will still feel quite soft when ready but will harden as it cools. Cool completely in the tin and then turn out on to a serving plate. Dust with icing sugar before serving.

1 Preheat the oven to 180°C/ 350°F/Gas 4. Grease a 20cm/ 8in round cake tin with the butter. Line the base of the tin with non-stick baking paper. Spread the nuts on a baking tray and place in the oven for about 10 minutes until lightly toasted. Remove and set aside. Lower the oven temperature to 150°C/300°F/Gas 2. In a large mixing bowl, combine the candied fruits, all the spices and the flour and stir together with a wooden spoon. Add the nuts to the bowl and stir well, so they are evenly distributed.

Zabaglione

This sumptuous warm dessert is quick and easy to make, but needs to be served straight away. For a dinner party, assemble the ingredients ahead of time so that all you need to do is mix everything together once the main course is over.

INGREDIENTS

Serves 6
4 egg yolks
65g/2½oz/⅓ cup caster sugar
120ml/4fl oz/½ cup dry Marsala
savoiardi (Italian sponge fingers),
   to serve

1 Half fill a saucepan with water and bring it to simmering point. Put the egg yolks and sugar in a large heatproof bowl and beat with a hand-held electric mixer until the mixture is pale and creamy.

2 Put the bowl over the pan and gradually pour in the Marsala, whisking the mixture until it is very thick and has increased in volume.

3 Remove the bowl from the water and pour the zabaglione into six heatproof, long-stemmed glasses. Serve at once, with sponge fingers.

Lovers' Knots

The literal translation of these *cenci* is "rags and tatters", but they are often referred to by the more endearing term of lovers' knots. They are eaten at carnival time in February.

INGREDIENTS

150g/5oz/1¼ cups plain flour
2.5ml/½ tsp baking powder
pinch of salt
30ml/2 tbsp caster sugar, plus extra
   for dusting
1 egg, beaten
about 25ml/1½ tbsp rum
vegetable oil, for deep frying

--- COOK'S TIP ---

If you do not have a deep-fat fryer with a built-in thermostat, or a deep-fat thermometer, test the temperature of the oil by dropping in a scrap of the dough trimmings – it should turn crisp and golden in about 30 seconds.

1 Sift the flour, baking powder and salt into a large mixing bowl, then stir in the sugar. Add the egg. Stir with a fork until it is evenly mixed with the flour, then add the rum gradually and continue mixing until the dough draws together. Knead the dough on a lightly floured surface until it is smooth and elastic. Divide the dough into quarters.

2 Roll each piece of dough out to a 15 x 7.5cm/6 x 3in rectangle and trim the rectangles to make them straight. Cut the rectangles lengthways into six strips, 1cm/½in wide, and tie into a simple knot.

3 Heat the oil in a deep-fat fryer to a temperature of 190°C/375°F. Deep fry the knots in batches for 1–2 minutes until they are crisp and golden. Transfer to kitchen paper with a slotted spoon. Serve warm, dusted with sugar.

Tiramisu

The name of this popular dessert translates as "pick me up", which is said to derive from the fact that it tastes so good that it makes you swoon when you eat it.

INGREDIENTS

Serves 6–8

3 eggs, separated
450g/1lb/2 cups mascarpone cheese, at room temperature
1 sachet of vanilla sugar
175ml/6fl oz/¾ cup cold, very strong, black coffee
120ml/4fl oz/½ cup Kahlúa liqueur
18 savoiardi (Italian sponge fingers)
sifted cocoa powder and grated bittersweet chocolate, to decorate

1 Whisk the egg whites in a grease-free bowl until stiff and in peaks.

2 Mix the mascarpone, vanilla sugar and egg yolks in a separate large mixing bowl and whisk with the electric mixer until evenly combined. Fold in the egg whites, then put a few spoonfuls of the mixture in the bottom of a large serving bowl and spread it out evenly.

3 Mix the coffee and liqueur in a shallow dish. Dip a sponge finger in the mixture, turn it so that it becomes saturated, and place it on top of the mascarpone in the bowl. Add five more dipped sponge fingers, placing them side by side.

4 Spoon in one-third of the remaining mixture and spread it out. Make more layers in the same way, ending with mascarpone. Sift with cocoa powder. Cover and chill overnight. Before serving, sprinkle with cocoa and grated chocolate.

Stuffed Peaches with Amaretto

INGREDIENTS

Serves 4

4 ripe but firm peaches
50g/2oz amaretti biscuits
25g/1oz/2 tbsp butter, softened
25g/1oz/2 tbsp caster sugar
1 egg yolk
60ml/4 tbsp amaretto liqueur
250ml/8fl oz/1 cup dry white wine
8 tiny basil sprigs, to decorate
vanilla ice cream, to serve

3 Cream the butter and sugar together in a separate bowl until smooth. Stir in the reserved chopped peach flesh, the egg yolk and half the amaretto liqueur with the amaretti crumbs. Lightly butter a baking dish that is just large enough to hold the peach halves in a single layer.

4 Spoon the stuffing into the peaches, then stand them in the dish. Mix the remaining liqueur with the wine, pour over the peaches and bake for 25 minutes, until the peaches feel tender. Decorate with sprigs of basil and serve at once, with vanilla ice cream, if liked.

1 Preheat the oven to 180°C/ 350°F/Gas 4. Following the indentation line on each peach, cut in half down to the stone, then twist the halves in opposite directions to separate. Remove the stones, then cut away a little of the central flesh to make a larger hole for the stuffing. Chop this flesh finely and set aside.

2 Put the amaretti biscuits in a bowl and crush them finely with the end of a rolling pin.

SPAIN

Marinated Olives

For the best flavour, marinate the olives for at least 10 days and serve at room temperature.

INGREDIENTS

Serves 4

225g/8oz/1⅓ cups unpitted green olives
3 garlic cloves
5ml/1 tsp coriander seeds
2 small red chillies
2–3 thick slices of lemon, cut into pieces
1 thyme or rosemary sprig
75ml/5 tbsp white wine vinegar

COOK'S TIP

For a change, use a mix of caraway and cumin seeds in place of the coriander.

---

1 Spread out the olives and garlic on a chopping board. Using a rolling pin, crack and flatten them slightly.

2 Crack the coriander seeds in a mortar with a pestle.

3 Mix the olives, garlic, coriander seeds, chillies, lemon pieces, herb sprig and wine vinegar in a large bowl. Toss well, then transfer the mixture to a clean glass jar. Pour in water to cover. Store in the fridge for at least 5 days before serving.

Salted Almonds

These crunchy salted nuts are at their best when fresh, so, if you can, cook them on the day you plan to eat them.

INGREDIENTS

Serves 2–4

115g/4oz/1 cup whole almonds in their skins
15ml/1 tbsp egg white, lightly beaten
2.5ml/½ tsp coarse sea salt

COOK'S TIP

This traditional method of salt-roasting nuts gives a matt, dry-looking finish; if you want them to shine, tip the roasted nuts into a bowl, add 15ml/1 tbsp of olive oil and shake well to mix.

1 Preheat the oven to 180°C/350°F/ Gas 4. Spread out the almonds on a baking sheet and roast for about 20 minutes, until cracked and golden.

2 Mix the egg white and salt in a bowl, add the almonds and shake well to coat.

3 Tip out on to the baking sheet, give a shake to separate the nuts, then return them to the oven for 5 minutes, until they have dried. Leave until cold, then store in an airtight container until ready to serve.

Butterflied Prawns in Chocolate Sauce

Although the combination of flavours may seem odd, this is a truly delicious tapas. The use of bitter chocolate as a flavouring in savoury dishes is very popular.

Ingredients

Serves 4

8 large raw prawns, in the shell
15ml/1 tbsp seasoned flour
15ml/1 tbsp dry sherry
juice of 4 clementines or 1 large orange
15g/½oz unsweetened dark
    chocolate, chopped
30ml/2 tbsp olive oil
2 garlic cloves, finely chopped
2.5cm/1in piece fresh root ginger,
    finely chopped
1 small red chilli, seeded and chopped
salt and freshly ground black pepper

1 Peel the prawns, leaving just the tail sections intact. Make a shallow cut down the back of each prawn and carefully pull out and discard the dark intestinal tract. Turn over the prawns so that the undersides are uppermost, then carefully split them open from tail to top, using a small sharp knife, cutting almost, but not quite, through to the back.

2 Press the prawns down firmly to flatten them out. Coat with the seasoned flour and set aside.

3 Gently heat the sherry and clementine or orange juice in a small saucepan. When warm, remove from the heat and stir in the chopped chocolate until melted.

4 Heat the olive oil in a frying pan. Fry the garlic, ginger and chilli over a moderate heat for 2 minutes until golden. Remove with a slotted spoon and reserve. Add the prawns, cut side down, to the pan; cook for 2–3 minutes until golden brown with pink edges. Turn and cook for a further 2 minutes.

5 Return the garlic mixture to the pan and pour over the chocolate sauce. Cook for 1 minute, turning the prawns to coat them in the glossy sauce. Season to taste and serve hot.

Charred Artichokes with Lemon Oil Dip

INGREDIENTS

Serves 4

15ml/1 tbsp lemon juice or white
   wine vinegar
2 globe artichokes, trimmed
12 garlic cloves, unpeeled
45ml/3 tbsp olive oil
1 lemon
45ml/3 tbsp olive oil
sea salt
flat leaf parsley sprigs, to garnish

1 Preheat the oven to 200°C/400°F/
Gas 6. Add the lemon juice or
vinegar to a bowl of cold water. Cut
each artichoke lengthways into wedges.
Pull the hairy choke out from the
centre of each wedge, then drop them
into the acidulated water.

2 Drain the artichoke wedges and
place in a roasting tin with the
garlic. Add the oil and toss well to coat.
Sprinkle with salt and roast for 40
minutes, stirring once or twice, until
they are tender and a little charred.

3 Meanwhile, make the dip. Using
a small, sharp knife thinly pare
away two strips of rind from the
lemon. Lay the strips on a board and
carefully scrape away any remaining
pith. Place the rind in a small pan with
water to cover. Bring to the boil, then
simmer for 5 minutes. Drain the rind,
refresh it in cold water, then chop it
roughly. Set it aside.

4 Arrange the cooked artichokes on
a serving plate and set aside to cool
for 5 minutes. Using the back of a fork,
gently flatten the garlic cloves so that
the flesh squeezes out of the skins.
Transfer the garlic flesh to a bowl,
mash to a purée then add the lemon
rind. Squeeze the juice from the
lemon, then, using the fork, whisk the
remaining olive oil and the lemon juice
into the garlic mixture. Serve the
artichokes warm with the lemon dip.

—— COOK'S TIP ——

Artichokes are usually boiled, but dry-heat
cooking also works very well. If you can
get young artichokes, try roasting them
over a barbecue.

Marinated Anchovies

Make these at least 1 hour and up to 24 hours in advance. Fresh anchovies are tiny, so be prepared to spend time filleting them – the results will be worth the effort.

INGREDIENTS

Serves 4
225g/8oz fresh anchovies
juice of 3 lemons
30ml/2 tbsp extra virgin olive oil
2 garlic cloves, finely chopped
15ml/1 tbsp chopped fresh parsley
flaked sea salt

1 Cut off the heads and tails from the anchovies, then split them open down one side.

2 Open each anchovy out flat and carefully lift out the bone.

3 Arrange the anchovies skin side down in a single layer on a plate. Pour over two-thirds of the lemon juice and sprinkle with the salt. Cover and leave for 1–24 hours, basting occasionally with the juices, until the flesh is white and no longer translucent.

4 Transfer the fish to a serving plate and drizzle over the olive oil and the remaining lemon juice. Scatter over the garlic and parsley, cover and chill until ready to serve.

Russian Salad

This colourful salad will make a popular accompaniment.

INGREDIENTS

Serves 4

8 new potatoes, scrubbed
  and quartered
1 large carrot, diced
115g/4oz fine green beans, cut into
  2cm/³/₄in lengths
75g/3oz/³/₄ cup peas
½ Spanish onion, chopped
4 cornichons or small gherkins, sliced
1 small red pepper, seeded and diced
50g/2oz/¹/₃ cup pitted black olives
15ml/1 tbsp capers
60–90ml/4–6 tbsp aïoli or
  mayonnaise
15ml/1 tbsp freshly squeezed
  lemon juice
30ml/2 tbsp chopped fresh dill
salt and freshly ground black pepper
fresh dill, to garnish

——— COOK'S TIP ———

For a sweeter flavour, roast and skin the pepper before adding it to the salad.

1 Cook the potatoes and diced carrot in a saucepan of boiling lightly salted water for 5–8 minutes until almost tender. Add the beans and peas to the pan and cook for 2 minutes more, or until all the vegetables are tender. Drain well.

2 Tip the cooked vegetables into a large bowl. Add the onion, cornichons or gherkins, red pepper, olives and capers. Stir the aïoli or mayonnaise and lemon juice together.

3 Add most of the dressing and the dill to the vegetables with plenty of freshly ground black pepper. Toss well to lightly coat the vegetables. Chill until ready to serve, then drizzle with the remaining dressing and garnish with the dill.

Chorizo in Red Wine

This simple dish is flamed just before serving. If you wish, use small chorizo sausages and leave them whole. Provide cocktail sticks for spearing the chorizo.

INGREDIENTS

Serves 4
225g/8oz cured chorizo sausage
90ml/6 tbsp red wine
30ml/2 tbsp brandy
chopped fresh parsley, to garnish

COOK'S TIP

After cooking, the chorizo can be cooled, then chilled for up to 24 hours.

1 Prick the chorizo sausage(s) in several places with a fork and place in a saucepan with the wine. Bring to the boil, lower the heat, then cover and simmer gently for 15 minutes. Remove from the heat and leave to cool in the covered pan for 2 hours.

2 Remove the chorizo sausage(s) from the pan and reserve the wine.

3 Cut the chorizo sausage(s) into 1cm/½in slices.

4 Heat the chorizo in a heavy-based frying pan, then pour over the brandy and light very carefully with a match. When the flames have died down, add the reserved wine and cook for 2–3 minutes until piping hot. Serve garnished with chopped parsley.

Fried Black Pudding

Black pudding (*morcilla*) is a very popular tapas dish. In Spain the sausage is often home-made.

INGREDIENTS

Serves 4
15ml/1 tbsp olive oil
1 onion, thinly sliced
2 garlic cloves, thinly sliced
5ml/1 tsp dried oregano or marjoram
5ml/1 tsp paprika
225g/8oz black pudding, cut in 12 thick slices
1 small French stick, sliced into 12 rounds
30ml/2 tbsp dry sherry
sugar, to taste
salt and freshly ground black pepper
chopped oregano, to garnish

1 Heat the oil in a large frying pan and fry the onion, garlic, oregano and paprika for 7 – 8 minutes until the onion is softened and golden.

2 Add the black pudding slices, raise the heat and cook for 3 minutes on each side until crisp.

3 Arrange the rounds of bread on a large serving plate and top each with a slice of black pudding. Stir the sherry into the mixture remaining in the frying pan, with sugar to taste. Heat, swirling around until bubbling, then season with salt and pepper.

4 Spoon a little of the onion mixture on top of each slice of black pudding. Scatter over the oregano and serve immediately.

--- COOK'S TIP ---

If you do find real *morcilla*, which is usually flavoured with spices and herbs (including paprika, garlic and marjoram), serve it neat: simply fry the slices in olive oil and use to top little rounds of bread.

Spicy Meatballs

These meatballs are delicious served piping hot with chilli sauce on the side so guests can add as much heat as they like.

INGREDIENTS

Serves 6

115g/4oz fresh spicy sausages
115g/4oz minced beef
2 shallots, finely chopped
2 garlic cloves, finely chopped
75g/3oz/1½ cups fresh white
    breadcrumbs
1 egg, beaten
30ml/2 tbsp chopped fresh parsley, plus
    extra to garnish
15ml/1 tbsp olive oil
salt and freshly ground black pepper
Tabasco sauce or other hot chilli sauce,
    to serve

1 Remove the skins from the sausages and place the sausagemeat in a small mixing bowl.

—— COOK'S TIP ——

If you like, you can make the meatballs up to a day in advance, then cover and chill them until ready to cook.

2 Add the minced beef, shallots, garlic, breadcrumbs, beaten egg and parsley, with plenty of salt and pepper. Mix well, then shape into 18 small balls.

3 Heat the olive oil in a large frying pan and cook the meatballs, in batches if necessary, for about 15–20 minutes, stirring regularly until evenly browned and cooked through.

4 Transfer the meatballs to a warm plate and sprinkle with chopped parsley. Serve with chilli sauce. Offer cocktail sticks for spearing.

Sweet Crust Lamb

These little noisettes are just big enough for two mouthfuls, so are ideal for tapas. If you would prefer something a little more substantial, small lamb cutlets or chops can be prepared in the same way.

INGREDIENTS

Serves 8
175g/6oz tender lamb fillet, sliced into
   1cm/½ in rounds
5ml/1 tsp English mustard
30ml/2 tbsp light muscovado sugar
salt and freshly ground black pepper
cocktail sticks, to serve

1 Preheat the grill to high. Sprinkle the rounds of lamb generously with salt and pepper and grill on one side for 2 minutes until well browned.

2 Remove the grill pan from the grill. Turn the lamb rounds over and spread with the mustard.

3 Sprinkle the sugar evenly over the lamb rounds, then return the grill pan to the grill.

--- COOK'S TIP ---

Watch the lamb carefully while it is grilling, as the sugar may burn if cooked for more than a few minutes.

4 Cook the lamb for 2–3 minutes more, until the sugar has melted, but the lamb is still pink in the centre. Serve with cocktail sticks for spearing.

Skewered Lamb with Red Onion Salsa

This summery dish is ideal for barbecuing outdoors, although, if the weather fails, the skewers can be cooked under a conventional grill. The simple salsa makes a refreshing accompaniment – make sure that you use a mild-flavoured red onion which is fresh and crisp, and a tomato which is ripe and full of flavour.

INGREDIENTS

Serves 4
225g/8oz lean lamb, cubed
2.5ml/½ tsp ground cumin
5ml/1 tsp ground paprika
15ml/1 tbsp olive oil
salt and freshly ground black pepper

For the salsa
1 red onion, very thinly sliced
1 large tomato, seeded and chopped
15ml/1 tbsp red wine vinegar
3–4 fresh basil or mint leaves,
   roughly torn
small mint leaves, to garnish

1 Place the lamb in a bowl with the cumin, paprika, olive oil and plenty of salt and pepper. Toss well until the lamb is coated with spices.

2 Cover the bowl with clear film and leave in a cool place for several hours, or in the fridge overnight, so that the lamb absorbs the spicy flavours.

3 Spear the lamb cubes on four small skewers – if using wooden skewers, soak them first in cold water for at least 30 minutes to prevent them burning.

4 To make the salsa, put the sliced onion, tomato, vinegar and basil or mint leaves in a small bowl and stir together until thoroughly blended. Season to taste with salt, garnish with mint, then set aside while you cook the skewered lamb.

5 Cook the skewered lamb over hot coals or under a preheated grill for about 5–10 minutes, turning the skewers frequently, until the lamb is well browned but still slightly pink in the centre. Serve hot, with the salsa.

COOK'S TIP

For an alternative to the red onion salsa, stir chopped fresh mint or basil and a little lemon juice into a small pot of Greek-style yogurt. Drizzle the mixture over the cooked kebabs before serving.

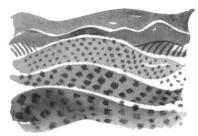

Sausage Stew

This robust sausage dish is good served with a glass of cold beer.

INGREDIENTS

Serves 4
15ml/1 tbsp olive oil
1 onion, chopped
2 garlic cloves, finely chopped
1 carrot, chopped
4 fresh spicy sausages
150ml/¼ pint/⅔ cup tomato juice
15ml/1 tbsp brandy
1.5ml/¼ tsp Tabasco sauce
5ml/1 tsp sugar
salt and freshly ground black pepper
30ml/2 tbsp chopped fresh coriander,
   to garnish

1 Heat the oil in a large saucepan. Cook the onion, garlic, carrot and sausages for 10 minutes, stirring occasionally until evenly browned.

2 Stir in the tomato juice, brandy, Tabasco and sugar, with salt and pepper to taste. Cover and simmer for 25 minutes until the sausages are cooked through and the sauce has thickened. Serve at once, garnished with chopped coriander.

Stewed Beans and Pork

Fabada is a classic Spanish stew which takes its name from a type of white bean. It always contains black pudding (*morcilla*) and chorizo sausage and usually takes a good 2 hours to prepare. Here is a simple, speedy version that serves well as a supper dish.

INGREDIENTS

Serves 4
15ml/1 tbsp olive oil
175g/6oz belly pork, rind removed
   and diced
115g/4oz cured chorizo sausage, diced
1 onion, chopped
2 garlic cloves, finely chopped
1 large tomato, roughly chopped
1.5ml/¼ tsp dried chilli flakes
400g/14oz can cannellini
   beans, drained
150ml/¼ pint/⅔ cup chicken stock
salt and freshly ground black pepper
flat leaf parsley, to garnish

1 Heat the oil in a large frying pan and fry the pork, chorizo, onion and garlic for 5–10 minutes until the onion has softened and browned. Add the tomato and chilli flakes and cook for 1 minute more.

2 Stir in the beans and stock. Bring to the boil, lower the heat, cover and simmer for 15–20 minutes until the pork is cooked through. Add salt and pepper to taste and serve, garnished with parsley.

--- COOK'S TIP ---

If preferred, smoked gammon can be used in place of belly pork in this recipe. Although it isn't quite as authentic, the meat is a lot less fatty and it adds a good smokey flavour.

Cheese and Ham Potato Patties

These soft patties can be served hot or cold – for a real treat, top each with a fried quail's egg.

INGREDIENTS

Serves 4

500g/1¼lb potatoes, peeled and cubed
25g/1oz/2 tbsp butter
50g/2oz/¼ cup grated cheese, such as
  Manchego or mature Cheddar
4 slices of serrano ham, chopped
50g/2oz/½ cup plain flour
oil, for greasing
salt and freshly ground black pepper

1 Cook the potatoes in a saucepan of boiling, lightly salted water for 10–15 minutes until tender. Drain well and mash with the butter and cheese until smooth.

2 Stir in the ham and flour with plenty of salt and pepper. Shape the mixture into eight rounds, each about 1cm/½in thick.

3 Lightly oil a griddle or heavy-based frying pan and cook the patties for 4–5 minutes on each side until golden brown. Drain on kitchen paper and serve at once.

COOK'S TIP

The patties have a very fluffy, soft centre, so take care when turning them over. If preferred, brush them with oil and cook them under a moderately hot grill, turning them halfway through cooking.

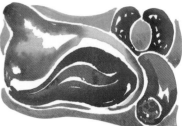

Chicken Croquettes

This recipe uses chicken but you can substitute a number of different meat fillings if you prefer.

INGREDIENTS

Serves 4

25g/1oz/2 tbsp butter
25g/1oz/¼ cup plain flour
150ml/¼ pint/⅔ cup milk
15ml/1 tbsp olive oil
1 boneless chicken breast with skin, about 75g/3oz, diced
1 garlic clove, finely chopped
1 small egg, beaten
50g/2oz/1 cup fresh white breadcrumbs
vegetable oil, for deep frying
salt and freshly ground black pepper
flat leaf parsley, to garnish
lemon wedges, to serve

1 Melt the butter in a small saucepan. Add the flour and cook gently, stirring, for 1 minute. Gradually beat in the milk to make a smooth, very thick sauce. Cover with a lid and remove from the heat.

2 Heat the oil in a frying pan and cook the chicken with the garlic for 5 minutes, until the chicken is lightly browned and cooked through.

3 Tip the contents of the frying pan into a food processor and process until finely chopped. Stir into the sauce. Add plenty of salt and pepper to taste, then leave to cool completely.

4 Shape into eight small sausages, then dip each in egg and then breadcrumbs. Deep fry in hot oil for 4 minutes until crisp and golden. Drain on kitchen paper and serve with lemon wedges, garnished with flat leaf parsley.

Spicy Chicken Wings

These deliciously sticky bites will appeal to adults and children alike, although younger eaters might prefer a little less chilli.

INGREDIENTS

Serves 4
8 plump chicken wings
2 large garlic cloves, cut into slivers
15ml/1 tbsp olive oil
15ml/1 tbsp paprika
5ml/1 tsp chilli powder
5ml/1 tsp dried oregano
5ml/1 tsp salt
5ml/1 tsp ground black pepper
lime wedges, to serve

─────── COOK'S TIP ───────

Chunks of chicken breast and small thighs may also be cooked in this way.

1 Using a small sharp knife, make one or two cuts in the skin of each chicken wing and carefully slide a sliver of garlic under the skin. Brush the wings with the olive oil.

2 In a large bowl, stir together the paprika, chilli powder, oregano, salt and pepper. Add the chicken wings and toss together until very lightly coated in the mixture.

3 Grill or barbecue the chicken wings for 15 minutes until they are cooked through with a blackened, crispy skin. Serve with lime wedges to squeeze over.

Chicken with Lemon and Garlic

Extremely easy to cook and delicious to eat, serve this succulent dish with fried potatoes and aïoli.

INGREDIENTS

Serves 4
225g/8oz skinless chicken breast fillets
30ml/2 tbsp olive oil
1 shallot, finely chopped
4 garlic cloves, finely chopped
5ml/1 tsp paprika
juice of 1 lemon
30ml/2 tbsp chopped fresh parsley
salt and freshly ground black pepper
flat leaf parsley, to garnish
lemon wedges, to serve

1 Sandwich the chicken breasts between two sheets of clear film or greaseproof paper. Bat out with a rolling pin until the fillets are about 5mm/¼ in thick.

─────── COOK'S TIP ───────

For a variation on this dish, try using strips of turkey breast or pork.

2 Cut the chicken into strips about 1cm/½ in wide. Heat the oil in a large frying pan. Stir-fry the chicken strips with the shallot, garlic and paprika over a high heat for about 3 minutes until lightly browned and cooked through. Add the lemon juice and parsley with salt and pepper to taste. Serve hot with lemon wedges, garnished with flat leaf parsley.

Monkfish Parcels

INGREDIENTS

Serves 4

175g/6oz/1½ cups strong plain flour
2 eggs
115g/4oz skinless monkfish fillet, diced
grated rind of 1 lemon
1 garlic clove, chopped
1 small red chilli, seeded and sliced
45ml/3 tbsp chopped fresh parsley
30ml/2 tbsp single cream

For the tomato oil

2 tomatoes, peeled, seeded and
  finely diced
45ml/3 tbsp extra virgin olive oil
30ml/1 tbsp fresh lemon juice
salt and freshly ground black pepper

COOK'S TIP

If the dough is sticky, sprinkle a little flour
into the food processor bowl.

---

1 Place the flour, eggs and 2.5ml/
½ tsp salt in a food processor; pulse
until the mixture forms a soft dough.
Knead for 2–3 minutes then wrap in
clear film. Chill for 20 minutes.

2 Place the monkfish, lemon rind,
garlic, chilli and parsley in the
clean food processor; process until very
finely chopped. Add the cream, with
plenty of salt and pepper and whizz
again to form a very thick purée.

3 Make the tomato oil by stirring the
diced tomato with the olive oil and
lemon juice in a bowl. Add salt to taste.
Cover and chill.

4 Roll out the dough on a lightly
floured surface and cut out
32 rounds, using a 4cm/1½in plain
cutter. Divide the filling among half
the rounds, then cover with the
remaining rounds. Pinch the edges
tightly to seal, trying to exclude as
much air as possible.

5 Bring a large saucepan of water to
simmering point and poach the
parcels, in batches, for 2–3 minutes or
until they rise to the surface. Drain and
serve hot, drizzled with the tomato oil.

Cod with Potato and Mustard Seeds

INGREDIENTS

Serves 4

30ml/2 tbsp olive oil
5ml/1 tsp mustard seeds
1 large potato, cubed
2 slices of serrano ham, shredded
1 onion, thinly sliced
2 garlic cloves, thinly sliced
1 red chilli, seeded and sliced
115g/4oz skinless, boneless cod, cubed
120ml/4fl oz/½ cup vegetable stock
50g/2oz/½ cup grated tasty cheese,
    such as Manchego or Cheddar
salt and freshly ground black pepper

--- COOK'S TIP ---

For a crisp topping, substitute half the
cheese with wholemeal breadcrumbs.

1 Heat the oil in a heavy-based
frying pan. Add the mustard seeds.
Cook for a minute or two until the
seeds begin to pop and splutter, then
add the potato, ham and onion.

2 Cook, stirring regularly for about
10–15 minutes, until the potatoes
are brown and almost tender.

3 Add the garlic and chilli and cook
for 2 minutes more.

4 Stir in the cod cubes and cook for
2–3 minutes until white, then add
the stock and plenty of salt and pepper.
Cover the pan and cook for 5 minutes,
until the fish is just cooked and the
potatoes are tender.

5 Transfer the mixture to a flameproof dish. Sprinkle over the
grated cheese and place under a hot
grill for about 2–3 minutes until the
cheese is golden and bubbling.

Spanish Seafood Paella

Ingredients

Serves 4

60ml/4 tbsp olive oil
225g/8oz monkfish or cod, skinned
 and cut into chunks
3 prepared baby squid, body cut into
 rings and tentacles chopped
1 red mullet, filleted, skinned and cut
 into chunks (optional)
1 onion, chopped
3 garlic cloves, finely chopped
1 red pepper, seeded and sliced
4 tomatoes, skinned and chopped
225g/8oz/1¼ cups arborio rice
450ml/¾ pint/1⅞ cups fish stock
150ml/¼ pint/⅔ cup white wine
75g/3oz/¾ cup frozen peas
4–5 saffron strands soaked in 30ml/
 2 tbsp hot water
115g/4oz/1 cup cooked, peeled prawns
8 fresh mussels in shells, scrubbed
salt and black pepper
15ml/1 tbsp chopped fresh parsley,
 to garnish
lemon wedges, to serve

1 Heat 30ml/2 tbsp of the oil in a large frying pan and add the monkfish or cod, the squid and the red mullet, if using, to the pan. Stir-fry for 2 minutes, then transfer the fish to a bowl with all the juices and reserve.

2 Heat the remaining 30ml/2 tbsp of oil in the pan and add the onion, garlic and pepper. Fry for 6–7 minutes, stirring frequently, until the onions and peppers have softened.

3 Stir in the tomatoes and fry for 2 minutes, then add the rice, stirring to coat the grains with oil, and cook for 2–3 minutes. Pour on the fish stock and wine and add the peas, saffron and water. Season well and mix.

4 Gently stir in the reserved cooked fish with all the juices, followed by the prawns and then push the mussels into the rice. Cover and cook over a gentle heat for about 30 minutes, or until the stock has been absorbed but the mixture is still moist.

5 Remove from the heat, keep covered and leave to stand for 5 minutes. Sprinkle with parsley and serve with lemon wedges.

Salt Cod Fishcakes with Aïoli

Bite-size fish cakes, dipped in a rich garlic mayonnaise, are irresistible. Start these in good time, as the salt cod needs a lengthy soaking.

INGREDIENTS

Serves 6

450g/1lb potatoes, peeled and cubed
115g/4oz salt cod, soaked in cold water
   for 48 hours
15ml/1 tbsp olive oil
1 small onion, finely chopped
2 garlic cloves, finely chopped
30ml/2 tbsp chopped fresh parsley
1 egg, beaten
Tabasco or chilli sauce
plain flour, for dusting
vegetable oil, for frying
salt and freshly ground black pepper
flat leaf parsley and lemon wedges,
   to garnish
aïoli, to serve

COOK'S TIP

Try making these with drained canned fish, such as salmon or tuna.

1 Cook the potatoes in a saucepan of boiling water for 10–12 minutes until tender. Drain well, then mash until smooth. Set aside.

2 Place the cod in a frying pan, add water to cover and bring to the boil. Drain the fish, then remove the skin and bones. Using a fork, break the flesh into small pieces.

3 Heat the olive oil in a small saucepan and cook the onion and garlic for 5 minutes until softened.

4 In a large bowl, mix together the mashed potato, flaked fish, fried onion mixture and parsley. Bind with the egg, then add salt, pepper and Tabasco or chilli sauce to taste. With floured hands, shape the mixture into 18 small balls.

5 Flatten the balls slightly and place on a large floured plate. Chill for about 15 minutes.

6 Heat 1cm/½in vegetable oil in a large frying pan. Cook the fish cakes for 3–4 minutes on each side until golden. Drain on kitchen paper and serve hot, with the aïoli, garnished with parsley and lemon wedges.

Grilled Pepper Tartlets

INGREDIENTS

Serves 4

175g/6oz/1½ cups plain flour
pinch of salt
75g/3oz/6 tbsp chilled butter, diced
30–45ml/2–3 tbsp water
1 red pepper, seeded and quartered
1 yellow pepper, seeded and quartered
60ml/4 tbsp double cream
1 egg
15ml/1 tbsp freshly grated
  Parmesan cheese
salt and freshly ground black pepper

— COOK'S TIP —

For a change, try filling the pastry cases
with strips of grilled aubergine mixed with
sun-dried tomato, or strips of grilled
courgette mixed with toasted pine nuts.

1 Sift the flour and salt into a bowl.
Add the butter and rub it in with
your fingertips until the mixture
resembles fine breadcrumbs. Stir in
enough of the water to make a firm,
not sticky, dough.

2 Preheat the oven to 200°C/400°F/
Gas 6. Roll the dough out thinly
on a lightly floured surface and line
12 individual moulds or a 12-hole
tartlet tin. Prick the bases with a fork
and fill the pastry cases with crumpled
foil. Bake for 10 minutes.

3 Meanwhile, place the peppers
skin-side up on a baking sheet and
grill for 10 minutes until the skin is
blistered and blackened. Cover with a
dish towel and leave for 5 minutes,
then peel away the skin.

4 Cut each piece of pepper
lengthways into very thin strips.
Remove the foil from the pastry cases
and divide the pepper strips among
the pastry cases.

5 Whisk the cream and egg in a
bowl. Add plenty of salt and
pepper and pour over the peppers.
Sprinkle the Parmesan over each filled
tartlet and bake for 15–20 minutes
until firm and golden brown. Cool for
2 minutes before removing from the
moulds and transferring to wire racks;
serve warm or cold.

Baked Peppers and Tomatoes

Make sure there is a basket of warm bread on hand so that none of the delicious juices from this dish are wasted.

INGREDIENTS

Serves 8
2 red peppers
2 yellow peppers
1 red onion, sliced
2 garlic cloves, halved
6 plum tomatoes, quartered
50g/2oz/¼ cup black olives
5ml/1 tsp soft light brown sugar
45ml/3 tbsp sherry
3–4 rosemary sprigs
30ml/2 tbsp olive oil
salt and freshly ground black pepper

1 Seed the red and yellow peppers, then cut each into 12 strips.

2 Preheat the oven to 200°C/400°F/ Gas 6. Place the peppers, onion, garlic, tomatoes and olives in a large roasting tin. Sprinkle over the sugar, then pour over the sherry. Season well, cover with foil and bake for 45 minutes.

3 Remove the foil from the tin and stir the mixture well. Add the rosemary sprigs.

4 Drizzle over the olive oil. Return the tin to the oven for a further 30 minutes until the vegetables are tender. Serve hot.

--- COOK'S TIP ---

Use four or five well-flavoured beefsteak tomatoes instead of plum tomatoes if you prefer. Cut them into thick wedges instead of quarters.

Artichoke Rice Cakes with Melting Manchego

For a really impressive side dish, serve these rice cakes topped with aïoli and salt-cured salmon.

INGREDIENTS

Serves 6

1 globe artichoke
50g/2oz/¼ cup butter
1 small onion, finely chopped
1 garlic clove, finely chopped
115g/4oz/⅔ cup risotto rice
450ml/¾ pint/scant 2 cups hot chicken stock
50g/2oz/¼ cup freshly grated Parmesan cheese
150g/5oz Manchego cheese, very finely diced
45–60ml/3–4 tbsp fine cornmeal
olive oil for frying
salt and freshly ground black pepper
flat leaf parsley, to garnish

1 Remove the stalk, leaves and choke to leave just the heart of the artichoke; chop the heart finely.

2 Melt the butter in a saucepan and gently fry the chopped artichoke heart, onion and garlic for 5 minutes until softened. Stir in the rice and cook for about 1 minute.

3 Keeping the heat fairly high, gradually add the stock, stirring constantly until all the liquid has been absorbed and the rice is cooked – this should take about 20 minutes. Season well, then stir in the Parmesan. Transfer to a bowl. Leave to cool, then cover and chill for at least 2 hours.

4 Spoon about 15ml/1 tbsp of the mixture into the palm of one hand, flatten slightly, and place a few pieces of diced cheese in the centre. Shape the rice around the cheese to make a small ball. Flatten slightly then roll in the cornmeal, shaking off any excess. Repeat with the remaining mixture to make about 12 cakes.

5 Shallow fry in hot olive oil for 4–5 minutes until the rice cakes are crisp and golden brown. Drain on kitchen paper and serve hot, garnished with flat leaf parsley.

COOK'S TIP

Fresh Parmesan should be piquant, grainy and not so hard that it is difficult to grate.

Classic Potato Tortilla

A traditional Spanish tortilla contains potatoes and onions. Other ingredients can be added to the basic egg mixture, but it is generally accepted that the classic tortilla cannot be improved.

INGREDIENTS

Serves 6
450g/1lb small waxy potatoes, peeled
1 Spanish onion
45ml/3 tbsp vegetable oil
4 eggs
salt and freshly ground black pepper
flat leaf parsley, to garnish

1 Cut the potatoes into thin slices and the onions into rings.

2 Heat 30ml/2 tbsp of the oil in a 20cm/8in heavy-based frying pan. Add the potatoes and the onions and cook over a low heat for about 10 minutes until the potatoes are just tender. Remove from the heat.

3 In a large bowl, beat together the eggs with a little salt and pepper. Stir in the sliced potatoes and onion.

4 Heat the remaining oil in the frying pan and pour in the potato mixture. Cook very gently for 5–8 minutes until the mixture is almost set.

5 Place a large plate upside-down over the pan, invert the tortilla on to the plate and then slide it back into the pan. Cook for 2 or 3 minutes more, until the underside of the tortilla is golden brown. Cut into wedges and serve, garnished with flat leaf parsley.

Stewed Aubergines

INGREDIENTS

Serves 4
60–90ml/4–6 tbsp olive oil
1 large aubergine, sliced into 1cm/
    ½ in rounds
2 shallots, thinly sliced
4 tomatoes, quartered
2 garlic cloves, thinly sliced
60ml/4 tbsp red wine
30ml/2 tbsp chopped fresh parsley, plus
    extra to garnish
salt and freshly ground black pepper

COOK'S TIP

For a tasty variation, spoon the cooked
mixture into a flameproof dish, sprinkle
with grated cheese and grill for 5 minutes,
until bubbling and golden.

1 Heat 15ml/1 tbsp of the oil in a
large frying pan. Cook the
aubergine slices in batches (adding
more oil as necessary, but reserving
15ml/1 tbsp), until golden brown.
Drain the slices, cut them into strips
about 1cm/½ in wide, and set aside.

2 Heat the reserved 15ml/1 tbsp of
oil in a saucepan and cook the
shallots for 5 minutes until golden. Add
the aubergine strips with the tomatoes,
garlic and wine. Season to taste. Cover
and simmer for 30 minutes. Stir in the
parsley, check the seasoning and serve,
sprinkled with chopped parsley.

Courgette Fritters

Serve these crisp fritters with
a dipping sauce such as aïoli,
tomato sauce, or a fiery salsa.

INGREDIENTS

Serves 4
2 courgettes
25g/1oz/¼ cup seasoned flour
2 eggs, beaten
30ml/2 tbsp milk
vegetable oil, for frying
coarse sea salt

1 Cut the courgettes on the diagonal
into slices about 5mm/¼ in thick.
Toss the slices in the seasoned flour in
a strong plastic bag. Beat together the
egg and milk in a small bowl. Heat
1cm/½ in oil in a frying pan.

2 Shake off the excess flour from the
courgette slices. Dip them one at a
time into the egg mixture, until they
are well coated.

3 Shallow fry the fritters in the hot
oil for 1–2 minutes on each side
until crisp and golden. Drain on
kitchen paper and serve, lightly
sprinkled with sea salt.

Grilled Asparagus with Salt-cured Ham

Serve this dish when asparagus is
plentiful and not too pricey.

INGREDIENTS

Serves 4

6 slices of serrano ham
12 asparagus spears
15ml/1 tbsp olive oil
sea salt and coarsely ground black
  pepper

—————— COOK'S TIP ——————

If you can't find serrano ham, use Italian
prosciutto or Portuguese *presunto*.

1 Preheat the grill to high. Halve
each slice of ham lengthways and
wrap one half around each of the
asparagus spears.

2 Brush the ham and asparagus
lightly with oil and sprinkle with
salt and pepper. Place on the grill rack.
Grill for 5–6 minutes, turning
frequently, until the asparagus is tender
but still firm. Serve at once.

Braised Buttery Cabbage with Chorizo

This dish is equally delicious
without the chorizo sausage, so
just omit it when serving this to
vegetarian guests.

INGREDIENTS

Serves 4

50g/2oz/¼ cup butter
1 tsp caraway seeds
225g/8oz green cabbage, shredded
2 garlic cloves, finely chopped
50g/2oz cured chorizo sausage,
  roughly chopped
60ml/4 tbsp dry sherry or white wine
salt and freshly ground black pepper

—————— COOK'S TIP ——————

Smoked bacon makes a good substitute for
chorizo sausage in this recipe. Add it to the
pan after the caraway seeds and cook for a
few minutes before addding the cabbage.

1 Melt the butter in a frying pan, add
the caraway seeds and cook for
1 minute. Add the cabbage to the pan
with the garlic and chorizo. Stir-fry for
5 minutes until the cabbage is tender.

2 Add the sherry or wine and plenty
of salt and pepper. Cover the pan
and cook for 15–20 minutes until the
cabbage is tender. Check the seasoning
and serve.

Fried Potatoes with Aïoli

Aïoli is a Catalan speciality which began life as a mixture of garlic, salt and olive oil, pounded together with a pestle in a mortar. Nowadays, it is usually made in a food processor and is more like garlic mayonnaise.

Ingredients

Serves 4
4 potatoes, cut into 8 wedges each
vegetable oil, for deep frying
coarse sea salt

For the aïoli
1 large egg yolk, at room
  temperature
5ml/1 tsp white wine vinegar
75ml/5 tbsp olive oil
75ml/5 tbsp sunflower oil
4 garlic cloves, crushed

1 Make the aïoli. Place the egg yolk and vinegar in a food processor. With the motor running, add the olive oil, about 10ml/2 tsp at a time.

2 When all the olive oil has been added, add the sunflower oil in the same way, until the aïoli resembles a thick mayonnaise. If it is too thick, add a little more vinegar. Stir in the garlic and salt to taste. Cover and chill.

3 Heat the oil in a saucepan until a cube of bread turns golden in 60 seconds. Add the potatoes and cook for 7 minutes until pale golden.

4 Remove the potato wedges from the pan and drain on kitchen paper. Raise the heat of the oil slightly – it should be hot enough to brown a cube of bread in 30 seconds. Return the potatoes to the pan and cook for 2–3 minutes until golden brown. Drain on kitchen paper and sprinkle with salt. Serve hot with the aïoli.

Cook's Tip

This aïoli recipe has equal quantities of olive oil and sunflower oil, but aïoli can be made with 3 parts sunflower oil to 1 part olive oil for a milder flavour. If made solely with olive oil, the finished aïoli will have a waxy appearance and strong, slightly bitter flavour.

Spicy Potatoes

Spicy potatoes, *patatas picantes*, are among the most popular dishes in Spain, where they are sometimes described as *patatas bravas* (wild potatoes). There are many variations of this classic: boiled new potatoes or large wedges of fried potato may be used, but they are perhaps best simply roasted as in this recipe.

INGREDIENTS

Serves 2–4
225g/8oz small new potatoes
15ml/1 tbsp olive oil
5ml/1 tsp paprika
5ml/1 tsp chilli powder
2.5ml/¹/₂ tsp ground cumin
2.5ml/¹/₂ tsp salt
flat leaf parsley, to garnish

1 Preheat the oven to 200°C/400°F/ Gas 6. Prick the skin of each potato in several places with a fork, then place them in a bowl.

2 Add the olive oil, paprika, chilli, cumin and salt and toss well.

3 Transfer the potatoes to a roasting tin and bake for 40 minutes.

——— COOK'S TIP ———

This dish is delicious served with a tomato sauce or salsa – provide small forks for dipping.

4 Occasionally during cooking, remove the potatoes from the oven and turn them. Serve hot, garnished with flat leaf parsley.

FRANCE

French Onion Soup

In France, this standard bistro fare is served so frequently, it is simply referred to as *gratinée*.

INGREDIENTS

Serves 6–8

15g/½oz/1 tbsp butter
30ml/2 tbsp olive oil
4 large onions, thinly sliced
2–4 garlic cloves, finely chopped
5ml/1 tsp sugar
2.5ml/½ tsp dried thyme
30ml/2 tbsp plain flour
125ml/4fl oz/½ cup dry white wine
2 litres/3⅓ pints/8 cups chicken or
   beef stock
30ml/2 tbsp brandy (optional)
6–8 thick slices French bread, toasted
1 garlic clove
340g/12oz Gruyère or Emmental
   cheese, grated

1 In a large heavy saucepan or flameproof casserole, heat the butter and oil over a medium-high heat. Add the onions and cook for 10–12 minutes until they are softened and beginning to brown. Add the garlic, sugar and thyme and continue cooking over a medium heat for 30–35 minutes until the onions are well browned, stirring frequently.

2 Sprinkle over the flour and stir until well blended. Stir in the white wine and stock and bring to the boil. Skim off any foam that rises to the surface, then reduce the heat and simmer gently for 45 minutes. Stir in the brandy, if using.

3 Preheat the grill. Rub each slice of toasted French bread with the garlic clove. Place six or eight ovenproof soup bowls on a baking sheet and fill about three-quarters full with the onion soup.

4 Float a piece of toast in each bowl. Top with grated cheese, dividing it evenly, and grill about 15cm/6in from the heat for about 3–4 minutes, until the cheese begins to melt and bubble.

Prawn Bisque

INGREDIENTS

Serves 6–8

675g/1½lb small or medium cooked
   prawns in the shell
25ml/1½ tbsp vegetable oil
2 onions, halved and sliced
1 large carrot, sliced
2 celery sticks, sliced
2 litres/3⅓ pints/8 cups water
a few drops of lemon juice
30ml/2 tbsp tomato purée
bouquet garni
55g/2oz/4 tbsp butter
55g/2oz/⅓ cup plain flour
45–60ml/3–4 tbsp brandy
150ml/¼ pint/⅔ cup whipping cream

1 Make the prawn stock. Remove the heads from the prawns and peel away the shells, reserving the heads and shells for the stock. Chill the peeled prawns. Heat the oil in a large saucepan or flameproof casserole, add the prawn heads and shells and cook over a high heat, stirring frequently, until they start to brown. Reduce the heat to medium, add the onions, carrot and celery and fry gently, stirring occasionally, for about 5 minutes until the onions have softened.

2 Add the water, lemon juice, tomato purée and bouquet garni to the saucepan. Bring the stock to the boil, then reduce the heat, cover and simmer gently for 25 minutes. Strain the stock through a sieve. Meanwhile, melt the butter in a heavy saucepan over a medium heat. Stir in the flour and cook until just golden, stirring occasionally.

3 Add the brandy and half of the prawn stock, then whisk in the remaining stock. Reduce the heat, cover and simmer for 5 minutes.

4 Strain the soup into a clean saucepan. Add the cream and a little extra lemon juice to taste, then stir in most of the reserved prawns and cook over a medium heat, stirring frequently, until the soup is hot. Serve at once, garnished with the reserved prawns.

Chicken and Pistachio Pâté

INGREDIENTS

Serves 10–12

900g/2lb boneless chicken meat
1 skinless boneless chicken breast
  (about 175g/6oz)
30g/1oz/⅔ cup white breadcrumbs
125ml/4fl oz/½ cup whipping cream
1 egg white
4 spring onions, finely chopped
1 garlic clove, finely chopped
85g/3oz cooked ham, cubed
55g/2oz/½ cup shelled pistachio nuts
45ml/3 tbsp chopped fresh tarragon
pinch of grated nutmeg
3.5ml/¾ tsp salt
7.5ml/1½ tsp pepper
green salad, to serve

1 Trim all the fat, tendons and connective tissue from the 900g/2lb chicken meat and cut into 5cm/2in cubes. Put in a food processor fitted with the metal blade and pulse to chop the meat to a smooth purée, in two or three batches (depending on capacity). Or alternatively, pass the meat through the medium or fine blade of a mincer. Remove any white stringy pieces from the minced meat.

2 Preheat the oven to 180°C/ 350°F/Gas 4. Cut the chicken breast fillet into 1cm/⅜in cubes.

— COOK'S TIP —

You could use turkey meat in place of some or all of the chicken, if you prefer. As a guide to quantity, a 2kg/4½lb chicken or whole turkey breast yields about 900g/2lb of boneless meat.

3 In a large mixing bowl, soak the breadcrumbs in the cream. Add the minced chicken, egg white, spring onions, garlic, ham, pistachio nuts, tarragon, nutmeg and salt and pepper. Using a wooden spoon or your fingers, mix until the ingredients are thoroughly combined.

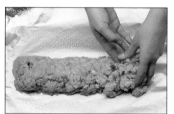

4 Lay out a piece of extra-wide strong foil about 45cm/18in long on a work surface and lightly brush oil on a 30cm/12in square in the centre. Spoon the chicken mixture on to the foil to form a log shape, about 30cm/12in long and about 9cm/3½in thick across the width of the foil. Bring together the long sides of the foil and fold over securely to enclose. Twist the ends of the foil and tie with string.

5 Transfer to a baking dish and bake for 1½ hours. Leave to cool in the dish and chill until cold, preferably overnight. Serve the pâté in slices, with a crisp green salad.

Scallops with Mushrooms

This dish has been a classic on bistro menus since Hemingway's days in Paris – it makes an appealing starter, or serve it as a rich and elegant main course.

INGREDIENTS

Serves 2-4
250ml/8fl oz/1 cup dry white wine
125ml/4fl oz/½ cup water
2 shallots, finely chopped
1 bay leaf
450g/1lb shelled scallops, rinsed
40g/1½oz/3 tbsp butter
40g/1½oz/3 tbsp plain flour
90ml/6 tbsp whipping cream
freshly grated nutmeg
175g/6oz mushrooms, thinly sliced
45–60ml/3–4 tbsp dry breadcrumbs
salt and freshly ground black pepper

1 Combine the wine, water, shallots and bay leaf in a medium saucepan. Bring to the boil, then reduce the heat to medium-low and simmer for 10 minutes. Add the scallops, cover and simmer for 3–4 minutes until they are opaque.

2 Remove the scallops from the cooking liquid with a slotted spoon, and boil the liquid until reduced to about 175ml/6fl oz. Strain and reserve the liquid

3 Carefully pull off the tough muscle from the side of the scallops and discard. Slice the scallops in half crossways, using a sharp kitchen knife.

4 Melt 30g/1oz/2 tbsp of the butter in a heavy saucepan over a medium-high heat. Stir in the flour and cook for 2 minutes. Add the reserved cooking liquid, whisking vigorously until smooth, then whisk in the cream and season with salt, pepper and nutmeg. Reduce the heat to low and simmer for 10 minutes, stirring frequently.

5 Melt the remaining butter in a frying pan over a medium-high heat. Add the mushrooms and cook for about 5 minutes until lightly browned, stirring frequently. Stir the mushrooms into the sauce.

6 Preheat the grill. Add the scallops to the sauce and check the seasoning. Spoon the mixture into individual gratin dishes or scallop shells and sprinkle with breadcrumbs. Grill until golden and bubbling.

Goat's Cheese Soufflé

Make sure everyone is seated before the soufflé comes out of the oven because it will begin to deflate almost immediately. This recipe works equally well with strong blue cheeses such as Roquefort.

INGREDIENTS

Serves 4–6
30g/1oz/2 tbsp butter
30g/1oz/3 tbsp plain flour
175ml/6fl oz/¾ cup milk
1 bay leaf
freshly grated nutmeg
grated Parmesan cheese, for
  sprinkling
40g/1½oz herb and garlic soft cheese
150g/5oz firm goat's cheese, diced
6 egg whites, at room temperature
1.5ml/¼ tsp cream of tartar
salt and freshly ground black pepper

2 Remove the sauce from the heat and discard the bay leaf. Add the cheeses and stir until smooth.

1 Melt the butter in a saucepan over a medium heat. Add the flour and cook until golden, stirring. Pour in half the milk, stirring vigorously until smooth, then stir in the remaining milk and add the bay leaf. Season with a pinch of salt and plenty of pepper and nutmeg. Reduce the heat to medium-low, cover and simmer for 5 minutes, stirring occasionally. Preheat the oven to 190°C/375°F/Gas 5. Generously butter a 1.5 litre/2½ pint soufflé dish and sprinkle with Parmesan cheese.

3 In a clean, greasefree bowl, using an electric mixer or balloon whisk, beat the egg whites slowly until they become frothy. Add the cream of tartar, increase the speed and continue beating until they form soft peaks. Continue to beat the egg whites mixture until the peaks begin to flop over a little at the top.

4 Stir a spoonful of beaten egg whites mixture into the cheese sauce to lighten it, then pour the cheese sauce over the remaining egg whites mixture. Using a rubber spatula or large metal spoon, fold the sauce into the whites until well combined: try to work in one flowing movement, cutting down through the centre of the bowl to the bottom, then along the side of the bowl and up to the top.

5 Gently pour the soufflé mixture into the prepared dish and bake in the preheated oven for 25–30 minutes until puffed and golden brown. Serve the soufflé at once.

Provençal Chard Omelette

This traditional flat omelette can be made with fresh spinach, but chard leaves are typical in Provence. It is delicious served with small black Niçoise olives.

INGREDIENTS

Serves 6
675g/1½lb chard leaves without stalks
60ml/4 tbsp olive oil
1 large onion, sliced
5 eggs
salt and freshly ground black pepper
fresh parsley sprigs, to garnish

1 Wash the chard well and pat dry. Stack four or five leaves at a time and slice across into thin ribbons. Steam the chard until wilted, then drain in a sieve and press out any liquid with the back of a spoon.

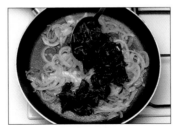

2 Heat 30ml/2 tbsp of the olive oil in a large frying pan. Add the onion and cook over a medium-low heat for about 10 minutes until soft, stirring occasionally. Add the chard and cook for a further 2–4 minutes until the leaves are tender.

3 In a large bowl, beat the eggs and season with salt and pepper, then stir in the cooked vegetables.

4 Heat the remaining 30ml/2 tbsp of oil in a large non-stick frying pan over a medium-high heat. Pour in the egg mixture and reduce the heat to medium-low. Cook the omelette, covered, for 5–7 minutes until the egg mixture is set around the edges and almost set on top

5 To turn the omelette over, loosen the edges and slide it on to a large plate. Place the frying pan over the omelette and, holding them tightly, carefully invert the pan and plate together. Lift off the plate and continue cooking for a further 2–3 minutes. Slide the omelette on to a serving plate and serve hot or at room temperature, cut into wedges and garnished with fresh parsley.

Pepper Steak

There are many versions of this French bistro classic. Some omit the cream, but it helps to balance the heat of the pepper. Use fairly thick steaks, such as fillet or lean sirloin.

INGREDIENTS

Serves 2
30ml/2 tbsp black peppercorns
2 fillet or sirloin steaks, about
    225g/8oz each
15g/½oz/1 tbsp butter
10ml/2 tsp vegetable oil
45ml/3 tbsp brandy
150ml/¼ pint/⅔ cup whipping cream
1 garlic clove, finely chopped
salt, if needed

1 Place the peppercorns in a sturdy polythene bag. Crush with a rolling pin until medium-coarse or, using the flat base of a small heavy saucepan, press down on the peppercorns, rocking the pan to crush them.

2 Put the steaks on a board and trim away any extra fat. Press the pepper on to both sides of the meat, coating it completely.

3 Melt the butter with the oil in a heavy frying pan over a medium-high heat. Add the meat and cook for 6–7 minutes, turning once, until done as preferred (medium-rare meat will still be slightly soft when pressed, medium will be springy and well-done firm). Transfer the steaks to a warmed serving platter or plates and cover to keep warm.

4 Pour in the brandy to deglaze the pan. Allow to boil until reduced by half, scraping the base of the pan, then add the cream and garlic. Boil gently over a medium heat for about 4 minutes until the cream has reduced by one-third. Stir any accumulated juices from the meat into the sauce, taste and add salt, if necessary. Pour the sauce over the steaks to serve.

Châteaubriand with Béarnaise

Châteaubriand is a lean and tender cut that is pounded to give it its characteristic shape. It is usually served for two, but could easily stretch to three.

INGREDIENTS

Serves 2

150g/5oz/⅔ cup butter, cut into pieces
25ml/1½ tbsp tarragon vinegar
25ml/1½ tbsp dry white wine
1 shallot, finely chopped
2 egg yolks
450g/1lb beef fillet, about 12.5–15cm/5–6in long, cut from the thickest part of the fillet
15ml/1 tbsp vegetable oil
salt and freshly ground black pepper
sautéed potatoes, to serve

1 Clarify the butter by melting in a saucepan over a low heat; do not boil. Skim off the foam and set aside.

2 Put the vinegar, wine and shallot in a heavy saucepan over a high heat and boil to reduce until the liquid has almost all evaporated. Remove from the heat and cool slightly. Add the egg yolks and whisk for 1 minute. Place the saucepan over a very low heat and whisk constantly until the yolk mixture begins to thicken and the whisk begins to leave tracks on the base of the pan. Remove the pan from the heat.

3 Whisk in the melted butter, drop by drop until the sauce begins to thicken.

4 Season the sauce with salt and pepper and keep warm, stirring occasionally. Meanwhile, place the meat between two sheets of greaseproof paper or clear film and pound with the flat side of a meat pounder or roll with a rolling pin to flatten to about 4cm/1½in thick. Season with salt and pepper.

5 Heat the oil in a heavy frying pan over a medium-high heat. Add the meat and cook for about 10–12 minutes, turning once, until done as preferred (medium-rare meat will be slightly soft when pressed, medium will be springy and well-done firm).

6 Transfer the steak to a board and carve in thin diagonal slices. Strain the sauce, if you prefer, and serve with the steak, accompanied by sautéed potatoes.

COOK'S TIP

Beef fillet is often cheaper when bought whole than when it has been divided into steaks. If you buy a whole fillet, you can cut a *Châteaubriand* from the thickest part, *filet mignon* steaks from less thick parts, *tournedos* from the thinner part and reserve the thinnest tail part for stir-frying or Stroganoff. If you wish, wrap tightly and freeze until needed.

Toulouse Cassoulet

This is a regional speciality from Southwest France.

INGREDIENTS

Serves 6–8

450g/1lb dried white beans (haricot or cannellini), soaked overnight in cold water, then rinsed and drained
675g/1½lb Toulouse sausages
550g/1¼lb each boneless lamb and pork shoulder, cut into 5cm/2in pieces
1 large onion, finely chopped
3 or 4 garlic cloves, finely chopped
4 tomatoes, peeled, seeded and chopped
300ml/½ pint/1¼ cups chicken stock
bouquet garni
60ml/4 tbsp fresh breadcrumbs
salt and freshly ground black pepper

1 Put the beans in a pan with water to cover. Boil vigorously for 10 minutes and drain, then return to a clean pan, cover with water and bring to the boil. Reduce the heat and simmer for 45 minutes. Add salt and leave to soak in the cooking water.

2 Preheat the oven to 180°C/ 350°F/Gas 4. Prick the sausages, place them in a large heavy frying pan over a medium heat and cook for 20–25 minutes until browned, turning occasionally. Drain on kitchen paper and pour off all but 15ml/1 tbsp of the fat from the pan.

3 Increase the heat to medium-high. Season the lamb and pork and add enough of the meat to fit in the pan easily in one layer. Cook until browned, then transfer to a large dish. Continue browning in batches. Add the onion and garlic to the pan and cook for 3–4 minutes until just soft, stirring. Stir in the tomatoes and cook for 2–3 minutes more.

4 Transfer the vegetables to the meat dish. Add the stock and gently bring to the boil, then skim off the fat. Spoon a quarter of the beans into a large casserole, and top with a third of the sausages, meat and vegetables. Continue layering, ending with a layer of beans. Tuck in the bouquet garni, pour over the stock and top up with enough of the bean cooking liquid to just cover.

5 Cover the casserole and bake for 2 hours (check and add more bean cooking liquid if it seems dry). Uncover the casserole, sprinkle over the breadcrumbs and press with the back of a spoon to moisten them. Continue cooking the cassoulet, uncovered, for about 20 minutes more until browned.

Veal Kidneys with Mustard

INGREDIENTS

Serves 4

2 veal kidneys or 8–10 lamb's
  kidneys, trimmed
30g/1oz/2 tbsp butter
15ml/1 tbsp vegetable oil
120g/4oz button mushrooms,
  quartered
60ml/4 tbsp chicken stock
30ml/2 tbsp brandy (optional)
175ml/6fl oz/¾ cup crème fraîche
30ml/2 tbsp Dijon mustard
salt and freshly ground black pepper
snipped fresh chives, to garnish

1 Cut the veal kidneys into pieces,
  discarding any fat. If using lamb's
kidneys, remove the central core by
cutting a V-shape from the middle of
each kidney. Cut each kidney into
three or four pieces.

2 In a large frying pan, melt the
  butter with the oil over a high
heat and swirl to blend. Add the
kidneys and sauté for about 3–4
minutes, stirring frequently until
well browned, then transfer them
to a plate using a slotted spoon.

3 Add the mushrooms to the pan
  and sauté for 2–3 minutes until
golden, stirring frequently. Pour in
the chicken stock and brandy, if
using, then bring to the boil and
boil gently for 2 minutes.

4 Stir the crème fraîche into the
  frying pan and cook for about
2–3 minutes, until the sauce is slightly
thickened. Stir in the mustard and
season with salt and pepper, then add
the kidneys and cook for 1 minute
more to reheat. Scatter over the
chives before serving.

Roast Leg of Lamb with Beans

INGREDIENTS

Serves 8–10
2.7–3kg/6–7lb leg of lamb
3 or 4 garlic cloves
olive oil
fresh or dried rosemary leaves
450g/1lb dried haricot or flageolet
   beans, soaked in cold water
1 bay leaf
30ml/2 tbsp red wine
150ml/¼ pint/⅔ cup lamb stock
30g/1oz/2 tbsp butter
salt and freshly ground black pepper
watercress, to garnish

1 Preheat the oven to 220°C/
425°F/Gas 7. Wipe the leg of
lamb with damp kitchen paper and
dry the fat covering well. Cut 2 or 3
of the garlic cloves into 10–12 slivers,
then with the tip of a knife, cut
10–12 slits into the lamb and insert
the garlic slivers into the slits. Rub
with olive oil, season with salt and
pepper and sprinkle with rosemary.

2 Set the lamb on a rack in a
shallow roasting tin and put in
the oven. After 15 minutes, reduce
the heat to 180°C/350°F/Gas 4 and
continue to roast for 1½–1¾ hours
(about 18 minutes per 450g/1lb) or
until a meat thermometer inserted
into the thickest part of the meat
registers 57–60°C/135–140°F for
medium-rare to medium meat or
66°C/150°F for well-done.

3 Meanwhile, rinse the beans and
place in a saucepan with enough
fresh water to cover generously. Add
the remaining garlic and the bay leaf,
then bring to the boil. Reduce the
heat and simmer for 45 minutes, or
until tender.

4 Transfer the roast to a board and
allow to stand, loosely covered,
for 10–15 minutes. Skim off the fat
from the cooking juices, then add
the wine and stock to the roasting
tin. Boil over a medium heat, stirring
and scraping the base of the tin, until
slightly reduced. Strain into a warmed
gravy boat.

5 Drain the beans, discard the bay
leaf, then toss the beans with the
butter until it melts, and season to
taste with salt and pepper. Garnish
the lamb with watercress and serve
with the beans and the sauce.

Pork with Camembert

INGREDIENTS

Serves 3–4

350–450g/¾–1lb pork fillet
15g/½oz/1 tbsp butter
45ml/3 tbsp sparkling dry cider or
   dry white wine
125–175ml/4–6fl oz/½–¾ cup crème
   fraîche or whipping cream
15ml/1 tbsp chopped fresh mixed
   herbs, such as marjoram, thyme
   and sage
½ Camembert cheese (120g/4oz),
   rind removed (70g/2½oz without
   rind), sliced
7.5ml/1½ tsp Dijon mustard
freshly ground black pepper
fresh parsley, to garnish

1 Slice the pork fillet crossways into small steaks about 2cm/¾in thick. Place between two sheets of greaseproof paper or clear film and pound with the flat side of a meat mallet or roll with a rolling pin to flatten to a thickness of 1cm/½in. Sprinkle the pork liberally with freshly ground black pepper.

2 Melt the butter in a heavy frying pan over a medium-high heat until it begins to brown, then add the meat. Cook for 5 minutes, turning once, or until just cooked through and the meat is springy when pressed. Transfer to a warmed dish and cover to keep warm.

3 Add the cider or wine and bring to the boil, scraping the base of the pan. Stir in the cream and herbs and bring back to the boil.

4 Add the cheese and mustard and any accumulated juices from the meat. Add a little more cream if needed and adjust the seasoning. Serve the pork with the sauce and garnish with parsley.

Mussels Steamed in White Wine

INGREDIENTS

Serves 4
2kg/4½lb mussels
300ml/½ pint/1¼ cups dry white wine
4–6 large shallots, finely chopped
bouquet garni
freshly ground black pepper

1 To prepare the mussels, discard any broken mussels and those with open shells that refuse to close when tapped. Under cold running water, scrape the mussel shells with a knife to remove any barnacles and pull out the stringy "beards". Soak the mussels in several changes of cold water for at least 1 hour.

2 In a large heavy flameproof casserole combine the wine, shallots, bouquet garni and plenty of pepper. Bring to the boil over a medium-high heat and cook for about 2 minutes.

3 Add the mussels to the casserole and cook, tightly covered, for about 5 minutes, or until the mussels open, shaking and tossing the pan occasionally. Discard any mussels that do not open.

4 Using a slotted spoon, divide the mussels among warmed soup plates. Tilt the casserole a little and hold for a few seconds to allow any sand to settle to the bottom.

5 Spoon or pour the cooking liquid over the mussels, dividing it evenly, then serve at once.

VARIATION

For Mussels with Cream Sauce (Moules à la Crème), cook as above, but transfer the mussels to a warmed bowl and cover to keep warm. Strain the cooking liquid through a muslin-lined sieve into a large saucepan and boil for 7–10 minutes, until reduced by half. Stir in 90ml/6 tbsp whipping cream and 30ml/2 tbsp chopped parsley, then add the mussels. Cook for about 1 minute more to reheat the mussels.

Lobster Thermidor

INGREDIENTS

Serves 2–4

2 live lobsters (about 675g/1½lb each)
20g/¾oz/1½ tbsp butter
30ml/2 tbsp plain flour
30ml/2 tbsp brandy
125ml/4fl oz/½ cup milk
90ml/6 tbsp whipping cream
15ml/1 tbsp Dijon mustard
lemon juice
salt and white pepper
grated Parmesan cheese, for
  sprinkling
fresh parsley and dill, to garnish

3 Melt the butter in a heavy saucepan over a medium-high heat. Stir in the flour and cook, stirring, until slightly golden. Pour in the brandy and milk, whisking vigorously until smooth, then whisk in the cream and mustard.

4 Push the lobster coral and liver through a sieve into the sauce and whisk to blend. Reduce the heat and simmer gently for 10 minutes until thickened. Season with salt, white pepper and lemon juice.

5 Preheat the grill. Arrange the lobster shells in a gratin dish or shallow flameproof baking dish.

6 Stir the lobster meat into the sauce and divide the mixture evenly among the shells. Sprinkle lightly with Parmesan and grill until golden. Serve garnished with herbs.

1 Bring a large saucepan of salted water to the boil. Put the lobsters into the saucepan head first and cook for 8–10 minutes.

2 Cut the lobsters in half lengthways and discard the dark sac behind the eyes. Pull out the string-like intestine from the tail. Remove the meat from the shells, reserving the coral and liver, then rinse the shells and wipe dry. Cut the meat into bite-size pieces.

Asparagus with Orange Sauce

INGREDIENTS

Serves 6
175g/6oz/¾ cup unsalted butter
3 egg yolks
15ml/1 tbsp cold water
15ml/1 tbsp fresh lemon juice
grated rind and juice of 1 unwaxed
  orange
30–36 thick asparagus spears
salt and cayenne pepper, to taste
shreds of orange rind, to garnish

1 Melt the butter in a small saucepan over a low heat; do not boil. Skim off any foam and set aside.

2 In a heatproof bowl set over a saucepan of barely simmering water or in the top of a double boiler, whisk together the egg yolks, water, lemon juice, 15ml/1 tbsp of the orange juice and season with salt. Place the saucepan or double boiler over a very low heat and whisk constantly until the mixture begins to thicken and the whisk begins to leave tracks on the base of the pan. Remove the pan from the heat.

3 Whisk in the melted butter, drop by drop until the sauce begins to thicken, then pour it in a little more quickly, leaving behind the milky solids at the base of the pan. Whisk in the orange rind and 30–60ml/ 2–4 tbsp of the orange juice. Season with salt and cayenne pepper and keep warm, stirring occasionally.

4 Cut off the tough ends from the asparagus spears and trim to the same length. If peeling, hold each spear gently by the tip, then using a vegetable peeler, strip off the peel and scales from just below the tip to the end. Rinse in cold water.

5 Fill a large deep frying pan or wok with 5cm/2in of water and bring to the boil over a medium-high heat. Add the asparagus and bring back to the boil, then simmer for 4–7 minutes, until just tender.

6 Carefully transfer the spears to a large colander to drain, then lay them on a tea towel and pat dry. Arrange on a large serving platter or individual plates and spoon over a little sauce. Scatter the orange rind over the sauce and serve at once.

COOK'S TIP

This sauce is a kind of hollandaise and needs gentle treatment. If the egg yolk mixture thickens too quickly, remove from the heat and plunge the base of the pan into cold water to prevent the sauce from curdling. The sauce should keep over hot water for 1 hour, but don't let it get too hot.

Stuffed Artichoke Bottoms

INGREDIENTS

Serves 4–6

225g/8oz button mushrooms
15g/½oz/1 tbsp butter
2 shallots, finely chopped
55g/2oz full- or medium-fat soft
   cheese
30ml/2 tbsp chopped walnuts
45ml/3 tbsp grated Gruyère cheese
4 large or 6 small artichoke bottoms
   from cooked artichokes, leaves and
   choke removed, or cooked frozen
   or canned artichoke bottoms
salt and freshly ground black pepper
fresh parsley sprigs, to garnish

3 Preheat the oven to 200°C/
400°F/Gas 6. Lightly grease a
shallow baking tin or dish. In a small
bowl, combine the soft cheese and
mushrooms. Add the walnuts and
half the grated cheese.

4 Divide the mushroom mixture
among the artichoke bottoms
and arrange them in the baking tin
or dish. Sprinkle over the remaining
cheese and bake for 12–15 minutes,
or until bubbly and browned. Serve
hot, garnished with parsley sprigs.

1 Wipe or rinse the mushrooms
and pat dry. Put them in a food
processor fitted with the metal blade
and pulse until finely chopped.

2 Melt the butter in a non-stick
frying pan and cook the shallots
over a medium heat for 2–3 minutes
until just softened. Add the
mushrooms, raise the heat slightly,
and cook for 5–7 minutes until they
have rendered and re-absorbed their
liquid and are almost dry, stirring
frequently. Season to taste.

Ratatouille

INGREDIENTS

Serves 6

2 medium aubergines
60–75ml/4–5 tbsp olive oil
1 large onion, halved and sliced
2 or 3 garlic cloves, finely chopped
1 large red or yellow pepper, seeded
   and cut into thin strips
2 large courgettes, cut into 1cm/½in
   slices
675g/1½lb ripe tomatoes, peeled,
   seeded and chopped, or
400g/14oz/2 cups canned chopped
   tomatoes
5ml/1 tsp dried *herbes de Provence*
salt and freshly ground black pepper

1 Preheat the grill. Cut the aubergines into 2cm/¾in slices, then brush the slices with olive oil on both sides and grill until lightly browned, turning once. Cut the slices into cubes.

VARIATION

To remove the pepper skin and add flavour to the ratatouille, quarter the pepper and grill, skin-side up, until blackened. Enclose in a sturdy polythene bag and set aside until cool. Peel off the skin, then remove the core and seeds and cut into strips. Add to the mixture with the cooked aubergine.

2 Heat 15ml/1 tbsp of the olive oil in a large heavy saucepan or flameproof casserole and cook the onion over a medium-low heat for about 10 minutes until lightly golden, stirring frequently. Add the garlic, pepper and courgettes and cook for a further 10 minutes, stirring occasionally.

3 Add the tomatoes and aubergine cubes, dried herbs and season to taste with salt and pepper. Simmer gently, covered, over a low heat for 20 minutes, stirring occasionally. Uncover and continue cooking for a further 20–25 minutes, stirring occasionally, until all the vegetables are tender and the cooking liquid has thickened slightly. Serve ratatouille hot or at room temperature.

Potatoes Dauphinois

INGREDIENTS

Serves 6

1kg/2¼lb potatoes
900ml/1½ pints/3⅔ cups milk
pinch of freshly grated nutmeg
1 bay leaf
15–30ml/1–2 tbsp butter,
    softened
2 or 3 garlic cloves, very finely
    chopped
45–60ml/3–4 tbsp crème fraîche or
    whipping cream (optional)

1 Preheat the oven to 180°C/
350°F/Gas 4. Cut the potatoes
in half and then into fairly thin slices.

3 Generously butter a 36cm/14in
oval gratin dish or a 2 litre/
3¼ pint/8 cup shallow baking dish
and sprinkle the garlic over the base.

4 Using a slotted spoon, transfer
the potatoes to the gratin or
baking dish. Season the milk to taste,
then pour over enough of the milk
to come just to the surface of the
potatoes, but not cover them. Spoon
a layer of cream over the top, or add
more of the thickened milk to cover.

5 Bake the potatoes in the oven for
about 1 hour, until the milk is
absorbed and the topping has turned
a deep golden brown.

2 Put the potatoes in a large
saucepan and pour over the milk,
adding more to cover if needed. Add
the salt and pepper, nutmeg and the
bay leaf. Bring slowly to the boil over
a medium heat and simmer for about
15 minutes until the potatoes just
start to soften, but are not completely
cooked, and the milk has thickened.

Individual Brioches

These buttery rolls with their distinctive little topknots are delicious with a spoonful or two of jam and a *café au lait*.

INGREDIENTS

Serves 8
7g/¼oz/scant 1 tbsp active dry yeast
15ml/1 tbsp caster sugar
30ml/2 tbsp warm milk
2 eggs
about 200g/7oz/1½ cups plain flour
2.5ml/½ tsp salt
85g/3oz/6 tbsp butter, cut into pieces
1 egg yolk beaten with 10ml/2 tsp
    water, for glazing

1 Lightly butter eight individual brioche tins or muffin tins. Put the yeast and sugar in a small bowl, add the milk and stir until dissolved. Leave to stand for about 5 minutes until foamy, then beat in the eggs.

2 Put the flour and salt into a food processor fitted with the metal blade, then with the machine running, pour in the yeast mixture. Scrape down the sides and continue processing for about 2–3 minutes, or until the dough forms a ball. Add the butter and pulse about 10 times, or until the butter is incorporated.

3 Transfer the dough to a lightly buttered bowl and cover with a cloth. Set aside to rise in a warm place for about 1 hour until doubled in size, then punch down.

4 Set aside one quarter of the dough. Shape the remaining dough into eight balls, using your hands, and put into the prepared tins. Shape the reserved dough into eight smaller balls, then make a depression in the top of each large ball and set a small ball into it for the topknots.

5 Cover the brioches with a cloth and allow to rise in a warm place for about 30 minutes until doubled in size. Preheat the oven to 200°C/400°F/Gas 6.

6 Brush the brioches lightly with the egg glaze and bake them in the oven for 15–18 minutes until golden brown. Transfer to a wire rack and leave to cool before serving.

— COOK'S TIP —

The dough may also be baked in a characteristic large brioche tin with sloping fluted sides. Put about three-quarters of the dough into the tin and set the remainder in a depression in the top, for the topknot. Cover and leave to rise for about 1 hour, then bake in the oven for 35–45 minutes.

Brittany Butter Biscuits

These little biscuits are similar to shortbread, but richer. Like most of the cakes and pastries from the Brittany region of northern France, they are made with the lightly salted butter, *beurre demi-sel*, produced in the Nantes area.

INGREDIENTS

Serves 18–20
6 egg yolks, lightly beaten
15ml/1 tbsp milk
250g/9oz/2 cups plain flour
175g/6oz/⅞ cup caster sugar
200g/7oz/⅞ cup lightly salted
   butter, at room temperature,
   cut into small pieces

1 Preheat the oven to 180°C/ 350°F/Gas 4. Lightly butter a large heavy baking sheet. Mix 15ml/ 1 tbsp of the egg yolks with the milk to make a glaze and set aside.

2 Sift the flour into a large bowl and make a well in the centre. Add the egg yolks, sugar and butter and, using your fingertips, work them together until smooth and creamy.

3 Gradually bring in a little flour at a time from the edge of the well, working it with your fingertips into the centre to form a smooth and slightly sticky dough.

4 With floured hands, pat out the dough to a 8mm/⅜in thickness and cut out rounds using a cutter. Transfer the rounds to a baking sheet, brush each with a little egg glaze, then using the back of a knife, score with lines to create a lattice pattern.

5 Bake the biscuits for 12 minutes until golden. Cool in the tin on a wire rack, then remove the biscuits and leave to cool completely on the rack. Store in an airtight container.

----- COOK'S TIP -----

To make a Brittany Butter Cake, pat the dough into a 23cm/9in loose-based cake tin. Brush with egg glaze and score the lattice pattern on top. Bake for about 45 minutes until firm and golden brown.

Lemon Tart

This tart has a refreshing tangy flavour. You can find it in *pâtisseries* all over France.

INGREDIENTS

Serves 8–10

340g/12oz shortcrust or
 sweet shortcrust pastry
grated rind of 2 or 3 lemons
150ml/¼ pint/⅔ cup freshly
 squeezed lemon juice
100g/3½oz/½ cup caster sugar
60ml/4 tbsp crème fraîche or
 double cream
4 eggs, plus 3 egg yolks
icing sugar, for dusting

1 Preheat the oven to 190°C/
375°F/Gas 5. Roll out the pastry thinly and use to line a 23cm/9in flan tin. Prick the base of the pastry all over with a fork.

2 Line the pastry case with foil and fill with baking beans. Bake for about 15 minutes until the edges are set and dry. Remove the foil and beans and continue baking for a further 5–7 minutes until golden.

3 Place the lemon rind, juice and sugar in a bowl. Beat until combined and then gradually add the crème fraîche or double cream and beat until well blended.

4 Beat in the eggs, one at a time, then beat in the egg yolks and pour the filling into the pastry case. Bake in the oven for 15–20 minutes, until the filling is set. If the pastry begins to brown too much, cover the edges with foil. Leave to cool. Dust with icing sugar before serving.

Apple Charlotte

This dessert takes its name from the straight-sided tin with heart-shaped handles in which it is baked. The buttery bread crust encases a thick, sweet, yet sharp apple purée.

INGREDIENTS

Serves 6

1.2kg/2½lb apples
30ml/2 tbsp water
120g/4oz/⅔ cup soft light brown sugar
2.5ml/½ tsp ground cinnamon
1.5ml/¼ tsp freshly grated nutmeg
7 slices firm textured sliced white bread
70–85g/2½–3oz/5–6 tbsp butter, melted
custard, to serve (optional)

2 Preheat the oven to 200°C/400°F/Gas 6. Trim the crusts from the sliced bread and brush with melted butter on one side. Cut two slices into triangles and use as many triangles as necessary to cover the base of a 1.4 litre/2¼ pint/6 cup charlotte tin or soufflé dish, placing them buttered-sides down and fitting them tightly. Cut fingers of bread the same height as the tin or dish and use them to completely line the sides, overlapping them slightly.

3 Pour the apple purée into the tin or dish. Cover the top with bread slices, buttered-side up, cutting them as necessary to fit.

4 Bake the charlotte in the preheated oven for 20 minutes, then reduce the oven temperature to 180°C/350°F/Gas 4 and bake for 25 minutes until well browned and firm. Leave to stand for 15 minutes. To turn out, place a serving plate over the tin or dish, hold tightly, and invert, then lift off the tin or dish. Serve the charlotte warm, with custard if wished.

COOK'S TIP

If preferred, microwave the apples without water in a large glass dish at HIGH, tightly covered, for 15 minutes. Add the sugar and spices and microwave, uncovered, for about 15 minutes more until very thick, stirring once or twice.

1 Peel, quarter and core the apples. Cut into thick slices and put in a large saucepan with the water. Cook, covered, over a medium-low heat for 5 minutes, and then uncover the pan and cook for 10 minutes until the apples are very soft. Add the sugar, cinnamon and nutmeg and continue cooking for 5 minutes, stirring, until the apples are soft and thick.

Chocolate Profiteroles

INGREDIENTS

Serves 4–6

275g/10oz plain chocolate
120ml/8 tbsp warm water
750ml/1¼ pints/3 cups vanilla
  ice cream

For the profiteroles

110g/3¾oz/¾ cup plain flour
1.5ml/¼ tsp salt
pinch of freshly grated nutmeg
175ml/6fl oz/¾ cup water
85g/3oz/6 tbsp unsalted butter, cut
  into 6 pieces
3 eggs

1 Preheat the oven to 200°C/
400°F/Gas 6 and butter a large
baking sheet.

2 To make the profiteroles, sift
together the flour, salt and
nutmeg. In a saucepan, bring the
water and butter to the boil. Remove
the pan from the heat and add the
dry ingredients all at the same time.
Beat with a wooden spoon for about
1 minute until well blended, then set
the pan over a low heat and cook the
mixture for about 2 minutes, beating
constantly. Remove the saucepan
from the heat.

3 Beat 1 egg in a small bowl and
set aside. Add the remaining
eggs, one at a time, to the flour
mixture, beating well after each.
Add the beaten egg by teaspoonfuls
until the dough is smooth and shiny;
it should pull away and fall slowly
when dropped from a spoon.

4 Using a tablespoon, drop the
dough on to the baking sheet in
12 mounds. Bake in the preheated
oven for 25–30 minutes until the
pastry is well risen and browned.
Turn off the oven and leave the puffs
to cool with the oven door open.

5 To make the sauce, place the
chocolate and water in a double-
boiler or in a bowl placed over a pan
of hot water and leave to melt,
stirring occasionally. Keep the sauce
warm until ready to serve, or reheat,
over simmering water.

6 Split the profiteroles in half and
put a small scoop of vanilla ice
cream in each. Arrange on a serving
platter or divide among individual
plates. Pour the chocolate sauce over
the top and serve at once.

Crème Caramel

Also called *crème renversée*, this is one of the most popular French desserts and is wonderful when freshly made. This is a lighter version of the traditional recipe.

INGREDIENTS

Serves 6–8
250g/9oz/1¼ cups granulated sugar
60ml/4 tbsp water
1 vanilla pod or 10ml/2 tsp vanilla
  essence
425ml/14fl oz/1¾ cups milk
250ml/8fl oz/1 cup whipping cream
5 large eggs
2 egg yolks

1 Put 175g/6oz/⅞ cup of the sugar in a heavy saucepan with the water to moisten. Bring to the boil, swirling the pan to dissolve the sugar. Boil, without stirring, until the syrup turns a dark caramel colour. Pour the caramel immediately into a 1 litre/1¾ pint/4 cup soufflé dish.

2 Swirl the dish to coat with the caramel and set aside. Place the dish in a small roasting tin.

3 Preheat the oven to 170°C/325°F/Gas 3. With a small sharp knife, carefully split the vanilla pod lengthways and scrape the black seeds into a medium saucepan. Add the milk and cream and bring just to the boil over a medium-high heat, stirring frequently. Remove the pan from the heat, cover and set aside for about 15–20 minutes.

4 In a bowl, whisk the eggs and egg yolks with the remaining sugar for 2–3 minutes until smooth and creamy. Whisk in the hot milk and strain the mixture into the caramel-lined dish. Cover with foil.

5 Place the dish in a roasting tin and pour in enough boiling water to come halfway up the sides of the dish. Bake the custard for 40–45 minutes until a knife inserted about 5cm/2in from the edge comes out clean (the custard should be just set). Remove from the roasting tin and cool for ½ hour, then chill overnight.

6 To turn out, carefully run a sharp knife around the edge of the dish to loosen the custard. Cover the dish with a serving plate and, holding them tightly, invert the dish and plate together. Gently lift one edge of the dish, allowing the caramel to run over the sides, then slowly lift off the dish.

Crêpes Suzette

This is one of the best-known French dessert and is easy to do at home. You can make the crêpes in advance, then you will be able to put the dish together quickly at the last minute.

INGREDIENTS

Serves 6

120g/4oz/⅔ cup plain flour
1.5ml/¼ tsp salt
30g/1oz/2 tbsp caster sugar
2 eggs, lightly beaten
250ml/8fl oz/1 cup milk
60ml/4 tbsp water
30ml/2 tbsp orange flower water or
   orange liqueur (optional)
30g/1oz/2 tbsp unsalted butter, melted

For the orange sauce

85g/3oz/6 tbsp unsalted butter
55g/2oz/¼ cup caster sugar
grated rind and juice of 1 large
   unwaxed orange
grated rind and juice of 1 unwaxed
   lemon
150ml/¼ pint/⅔ cup fresh orange juice
60ml/4 tbsp orange liqueur, plus
   more for flaming (optional)
brandy, for flaming (optional)
orange segments, to decorate

1 In a large mixing bowl, sift together the flour, salt and sugar. Make a well in the centre and pour in the beaten eggs. Using an electric whisk, beat the eggs, bringing in the flour from the edge of the bowl a little at a time. Whisk in the milk and water to make a smooth batter.

2 Whisk in the orange flower water or liqueur, if using. Strain the batter into a large jug and set aside for 20–30 minutes. If the batter thickens, add a little milk or water to thin.

3 Heat a 18–20cm/7–8in crêpe pan (preferably non-stick) over a medium heat. Stir the melted butter into the crêpe batter. Brush the hot pan with a little extra melted butter and pour in about 30ml/2 tbsp of batter. Quickly tilt and rotate the pan to cover the base with a thin layer of batter. Cook for about 1 minute until the top is set and the base is golden brown. With a palette knife, lift the edge of the crêpe to check the colour, then carefully turn over the crêpe and cook for 20–30 seconds, until just set. Tip out on to a plate.

4 Continue to cook the crêpes, placing clear film between each crêpe to prevent sticking. (Crêpes can be prepared ahead to this point – wrap and chill until ready to use.)

5 To make the orange sauce, melt the butter in a large frying pan over a medium-low heat, then stir in the sugar, orange and lemon rind and juice, the additional orange juice and the orange liqueur.

6 Place a crêpe in the pan browned-side down, swirling gently to coat with the sauce. Fold the crêpe in half, then in half again to form a triangle and push to the side of the pan. Continue heating and folding the crêpes until all are warm and covered with the sauce.

7 To flame the crêpes, heat 30ml/ 2 tbsp each of orange liqueur and brandy in a pan. Remove the pan from the heat, ignite the liquid with a match and pour over the crêpes.

NORTH AMERICA

New England Clam Chowder

INGREDIENTS

Serves 8

4 dozen clams, scrubbed
125ml/2¼ pints/6 cups water
35g/1¼oz bacon, diced
2 large onions, chopped
1 bay leaf
550g/1¼lb potatoes, cubed
475ml/16fl oz/2 cups milk, warmed
250ml/8fl oz/1 cup single cream
salt and freshly ground black pepper
chopped fresh parsley, to garnish

1 Rinse the clams well in cold
water. Drain. Place them in a deep
saucepan with the water and bring to
the boil. Cover and steam the clams
for 10 minutes, until the shells open.
Remove the pan from the heat.

2 When the clams have cooled
slightly, remove them from their
shells. Discard any clams that have not
opened. Chop the clams coarsely.
Strain the cooking liquid through a
strainer lined with muslin, and reserve
the liquid.

3 In a large heavy saucepan, fry the
bacon until it renders its fat and
begins to brown. Add the onions and
cook over a low heat for 8–10 minutes
until softened.

4 Add the bay leaf, potatoes, and
clam cooking liquid. Stir. Bring
to the boil and cook 5–10 minutes.

5 Stir the chopped clams into the
mixture in the casserole. Continue
to cook until the potatoes are tender,
stirring occasionally. Season well with
salt and pepper.

6 Reduce the heat to low and stir
in the warmed milk and cream.
Simmer gently for 5 minutes more.
Discard the bay leaf, taste and adjust
the seasoning and sprinkle with
chopped fresh parsley to garnish.

--- COOK'S TIP ---

If the clams have been dug, purging will
help to rid them of sand and stomach
contents. Put the clams in a bowl of cold
water, sprinkle with 120ml/½ cup cornmeal and some salt. Stir lightly and let
stand in a cool place for 3–4 hours.

Eggs Benedict

INGREDIENTS

Serves 4

5ml/1 tsp vinegar
4 eggs
2 English muffins or 4 rounds of bread
butter, for spreading
2 slices of cooked ham, 5mm/¼in
   thick, each cut in half crossways
fresh chives, to garnish

For the sauce

3 egg yolks
30ml/2 tbsp fresh lemon juice
1.5ml/¼ tsp salt
115g/4oz/½ cup butter
30ml/2 tbsp single cream
freshly ground black pepper

4 Bring a shallow pan of water to the boil. Stir in the vinegar. Break each egg into a cup, then slide it carefully into the water. Delicately turn the white around the yolk with a slotted spoon. Cook for 3–4 minutes, or until the egg is set to your taste. Remove to kitchen towels to drain. Very gently cut any ragged edges off the eggs with a small knife or scissors.

5 While the eggs are poaching, split and toast the muffins or toast the bread slices. Butter while still warm.

6 Place a piece of ham, which you may brown in butter if you wish, on each muffin half or slice of toast. Trim the ham to fit neatly. Place an egg on each ham-topped muffin. Spoon the warm sauce over the eggs, garnish with chives, and serve.

1 For the sauce, put the egg yolks, lemon juice and salt in the container of a food processor or blender. Blend for 15 seconds.

2 Melt the butter in a saucepan until it bubbles (do not let it brown). With the motor running, pour the hot butter into the food processor or blender through the feed tube in a slow, steady stream. Turn off the machine as soon as all the butter has been added.

3 Scrape the sauce into a double boiler set over simmering water. Stir for 2–3 minutes, until thickened. (If the sauce curdles, whisk in 15ml/ 1 tbsp boiling water.) Stir in the single cream and season with pepper. Keep the sauce warm over the hot water.

Oyster Stew

INGREDIENTS

Serves 6

475ml/16fl oz/2 cups milk
475ml/16fl oz/2 cups single cream
950ml/1⅝ pints/4 cups oysters, shelled,
   drained, liquid reserved
⅛ tsp paprika
25g/1oz/2 tbsp butter
15ml/1 tbsp chopped fresh parsley
salt and freshly ground black pepper
water biscuits, to serve

1 Combine the milk, cream and
oyster liquid in a heavy saucepan.

2 Heat the mixture over a medium
heat until small bubbles appear
around the edge of the pan. Do not
allow the mixture to boil. Reduce the
heat and add the oysters.

3 Cook, stirring occasionally, until
the oysters plump up and their
edges begin to curl. Add the paprika,
and salt and pepper to taste.

4 Meanwhile, warm 6 soup plates or
bowls. Cut the butter into 6 pieces
and put one piece in each bowl.

5 Ladle in the oyster stew and
sprinkle with chopped parsley.
Serve immediately, with water biscuits.

Oysters Rockefeller

INGREDIENTS

Serves 6

450g/1lb fresh spinach leaves
40g/1½oz/½ cup chopped spring
   onions
50g/2oz/½ cup chopped celery
25g/1oz/½ cup chopped fresh parsley
1 garlic clove
2 anchovy fillets
50g/2oz/4 tbsp butter or margarine
30g/1¼oz/½ cup dry breadcrumbs
5ml/1 tsp Worcestershire sauce
10ml/2 tbsp Pernod or anise-flavoured
   liqueur
2.5ml/½ tsp salt
hot pepper sauce
36 oysters in shells

> —— COOK'S TIP ——
>
> To open an oyster, push the point of an
> oyster knife about 1cm/½in into the
> "hinge" of the shell. Push down firmly.
> The lid should pop open.

1 Wash the spinach well. Drain, and
place in a heavy saucepan. Cover
and cook over low heat until just
wilted. Remove from the heat. When
the spinach is cool enough to handle,
squeeze it to remove the excess water.

2 Put the spinach, spring onions,
celery, parsley, garlic and anchovy
fillets in a food processor and process
until finely chopped.

3 Heat the butter or margarine in
a frying pan. Add the spinach
mixture, breadcrumbs, Worcestershire
sauce, liqueur, salt and hot pepper
sauce to taste. Cook for 1–2 minutes.
Cool and refrigerate until ready to use.

4 Preheat the oven to 230°C/450°F/
Gas 8. Line a baking sheet with foil.

5 Open the oysters and remove the
top shells. Arrange them, side by
side, on the foil (it will keep them
upright). Spoon the spinach mixture
over the oysters, smoothing the tops
with the back of the spoon.

6 Bake for about 20 minutes, until
piping hot. Serve immediately,
garnished with lemon rind.

Cape Cod Fried Clams

INGREDIENTS

Serves 4

36 clams, scrubbed
250ml/8fl oz/1 cup buttermilk
1.5ml/¼ tsp celery salt
1.5ml/¼ tsp cayenne pepper
65g/2½oz/1 cup dry breadcrumbs
2 eggs, beaten with 30ml/2 tbsp water
oil, for deep frying
lemon wedges and tartare sauce,
  to serve

1 Rinse the clams. Put in a large pan with 475ml/16fl oz/2 cups water and bring to the boil. Cover and steam until the shells open.

2 Remove the clams from their shells, and cut away the black skins from the necks. Discard any clams that have not opened. Strain the cooking liquid and reserve.

3 Place the buttermilk in a bowl and stir in the celery salt and cayenne pepper. Add the clams and 120ml/ 4fl oz/½ cup of their cooking liquid. Mix well. Leave to stand for 1 hour

4 Heat the oil in a large saucepan to 190°C/375°F/Gas 5. (To test the temperature without a thermometer, drop in a cube of bread; it should turn golden brown in 40 seconds.)

5 Drain the clams and roll them in the breadcrumbs to coat all over. Dip them in the beaten egg and then in the breadcrumbs again.

6 Fry the clams in the hot oil, a few at a time, stirring, until they are crisp and brown, about 2 minutes per batch. Remove with a slotted spoon and drain on kitchen towels.

7 Serve the fried clams hot, accompanied by lemon wedges and tartare sauce.

Maine Lobster Dinner

INGREDIENTS

Serves 4

4 live lobsters, 675g/1½lb each
45ml/3 tbsp chopped mixed fresh
 herbs, such as parsley, chives, and
 tarragon
225g/8oz/1 cup butter, melted and
 kept warm
8 corn on the cob, trimmed
salt and freshly ground black pepper
lemon halves, to serve

1 Preheat the grill. Kill each lobster quickly by inserting the tip of a large kitchen knife between the eyes.

2 Turn each lobster over on to its back and cut it in half, from the head straight down to the tail. Remove and discard the hard sac near the head, and the intestinal vein that runs through the middle of the underside of the tail. All the rest of the lobster meat is edible.

3 Combine the chopped fresh herbs with the melted butter.

4 Place the lobster halves, shell side up, in a foil-lined grill pan or a large roasting pan. (You may have to do this in two batches.) Grill for about 8 minutes. Turn the lobster halves over, brush generously with the herb butter, and grill for 7–8 minutes more.

5 While the lobsters are cooking, drop the corn on the cob into a pan of boiling water and cook for 4–7 minutes, until just tender. Drain.

6 Serve the lobsters and corn hot, with salt, freshly ground black pepper, lemon halves and individual bowls of herb butter. Provide crackers for the claws, extra plates for cobs and shells, finger bowls and lots of napkins.

Lone Star Steak and Potato Dinner

INGREDIENTS

Serves 4

45ml/3 tbsp olive oil
5 large garlic cloves, crushed
5ml/1 tsp coarse black pepper
2.5ml/½ tsp ground allspice
5ml/1 tsp ground cumin
2.5ml/½ tsp chilli powder
10ml/2 tsp dried oregano
15ml/1 tbsp cider vinegar
4 boneless sirloin steaks,
    about 2cm/¾in thick
salt
tomato salsa and freshly cooked corn
    on the cob, to serve

For the potatoes

120ml/4fl oz/¼ cup vegetable oil
1 onion, chopped
5ml/1 tsp salt
900g/2lb potatoes, cooked and cubed
30–75ml/2–5 tbsp chopped canned
    green chillies

1 Heat the olive oil in a heavy frying pan. When hot, add the garlic and cook for about 3 minutes until tender and just brown, stirring often; do not let the garlic burn.

2 Transfer the garlic and oil to a shallow dish large enough to hold the steaks in a single layer.

3 Add the pepper, spices, herbs, and vinegar to the garlic and stir to blend thoroughly. If necessary, add just enough water to obtain a moderately thick paste.

4 Add the steaks to the dish and turn to coat evenly on both sides with the spice mixture. Cover and let stand for 2 hours, or refrigerate the steaks overnight. (Bring them back to room temperature before cooking.)

COOK'S TIP

The steaks are ideal for cooking on a barbecue. Prepare the fire, and when the coals are glowing red and covered with grey ash, spread the steaks in a single layer. Cook in the centre of an oiled grill set about 13cm/5in above the coals for 1 minute each side to char them. Move the steaks away from the centre of the grill and cook for 10–12 minutes more, for medium-rare, turning once.

5 For the potatoes, heat the oil in a large frying pan. Add the onion and salt. Cook over medium heat for about 5 minutes, until softened. Add the potatoes and chillies. Cook, stirring occasionally, for 15–20 minutes until well browned.

6 Season the steaks on both sides with salt to taste. Heat a ridged grill pan. When hot, add the steaks and cook, turning once, until done to taste. Allow about 2 minutes on each side for medium-rare, and 3–4 minutes for well-done.

7 If necessary, briefly reheat the potatoes. Serve immediately, with the tomato salsa and corn, if using.

Idaho Beef Stew

INGREDIENTS

Serves 6

60ml/4 tbsp vegetable oil
2 onions, chopped
4 large carrots, thickly sliced
1.5kg/3lb braising steak, cubed
20g/¾oz/3 tbsp flour
750ml/1¼ pints/3 cups unsalted beef
    stock
250ml/8fl oz/1 cup strong black
    coffee
10ml/2 tsp dried oregano
1 bay leaf
115g/4oz fresh or frozen peas
salt and freshly ground black pepper
mashed potatoes, to serve

1 Heat 30ml/2 tbsp of the oil in a large saucepan. Add the onions and carrots and cook over a medium heat for about 8 minutes, until lightly browned. Remove the vegetables with a slotted spoon, transfer them to a plate or dish, and reserve.

2 Add another 15ml/1 tbsp of oil to the saucepan and then add the beef cubes. Increase the heat to medium-high and cook until browned all over. If necessary, fry the meat in batches to ensure it browns evenly. Season.

3 Return the vegetables to the saucepan. Add the flour and the remaining oil. Cook for 1 minute, stirring constantly. Add the stock, coffee, oregano, and bay leaf. Bring to the boil and cook, stirring often, until thickened. Reduce the heat to very low, then cover the saucepan and allow the stew to simmer gently for 1–1½ hours until the beef is tender.

4 Add the peas and simmer for a further 5–10 minutes. Discard the bay leaf and adjust the seasoning. Serve hot, with mashed potatoes.

Red Flannel Hash with Corned Beef

INGREDIENTS

Serves 4

6 streaky bacon rashers
1 onion, finely chopped
450g/1lb potatoes, cooked and cubed
225g/8oz corned beef, chopped
225g/8oz cooked beetroot (not in
   vinegar), diced
50ml/2fl oz/¼ cup single cream
45ml/3 tbsp finely chopped fresh
   parsley
salt and freshly ground black pepper

1 Cook the bacon until golden and crisp. Remove. Pour off all but 30ml/2 tbsp of the bacon fat into a small jug, reserving the rest for later.

2 Slice the bacon and place in a bowl. Cook the onion gently in the bacon fat. Remove the onion from the pan and add to the bacon.

3 Mix in the potatoes, corned beef, beetroot, cream and the chopped parsley. Season with salt and pepper and mix well. Heat 60ml/4 tbsp of the reserved bacon fat, or other fat, in the frying pan. Add the hash mixture, spreading it evenly with a fish slice. Cook over a low heat until the base is brown. Flip the hash out on to a plate.

4 Gently slide the hash back into the frying pan and cook on the other side until lightly browned. Serve the hash immediately.

Country Meat Loaf

INGREDIENTS

Serves 6

25g/1oz/2 tbsp butter
½ onion, finely chopped
2 garlic cloves, finely chopped
2 celery sticks, finely chopped
450g/1lb lean minced beef
225g/8oz minced veal
225g/8oz lean minced pork
2 eggs
50g/2oz/1 cup fresh white
 breadcrumbs
90ml/6 tbsp chopped fresh parsley
30ml/2 tbsp chopped fresh basil
2.5ml/½ tsp fresh or dried thyme
 leaves
30ml/2 tbsp Worcestershire sauce
45ml/3 tbsp chilli sauce
6 streaky bacon rashers
salt and freshly ground black pepper
fresh basil and parsley sprigs, to garnish

1 Preheat the oven to 180°C/350°F/
 Gas 4.

2 Melt the butter. Add the onion,
 garlic and celery and cook until
softened. Remove the pan from the
heat and allow to cool slightly.

3 In a large mixing bowl, combine
 the onion, garlic, and celery with
all the other ingredients except the
bacon. Mix together lightly, using a
fork or your fingers. Do not overwork
or the meat loaf will be too compact.

4 Form the meat mixture into an
 oval loaf shape. Carefully transfer
it to a greased baking tin.

5 Lay the bacon rashers across the
 meat loaf. Bake in the oven for
1¼ hours, basting occasionally with the
meat juices and bacon fat in the tin.

6 Remove from the oven and drain
 off the fat. Let the meat loaf stand
for 10 minutes before serving.

San Antonio Tortilla

INGREDIENTS

Serves 4

15ml/1 tbsp vegetable oil
½ onion, sliced
1 small green pepper, seeded and sliced
1 garlic clove, finely chopped
1 tomato, chopped
6 stoned black olives, chopped
275g/10oz potatoes, cooked and sliced
50g/2oz sliced chorizo, cut into strips
fresh green chilli, seeded and chopped
50g/2oz/½ cup grated Cheddar cheese
6 large eggs
45ml/3 tbsp milk
1.5ml/¼ tsp ground cumin
1.5ml/¼ tsp dried oregano
1.5ml/¼ tsp paprika
salt and freshly ground black pepper

1 Preheat the oven to 190°C/ 375°F/Gas 5. Lightly grease a 23cm/9in round cake tin.

2 Heat the oil in a non-stick frying pan. Add the onion, pepper and garlic and cook over a medium heat for 5–8 minutes, until softened.

3 Transfer the vegetables to the prepared cake tin. Add the tomato, olives, potatoes, chorizo and chilli. Sprinkle with the grated Cheddar cheese and set aside.

4 Place the eggs and milk in a bowl and whisk until frothy. Add the cumin, oregano, paprika, salt and pepper to taste. Whisk to blend.

5 Pour the egg mixture on to the vegetables, tilting the tin so that the egg mixture spreads it evenly.

6 Bake for 30 minutes, until set and golden. Serve hot or cold.

Baked Pork Loin with Red Cabbage and Apples

INGREDIENTS

Serves 8

2kg/4½lb boned loin of pork
2.5ml/½ tsp ground ginger
50g/2oz/4 tbsp butter, melted
350ml/12fl oz/1½ cups sweet apple cider or dry white wine
salt and freshly ground black pepper

For the cabbage

65g/2½oz/3 tbsp butter or margarine
1 large onion, finely sliced
5ml/1 tsp caraway seeds
3 tart eating apples, quartered, cored and sliced
15ml/1 tbsp soft dark brown sugar
1.5kg/3½lb red cabbage, shredded
90ml/6 tbsp cider vinegar, or 50ml/2fl oz/¼ cup wine vinegar and 30ml/2 tbsp water
120ml/4fl oz/½ cup beef stock
120ml/4fl oz/½ cup sweet apple cider or white wine
5ml/½ tsp salt
1.25ml/¼ tsp fresh thyme leaves

1 Preheat the oven to 180°C/350°F/Gas 4.

2 Trim any excess fat from the pork. Tie it into a neat shape, if necessary. Sprinkle with the ground ginger, salt and pepper.

3 Place the pork, fat side down, in a large casserole. Cook over medium heat, turning frequently, for about 15 minutes, until browned on all sides. Add a little of the melted butter if the roast starts to stick.

4 Cover the casserole, transfer to the oven, and roast for 1 hour, basting frequently with the meat juices, melted butter, and cider or wine.

5 Meanwhile, prepare the cabbage. Melt the butter or margarine in a large frying pan and add the onion and caraway seeds. Cook over a low heat for 8–10 minutes, until softened. Stir in the apple slices and brown sugar. Cover the pan and cook for 4–5 minutes more.

6 Stir in the cabbage and add the vinegar. Cover and cook for 10 minutes. Pour in the stock and cider or wine, add the salt and thyme leaves, and stir well. Cover again and cook over medium-low heat for 30 minutes.

7 When the pork has cooked for 1 hour, remove from the oven. Transfer the pork to a plate and keep warm. Tilt the casserole and discard all but 30ml/2 tbsp of the fat.

8 Transfer the cabbage mixture from the frying pan to the casserole and stir well to mix the cabbage with the roasting juices.

9 Place the pork on the cabbage, cover and return to the oven. Cook for another hour, basting occasionally. Serve garnished with fresh thyme.

San Francisco Chicken Wings

INGREDIENTS

Serves 4

75ml/3fl oz/⅓ cup soy sauce
15ml/1 tbsp soft brown sugar
15ml/1 tbsp rice vinegar
30ml/2 tbsp dry sherry wine
juice of 1 orange
5cm/2in strip of orange peel
1 star anise
5ml/1 tsp cornstarch
50ml/2fl oz/¼ cup water
1 tbsp/¹⁄₁₆ cup chopped fresh gingerroot
Oriental chilli-garlic sauce, to taste
1.5kg/3½lb chicken wings, tips
  removed

1 Preheat the oven to 200°C/400°F/
Gas 6.

2 Combine the soy sauce, brown
sugar, vinegar, sherry, orange juice
and peel and star anise in a saucepan.
Bring to the boil over a medium heat.

3 Combine the cornstarch and
water in a small bowl and stir
until blended. Add to the boiling soy
sauce mixture, stirring well. Boil for
1 minute more, stirring constantly.

4 Remove the soy sauce mixture
from the heat and stir in the
chopped ginger and chilli-garlic sauce.

5 Arrange the chicken wings, in one
layer, in a large baking dish. Pour
over the soy sauce mixture and stir to
coat the wings evenly. Bake for 30–40
minutes, until tender and browned,
basting occasionally. Serve the chicken
wings hot or warm.

Galveston Chicken

INGREDIENTS

Serves 4

1.5kg/3½lb chicken
juice of 1 lemon
4 garlic cloves, finely chopped
15ml/1 tbsp cayenne pepper
15ml/1 tbsp paprika
15ml/1 tbsp dried oregano
10ml/2 tsp olive oil
fresh coriander sprigs, to garnish
salt and freshly ground black pepper
mixed sweet peppers, to serve

— COOK'S TIP —

Roasting chicken in an oven that has not been preheated produces a particularly crispy skin.

1 With a sharp knife or poultry shears, remove the backbone from the chicken. Turn it breast side up. With the heel of your hand, press down to break the breastbone, and open the chicken flat like a book. Insert a skewer through the chicken, at the thighs, to keep it flat.

2 Place the chicken in a shallow dish and pour over the lemon juice.

3 In a small bowl, combine the garlic, cayenne, paprika, oregano, oil and pepper. Mix well. Rub evenly over the surface of the chicken.

4 Cover and leave to marinate for 2–3 hours at room temperature, or refrigerate overnight and return to room temperature before roasting.

5 Season the chicken with salt on both sides. Transfer it to a shallow roasting tin, skin side up.

6 Put the tin in a cold oven and set the temperature to 200°C/400°F/Gas 6. Roast for about 1 hour, until the chicken is done, turning occasionally and basting with the pan juices. To test whether the chicken is cooked, prick the thickest part of the flesh with a skewer: the juices that run out should be clear. Garnish with sprigs of fresh coriander and serve hot, with mixed sweet peppers.

Macaroni and Blue Cheese

INGREDIENTS

Serves 6

450g/1lb macaroni
1.2 litres/2 pints/5 cups milk
50g/2oz/4 tbsp butter
75g/3oz/6 tbsp plain flour
225g/8oz blue Stilton cheese,
  crumbled
salt and freshly ground black pepper

1 Preheat the oven to 180°C/350°F/
Gas 4. Grease a 33 x 23cm /
13 x 9in ovenproof dish.

2 Bring a saucepan of salted water to
the boil. Add the macaroni and
cook for 10–12 minutes, until just
tender. Drain and rinse under cold
running water. Place in a large bowl
and set aside.

3 In another saucepan, bring the
milk to the boil and set aside.

4 Melt the butter in a heavy-based
saucepan over low heat. Whisk
in the flour and cook for 5 minutes,
whisking constantly and taking care
not to let the mixture become brown.

5 Remove the pan from the heat
and whisk the hot milk into the
butter and flour mixture. When the
mixture is smoothly blended, return
to a medium heat and continue
cooking, whisking constantly for
about 5 minutes, until the sauce is
thick. Add salt and pepper to taste.

6 Stir the sauce into the macaroni.
Add three-quarters of the blue
cheese and stir well. Transfer the
macaroni mixture to the prepared
ovenproof dish and spread in an
even layer.

7 Sprinkle the remaining cheese
evenly over the surface. Bake for
about 25 minutes until bubbling hot.

8 Preheat the grill and brown the
top of the macaroni and cheese.
Serve immediately, sprinkled with
freshly ground black pepper.

Milwaukee Onion Tart

INGREDIENTS

Serves 6

25g/1oz/2 tbsp olive oil
2 onions, thinly sliced
2.5ml/½ tsp fresh or dried thyme
    leaves
1 egg
120ml/4fl oz/½ cup soured cream or
    natural yogurt
10ml/2 tsp poppy seeds
1.5ml/¼ tsp ground mace or nutmeg
salt and freshly ground black pepper

For the pastry base

115g/4 oz/1 cup plain flour
6.5ml/1¼ tsp baking powder
2.5ml/½ tsp salt
40g/1½oz/3 tbsp cold butter or white
    cooking fat
90ml/6 tbsp milk

1 Heat the butter or oil in a medium-sized frying pan. Add the onions and cook over a low heat for 10–12 minutes, until soft and golden. Add the thyme and season with salt and pepper. Remove the pan from the heat and leave to cool.

2 Preheat the oven to 220°C/425°F/ Gas 7.

3 To make the pastry base, sift the flour, baking powder and salt into a bowl. Dice the butter or cooking fat, add to the dry ingredients and rub in with your fingertips. Add the milk and stir in lightly with a wooden spoon to make a soft dough.

4 Turn the dough out on to a floured work surface and knead lightly until smooth.

5 Lightly grease a 20cm/8in baking tin that is at least 5cm/2in deep. Pat out the dough into a round of the same size and press it into the base of the tin. Cover with the onions.

6 Beat together the egg and soured cream or yogurt and spread evenly over the onions. Sprinkle with the poppy seeds and mace or nutmeg. Bake for 25–30 minutes, until the egg topping is puffed and golden.

7 Leave to cool in the tin for 10 minutes. Slip a knife between the tart and the pan to loosen, then turn out on to a plate. Cut the tart into wedges and serve warm.

Boston Baked Beans

INGREDIENTS

Serves 8
675g/1½lb/3 cups dried soya beans
1 bay leaf
4 cloves
2 onions
175g/6oz/½ cup molasses or black
   treacle
165g/5½oz/¾ cup dark brown sugar
15ml/1 tbsp Dijon mustard
5ml/1 tsp salt
5ml/1 tsp freshly ground black pepper
250ml/8fl oz/1 cup boiling water
225g/8oz piece salt pork

1 Rinse the beans under cold running water. Drain and place in a large bowl. Cover with cold water and let soak overnight.

2 Drain and rinse the beans. Place in a large pan with the bay leaf and cover with fresh cold water. Boil rapidly for 10 minutes.

3 Reduce the heat and simmer for 1½–2 hours, until tender. Preheat the oven to 140°C/275°F/Gas 1.

4 Put the beans in a large casserole. Stick 2 cloves in each of the onions and add them to the pot. In a mixing bowl, combine the molasses, sugar, mustard, salt and pepper. Add the boiling water and stir to blend. Pour this mixture over the beans. Add more water if necessary so the beans are almost covered with liquid.

5 Blanch the piece of salt pork in boiling water for 3 minutes. Drain. Score the rind in deep 1cm/⅓in cuts. Add the salt pork to the casserole and push down just below the surface of the beans, skin-side up.

6 Cover the casserole and bake in the centre of the preheated oven for 4½–5 hours. Uncover for the last half hour, so the pork rind becomes brown and crisp. Slice or shred the pork and serve hot.

Harvard Beets

INGREDIENTS

Serves 6
5 beetroot, cooked (about 675g/1½lb)
50g/2oz/⅓ cup sugar
15ml/1 tbsp cornflour
2.5ml/½ tsp salt
50ml/2fl oz/¼ cup cider or white wine
   vinegar
120ml/4fl oz/½ cup beetroot cooking
   liquid or water
25g/1oz/2 tbsp butter or margarine
fresh parsley sprigs, to garnish

1 Peel the beetroot and cut them into thick slices. Set aside.

2 Place the sugar, cornflour, salt, vinegar and beetroot liquid or water in the top of a double boiler and stir until smooth. Cook over a pan of hot water, stirring constantly, until the mixture is smooth and clear.

3 Add the beetroot and butter or margarine. Continue to cook, stirring occasionally, until the beetroot are heated through. Serve hot.

Coleslaw

INGREDIENTS

Serves 8

250ml/8fl oz/1 cup mayonnaise
120ml/4fl oz/½ cup white wine
  vinegar
15ml/1 tbsp Dijon mustard
10ml/2 tsp caster sugar
15ml/1 tbsp caraway seeds
1 white cabbage, finely sliced
2 carrots, grated
1 small onion, finely sliced
salt and freshly ground black pepper
fresh parsley sprigs, to garnish

1 Mix together the mayonnaise, vinegar, mustard, sugar and caraway seeds. Season to taste.

2 Place the cabbage, carrots and sliced onion in a large bowl.

3 Add the dressing to the vegetables and mix well. Taste for seasoning. Cover and refrigerate for 1–2 hours. The cabbage will become more tender the longer it marinates. Stir well, and serve with fresh parsley sprigs.

Pennsylvania Dutch Fried Tomatoes

INGREDIENTS

Serves 4

225g/8oz large firm red tomatoes
40g/1½oz/3 tbsp plain flour
50g/2oz/4 tbsp butter or bacon
  dripping
sugar, to taste
4 slices of hot buttered toast
175ml/6fl oz/¾ cup single cream
salt and freshly ground black pepper
fresh parsley sprigs

1 Slice the tomatoes into 1cm/½in rounds and coat lightly with flour.

2 Heat the butter or bacon dripping in a frying pan. When it is hot, add the tomato slices and cook until browned. Turn them once, and season generously with salt and pepper.

3 If the tomatoes are green, sprinkle each slice with a little sugar. Cook for a further 3–4 minutes, until the other side is well browned. Divide the tomatoes among the slices of toast and keep hot.

4 Pour the single cream into the hot frying pan and bring to a simmer. Cook 1–2 minutes, stirring to mix in the cooking juices. Spoon the sauce over the tomatoes, and serve immediately, garnished with parsley.

——— VARIATION ———

For Fried Tomatoes with Ham, top the toast with ham slices before covering with the tomatoes.

Sweet Potato Biscuits

INGREDIENTS

Makes about 24

150g/5oz/1¼ cups plain flour
20ml/4 tsp baking powder
5ml/1 tsp salt
15g/½oz/1 tbsp brown sugar
150g/5oz/¾ cup mashed cooked
  sweet potatoes
150ml/¼ pint/⅔ cup milk
50g/2oz/4 tbsp butter or margarine,
  melted

1 Preheat the oven to 230°C/450°F/
Gas 8.

2 Sift the plain flour, baking powder,
and salt into a mixing bowl. Add
the sugar and stir well to combine.

4 Stir the dry ingredients into the
sweet potato mixture to make a
dough. Turn on to a lightly floured
surface and knead lightly for 1–2
minutes, until soft and pliable.

3 In a separate bowl, mix the sweet
potatoes with the milk and melted
butter or margarine. Beat well until
evenly blended.

5 Roll or pat out the dough to a
1cm/½in thickness. Cut out rounds
with a biscuit cutter.

6 Arrange the rounds on a greased
baking sheet. Bake for 15 minutes,
until puffed and lightly golden. Serve
the biscuits warm.

Boston Brown Bread

INGREDIENTS

Makes 2 small loaves

15g/½oz/1 tbsp butter, at room
  temperature
115g/4oz/1 cup yellow cornmeal
115g/4oz/1 cup wholemeal flour
115g/4oz/1 cup rye flour
10ml/2 tsp baking soda
5ml/1 tsp salt
500ml/16fl oz/2 cups buttermilk, at
  room temperature
175ml/8fl oz/¾ cup black treacle
150g/5oz/1 cup chopped raisins
butter or cream cheese, to serve

1 Grease two 450g/1lb food cans,
or two 900ml/1½ pint pudding
moulds, with the soft butter.

2 Sift all the dry ingredients together
into a large bowl. Tip in any bran
from the wholemeal flour. Stir well.

3 In a separate bowl, combine the
buttermilk, black treacle and
raisins. Add to the dry ingredients
and mix well.

4 Pour the batter into the prepared
moulds, filling them two-thirds
full. Cover the tops with buttered foil,
and tie or tape it down so that the
rising bread cannot push off the foil lid.

5 Set the moulds on a rack in a
large saucepan with a tight-fitting
lid. Pour in enough warm water to
come halfway up the sides of the
moulds. Cover the pan, bring to the
boil, and steam for 2½ hours. Check
occasionally that the water has not
boiled dry, adding more if necessary.

6 Turn the bread out on to a
warmed serving dish. Slice and
serve with butter or cream cheese.

Marbled Brownies

INGREDIENTS

Makes 24

225g/8oz plain chocolate
85g/3oz/6tbsp butter
4 eggs
300g/10½oz/1½ cups sugar
140g/5oz/1¼ cups plain flour
2.5ml/½ tsp salt
5ml/1 tsp baking powder
10ml/2 tsp vanilla essence
115g/4oz/1 cup walnuts, chopped
butter, for greasing

For the plain mixture

55g/2oz/4tbsp butter, at room
   temperature
170g/6oz/¾ cup cream cheese
100g/3½oz/½ cup sugar
2 eggs
30g/1oz/¼ cup plain flour
5ml/1 tsp vanilla essence

1 Preheat the oven to 180°C/350°F/
Gas 4. Line a 33 x 23cm/13 x 9in
tin with greaseproof paper and grease
it with butter.

2 Melt the chocolate and butter over
a gentle heat, stirring constantly.
Set aside to cool.

3 Meanwhile, beat the eggs until
light and fluffy. Gradually add
the sugar and continue to beat until
blended. Sift over the flour, salt and
baking powder and fold to combine.

4 Stir in the cooled chocolate
mixture. Add the vanilla essence
and walnuts. Reserve 450ml/16fl oz
of the chocolate mixture.

5 For the plain mixture, cream the
butter and cream cheese with an
electric mixer.

6 Add the sugar and continue to
beat until blended. Beat in
the eggs, flour and vanilla essence.

7 Spread the unmeasured chocolate
mixture in the tin. Pour over the
plain mixture. Drop spoonfuls of the
reserved chocolate mixture on top.

8 With a metal palette knife, swirl
the mixtures to marble. Do not
blend completely. Bake for 35–40
minutes, until just set. Turn out when
cool and cut into squares for serving.

Apple and Cranberry Muffins

INGREDIENTS

Makes 12

55g/2oz/4tbsp butter or margarine
1 egg
100g/3½oz/½ cup sugar
grated rind of 1 large orange
125ml/4fl oz/½ cup freshly squeezed
    orange juice
140g/5oz/1¼ cups plain flour
5ml/1 tsp baking powder
2.5ml/½ tsp bicarbonate of soda
5ml/1 tsp ground cinnamon
2.5ml/½ tsp grated nutmeg
2.5ml/½ tsp ground allspice
1.5ml/¼ tsp ground ginger
1.5ml/¼ tsp salt
1–2 dessert apples
170g/6oz/1½ cups cranberries
55g/2oz/½ cup walnuts, chopped
icing sugar, for dusting

1 Preheat the oven to 180°C/350°F/
Gas 4. Grease a 12 cup muffin tin
or use paper cases.

2 Place the butter or margarine in
a small saucepan and set over a
gentle heat to melt. Set aside to cool.

3 Place the egg in a mixing bowl
and whisk lightly. Add the melted
butter or margarine and whisk to
combine. Add the sugar, orange rind
and juice to the bowl. Whisk to blend,
then set the egg mixture aside.

4 In a separate bowl, sift together the
flour, baking powder, bicarbonate
of soda, cinnamon, nutmeg, allspice,
ginger and salt. Set aside.

5 Quarter, core and peel the apples.
With a sharp knife, chop coarsely.

6 Make a well in the dry ingredients
and pour in the egg mixture. Stir
with a spoon until just blended.

7 Add the apples, cranberries and
walnuts and stir to blend.

8 Fill the cups three-quarters full and
bake for 25–30 minutes, until the
tops spring back when touched lightly.
Transfer to a wire rack and allow to
cool. Dust lightly with icing sugar, if
liked. Store in an airtight container
until ready to serve.

Shaker Summer Pudding

INGREDIENTS

Serves 6–8

1 sliced white loaf, 1–2 days old
675g/1½lb fresh redcurrants
50g/2oz/¼ cup plus 25g/1oz/2 tbsp
   sugar
50ml/2fl oz/¼ cup water
675g/1½lb mixed berries such as
   raspberries, blueberries and
   blackberries
juice of ½ lemon
whipped cream, to serve

1 Trim the crusts from the bread
slices. Cut a round of bread to
fit in the bottom of a 1.5 litre/2½ pint/
6 cup pudding mould or mixing bowl.
Line the mould with the bread slices,
cutting them to fit and overlapping
them slightly. Reserve enough bread
slices to cover the top of the mould.

2 Combine the redcurrants with
50g/2oz/¼ cup of the sugar and
the water in a non-reactive saucepan.
Heat gently, crushing the berries to
help the juices to flow. When the sugar
has dissolved, remove from the heat.

3 Tip the currant mixture into a
food processor and process until
smooth. Press through a fine-mesh
nylon sieve set over a bowl. Discard
the fruit pulp left in the sieve.

4 Put the berries in a bowl with the
remaining sugar and the lemon
juice. Stir well.

5 One at a time, remove the cut
bread pieces from the mould and
dip in the redcurrant purée. Replace
to line the mould evenly.

6 Spoon the berries into the lined
mould, pressing them down
evenly. Top with the reserved cut
bread slices, which have been dipped
in the currant purée.

7 Cover the mould with clear film.
Set a small plate, just big enough
to fit inside the rim of the mould, on
top of the pudding. Weigh it down
with cans of food. Refrigerate for
8–24 hours.

8 To unmould, remove the weights,
plate and clear film. Run a knife
between the mould and the pudding
to loosen it. Turn out on to a serving
plate. Serve in thick wedges, with
whipped cream if liked.

Apple Maple Dumplings

INGREDIENTS

Serves 8

500g/1¼lb/4½ cups plain flour
2.5ml/½ tsp salt
350g/12oz/1½ cups butter
175–250ml/6–8fl oz/¾–1 cup iced
  water
8 firm cooking apples
1 egg white
130g/4½oz/⅔ cup caster sugar
45ml/3 tbsp whipping cream, plus
  extra to serve
2.5ml/½ tsp vanilla essence
12oz/1 cup maple syrup

1 Preheat the oven to 220°C/425°F/
Gas 7.

2 Sift the flour and salt into a large
bowl. Rub in the butter until
the mixture resembles breadcrumbs.
Sprinkle with about 175ml/6fl oz/
¾ cup water and mix until the dough
holds together, adding a little more
water if necessary. Gather into a ball.
Place the dough in a sealed plastic bag
and chill for 20 minutes.

3 Peel the apples. Remove the
cores, cutting from the stem end,
without cutting through the base.

4 Roll out the pastry thinly. Cut
squares almost large enough to
enclose the apples, then brush the
squares with egg white. Set an apple
in the centre of each pastry square.

5 Combine the sugar, cream, and
vanilla essence in a bowl. Spoon
some into the hollow of each apple.

6 Pull the points of the pastry
squares up around the apples and
moisten the edges where they overlap.
Mould the dough around the apples,
pleating the top neatly. Do not cover
the centre hollows. Crimp the edges
tightly to seal, if you prefer.

7 Set the apples in a greased
baking dish, at least 2cm/¾in
apart. Bake for 30 minutes. Lower
the oven temperature to 180C°/350°F/
Gas 4 and continue baking for another
20 minutes, until the pastry is golden
brown and the apples are tender.

8 Transfer the dumplings to a
serving dish. Mix the maple syrup
with the juices in the baking dish and
drizzle over the dumplings.

9 Serve the dumplings piping hot,
with whipped cream.

Huckleberry Coffee Cake

INGREDIENTS

Serves 10
225g/8oz/2 cups flour
15ml/1 tbsp baking powder
5ml/1 tsp salt
75g/3oz/⅓ cup butter or margarine, at
   room temperature
150g/5oz/¾ cup granulated sugar
1 egg
250ml/8fl oz/1 cup milk
2.5ml/½ tsp grated lemon rind
225g/8oz/2 cups fresh or frozen
   huckleberries, well drained
100g/4oz/1 cup icing sugar
30ml/2 tbsp fresh lemon juice

1 Preheat the oven to 180°C/350°F/
   Gas 4.

2 Sift the flour with the baking
   powder and salt.

3 In a large bowl, beat the butter
   with the granulated sugar until light
and fluffy. Beat in the egg and milk.
Fold in the flour mixture until blended
to a batter. Mix in the lemon rind.

4 Spread half of the batter in a
   greased 33 x 23 x 5cm/13 x 9 x 2in
baking dish. Sprinkle with 115g/4oz/
1 cup of the berries. Top with the
remaining batter and sprinkle with
the rest of the berries. Bake for about
35 minutes, until a skewer inserted in
the centre comes out clean.

5 Mix the icing sugar gradually into
   the lemon juice to make a smooth
glaze with a pourable consistency.
Drizzle the glaze over the top of the
warm cake and allow it to set before
serving, warm or at room temperature.

Northwestern Brown Betty

INGREDIENTS

Serves 6

1kg/2¼lb pears (about 8)
50ml/2fl oz/¼ cup lemon juice
6oz/175g/3 cups brioche breadcrumbs
75g/3oz/6 tbsp butter, melted
75g/3oz/⅔ cup dried cherries
75g/3oz/⅔ cup chopped hazelnuts
115g/4oz/½ cup brown sugar, firmly
    packed
15–25g/½–1oz/1–2 tbsp butter, cubed
whipped cream, to serve

1 Preheat the oven to 190°C/375°F/
    Gas 5. Grease an 20cm/8in square
cake tin.

2 Peel, core and dice the pears.
    Sprinkle them with the lemon
juice to prevent discoloration.

3 Combine the breadcrumbs and
    melted butter in a bowl. Spread
one-third of the crumb mixture on the
bottom of the prepared cake tin.

4 Top with half of the pears.
    Sprinkle over half of the dried
cherries, half of the hazelnuts and half
of the sugar. Repeat the layers, then
finish with a layer of crumb mixture.

5 Dot with the pieces of butter.
    Bake for 30–35 minutes, until
golden. Serve piping hot, with
whipped cream if liked.

CAJUN & CREOLE

Corn and Crab Bisque

A Louisiana classic, and certainly luxurious enough for a dinner party, which makes it worth the trouble. The crab shells together with the corn cobs, from which the kernels are stripped, make a fine-flavoured stock.

SERVES 8

INGREDIENTS

4 large cobs sweetcorn
2 bay leaves
salt, freshly ground black and white
  pepper, and cayenne
1 cooked crab weighing about 1 kg/2¼ lb
25 g/1 oz/2 tbsp butter
2 tbsp plain flour
300 ml/10 fl oz/1¼ cups whipping cream
6 spring onions, shredded
hot French bread or grissini bread sticks
  to serve

I Pull away the husks and silk from the cobs of corn and strip off the kernels (see step 1 of Sweetcorn Cakes with Grilled Tomatoes, for the method).

2 Keep the kernels on one side and put the stripped cobs into a deep saucepan or flameproof casserole with 3 litres/5 pints/12½ cups cold water, the bay leaves and 2 tsp salt. Bring to the boil and leave to simmer while you prepare the crab.

3 Pull away the two flaps between the big claws of the crab, stand it on its 'nose' where the flaps were and bang down firmly with the heel of your hand on the rounded end.

4 Separate the crab from its top shell, keeping the shell.

5 Push out the crab's mouth and its abdominal sac immediately below the mouth, and discard.

6 Pull away the feathery gills surrounding the central chamber and discard. Scrape out all the semi-liquid brown meat from the shell and keep it.

7 Crack the claws in as many places as necessary to extract all the white meat. Pick out the white meat from the fragile cavities in the central body of the crab. Set aside all the crabmeat, brown and white. Put the spidery legs, back shell and all the other pieces of shell into the pan with the corn cobs. Simmer for a further 15 minutes, then strain the stock into a clean pan and boil hard to reduce to 2 litres/3½ pints/9 cups.

8 Meanwhile melt the butter in a small pan and sprinkle in the flour. Stir constantly over a low heat until the roux is the colour of rich cream.

9 Off the heat, slowly stir in 250 ml/8 fl oz/1 cup of the stock. Return to the heat and stir until it thickens, then stir this thickened mixture into the pot of strained stock.

10 Add the corn kernels, return to the boil and simmer for 5 minutes.

11 Add the crabmeat, cream and spring onions and season with salt, black or white pepper (or a bit of both) and cayenne. Return to the boil and simmer for a further 2 minutes. Serve with hot French bread or grissini bread sticks.

COOK'S TIP

You can, if you prefer, ask your fish-monger to remove all the inedible bits of the crab – the mouth, stomach sac and gills.

Sweetcorn Cakes with Grilled Tomatoes

SERVES 4

INGREDIENTS

1 large cob sweetcorn
75 g/3 oz/³/4 cup plain flour
1 egg
a little milk
salt and freshly ground black pepper
2 large firm tomatoes
1 garlic clove
1 tsp dried oregano
2–3 tbsp oil, plus extra for shallow-frying
8 cupped leaves iceberg lettuce
shredded fresh basil leaves to garnish

1   Pull the husks and silk away from the corn, then hold the cob upright on a board and cut downwards with a heavy knife to strip off the kernels. Put them into a pan of boiling water and cook for 3 minutes after the water has returned to the boil, then drain and rinse under the cold tap to cool quickly.

2 Put the flour into a bowl and break the egg into a well in the middle, then start stirring in the flour with a fork, adding a little milk to make a soft dropping consistency. Stir in the drained corn and season.

3   Preheat the grill. Halve the tomatoes horizontally and make 2 or 3 criss-cross slashes across the cut side of each half. Crush the garlic and rub it, the oregano and some salt and pepper over the cut surface of each half, then trickle with oil and grill until lightly browned.

4   While the tomatoes grill, heat some oil in a wide frying pan and drop a tablespoon of batter into the centre. Cook, one at a time, over a low heat and turn as soon as the top is set. Drain on kitchen paper and keep warm while cooking remaining fritters. The mixture should make at least 8 corn cakes.

5 Put 2 corn cakes onto lettuce leaves, garnish with basil and serve with a grilled tomato half.

Muffuletto Sandwich

In New Orleans you buy your Muffuletto sandwich ready-made from one of the grocery stores on Chartres Street that are famous for it, and where they also make up the olive pickle (an essential ingredient) by the barrel-load. There it comes in a special 25 cm/10 in diameter soft loaf, like an extra large hamburger bun, served in quarters. You can make it in a French loaf.

SERVES 4

INGREDIENTS
For the olive pickle
1 celery stick, finely chopped
1 garlic clove, crushed
1 canned sweet red pepper, drained and finely chopped
75 g/3 oz/⅔ cup stoned green olives, chopped
2 tbsp pickled cocktail onions, drained and coarsely chopped
2 tsp capers, drained and halved
3 tbsp olive oil
2 tsp red wine vinegar

For the sandwich
1 large French loaf
4 thin slices Parma ham
50 g/2 oz Provolone or Emmental cheese, thinly sliced
black pepper
50 g/2 oz Italian salami, rinded and thinly sliced

2   To make the sandwich, halve the loaf and cut it lengthways. Line the base with Parma ham. Lay the cheese on top and grind on some black pepper, then overlay with slices of salami.

3   Finally spoon the olive pickle on top of the salami and press the sandwich shut.

I   Mix all the vegetable and pickled ingredients for the olive pickle, then stir in the oil and vinegar and refrigerate.

Creole Omelette

SERVES 3–4

INGREDIENTS

1 large Spanish onion, finely chopped
25 g/1 oz/2 tbsp butter
1 garlic clove, crushed
2 tbsp soft white breadcrumbs
4 large tomatoes, skinned and chopped
50 g/2 oz/½ cup lean cooked ham
    finely chopped
salt, freshly ground black pepper and
    cayenne
6 eggs, lightly beaten
chopped fresh parsley to garnish

1 Soften the onion in the butter in a heavy frying pan, stirring regularly over a low heat for about 10 minutes.

2   Add the garlic and breadcrumbs and continue to stir over the heat until the breadcrumbs begin to crisp.

3   Add the tomatoes and cook for 10–15 minutes until they have broken down. Stir in the ham and season the mixture quite highly to compensate for the eggs.

4   Preheat the grill. Stir the beaten eggs through the mixture and continue to stir over the heat, breaking up the base as it sets to allow the uncooked mixture through.

5 When the omelette begins to set, leave it over a low heat until it is almost completely set.

6 Finish the omelette under the grill to cook the top. Serve either turned out onto a warm serving plate or straight from the pan, cut in wedges. Garnish with chopped parsley.

COOK'S TIP

You can leave out the ham to make the omelette suitable for vegetarians. Or, you can replace the ham with cut-up spicy sausages.

Creole Cheese Potato Puffs

It's worth boiling extra potatoes just to have some left over to mash for this heartening starter.

SERVES 4–6

INGREDIENTS
3 tbsp milk
25 g/1 oz/2 tbsp butter
450 g/1 lb/2½ cups cold mashed potatoes
50 g/2 oz/½ cup grated Cheddar cheese
4 spring onions, shredded
salt, freshly ground black pepper and grated nutmeg
2 eggs, separated
watercress and cherry tomatoes to garnish

3 Whisk the egg whites to soft peaks. Mix a tablespoon or two of the whites thoroughly into the potato mixture to loosen it, then fold the rest of the whites through the potato as lightly as you can.

4 Spoon the mixture into the bun tins and bake in the oven for about 15 minutes, until the puffs have risen and are tinged golden brown. Serve immediately, garnished with watercress and cherry tomatoes.

1 Preheat the oven to 220°C/425°F/ Gas 7 and generously butter a 12-hole non-stick bun sheet, buttering the sections between the indents as well.

2 Warm the milk and butter to just below boiling point in a small pan, then mix thoroughly into the mashed potatoes with the cheese, spring onions and seasoning. Mix in the egg yolks and beat thoroughly.

COOK'S TIP

Garnished elegantly, these puffs make a pretty starter, but on a more homely occasion they are just as good served with sausages and tomato ketchup.

Eggs Sardou

Restaurants don't come and go much in New Orleans: Antoine's, where this dish was created in 1908, is still there, right in the heart of jazzland. The dish's popularity has spread and it now crops up on brunch menus as well as being a favourite starter.

SERVES 4

INGREDIENTS

4 large artichokes
500 g/1¼ lb raw spinach
50 g/2 oz/4 tbsp butter
2 tbsp plain flour
175 ml/6 fl oz/¾ cup milk
4 canned anchovy fillets, drained and mashed
salt, freshly ground black pepper, grated nutmeg and Tabasco sauce
4 eggs

For the Hollandaise sauce

2 tbsp white wine vinegar
4 black peppercorns
1 bay leaf
2 egg yolks, at room temperature
115 g/4 oz/½ cup butter, at warm room temperature, cubed
salt and freshly ground black pepper

1   With a sharp knife, cut the stems from the artichokes, then cut off the top half of each artichoke and scoop out the centre. Set aside.

2   Wash the spinach thoroughly, trimming off any discoloured bits and the coarser stems. Put the spinach into a deep pan with just the water that clings to it. Cover and cook until it wilts right down. Turn out into a colander and, when it's cool enough to handle, squeeze out much of the moisture. Slice across the ball of spinach both ways to chop it.

3   To make the Hollandaise sauce, boil the vinegar with 2 tsp water, the peppercorns and bay leaf in a small pan until the liquid is reduced to 1 tbsp. Leave to cool.

4   Cream the egg yolks with one cube of soft butter and a pinch of salt in a heatproof bowl, then strain on the vinegar, set the bowl over a pan of boiling water and turn off the heat.

5 Whisk in the remaining butter a cube at a time, adding each cube as the one before melts into the sauce. Carry on whisking until the sauce is shiny and thick. Season with salt and pepper. Leave over the pan of water to keep warm.

6   Bring a wide pan full of salted water to the boil. Add the artichokes, cover and cook for about 30 minutes or until tender. Lift them with a slotted spoon onto warmed serving plates and keep warm.

7   Meanwhile, to finish the spinach, melt the butter in a wide pan, mix in the flour and stir for 1 minute over the heat until the roux froths and bubbles. Take off the heat and pour in the milk gradually, stirring constantly. When the sauce loosens, return it to the heat and continue stirring in the milk.

8 When the sauce reaches simmering point, stir in the mashed anchovies and leave to simmer for about 5 minutes. Then add the chopped spinach, return to simmering point, season with black pepper, nutmeg, Tabasco sauce and salt if it needs it, and keep warm.

9   Poach the eggs 2 at a time in the pan of artichoke cooking water.

10 To assemble the dish, spoon some spinach into each artichoke, allowing it to spill over the edges. Set a poached egg on the plate and spoon Hollandaise sauce over.

Smothered Rabbit

Game has always formed a big part of the Cajun diet — it was the only meat available to the early settlers. The smothering technique gives plenty of flavour to a domestic rabbit, too. Get your butcher or game dealer to prepare the rabbit pieces for you.

SERVES 4

INGREDIENTS

1 rabbit, skinned, cleaned and cut into 8 pieces
2 tsp salt
¹/₂ tsp garlic salt
¹/₂ tsp dried oregano
good pinch each of freshly ground black pepper and cayenne
50 g/2 oz/¹/₂ cup plain flour
4 tbsp cooking oil
1 medium onion, chopped
1 celery stick, chopped
1 large garlic clove, crushed
1 bay leaf
350 ml/12 fl oz/1¹/₂ cups chicken stock
3 spring onions, shredded
2 tbsp chopped fresh parsley
mange-tout to serve

I   Mix the salt, garlic salt, oregano, black pepper and cayenne together. Sprinkle the rabbit pieces lightly, using about half the seasoning mix, and pat it in with your fingers.

2   Put the rest of the seasoning mix with the flour into a polythene bag, shake to mix, then shake the pieces of rabbit in this to dredge them, shaking the surplus back into the bag as you lift them out.

3   Heat the oil in a heavy flameproof casserole and fry the rabbit pieces until browned on all sides. Do this in batches so as not to crowd the pan, removing each one as it is ready.

4   When all the rabbit is browned, cook the onion and celery in the same pan for 5 minutes, stirring regularly. Add the garlic and bay leaf.

5   Heat the stock. Meanwhile, add 1 tbsp seasoned flour to the oil in the pan and stir over the heat for 1 minute. Remove from the heat and gradually stir in some of the hot stock. When the sauce loosens, return the pan to the heat and add the remaining stock, stirring constantly until boiling point is reached.

6   Lower the heat, return the rabbit pieces to the casserole, cover and simmer for about 1 hour, until the rabbit is very tender.

7   Check the seasoning and stir in the spring onions and parsley. Serve with mange-tout and perhaps some crusty bread.

COOK'S TIP

You could make Smothered Chicken in exactly the same way with 4 chicken pieces.

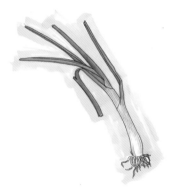

Poussins with Dirty Rice

This rice is called dirty not because of the bits in it (though the roux and chicken livers do 'muss' it up a bit) but because jazz is called 'dirty music', and the rice here is certainly jazzed up.

SERVES 4

INGREDIENTS
For the rice
4 tbsp cooking oil
25 g/1 oz/¼ cup plain flour
50 g/2 oz/4 tbsp butter
1 large onion, chopped
2 celery sticks, chopped
1 sweet green pepper, seeded and diced
2 garlic cloves, crushed
200 g/7 oz minced pork
225 g/8 oz chicken livers, trimmed and sliced
salt, freshly ground black pepper and Tabasco sauce
300 ml/10 fl oz/1¼ cups chicken stock
4 spring onions, shredded
3 tbsp chopped fresh parsley
225 g/8 oz/generous 1 cup American long-grain rice, cooked

For the birds
4 poussins
2 bay leaves, halved
25 g/1 oz/2 tbsp butter
salt and freshly ground black pepper
1 lemon

1 In a small heavy saucepan, make a roux with 2 tbsp of the oil and the flour. When it is a chestnut-brown colour, remove the pan from the heat and place it immediately on a cold surface.

2　Heat the remaining 2 tbsp oil with the butter in a frying pan and stir-fry the onion, celery and sweet pepper for about 5 minutes.

3　Add the garlic and pork and stir-fry for 5 minutes, breaking up the pork and stirring to cook it all over.

4　Add the chicken livers and fry for 2–3 minutes until they have changed colour all over. Season with salt, pepper and a dash of Tabasco sauce.

5　Stir the roux into the stir-fried mixture, then gradually add in the stock. When it begins to bubble, cover and cook for 30 minutes, stirring occasionally. Then uncover and cook for a further 15 minutes, stirring frequently.

6　Preheat the oven to 200°C/400°F/ Gas 6. Mix the spring onions and parsley into the meat mixture and stir it all into the cooked rice.

7　Put ½ bay leaf and 1 tbsp rice into each poussin. Rub the outside with the butter and season with salt and pepper.

8　Put the birds on a rack in a roasting tin, squeeze the juice from the lemon over them and roast in the oven for 35–40 minutes, basting twice with the pan juices.

9　Put the remaining rice into a shallow ovenproof dish, cover it and place on a low shelf in the oven for the last 15–20 minutes of the birds' cooking time.

10　Serve the birds on a bed of dirty rice with the roasting pan juices (drained of fat) poured over.

COOK'S TIP

You can substitute quails for the poussins, in which case offer 2 per person and stuff each little bird with 2 tsp of the dirty rice before roasting for about 20 minutes.

Chicken and Prawn Jambalaya

The mixture of chicken, seafood and rice suggests a close relationship to the Spanish paella, but the name is more probably derived from 'jambon' (the French for ham), 'à la ya' (Creole for rice). Jambalayas are a colourful mixture of highly flavoured ingredients, and are always made in large quantities for big family or celebration meals.

SERVES 10

INGREDIENTS

2 × 1.5 kg/3 lb chicken
salt and freshly ground black pepper
450 g/1 lb piece raw smoked gammon
50 g/2 oz/4 tbsp lard or bacon fat
50 g/2 oz/1/2 cup plain flour
3 medium onions, finely sliced
2 sweet green peppers, seeded and sliced
675 g/1 1/2 lb tomatoes, skinned and chopped
2–3 garlic cloves, crushed
2 tsp chopped fresh thyme or 1 tsp dried thyme
24 Mediterranean prawns, beheaded and peeled
500 g/1 1/4 lb/3 cups American long-grain rice
2–3 dashes Tabasco sauce
1 bunch spring onions, finely chopped (including the green parts)
3 tbsp chopped fresh parsley

I   Cut each chicken into 10 pieces and season with salt and pepper.

2   Dice the gammon, discarding the rind and fat.

3   In a large heavy-based pan or flameproof casserole, melt the lard or bacon fat and brown the chicken pieces all over, lifting them out with a slotted spoon and setting them aside as they are done.

4   Turn the heat down, sprinkle the flour onto the fat in the pan and stir continuously until the roux turns light golden brown.

5   Return the chicken pieces to the pan, add the diced gammon, onions, green peppers, tomatoes, garlic and thyme and cook, stirring regularly, for 10 minutes, then stir in the prawns.

6 Stir the rice into the pan with one and a half times the rice's volume in cold water. Season with salt, pepper and Tabasco sauce. Bring to the boil and cook over a gentle heat until the rice is tender and the liquid absorbed. Add a little extra boiling water if the rice looks like drying out before it is cooked.

7 Mix the spring onions and parsley into the finished dish, reserving a little of the mixture to scatter over the jambalaya. Serve hot.

COOK'S TIP

The roux thickening is a vital part of Cajun cooking, particularly essential to jambalaya. Cook the roux over a low heat, watching like a hawk to see it doesn't develop dark flecks, which indicate burning. Don't stop stirring for an instant.

Louisiana Seafood Gumbo

Gumbo is a soup, but is served over rice as a main course. This recipe is based on a gumbo that chef John Folse, of the renowned Louisiana restaurant Lafitte's Landing, served on a visit to London. In his neck of the bayous, where they are cheap and prolific, oysters are an important ingredient. However, his suggestion to substitute mussels for oysters, works very well too.

SERVES 6

INGREDIENTS
450 g/1 lb mussels
450 g/1 lb prawns
1 cooked crab weighing about 1 kg/2¼ lb
salt
1 small bunch of parsley, leaves chopped
*   and stalks reserved*
150 ml/5 fl oz/⅔ cup cooking oil
115 g/4 oz/1 cup plain flour
1 sweet green pepper, seeded and chopped
1 large onion, chopped
2 celery sticks, sliced
3 garlic cloves, finely chopped
75 g/3 oz smoked spiced sausage, skinned
*   and sliced*
6 spring onions, shredded
cayenne
Tabasco sauce
boiled American long-grain rice to serve

1   Wash the mussels in several changes of cold water, scrubbing away any barnacles and pulling off the black 'beards' that protrude between the shells. Discard any mussels that are broken or any open ones that don't close when you tap them firmly.

2   Heat 250 ml/8 fl oz/1 cup water in a deep saucepan and, when it boils, add the mussels, cover tightly and cook over a high heat, shaking regularly, for 3 minutes. As the mussels open, lift them out with tongs into a sieve set over a bowl. Discard any that refuse to open after a further 1 minute's cooking.

3   Shell the mussels, discarding the shells. Return the liquor from the bowl to the pan and make the quantity up to 2 litres/3½ pints/9 cups with water.

4   Shell the prawns and put the shells and heads into the saucepan.

5   Remove all the meat from the crab (see the Corn and Crab Bisque recipe), separating the brown and white meat. Add all the pieces of shell to the saucepan with 2 tsp salt.

6   Bring the shellfish stock to the boil, skimming regularly to remove the froth that rises as boiling point approaches.

7   When no more froth rises from the shellfish stock, add the parsley stalks and simmer for 15 minutes. Cool the stock, then strain off the liquor, discarding all the solids. Make up to 2 litres/3½ pints/9 cups with water.

8   Make a roux with the oil and flour. Stir constantly over the heat with a wooden spoon or whisk until it reaches a golden-brown colour. It is vital to stir constantly to darken the roux without burning. Should black specks occur at any stage of cooking, discard the roux and start again.

9   As soon as the roux is the right colour, add the pepper, onion, celery and garlic and continue cooking until they are soft – about 3 minutes. Then add the sausage. Reheat the stock.

10 Stir the brown crabmeat into the roux, then ladle in the hot stock a little at a time, stirring constantly until it is all smoothly incorporated. Bring to a low boil and simmer the soup for 30 minutes, partially covered.

11 Add the prawns, mussels, white crabmeat and spring onions. Return to the boil, season with salt if necessary, cayenne and a dash or two of Tabasco sauce, and simmer for a further minute.

12 Add the chopped parsley leaves and serve immediately, ladling the soup over the hot rice in soup plates.

COOK'S TIP

It's important to have the onion, green pepper and celery prepared and ready to add to the roux the minute it reaches the correct golden-brown stage, as this arrests its darkening.

Fried Fish with Tartare Sauce and Hush Puppies

The story goes that fishermen frying their catch used to drop pieces of stiffened batter into the fat to fry. They would then throw the fried batter to their dogs to hush their hungry howlings – hence the name of hush puppies, a traditional Southern food.

SERVES 4

INGREDIENTS

For the tartare sauce
150 ml/5 fl oz/²⁄₃ cup mayonnaise
1 tbsp chopped dill pickles
5 stoned green olives, chopped
2 spring onions, finely shredded
1 tbsp lemon juice
1–2 dashes Tabasco sauce

For the hush puppies
115 g/4 oz/1 cup cornmeal
50 g/2 oz/¹⁄₂ cup plain flour
1¹⁄₂ tsp baking powder
1 garlic clove, crushed with 1 tsp salt
2 spring onions, finely shredded
1 egg, lightly beaten
about 5 tbsp milk
25 g/1 oz/2 tbsp butter

For the fish coating
25 g/1 oz/¹⁄₄ cup plain flour
25 g/1 oz/¹⁄₄ cup cornflour
50 g/2 oz/¹⁄₂ cup cornmeal
¹⁄₂ tsp dried oregano
¹⁄₂ tsp dried thyme
1 tsp salt
1 tsp cayenne
1 tsp paprika
2 tsp dry mustard powder
1 egg
about 120 ml/4 fl oz/¹⁄₂ cup milk

For the fish fillets
oil for deep-frying
4 skinned plaice fillets, thawed if frozen
lemon slices and fresh parsley sprigs to garnish

I Mix all the ingredients for the tartare sauce and set aside.

2   Next make the hush puppy batter. Mix the cornmeal, flour and baking powder and stir in the crushed garlic and spring onions. Fork in the egg.

3   Heat 5 tbsp milk and the butter together slowly until the butter melts, then raise the heat and, when it boils, stir thoroughly into the dry ingredients, adding a little more milk if necessary to make a stiff dough. Leave to cool.

4   To make the fish coating, mix the flours, all the herbs and seasonings for the fish coating in a shallow dish. Beat the egg and milk together lightly in another shallow dish.

5   Scoop out pieces of hush puppy batter no bigger than a walnut and roll into balls between wetted hands.

6   Heat the oil for deep-frying. Fry the hush puppies in batches, turning them until they are deep golden brown

all over. They will swell in cooking, and it's important that they are cooked right to the middle, so don't have the oil fiercely hot to start with. It should sizzle and froth up round them as you drop them in, but not brown them immediately. Lift them out with a slotted spoon and drain on kitchen paper as they are done. Keep warm.

7   Coat the fish fillets, first in the egg mixture and then in the cornmeal mixture.

8   Fry the fillets 2 at a time for 2–3 minutes on each side, until crisp and golden brown. Drain on kitchen paper and serve with the hush puppies, garnished with lemon slices and sprigs of parsley.

COOK'S TIP

Louisiana cooks use a specially fine ground cornmeal in their coating mixture. The nearest I've found to it is masa harina, from which Mexican cooks make tortillas. It's available from specialist shops or by mail order from The Cool Chile Co, Unit 7, 34 Bassett Road, London W10 6JL.

Maque Choux

A Cajun classic, good with ham and chicken. Some cooks add a little sugar to heighten the sweetness, but for most the natural sweetness of the corn is enough.

INGREDIENTS

50 g/2 oz/4 tbsp butter
1 large onion, finely chopped
1 sweet green pepper, seeded and diced
2 large tomatoes, skinned and chopped
450 g/1 lb/4 cups frozen sweetcorn kernels, thawed
120 ml/4 fl oz/½ cup milk
salt, freshly ground black pepper and cayenne

1   Melt half the butter in a large pan and soften the onion in it, stirring regularly over a low heat for about 10 minutes until it begins to turn pale gold. Add the sweet pepper and stir over the heat for a further minute, then add the tomatoes and leave to cook gently while you prepare the corn.

2   Put the corn kernels and milk into a food processor or blender and process in brief bursts to break up the kernels to a porridgy consistency.

3   Stir the corn mixture thoroughly into the pan and cook, partially covered, over a low heat for 20 minutes. Stir regularly, making sure that it does not stick to the bottom. If the mixture threatens to become too dry, add a little more milk. Should it still be rather wet in the latter stages, uncover, raise the heat a little and stir constantly for the last 5 minutes.

4   Stir in the rest of the butter and season quite highly with salt, black pepper and cayenne. Serve hot.

COOK'S TIP

You are aiming at a consistency rather like that of scrambled eggs and, like scrambled eggs, Maque Choux is also good with bacon and fried bread for breakfast.

Baked Sweet Potatoes

Sweet potatoes go well with the favourite Cajun seasonings: plenty of salt, white pepper as well as black and cayenne, and lavish quantities of butter. Serve half a potato per person as an accompaniment to meat, sausages or fish, or a whole one as a supper dish, perhaps topped with crisped and crumbled bacon and accompanied by a green side salad peppered with watercress.

SERVES 3–6

INGREDIENTS

*3 pink-skinned sweet potatoes, each
    weighing about 450 g/1 lb
salt
75 g/3 oz/6 tbsp butter, sliced
black, white and cayenne peppers*

2   The potatoes can either be served in halves or whole. For halves, split each one lengthways and make close diagonal cuts in the flesh of each half. Then spread with slices of butter, and work the butter and seasonings roughly into the cuts with a knife point.

3   Alternatively, make an incision along the length of each potato if they are to be served whole. Open them slightly and put in butter slices along the length, seasoning with salt and the peppers.

I   Wash the potatoes, leaving the skins wet. Rub salt into the skins, prick them all over with a fork, and place on the middle shelf of the oven. Turn on the oven at 200°C/400°F/Gas 6 and bake for about an hour, until the flesh yields and feels soft when pressed.

COOK'S TIP

Sweet potatoes cook more quickly than ordinary ones, and there is no need to preheat the oven.

Hot Parsnip Fritters on Baby Spinach

Fritters are a natural favourite of Cajun cooks, with their love for deep-frying. The technique brings out the luscious sweetness of parsnips, here set, none too traditionally, on a walnut-dressed salad of baby spinach leaves.

SERVES 4

INGREDIENTS
2 large parsnips
1 egg, separated
115 g/4 oz/1 cup plain flour
120 ml/4 fl oz/¹/₂ cup milk
salt, freshly ground black pepper and cayenne
115 g/4 oz baby spinach leaves
2 tbsp olive oil
1 tbsp walnut oil
1 tbsp sherry vinegar
oil for deep-frying
1 tbsp coarsely chopped walnuts

1   Peel the parsnips, bring to the boil in a pan of salted water and simmer for 10–15 minutes until tender but not in the least mushy. Drain, cool and cut diagonally into slices about 5 cm/2 in long × 5 mm–1 cm/¹/₄–¹/₂ in thick.

2 Put the egg yolk into a well in the flour in a bowl and mix in with a fork, gradually pulling in the surrounding flour. Begin adding the milk, while continuing to mix in the flour. Season with salt, and black and cayenne peppers, and beat with a whisk until the batter is smooth.

3 Wash and dry the spinach leaves and put them in a bowl. In a screwtop jar, mix the olive and walnut oils, sherry vinegar, salt and pepper.

4   When you are ready to serve, whisk the egg white to the soft-peak stage, fold in a little of the yolk batter, then fold the white into the batter. Heat the oil for frying.

5 Meanwhile, shake the dressing jar vigorously, then toss the salad in the dressing. Arrange the dressed leaves on 4 salad plates and scatter with walnuts.

6   Dip the parsnip slices in batter and fry a few at a time until puffy and golden. Drain on kitchen paper and keep warm. To serve, arrange the fritters on top of the salad leaves.

Spiced Aubergine Fried in Cornmeal

SERVES 3–4

INGREDIENTS

1 large aubergine
salt
1 egg
120 ml/4 fl oz/½ cup milk
½ tsp paprika
½ tsp cayenne
½ tsp freshly ground black pepper
½ tsp garlic salt
115 g/4 oz/1 cup fine cornmeal
oil for deep-frying

1   Cut the aubergine into 1 cm/½ in thick slices. Sprinkle lightly with salt and stack them in a colander. Leave standing in the sink to drain for 30 minutes, then wipe the slices dry on kitchen paper.

2 Beat the egg lightly in a shallow bowl with the milk, spices, pepper and garlic salt. Spread the cornmeal on a plate. Heat the oil for deep-frying.

3   Pass each slice of aubergine through the spiced egg mixture, allowing the excess briefly to drip back into the bowl. Turn the slice in the cornmeal, then drop immediately into the hot oil.

4   Fry 3 or 4 slices at a time, turning once, until they are golden on both sides. Drain thoroughly on kitchen paper and keep warm until all the slices are fried. Serve hot.

COOK'S TIP

The crisp aubergine slices are very good with plain grills of meat, poultry or fish. They can also substitute for meat in a vegetarian meal.

Red Beans and Rice

This is the classic Monday dish in Louisiana; Monday being washday and beans not minding being left to their own devices for as long as it takes to finish the laundry. Hardly worth making in small quantities because of the long cooking time, this makes a splendid supper-party dish served with good grilled sausages and a green salad.

SERVES 8–10

INGREDIENTS

500 g/1¼ lb/3⅓ cups dried red kidney beans
2 bay leaves
2 tbsp oil, bacon fat or lard
1 medium onion, chopped
2 garlic cloves, finely chopped
2 celery sticks, sliced
225 g/8 oz piece salt pork or raw ham
salt and freshly ground black pepper
450 g/1 lb/2¼ cups American long-grain rice
3 tbsp chopped fresh parsley

1   Start the night before. Wash the beans thoroughly in a colander under a running cold tap, then put them into a deep bowl and fill it to the top with cold water. Leave to stand overnight.

2   Drain the beans and put them into a large pan with fresh cold water to cover generously. Bring to the boil and boil hard for 10 minutes, then drain and rinse both the beans and the pan.

3   Return the beans to the pan with the bay leaves and fresh cold water to cover generously. Bring to the boil, reduce the heat and simmer for 30 minutes, uncovered, topping up the water if necessary.

4   Meanwhile heat the oil or fat in a frying pan and cook the onion, garlic and celery gently, stirring frequently, until the onion is soft and translucent.

5   Stir the fried vegetables into the beans and push the piece of salt pork or ham well down in the middle of them. Bring back to the boil and continue to simmer, topping up the water as necessary, for a further 45 minutes or so until the beans are very tender. Add salt, if necessary, 15–20 minutes before the end of the cooking time.

6   Measure the rice into a pan with a cup and add 1½ times its volume of cold water, plus 1 tsp salt. Bring to the boil, stirring occasionally, then cover the pan tightly and leave over a very low heat for 12 minutes. Without lifting the lid, turn off the heat and leave the rice undisturbed for a further 12 minutes.

7   Lift the piece of salt pork or ham out from among the beans and dice it, removing the fat and rind. Drain the beans and correct the seasoning with plenty of black pepper and more salt if necessary. Mix the diced meat through the beans.

8   Fork up the rice to make it fluffy, stir in the parsley, then mound it in a warm serving dish and pour the beans over the top.

COOK'S TIP

The first fast boiling is a safety measure to eliminate toxins present in red kidney beans, so don't skip it.
The beans are just as good made the day before and reheated when you cook the rice. Indeed, some Cajun cooks say that this makes them taste even better.

Beignets

In New Orleans where a night on the town really can last all night, revellers are glad of a pit-stop at the Café du Monde, which serves its favourite treats of 'café au lait' and sugary beignets 24 hours a day. Chef John Folse of Lafitte's Landing restaurant, who is deeply interested in Louisiana history, says the recipe was brought to Louisiana in 1727 by Ursuline nuns. This is his version of their recipe.

MAKES 20

INGREDIENTS

1 packet dried yeast
400 g/14 oz/3½ cups plain flour
1 tsp salt
50 g/2 oz/¼ cup caster sugar
300 ml/10 fl oz/1¼ cups milk
3 eggs, beaten
25 g/1 oz/2 tbsp butter, melted
oil for deep-frying
115 g/4 oz/1 cup icing sugar

1 Dissolve the yeast in 4 tbsp warm water and set aside.

2 In a large mixing bowl, combine the flour, salt and caster sugar and mix well. Fold in the dissolved yeast, milk, eggs and melted butter.

3 Continue to mix until a smooth dough is formed.

4 Knead the dough until smooth and elastic. Cover the dough with a towel and leave to rise in a warm place for 1 hour.

5 Roll out the dough to 5 mm/¼ in thick on a well-floured surface. Cut into rectangular shapes about 5 × 7.5 cm/ 2 × 3 in and put them in a lightly floured Swiss roll tin.

6 Cover with a towel and leave to rise in a warm place for an hour or until they have doubled their size.

7 Put the icing sugar into a deep dish or oven tin. Heat the oil for deep-frying and fry the beignets in batches, turning each, until golden brown on both sides. Drain well on kitchen paper.

8 As each batch of beignets is cooked, transfer with a slotted spoon to the icing sugar and shake them about to coat liberally all round.

COOK'S TIP

The important thing with beignets, as with all doughnuts, is to have the oil at the right temperature to cook the dough right through to the middle before the outside is too dark brown.
Treat the first beignet or two as a test. Break them open and if they are still sticky in the middle lower the heat and allow the oil to cool down a bit before continuing with the next batch.
Eat the beignets soon after cooking, and certainly on the same day as they are made.

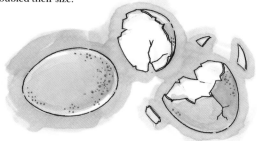

Pralines

Pronounced with a long 'a' and the stress on the first syllable, these resemble puddles of nut fudge more than the crisp biscuits Europeans think of as pralines. In Louisiana they are eaten as a dessert or whenever it seems a good idea to have something sweet with a cup of coffee.

MAKES ABOUT 30 PIECES

INGREDIENTS
225 g/8 oz/2 cups pecan halves
450 g/1 lb/2 well-packed cups soft light brown sugar
200 g/7 oz/1 cup white granulated sugar
300 ml/10 fl oz/1¼ cups double cream
175 ml/6 fl oz/¾ cup milk
1 tsp vanilla essence

1   Roughly chop half the pecans and set all the nuts aside. Line 2–3 baking sheets with non-stick baking paper.

2 Stir the brown and white sugars, cream and milk together in a heavy-based saucepan over a medium heat. Stir continuously until the mixture reaches 119°C/238°F or the soft-ball stage (see Cook's Tip).

3   Remove from the heat immediately and beat with an electric beater or a balloon whisk until the mixture loses its sheen and becomes creamy in texture and grainy looking. This could take 15 minutes by hand or about 5 minutes with an electric beater.

4   Stir in the vanilla and both lots of nuts and drop tablespoons of the mixture onto the lined baking sheets, allowing it to spread of its own accord. Leave to cool and set at room temperature. Store between layers of greaseproof paper in a tight-lidded tin.

COOK'S TIP

A mixture has reached the soft-ball stage when a teaspoonful dropped into cold water quickly sets to a soft ball. As this stage approaches, a spoonful of the mixture dribbled on the surface of the mixture in the pan will hold its trail. Test frequently towards the end of the cooking time unless you are using a sugar thermometer.

Bananas Foster

A now-famous dessert named after Dick Foster, who was on the Vice Committee and therefore in charge of cleaning up the French Quarter of New Orleans in the 1950s.

SERVES 4

INGREDIENTS

75 g/3 oz/¹/₃ cup soft light brown sugar
¹/₂ tsp ground cinnamon
¹/₂ tsp grated nutmeg
50 g/2 oz/4 tbsp butter
4 tbsp banana liqueur
5 tbsp dark rum
4 firm bananas, peeled and halved
*   lengthways*
4 scoops firmly frozen vanilla ice cream

3   Add the bananas and heat through, turning to coat with the sauce.

4 Tilt the pan if you are cooking over gas to set light to the sauce. If your stove is electric, light the sauce with a match. Hold the pan at arm's length while you do this.

5 As soon as the flames die down, put 2 pieces of banana on each plate with a scoop of ice cream between them. Pour on the sauce and serve immediately.

1   Mix the sugar, cinnamon and nutmeg together. Melt the butter in a heavy frying pan and add the sugar and spice mixture.

2 Add the liqueur and rum and stir over the heat until the sauce is syrupy.

COOK'S TIP

You can ring the changes with praline or walnut ice creams.

Pecan Pie

A favourite pie all over the southern states, where pecans flourish. Louisiana is no exception.

SERVES 6

INGREDIENTS
For the pastry
200 g/7 oz/1¾ cups plain flour
pinch of salt
115 g/4 oz/½ cup butter
dry pulses or rice for baking blind

For the filling
3 eggs
good pinch of salt
1 tsp vanilla essence
200 g/7 oz/¾ well-packed cup soft dark
*   brown sugar*
4 tbsp golden syrup or light corn syrup
50 g/2 oz/4 tbsp butter, melted
115 g/4 oz/1 cup chopped pecan kernels,
*   plus 12 pecan halves*

To serve
whipped cream or vanilla ice cream

1 Mix the flour with a pinch of salt, then rub in the butter with your fingertips to a coarse sand consistency. Add iced water a little at a time, mixing first with a fork, then with your hand, until the mixture gathers into a dough. Be mean with the water.

2 Wrap the dough in cling film and refrigerate for 30–40 minutes. Preheat the oven to 190°C/375°F/Gas 5 for 20 minutes before you bake the tart.

3 Grease a 20–23 cm/8–9 in loose-based flan tin. Roll out the pastry to line the tin, pressing it gently into place with your fingers.

4 Run the rolling pin over the top of the tin to sever the surplus pastry.

5 Prick the pastry base and line with foil. Fill it with dry pulses or rice and bake blind for 15 minutes, then remove the foil and pulses and bake for a further 5 minutes. Take the pastry case from the oven and lower the oven heat to 180°C/350°F/Gas 4.

6 Meanwhile, to make the filling, beat the eggs lightly with the salt and vanilla essence, then beat in the sugar, syrup and melted butter. Finally mix in the chopped pecans.

7 Spread the mixture in the half-baked pastry case and bake for 15 minutes, then take it from the oven and stud with the pecan halves in a circle.

8 Return to the oven and bake for a further 20–25 minutes until a thin metal skewer pushed gently into the centre comes out clean, with no uncooked mixture attached.

9 Cool the pie for 10–15 minutes and serve it warm with whipped cream or a scoop of vanilla ice cream.

COOK'S TIP

The corn syrup American cooks use in their pie filling is not widely available outside the USA. Substitute golden syrup. You can, however, find it in the larger department store food halls in major cities.

CARIBBEAN

Creamy Spinach Soup

An appetizing soup that you will find yourself making over and over again.

INGREDIENTS

Serves 4

25g/1oz/2 tbsp butter
1 small onion, chopped
675g/1½ lb fresh spinach, chopped
1.2 litres/2 pints/5 cups vegetable stock
50g/2oz creamed coconut
freshly grated nutmeg
300ml/½ pint/1¼ cups single cream
salt and freshly ground black pepper
fresh snipped chives, to garnish

1 Melt the butter in a saucepan over a moderate heat and sauté the onion for a few minutes until soft. Add the spinach, cover the pan and cook gently for 10 minutes, until the spinach has reduced.

2 Pour the spinach mixture into a blender or food processor and add a little of the stock. Blend until smooth.

3 Return mixture to the pan and add the remaining stock, creamed coconut, salt, pepper and nutmeg. Simmer for 15 minutes to thicken.

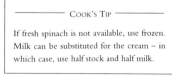

4 Add the cream, stir well and heat through – do not boil. Serve hot, garnished with chives.

COOK'S TIP

If fresh spinach is not available, use frozen. Milk can be substituted for the cream – in which case, use half stock and half milk.

Crab Cakes

These are quite delicious and they're just as good made with canned tuna fish, too.

INGREDIENTS

Makes about 15
225g/8oz white crab meat
115g/4oz cooked potatoes, mashed
25g/1oz/2 tbsp fresh herb seasoning
2.5ml/½ tsp mild mustard
2.5ml/½ tsp freshly ground black
  pepper
½ hot chilli pepper
15ml/1 tbsp shrimp paste (optional)
2.5ml/½ tsp dried oregano, crushed
1 egg, beaten
flour, for dusting
oil, for frying
lime wedges and basil leaves, to garnish

For the tomato dip
15ml/1 tbsp butter or margarine
½ onion, finely chopped
2 canned plum tomatoes, chopped
1 garlic clove, crushed
150ml/¼ pint/⅔ cup water
5–10ml/1–2 tsp malt vinegar
15ml/1 tbsp chopped fresh coriander
½ hot chilli pepper, chopped

1 To make the crab cakes, mix together the crab meat, potatoes, herb seasoning, mustard, peppers, shrimp paste, if using, oregano and egg in a large bowl. Chill for 30 minutes.

2 Make the tomato dip. Melt the butter or margarine in a small pan.

3 Add the onion, tomato and garlic and sauté for about 5 minutes until the onion is soft. Add the water, vinegar, coriander and hot pepper. Simmer for 10 minutes and then blend to a smooth purée in a food processor or blender and pour into a bowl. Keep warm or chill as required.

4 Using a spoon, shape the mixture into rounds and dust with flour. Heat a little oil in a frying pan and fry the crab cakes a few at a time for 2–3 minutes on each side until golden brown. Drain and keep warm while cooking the remaining cakes. Serve with the warm or cold tomato dip and garnish with lime wedges and basil leaves.

Spinach Patties

INGREDIENTS

Makes 10–12
For the pastry
250g/8oz/2 cups plain flour
115g/4oz/1/2 cup butter or margarine,
  chilled and diced
1 egg yolk
milk, to glaze

For the filling
25g/1oz/2 tbsp butter or margarine
1 small onion, finely chopped
175g–225g/6–8oz fresh or frozen leaf
  spinach, chopped
2.5ml/1/2 tsp ground cumin
1/2 vegetable stock cube, crumbled
freshly ground black pepper

1 Preheat the oven to 200°C/400°F/
Gas 6. Lightly grease the hollows of
a muffin or patty tin.

2 First make the spinach filling. Melt
the butter or margarine in a
saucepan, add the onion and cook
gently until softened. Stir in the spinach,
then add the cumin, stock cube and
pepper and cook for 5 minutes or until
the spinach has wilted. Leave to cool.

3 To make the pastry, put the flour
in a large bowl and rub in the
butter or margarine, until the mixture
resembles fine breadcrumbs. Add the
egg yolk and 30–45ml/2–3 tbsp cold
water and mix to a firm dough. Turn
out the pastry on to a floured surface.

4 Knead for a few seconds, divide the
dough in half and roll out one half to
a square or rectangle. Cut out 10–12
rounds using a 9cm/3 1/2 in pastry cutter.
Press into the hollows of the prepared
tin. Spoon about 15ml/1 tbsp of the
spinach mixture into the pastry cases.

5 Roll out the remaining dough and
cut out slightly smaller rounds to
cover the patties. Press the edges with a
fork, to seal. Prick the tops with the
fork. Brush with milk and bake for
15–20 minutes until golden brown
Serve hot or cold.

Saltfish Fritters (Stamp and Go)

These delicious fritters are also
known as Accras.

INGREDIENTS

Makes 15
115g/4oz/1 cup self-raising flour
115g/4oz/1 cup plain flour
2.5ml/1/2 tsp baking powder
175g/6oz soaked salt cod, shredded
1 egg, whisked
15ml/1 tbsp chopped spring onion
1 garlic clove, crushed
2.5ml/1/2 tsp freshly ground black
  pepper
1/2 hot chilli pepper, seeded and finely
  chopped
1.5ml/1/4 tsp turmeric
45ml/3 tbsp milk
vegetable oil, for shallow frying

1 Sift the flours and baking powder
together into a bowl, then add the
salt cod, egg, spring onion, garlic,
pepper, hot pepper and turmeric. Add
a little of the milk and mix well.

2 Gradually stir in the remaining
milk, adding just enough to make
a thick batter. Stir thoroughly so that all
ingredients are completely combined.

3 Heat a little oil in a large frying pan
until very hot. Add spoonfuls of
the mixture and fry for a few minutes
on each side until golden brown and
puffy. Lift out the fritters, drain on
kitchen paper and keep warm while
cooking the rest of the mixture in the
same way. Serve the fritters hot or
cold, as a snack.

Peppered Steak in Sherry Cream Sauce

This dish would be perfect for supper, served on a bed of noodles or with boiled plantains.

INGREDIENTS

Serves 4

675g/1½lb frying steak
5ml/1 tsp spice seasoning
25g/1oz/2 tbsp butter
6–8 shallots, sliced
2 garlic cloves, crushed
120ml/4fl oz/½ cup sherry
45ml/3 tbsp water
75ml/5 tbsp single cream
salt and freshly ground black pepper
cooked plantain, to serve
snipped fresh chives, to garnish

1 Cut the meat into thin strips, discarding any fat or gristle.

2 Season the meat with pepper and spice seasoning and leave to marinate in a cool place for 30 minutes.

3 Melt the butter in a large frying pan and sauté the meat for 4–5 minutes until browned on all sides. Transfer to a plate and set aside.

4 Add the shallots and garlic to the pan, fry gently for a few minutes then add the sherry and water and simmer for 5 minutes. Stir in the single cream.

5 Reduce the heat and adjust the seasoning. Stir in the meat and heat until hot but not boiling. Serve with plantain and garnish with chives.

Oxtail and Butter Beans

This is a traditional Caribbean stew; old-fashioned, economical and full of goodness. It requires patience because of the long cooking time and since there isn't much meat on the oxtail it's necessary to buy a large amount. Ask your butcher to chop the oxtail unless, of course, you can use a meat cleaver!

INGREDIENTS

Serves 4 or more

1.5kg/3lb oxtail, chopped into pieces
1.75 litres/3 pints/7½ cups water
1 onion, finely chopped
3 bay leaves
4 thyme sprigs
3 whole cloves
175g/6oz dried butter beans, soaked
 overnight
2 garlic cloves, crushed
15ml/1 tbsp tomato purée
400g/14oz can chopped tomatoes
5ml/1 tsp ground allspice
1 hot chilli pepper
salt and freshly ground black pepper

1 Place the oxtail in a large heavy pan, add the onion, bay leaves, thyme and cloves and cover with water. Bring to the boil, then reduce the heat.

2 Cover the pan and simmer for at least 2½ hours or until the meat is very tender, adding water whenever necessary.

3 Meanwhile, drain the beans and cover with water. Bring to the boil and simmer for 1–1¼ hours. Drain and set aside.

4 When the oxtail is cooked and the stock is well reduced, add the garlic, tomato purée, tomatoes, allspice, hot pepper, salt and black pepper. Add the butter beans and simmer for a further 20 minutes. The stew should be fairly thick, but if it looks dry add a little water. Adjust the seasoning and serve hot.

"Seasoned-up" Lamb in Spinach Sauce

Lamb, spinach and ginger go well together. Powdered ginger has a strong distinctive flavour and should be used sparingly – you could use grated fresh root ginger, if you prefer.

INGREDIENTS

Serves 4
675g/1½lb stewing lamb, cubed
2.5ml/½ tsp ground ginger
2.5ml/½ tsp dried thyme
30ml/2 tbsp olive oil
1 onion, chopped
2 garlic cloves, crushed
15ml/1 tbsp tomato purée
½ hot chilli pepper chopped (optional)
600ml/1 pint/2½ cups stock or water
115g/4oz fresh spinach, finely chopped
salt and freshly ground black pepper

1 Place the lamb in a glass or china dish, season with the ginger, thyme and salt and pepper and leave to marinate in a cool place for at least 2 hours or overnight in the fridge.

2 Heat the olive oil in a large heavy saucepan, add the onion and garlic and fry gently for 5 minutes or until the onion is soft.

3 Add the lamb together with the tomato purée and hot pepper, if using. Fry over a moderate heat for about 5 minutes, stirring frequently, then add the stock or water. Cover and simmer for about 30 minutes, until the lamb is tender. Stir in the spinach. Simmer for 8 minutes until the sauce is fairly thick. Serve hot with boiled rice or root vegetables.

Lamb Pelau

Rice is often cooked with meat and coconut milk.

INGREDIENTS

Serves 4
450g/1lb stewing lamb
15ml/1 tbsp curry powder
1 onion, chopped
2 garlic cloves, crushed
2.5ml/½ tsp dried thyme
2.5ml/½ tsp dried oregano
1 fresh or dried chilli
25g/1oz/2 tbsp butter or margarine, plus more for serving
600ml/1 pint/2½ cups beef or chicken stock or coconut milk
5ml/1 tsp freshly ground black pepper
2 tomatoes, chopped
10ml/2 tsp sugar
30ml/2 tbsp chopped spring onion
450g/1lb basmati rice
spring onion strips, to garnish

1 Cut the lamb into cubes and place in a shallow glass or china dish. Sprinkle with the curry powder, onion, garlic, herbs and chilli and stir well. Cover loosely with clear film and leave to marinate in a cool place for 1 hour.

2 Melt the butter or margarine in a saucepan and fry the lamb for 5–10 minutes, on all sides. Add the stock or coconut milk, bring to the boil, then lower the heat and simmer for 35 minutes or until the meat is tender.

3 Add the black pepper, tomatoes, sugar, spring onions and rice, stir well and reduce the heat. Make sure that the rice is covered by 2.5cm/1in of liquid and add a little water if necessary. Simmer the pelau for 25 minutes or until the rice is cooked, then stir a little extra butter or margarine into the rice before serving. Garnish with spring onion strips.

Barbecued Jerk Chicken

Jerk refers to the blend of herb and spice seasoning rubbed into meat, before it is roasted over charcoal sprinkled with pimiento berries. In Jamaica, jerk seasoning was originally used only for pork, but jerked chicken is equally good.

INGREDIENTS

Serves 4
8 chicken pieces

For the marinade
5ml/1 tsp ground allspice
5ml/1 tsp ground cinnamon
5ml/1 tsp dried thyme
1.5ml/¼ tsp freshly grated nutmeg
10ml/2 tsp demerara sugar
2 garlic cloves, crushed
15ml/1 tbsp finely chopped onion
15ml/1 tbsp chopped spring onion
15ml/1 tbsp vinegar
30ml/2 tbsp oil
15ml/1 tbsp lime juice
1 hot chilli pepper, chopped
salt and freshly ground black pepper
salad leaves, to serve

1 Combine all the marinade ingredients in a small bowl. Using a fork, mash them together well to form a thick paste.

2 Lay the chicken pieces on a plate or board and make several lengthways slits in the flesh. Rub the seasoning all over the chicken and into the slits.

3 Place the chicken pieces in a dish, cover with clear film and marinate overnight in the fridge.

4 Shake off any excess seasoning from the chicken. Brush with oil and either place on a baking sheet or on a barbecue grill if barbecuing. Cook under a preheated grill for 45 minutes, turning often. Or, if barbecuing, light the coals and when ready, cook over the coals for 30 minutes, turning often. Serve hot with salad leaves.

COOK'S TIP

The flavour is best if you marinate the chicken overnight. Sprinkle the charcoal with aromatic herbs such as bay leaves for even more flavour.

Thyme and Lime Chicken

INGREDIENTS

Serves 4
8 chicken thighs
30ml/2 tbsp chopped spring onion
5ml/1 tsp dried or chopped fresh thyme
2 garlic cloves, crushed
juice of 1 lime or lemon
90ml/6 tbsp melted butter
salt and freshly ground black pepper
cooked rice, to serve
lime slices and coriander sprigs,
    to garnish

1 Put the chicken thighs in an ovenproof dish or on a baking tray skin-side down and using a sharp knife, make a slit, lengthways along the thigh bone of each thigh. Mix the spring onion with a little salt and pepper and press the mixture into the slits.

2 Mix together the thyme, garlic, lime or lemon juice and all but 30ml/2 tbsp of the butter in a small bowl and spoon a little over each chicken thigh.

3 Spoon the remaining butter over the top. Cover the chicken loosely with clear film and leave to marinate in a cool place for several hours or overnight in the fridge.

4 Preheat the oven to 190°C/375°F/ Gas 5. Remove the clear film from the chicken and cover the dish with foil. Bake the chicken for 1 hour, then remove the foil and cook for a few more minutes to brown. Serve hot, with rice and garnish with lime and coriander.

COOK'S TIP

You may need to use two limes, depending on their size and juiciness. Or, for a less sharp flavour, use lemons instead.

Salmon in Mango and Ginger Sauce

Mango and salmon complement
each other, especially with the
subtle flavour of tarragon.

INGREDIENTS

Serves 2
2 salmon steaks (about 275g/10oz each)
a little lemon juice
1 or 2 garlic cloves, crushed
5ml/1 tsp dried tarragon, crushed
2 shallots, roughly chopped
1 tomato, roughly chopped
1 ripe mango (about 175g/6oz flesh),
   chopped
150ml/¼ pint/⅔ cup fish stock or water
15ml/1 tbsp ginger syrup
25g/1oz/2 tbsp butter
salt and freshly ground black pepper

1 Place the salmon steaks in a shallow
dish and season with the lemon
juice, garlic, tarragon and salt and
pepper. Set aside in the fridge to
marinate for at least 1 hour.

2 Meanwhile, place the shallots,
tomato and mango in a blender or
food processor and blend until smooth.
Add the fish stock or water and the
ginger syrup, blend again and set aside.

3 Melt the butter in a frying pan and
sauté the salmon steaks for about
5 minutes on each side.

4 Add the mango purée, cover and
simmer until salmon is cooked.

5 Transfer the salmon to warmed
serving plates. Heat the sauce
through, adjust the seasoning and pour
over the salmon. Serve hot.

Fried Snapper with Avocado

Caribbean fried fish is often
eaten with fried dumplins or
hard-dough bread, and, as in this
recipe, is sometimes accompanied
by avocado – it makes a delicious
light supper or lunch.

INGREDIENTS

Serves 4
1 lemon
4 red snappers, about 225g/8oz each,
   prepared
10ml/2 tsp spice seasoning
flour, for dusting
oil, for frying
2 avocados and sliced corn-on-the-cob,
   to serve
chopped fresh parsley and lime slices,
   to garnish

1 Squeeze the lemon juice both
inside and outside the fish and
sprinkle them all over with the spice
seasoning. Set the fish aside in a
shallow dish to marinate in a cool place
for a few hours.

2 Lift the fish out of the dish and dust
thoroughly with the flour, shaking
off the excess.

3 Heat the oil in a non-stick pan
over a moderate heat. Add the fish
and fry for about 10 minutes on each
side until browned and crispy.

4 Halve the avocados, remove the
stones and cut in half again. Peel
away the skin and cut the flesh into
thin strips.

5 Place the fish on warmed serving
plates with the avocado and corn
slices. Serve hot, garnished with parsley
and lime slices.

Fillets of Trout in Wine Sauce with Plantains

Tropical fish would add a distinctive flavour to this dish, but any filleted white fish can be cooked in this way.

INGREDIENTS

Serves 4

4 trout fillets
spice seasoning, for dusting
25g/1oz/2 tbsp butter or margarine
1 or 2 garlic cloves
150ml/¼ pint/⅔ cup white wine
150ml/¼ pint/⅔ cup fish stock
10ml/2 tsp honey
15–30ml/1–2 tbsp chopped fresh parsley
1 yellow plantain
salt and freshly ground black pepper
oil, for frying

1 Season the trout fillets with the spice seasoning and marinate for 1 hour.

—— COOK'S TIP ——

Plantains belong to the banana family and can be green, yellow, or brown, depending on ripeness. Unlike bananas, plantains must be cooked. Their subtle flavour works well in spicy dishes.

2 Melt the butter or margarine in a large frying pan and heat gently for 1 minute. Add the fillets and sauté for about 5 minutes, until cooked through, turning carefully once. Transfer to a plate and keep warm.

3 Add the wine, fish stock and honey to the pan, bring to the boil and simmer to reduce slightly. Return the fillets to the pan and spoon over the sauce. Sprinkle with parsley and simmer gently for a few minutes.

4 Meanwhile, peel the plantain, and cut into rounds. Heat a little oil in a frying pan and fry the plantain slices for a few minutes, until golden, turning once. Transfer the fish to warmed serving plates, stir the sauce, adjust the seasoning and pour over the fish. Garnish with the fried plantain.

Ackee and Saltfish

This is a classic of Jamaican cuisine, popular in the Caribbean served with boiled green bananas.

INGREDIENTS

Serves 4

450g/1lb salt cod
25g/1oz/2 tbsp butter or margarine
30ml/2 tbsp vegetable oil
1 onion, chopped
2 garlic cloves, crushed
225g/8oz chopped fresh tomatoes
½ hot chilli pepper, chopped (optional)
2.5ml/½ tsp freshly ground black pepper
2.5ml/½ tsp dried thyme
2.5ml/½ tsp ground allspice
30ml/2 tbsp chopped spring onion
540g/1lb 6oz can ackee, drained
Fried Dumplins, to serve

1 Place the salt cod in a bowl and cover with cold water. Leave it to soak for at least 12 hours, changing the water two or three times. Discard the water and rinse in fresh cold water.

2 Put the salt cod in a large saucepan of cold water, bring to the boil, then remove the fish and allow to cool on a plate. Remove and discard the skin and bones, then flake the fish and set aside.

3 Heat the butter or margarine and oil in a large heavy frying pan over a moderate heat. Add the onion and garlic and sauté for 5 minutes. Add the tomatoes and hot chilli pepper, if using, and cook gently for a further 5 minutes.

4 Add the salt cod, black pepper, thyme, allspice and spring onions, stir to mix then stir in the ackee, taking care not to crush them. If you prefer a moister dish, add a little water or stock. Serve hot with Fried Dumplins.

Macaroni Cheese Pie

INGREDIENTS

Serves 4

225g/8oz macaroni
25g/1oz/2 tbsp butter or margarine
45ml/3 tbsp plain flour
450ml/¾ pint/2 cups milk
5ml/1 tsp mild mustard
2.5ml/½ tsp ground cinnamon
175g/6oz mature Cheddar cheese,
    grated
1 egg, beaten
15ml/1 tbsp butter or margarine
25g/1oz/2 tbsp chopped spring onions
40g/1½oz/3 tbsp canned chopped
    tomatoes
115g/4oz/⅔ cup sweetcorn
freshly ground black pepper
chopped fresh parsley, to garnish

1 Heat the oven to 180°C/350°F/
Gas 4. Cook the macaroni in
boiling salted water for 10 minutes
until just tender. Rinse under cold
water and drain.

2 Melt the butter or margarine in a
saucepan and stir in the flour to
make a roux. Slowly pour in the milk,
whisking constantly, and simmer gently
for 5–10 minutes.

3 Add the mustard, cinnamon and
115g/4oz of the cheese and cook
gently, stirring frequently, then remove
from the heat and whisk in the egg. Set
aside and make the filling.

4 To make the filling, heat the butter
or margarine in a small frying pan
and cook the spring onions, chopped
plum tomatoes and sweetcorn over a
gentle heat for 5–10 minutes.

5 Tip half the cooked macaroni into
a greased ovenproof dish. Pour
over half the cheese sauce and mix
well, then spoon the tomato and
sweetcorn mixture over the macaroni.

6 Tip the remaining macaroni into
the saucepan with the remaining
sauce, stir well and then spread
carefully over the tomato and
sweetcorn mixture.

7 Top with the remaining grated
cheese and bake in the oven for
about 45 minutes, or until the top is
golden and bubbly. If possible leave to
stand for 30 minutes before serving.
Serve hot, garnished with the chopped
fresh parsley.

Red Bean Chilli

This vegetarian chilli can be adapted to accommodate meat eaters by adding either minced beef or lamb in place of the lentils. Add the meat once the onions are soft and fry until nicely browned before adding the tomatoes.

INGREDIENTS

Serves 4
30ml/2 tbsp vegetable oil
1 onion, chopped
400g/14oz can chopped tomatoes
2 garlic cloves, crushed
300ml/½ pint/1¼ cups white wine
about 300ml/½ pint/1¼ cups
   vegetable stock
115g/4oz red lentils
2 thyme sprigs or 5ml/1 tsp dried
   thyme
10ml/2 tsp ground cumin
45ml/3 tbsp dark soy sauce
½ hot chilli pepper, finely chopped
5ml/1 tsp mixed spice
15ml/1 tbsp oyster sauce (optional)
225g/8oz can red kidney beans,
   drained
10ml/2 tsp sugar
salt

1 Heat the oil in a large saucepan and fry the onion over a moderate heat for a few minutes until slightly softened.

2 Add the tomatoes and garlic, cook for 10 minutes, then stir in the wine and stock.

3 Add the lentils, thyme, cumin, soy sauce, hot pepper, mixed spice and oyster sauce, if using.

4 Cover and simmer for 40 minutes or until the lentils are cooked, stirring occasionally and adding more water if the lentils begin to dry out.

5 Stir in the kidney beans and sugar and continue cooking for 10 minutes, adding a little extra stock or water if necessary. Season to taste with salt and serve hot with boiled rice and sweetcorn.

--- COOK'S TIP ---

Fiery chillies can irritate the skin, so always wash your hands well after handling them and take care not to touch your eyes. If you like really hot, spicy food, then add the seeds from the chilli, too.

Spinach Plantain Rounds

This delectable way of serving plantains is a little fiddly to make, but well worth it! The plantains must be ripe, but still firm.

INGREDIENTS

Serves 4

2 large ripe plantains
oil, for frying
30ml/2 tbsp butter or margarine
25g/1oz/2 tbsp finely chopped onion
2 garlic cloves, crushed
450g/1lb fresh spinach, chopped
pinch of freshly grated nutmeg
1 egg, beaten
wholemeal flour, for dusting
salt and freshly ground black pepper

1 Using a small sharp knife, carefully cut each plantain lengthways into four slices.

2 Heat a little oil in a large frying pan and fry the plantain slices on both sides until lightly golden brown but not fully cooked. Drain on kitchen paper and reserve the oil.

3 Melt the butter or margarine in a saucepan and sauté the onion and garlic for a few minutes until the onion is soft. Add the spinach, salt, pepper and nutmeg. Cover and cook for about 5 minutes until the spinach has reduced. Cool, then tip into a sieve and press out any excess moisture.

4 Curl the plantain slices into rings and secure each ring with a wooden cocktail stick. Pack each ring with a little of the spinach mixture.

5 Place the egg and flour in two separate shallow dishes. Add a little more oil to the frying pan if necessary and heat until moderately hot. Dip the plantain rings in the egg and then in the flour and fry on both sides for 1–2 minutes until golden brown. Drain on kitchen paper and serve hot or cold with a salad, or as part of a meal.

COOK'S TIP

If fresh spinach is not available, use frozen spinach, thawed and drained. The plantain rings can be small or large, and if preferred mashed meat, fish or beans can be used instead of spinach for the filling.

Fried Dumplins

Fried Dumplins are easy to make and the "sister" to Bakes, as they are also known in the Caribbean and Guyana. They are usually served with saltfish or fried fish, but they can be eaten quite simply with butter and jam or cheese. Children love them!

INGREDIENTS

Makes about 10
450g/1lb/4 cups self-raising flour
10ml/2 tsp sugar
2.5ml/½ tsp salt
300ml/½ pint/1¼ cups milk
oil, for frying

1 Sift the dry ingredients together into a large bowl, add the milk and mix and knead until smooth.

2 Divide the dough into ten balls, kneading each ball with floured hands. Press the balls gently to flatten into 7.5cm/3in rounds.

3 Heat a little oil in a non-stick frying pan until moderately hot. Place half the dumplins in the pan, reduce the heat to low and fry for about 15 minutes until they are golden brown, turning once.

4 Stand them on their sides for a few minutes to brown the edges, before removing them and draining on kitchen paper. Serve warm.

Spicy Potato Salad

This tasty salad is quick to prepare, and makes a satisfying accompaniment to grilled or barbecued meat or fish.

INGREDIENTS

Serves 6

900g/2lb potatoes, peeled
2 red peppers
2 celery sticks
1 shallot
2 or 3 spring onions
1 green chilli, finely chopped
1 garlic clove, crushed
10ml/2 tsp finely snipped
  fresh chives
10ml/2 tsp finely chopped fresh basil
15ml/1 tbsp finely chopped fresh
  parsley
15ml/1 tbsp single cream
30ml/2 tbsp salad cream
15ml/1 tbsp mayonnaise
5ml/1 tsp mild mustard
7.5ml/½ tbsp sugar
snipped fresh chives, to garnish

1 Boil the potatoes until tender but still firm. Drain and cool, then cut into 2.5cm/1in cubes and place in a large salad bowl.

2 Halve the peppers, cut away and discard the core and seeds and cut into small pieces. Finely chop the celery, shallot, and spring onions and slice the chilli very thinly, discarding the seeds. Add the vegetables to the potatoes together with the garlic and chopped herbs.

3 Blend the cream, salad cream, mayonnaise, mustard and sugar in a small bowl, stirring until the mixture is well combined.

4 Pour the dressing over the potato and vegetable salad and stir gently to coat evenly. Serve, garnished with the snipped chives.

Rice and Peas

This popular dish is also known as Peas and Rice on the islands in the Eastern Caribbean.

INGREDIENTS

Serves 6

175g/6oz/1 cup red kidney beans
2 fresh thyme sprigs
50g/2oz creamed coconut
2 bay leaves
1 onion, finely chopped
2 garlic cloves, crushed
2.5ml/½ tsp ground allspice
115g/4oz chopped red or green pepper
450g/1lb long grain rice
salt and freshly ground black pepper

1 Place the red kidney beans in a large bowl. Cover with water and leave to soak overnight.

2 Drain the beans, place in a large pan and add enough water to cover the beans by about 2.5cm/1in. Bring to the boil and boil over a high heat for 10 minutes, then reduce the heat and simmer for about 1½ hours or until the beans are tender.

3 Add the thyme, creamed coconut, bay leaves, onion, garlic, allspice, red or green pepper and seasoning and stir in 600ml/1 pint/2½ cups water.

4 Bring to the boil and add the rice. Stir well, reduce the heat and simmer, covered for 25–30 minutes, until all the liquid is absorbed. Serve as an accompaniment to fish, meat or vegetarian dishes.

Dhal Puri

Otherwise known as roti, these thin fried breads can also be made with white flour. They are delicious served with meat, fish or vegetable dishes.

Ingredients

Makes about 15
450g/1lb/4 cups self-raising flour
115g/4oz/1 cup wholemeal flour
350ml/12fl oz/1½ cups cold water
30ml/2 tbsp oil, plus extra for frying
salt, to taste

For the filling
350g/12oz yellow split peas
15ml/1 tbsp ground cumin
2 garlic cloves, crushed

1 Sift together the dry ingredients into a bowl, then add the water a little at a time gradually kneading the mixture to make a soft dough. Knead for a short while until supple.

2 Add the oil to the dough and continue to knead until completely smooth. Put the dough in a polythene bag or wrap in clear film and keep in a cool place or in the fridge for at least 30 minutes, or leave overnight.

3 To make the filling, put the peas in a saucepan, cover with water and cook until the peas are half cooked – they should be tender on the outside, but still firm in the middle. Allow the water to evaporate during cooking, until the pan is dry, but watch carefully and add a little extra water to prevent burning, if necessary.

4 Spread the peas out on to a tray, and when cool, grind to a paste and mix with the cumin and garlic.

5 Divide the dough into about 15 balls. Slightly flatten each ball of dough, put about 15ml/1 tbsp of mixture into the centre and fold over the edges to enclose the mixture.

6 Dust a rolling pin and a board with flour and roll out the dhal puri, taking care not to overstretch, until they are about 18cm/7in in diameter.

7 Heat a little oil on a tawa (roti pan) or in a heavy-based frying pan, swirling the oil to cover the base. Cook the dhal puris for about 3 minutes on each side until light brown. Fold them into a clean dish towel, to keep warm. Serve warm.

Fried Yellow Plantains

When plantains are yellow they are ripe and ready to enhance most meat, fish or vegetarian dishes. The riper the plantains the darker and sweeter they are.

INGREDIENTS

Serves 4
2 yellow plantains
oil, for shallow frying
finely snipped chives, to garnish

1 Using a small sharp knife, top and tail the plantains, and cut in half.

2 Slit the skin only, along the natural ridges of each piece of plantain.

3 Ease up the edge of the skin and run the tip of your thumb along the plantains, lifting the skin.

4 Peel away the skin and slice the plantains lengthways. Heat a little oil in a large frying pan and fry the plantain slices for 2–3 minutes each side until golden brown.

5 When the plantains are brown and crisp, drain on kitchen paper and serve hot or cold, sprinkled with finely snipped chives.

Buttered Spinach and Rice

The layer of spinach was purely accidental – it was once missed from the dish and thus became a lovely topping for the rice!

INGREDIENTS

Serves 4
40g/1½oz/3 tbsp butter or margarine
1 onion, finely chopped
2 fresh tomatoes, chopped
450g/1lb basmati rice, washed
2 garlic cloves, crushed
600ml/1 pint/2½ cups stock or water
350g/12oz fresh spinach, shredded
salt and freshly ground black pepper
2 tomatoes, sliced, to garnish

1 Melt 25g/1oz/2 tbsp of the butter or margarine in a large saucepan and fry the onion for a few minutes until soft. Add the chopped tomatoes and stir.

2 Add the rice and garlic, cook for 5 minutes, then gradually add the stock, stirring all the time. Season well.

3 Cover and simmer gently for 10–15 minutes until the rice is almost cooked, then reduce the heat to low.

4 Spread the spinach in a thick layer over the rice. Cover the pan and cook over a low heat for 5–8 minutes until the spinach has wilted. Dot the remaining butter over the top and then serve, garnished with sliced tomatoes.

———— COOK'S TIP ————

If fresh spinach is not available, you can use frozen leaf spinach instead. Thaw and drain 225g/8oz frozen spinach and cook as recipe for about 5 minutes. Finely shredded spring greens can also be used.

Creamed Sweet Potatoes

White sweet potatoes are best for this recipe, rather than orange sweet potatoes. White yams make a good substitute, especially poona (Ghanaian) yam.

INGREDIENTS

Serves 4
900g/2lb sweet potatoes
50g/2oz/4 tbsp butter
45ml/3 tbsp single cream
freshly grated nutmeg
15ml/1 tbsp snipped fresh chives
salt and freshly ground black pepper

1 Peel the sweet potatoes under cold running water and place in a bowl of salted water. Cut or slice them and place in a large saucepan and cover with cold water. Cook, covered for about 30 minutes.

2 When the potatoes are cooked, drain and add the butter, cream, nutmeg, chives and seasoning. Mash with a potato masher and then fluff up with a fork. Serve warm as an accompaniment to a curry or stew.

Bread and Butter Custard

This dessert is a delicious family favourite. A richer version can be made with fresh cream, instead of evaporated milk. It can also be made using other dried fruit – mango is particularly good.

INGREDIENTS

Serves 4

15ml/1 tbsp softened butter
3 thin slices of bread, crusts removed
400g/14oz can evaporated milk
150ml/¼ pint/⅔ cup fresh milk
2.5ml/½ tsp mixed spice
40g/1½oz/3 tbsp demerara sugar
2 eggs, whisked
75g/3oz/½ cup sultanas
freshly grated nutmeg
a little icing sugar, for dusting

1 Preheat the oven to 180°C/350°F/ Gas 4 and lightly butter an ovenproof dish. Butter the bread and cut into small pieces.

2 Lay the buttered bread in several layers in the prepared dish.

3 Whisk together the evaporated milk and the fresh milk, mixed spice, sugar and eggs in a large bowl. Pour the mixture over the bread and butter. Sprinkle over the sultanas and leave to stand for 30 minutes.

4 Grate a little nutmeg over the top and bake for 30–40 minutes until the custard is just set and golden. Serve sprinkled with icing sugar.

Duckanoo

This tasty pudding originated in west Africa.

INGREDIENTS

Serves 4–6

450g/1lb/3 cups fine cornmeal
350g/12oz fresh coconut, chopped
600ml/1 pint/2½ cups fresh milk
115g/4oz currants or raisins
50g/2oz/4 tbsp butter or margarine, melted
115g/4oz/½ cup demerara sugar
60ml/4 tbsp water
1.5ml/¼ tsp freshly grated nutmeg
2.5ml/½ tsp ground cinnamon
5ml/1 tsp vanilla essence

1 Place the cornmeal in a large bowl. Blend the coconut and the milk in a blender or food processor until smooth. Stir the coconut mixture into the cornmeal, then add all the remaining ingredients and stir well.

2 Take 6 pieces of foil and fold into 13 x 15cm/5 x 6in pockets leaving an opening on one short side. Fold the edges of the remaining sides tightly to ensure that they are well sealed.

3 Put one or two spoonfuls of the mixture into each pocket and fold over the edge of the foil to seal.

4 Place the foil pockets in a large saucepan of boiling water. Cover and simmer for about 45–60 minutes. Lift out the pockets from the water and remove the foil. Serve the duckanoo by themselves or with fresh cream.

Fruits of the Tropics Salad

INGREDIENTS

Serves 4–6

1 medium pineapple
400g/14oz can guava halves in syrup
2 medium bananas, sliced
1 large mango, peeled, stoned and
   diced
115g/4oz stem ginger and 30ml/2 tbsp
   of the syrup
60ml/4 tbsp thick coconut milk
10ml/2 tsp sugar
2.5ml/½ tsp freshly grated nutmeg
2.5ml/½ tsp ground cinnamon
strips of coconut, to decorate

1 Peel, core and cube the pineapple, and place in a serving bowl. Drain the guavas, reserve the syrup and chop. Add the guavas to the bowl with one of the bananas and the mango.

2 Chop the stem ginger and add to the pineapple mixture.

3 Pour 30ml/2 tbsp of the ginger syrup, and the reserved guava syrup into a blender or food processor and add the other banana, the coconut milk and the sugar. Blend to make a smooth creamy purée.

4 Pour the banana and coconut mixture over the fruit, add a little grated nutmeg and a sprinkling of cinnamon. Serve chilled, decorated with strips of coconut.

Avocado Salad in Ginger and Orange Sauce

This is an unusual fruit salad since avocado is more often treated as a vegetable. However, in the Caribbean it is used as a fruit, which of course it is!

INGREDIENTS

Serves 4
2 firm ripe avocados
3 firm ripe bananas, chopped
12 fresh cherries or strawberries
juice of 1 large orange
shredded fresh root ginger (optional)

For the ginger syrup
50g/2oz fresh root ginger, chopped
900ml/1½ pints/3¾ cups water
225g/8oz/1 cup demerara sugar
2 cloves

1 First make the ginger syrup; place the ginger, water, sugar and cloves in a saucepan and bring to the boil. Reduce the heat and simmer for about 1 hour, until well reduced and syrupy.

2 Remove the ginger and discard. Leave to cool. Store in a covered, clean container in the fridge.

3 Peel the avocados, cut into cubes and place in a bowl with the bananas and cherries or strawberries.

4 Pour the orange juice over the fruits. Add 60ml/4 tbsp of the ginger syrup and mix gently, using a metal spoon. Chill for 30 minutes and add a little shredded ginger, if using.

MEXICO

Tlalpeño-style Soup

For a hearty version of this simple soup, add some cooked chick-peas or rice.

INGREDIENTS

Serves 6

1.5 litres/2½ pints/6 cups chicken stock
2 cooked chicken breast fillets, skinned and cut into large strips
1 drained canned *chipotle* chilli or *jalapeño* chilli, rinsed
1 avocado

─── COOK'S TIP ───

When using canned chillies, it is important to rinse them very thoroughly before adding them to the pan so as to remove the flavour of any pickling liquid.

1 Heat the stock in a large saucepan and add the chicken and chilli. Simmer over a very gentle heat for 5 minutes to heat the chicken and release the flavour from the chilli.

2 Cut the avocado in half, remove the stone and peel off the skin. Slice the avocado flesh neatly.

3 Remove the chilli from the stock, using a slotted spoon, and then discard it. Pour the soup into heated serving bowls, distributing the chicken evenly among them.

4 Carefully add a few avocado slices to each bowl and serve.

Avocado Soup

INGREDIENTS

Serves 4

2 large ripe avocados
1 litre/1¾ pints/4 cups chicken stock
250ml/8fl oz/1 cup single cream
salt and freshly ground white pepper
15ml/1 tbsp finely chopped coriander, to garnish (optional)

─── COOK'S TIP ───

The easiest way to mash the avocados is to hold each seeded half in turn in the palm of one hand and mash the flesh in the shell with a fork, before scooping it into the bowl. This avoids the avocado slithering about when it is being mashed.

1 Cut the avocados in half, remove the stones and mash the flesh (see Cook's Tip). Put the flesh into a sieve and with a wooden spoon, press it through into a warm soup bowl.

2 Heat the chicken stock with the cream in a saucepan. When the mixture is hot, but not boiling, whisk it into the puréed avocado.

3 Season to taste with salt and pepper. Serve immediately, sprinkled with the coriander, if used. The soup may be served chilled, if liked.

Mixed Tostadas

Like little edible plates, these fried tortillas can support anything that is not too juicy.

INGREDIENTS

Makes 14
oil, for shallow frying
14 freshly prepared unbaked
    corn tortillas
225g/8oz/1 cup mashed red kidney or
    pinto beans
1 iceberg lettuce, shredded
oil and vinegar dressing (optional)
2 cooked chicken breasts, skinned and
    thinly sliced
225g/8oz Guacamole
115g/4oz/1 cup coarsely grated
    Cheddar cheese
pickled *jalapeño* chillies, seeded and
    sliced, to taste

1 Heat the oil in a frying pan and fry the tortillas until golden brown on both sides and crisp but not hard.

2 Spread each tortilla with a layer of beans. Put a layer of shredded lettuce (which can be left plain or lightly tossed with a little dressing) over the beans.

3 Arrange pieces of chicken in a layer on top of the lettuce. Carefully spread over a layer of the Guacamole and finally sprinkle over a layer of the grated cheese.

4 Arrange the mixed tostadas on a large platter. Serve on individual plates but eat using your hands.

Quesadillas

These delicious filled and deep-fried tortilla turnovers make a popular snack and smaller versions make excellent canapés.

INGREDIENTS

Makes 14
14 freshly prepared unbaked tortillas

For the filling
225g/8oz/1 cup finely chopped or
    grated Cheddar cheese
3 *jalapeño* chillies, seeded and cut
    into strips
salt
oil, for shallow frying

1 Have the tortillas ready, covered with a clean cloth. Combine the grated cheese and chilli strips in a bowl. Season with salt. Set aside.

2 Heat the oil in a frying pan, then holding an unbaked tortilla on your palm, put a spoonful of filling along the centre, avoiding the edges.

--- COOK'S TIP ---

For other stuffing ideas try leftover beans with chillies, or chopped chorizo sausage fried with a little chopped onion.

3 Fold the tortilla and seal the edges by pressing or crimping well together. Fry in hot oil, on both sides, until golden brown and crisp.

4 Using a fish slice, lift out the quesadilla and drain it on kitchen paper. Transfer to a plate and keep warm while frying the remaining quesadillas. Serve hot.

Chimichangas

INGREDIENTS

Makes 14
½ quantity Picadillo
14 freshly prepared unbaked
   flour tortillas
oil, for frying

To garnish
whole radishes with leaves

COOK'S TIP

Chimichangas originally came from the state of Sonora, and are made with the large plate-sized tortillas that are a speciality of the region. Any size that suits the cook will do just as well.

1 Spoon about 60ml/4 tbsp Picadillo down the centre of each tortilla. Fold in the sides, then the top and bottom, envelope-fashion, or simply roll up and fasten with a cocktail stick.

2 Pour the corn oil into a frying pan to a depth of about 2.5cm/1in. Set the pan over a moderate heat. Fry the chimichangas, a few at a time, for about 1–2 minutes, or until golden.

3 Drain on kitchen paper and keep warm. Serve the chimichangas garnished with whole radishes.

Tacos

The taco has been called the Mexican sandwich; it is always eaten in the hand and makes a great speedy snack. All you need is a supply of tortillas or taco shells, and a selection of fillings.

INGREDIENTS

Makes as many as you like
freshly prepared corn tortillas or pre-prepared taco shells

For the fillings
Picadillo topped with Guacamole
chopped chorizo fried and mixed with
   chopped Cheddar cheese and chillies
Frijoles Refritos (Refried Beans) with
   sliced *jalapeño* chillies, Guacamole,
   and cubed cheese
leftover Mole Poblano de Guajalote
   with Guacamole
cooked shredded pork or chicken with
   salsa and shredded lettuce

1 To make tacos, all you need is a supply of fresh corn tortillas, and as many of the suggested fillings as you can muster. The idea is to use your imagination, and cooks often vie with one another to see who can produce the most interesting combination of flavours. Chillies and guacamole are always welcome, in the taco or served as an extra on the side.

2 To make traditional soft tacos, simply spoon the filling on to the tortilla, wrap the tortilla around the filling – and eat.

3 To make hard tacos, secure the rolled up and filled tortilla with a cocktail stick, then briefly shallow fry until crisp and golden.

4 Pre-prepared U-shaped taco shells are not Mexican, but make a speedy version of this snack. Hold one taco shell at a time in one hand, and fill with the fillings of your choice.

Tortilla Flutes

Flutes or *flautas* look as good as
they taste.

INGREDIENTS

Makes about 12
24 freshly prepared unbaked
   flour tortillas
2 tomatoes, peeled, seeded
   and chopped
1 small onion, chopped
1 garlic clove, chopped
30–45ml/2–3 tbsp corn oil
2 freshly cooked chicken breasts,
   skinned and shredded
salt

To garnish
sliced radishes
stuffed green olives

1 Place the unbaked flour tortillas in
pairs on a work surface, with the
right-hand tortilla overlapping its
partner by about 5cm/2in.

2 Put the tomatoes, onion, and garlic
into a food processor and process
to a purée. Season with salt to taste.

3 Heat 15ml/1 tbsp of the oil in a
frying pan and cook the tomato
purée for a few minutes, stirring to
blend the flavours. Remove from the
heat and stir in the shredded chicken,
mixing well.

4 Spread about 30ml/2 tbsp of the
chicken mixture on each pair of
tortillas, roll them up into flutes and
secure with a cocktail stick.

5 Heat a little oil in a frying pan
large enough to hold the flutes
comfortably. Cook more than one at a
time if possible, but don't overcrowd
the pan. Fry the flutes until light brown
all over. Add more oil if needed.

6 Drain the cooked flutes on kitchen
paper, and keep hot. When ready
to serve, transfer to a platter and
garnish with radishes and olives.

COOK'S TIP

If the flour tortillas are too hard to roll up
easily, fry them for just a few seconds in
hot oil, then quickly stuff and roll them.

Chilaquiles

INGREDIENTS

Serves 4

corn or peanut oil, for frying
6 leftover corn tortillas, cut or torn into
   1cm/¹/₂ in strips
275g/10oz can tomatillos (Mexican
   green tomatoes)
1 onion, finely chopped
2–3 drained canned *jalapeño* chillies,
   rinsed, seeded and chopped
30ml/2 tbsp chopped fresh coriander
115g/4oz/1 cup grated Cheddar cheese
175ml/6fl oz/ ³/₄ cup chicken stock
salt and freshly ground black pepper

To garnish

chopped spring onion
stuffed green olives
chopped fresh coriander

1 Heat 45ml/3 tbsp of the oil in a large frying pan. Fry the tortilla strips, a few at a time, on both sides, without browning. Add more oil if needed. Drain on kitchen paper.

2 Tip the tomatillos and juice into a food processor. Add the onion, chillies and coriander; purée.

3 Season the tomatillo purée with salt and pepper. Heat 15ml/1 tbsp oil in the clean frying pan, add the tomatillo mixture and cook gently for 2–3 minutes, stirring frequently.

4 Pour a layer of the sauce into the bottom of a flameproof casserole or shallow baking dish and top with a layer of tortilla strips and a layer of grated cheese. Continue until all the ingredients have been used, reserving some cheese for sprinkling on top.

5 Pour the chicken stock over the dish and sprinkle with the reserved cheese. If using a flameproof casserole, cover and cook over a moderate heat until all the liquid has been absorbed and the dish is heated through. Or, bake the chilaquiles, uncovered, in a preheated oven at 180°C/350°F/Gas 4 for 30 minutes or until heated through.

6 Serve directly from the casserole or dish, garnished with chopped spring onion, olives and coriander.

Seviche

This makes an excellent starter. With the addition of sliced avocado, it could make a light summer lunch for four.

INGREDIENTS

Serves 6

450g/1lb mackerel fillets, cut into
 1cm/½in pieces
350ml/12fl oz/1½ cups freshly
 squeezed lime or lemon juice
225g/8oz tomatoes, chopped
1 small onion, very finely chopped
2 drained canned *jalapeño* chillies or 4
 serrano chillies, rinsed and chopped
60ml/4 tbsp olive oil
2.5ml/½ tsp dried oregano
30ml/2 tbsp chopped fresh coriander
salt and freshly ground black pepper
lemon wedges and fresh coriander,
 to garnish
stuffed green olives, to serve

1 Put the fish into a glass dish and pour over the lime or lemon juice, making sure that the fish is completely covered. Cover and chill for 6 hours, turning once, by which time the fish will be opaque, "cooked" by the juice.

─────── COOK'S TIP ───────

For a more delicately flavoured Seviche, use a white fish such as sole.

2 When the fish is opaque, lift it out of the juice and set it aside.

3 Combine the tomatoes, onion, chillies, olive oil, oregano and coriander in a bowl. Add salt and pepper to taste and then pour in the reserved juice from the mackerel. Mix well and pour over the fish.

4 Cover the dish and return the seviche to the fridge for about an hour to allow the flavours to blend. Seviche should not be served too cold. Allow it to stand at room temperature for 15 minutes before serving. Garnish with lemon wedges and coriander sprigs, and serve with stuffed olives sprinkled with chopped coriander.

Red Snapper, Veracruz-style

This is Mexico's best-known fish dish. In Veracruz red snapper is always used but fillets of any firm-fleshed white fish can be substituted successfully.

INGREDIENTS

Serves 4
4 large red snapper fillets
30ml/2 tbsp freshly squeezed lime or
    lemon juice
120ml/4fl oz/½ cup olive oil
1 onion, finely chopped
2 garlic cloves, chopped
675g/1½lb tomatoes, peeled
    and chopped
1 bay leaf, plus a few sprigs to garnish
1.5ml/¼ tsp dried oregano
30ml/2 tbsp large capers, plus extra
    to serve (optional)
16 stoned green olives, halved
2 drained canned *jalapeño* chillies,
    seeded and cut into strips
butter, for frying
3 slices firm white bread, cut
    into triangles
salt and freshly ground black pepper

1 Arrange the fish fillets in a single layer in a shallow dish. Season with salt and pepper, drizzle with the lime or lemon juice and set aside.

2 Heat the oil in a large frying pan and sauté the onion and garlic until the onion is soft. Add the tomatoes and cook for about 10 minutes until the mixture is thick and flavoursome. Stir the mixture from time to time.

3 Stir in the bay leaf, oregano, capers, olives and chillies. Add the fish and cook over a very low heat for about 10 minutes or until tender.

— COOK'S TIP —

This dish can also be made with a whole fish, weighing about 1.5kg/3–3½lb. Bake together with the sauce, in a preheated oven at 160°C/325°F/Gas 3. Allow 10 minutes cooking time for every 2.5cm/1in thickness of the fish.

4 While the fish is cooking, heat the butter in a small frying pan and sauté the bread triangles until they are golden brown on both sides.

5 Transfer the fish to a heated platter, pour over the sauce and surround with the fried bread triangles. Garnish with bay leaves and serve with extra capers, if you like.

Striped Bass in Sauce

This is a typical Mayan dish.

INGREDIENTS

Serves 6

1.5kg/3–3½lb striped bass or any non-
  oily white fish, cut into 6 steaks
120ml/4fl oz/½ cup corn oil
1 large onion, thinly sliced
2 garlic cloves, chopped
350g/12oz tomatoes, sliced
2 drained canned *jalapeño* chillies,
  rinsed and sliced

For the marinade

4 garlic cloves, crushed
5ml/1 tsp black peppercorns
5ml/1 tsp dried oregano
2.5ml/½ tsp ground cumin
5ml/1 tsp ground *achiote* (annatto)
2.5ml/½ tsp ground cinnamon
120ml/4fl oz/½ cup mild white vinegar
salt
flat leaf parsley, to garnish

1 Arrange the fish steaks in a single layer in a shallow dish. Make the marinade. Using a pestle, grind the garlic and black peppercorns in a mortar. Add the dried oregano, cumin, *achiote* (annatto) and cinnamon and mix to a paste with the vinegar. Add salt to taste and spread the marinade on both sides of each of the fish steaks. Cover and leave in a cool place for 1 hour.

2 Select a flameproof dish large enough to hold the fish in a single layer and pour in enough of the oil to coat the bottom. Arrange the fish in the dish with any remaining marinade.

3 Top the fish with the onion, garlic, tomatoes and chillies and pour the rest of the oil over the top.

4 Cover the dish and cook over a low heat on top of the stove for 15–20 minutes, or until the fish is no longer translucent. Serve at once garnished with flat leaf parsley.

Salt Cod in Mild Chilli Sauce

INGREDIENTS

Serves 6
900g/2lb dried salt cod
1 onion, chopped
2 garlic cloves, chopped

For the sauce
6 dried *ancho* chillies
1 onion, chopped
2.5ml/½ tsp dried oregano
2.5ml/½ tsp ground coriander
1 *serrano* chilli, seeded and chopped
45ml/3 tbsp corn oil
750ml/1¼ pints/3 cups fish or
  chicken stock
salt

For the garnish
1 fresh green chilli, sliced

--- COOK'S TIP ---

Dried salt cod is a great favourite in Spain and Portugal and throughout Latin America. Look for it in Spanish and Portuguese markets.

1 Soak the cod in cold water for several hours, depending on how hard and salty it is. Change the water once or twice during soaking.

2 Drain the fish and transfer it to a saucepan. Pour in water to cover. Bring to a gentle simmer and cook for about 15 minutes until the fish is tender. Drain, reserving the stock. Remove any skin or bones from the fish and cut it into 4cm/1½ in pieces.

3 Make the sauce. Remove the stems and shake out the seeds from the *ancho* chillies. Tear the pods into pieces, put in a bowl of warm water and soak until they are soft.

4 Drain the soaked chillies and put them into a food processor with the onion, oregano, coriander and *serrano* chilli. Process to a purée.

5 Heat the oil in a frying pan and cook the purée, stirring, for about 5 minutes. Stir in the fish or chicken stock and simmer for 3–4 minutes.

6 Add the prepared cod and simmer for a few minutes longer to heat the fish through and blend the flavours. Serve garnished with the sliced chilli.

Crab with Green Rice

INGREDIENTS

Serves 4
225g/8oz/1 cup long grain rice
60ml/4 tbsp olive oil
2 x 275g/10oz cans tomatillos
  (Mexican green tomatoes)
1 onion, chopped
2 garlic cloves, chopped
30ml/2 tbsp chopped fresh coriander
about 350ml/12fl oz/1½ cups
  chicken stock
450g/1lb crab meat, thawed if frozen,
  broken into chunks
salt
chopped fresh coriander, to garnish
lettuce leaves, to serve

1 Soak the rice in enough hot water to cover for 15 minutes, then drain thoroughly. Heat the oil in a frying pan and sauté the rice over a moderate heat, stirring until the rice is golden and the oil has been absorbed.

2 Drain the tomatillos, reserving the juice, and put them into a food processor. Add the onion, garlic and coriander, and process to a purée. Pour into a measuring jug and add the tomatillo juice. Pour in enough stock to make the quantity up to 475ml/16fl oz/2 cups. Season to taste.

3 Place the rice, tomato mixture and crab meat in a shallow pan. Cover and cook over a very low heat for about 30 minutes or until the liquid has been absorbed and the rice is tender. Serve on lettuce leaves, garnished with chopped fresh coriander.

> ——— COOK'S TIP ———
>
> Mexican cooks always soak rice in water before cooking it. This seems to pay off, as their rice is always delicious, with every grain separate.

Prawns with Pumpkin Seed Sauce

INGREDIENTS

Serves 4
175g/6oz/1 generous cup *pepitas*
  (Mexican pumpkin seeds)
450g/1lb raw prawns, thawed if frozen,
  peeled and deveined
1 onion, chopped
1 garlic clove, chopped
30ml/2 tbsp chopped fresh coriander
225g/8oz tomatoes, peeled
  and chopped
1 drained canned *jalapeño* chilli, rinsed,
  seeded and chopped
1 red pepper, seeded and chopped
30ml/2 tbsp corn oil
salt
whole cooked prawns, lemon slices and
  fresh coriander sprigs, to garnish
rice, to serve

1 Grind the pumpkin seeds finely and shake through a sieve into a bowl and set to one side.

2 Cook the prawns in boiling salted water. As soon as they turn pink, remove with a slotted spoon and set them aside. Reserve the cooking water.

3 Purée the onion, garlic, coriander, tomatoes, chilli, red pepper and pumpkin seeds in a food processor. Heat the oil in a pan, stir and cook the mixture for 5 minutes. Season. Add prawn water to thin the mixture to a sauce consistency. Heat gently, add the prawns. Garnish and serve with rice.

Smoked Beef Tongue with Tomatillos

Tomatillos have a delicious, distinctive flavour and colour.

INGREDIENTS

Serves 6–8

1 smoked ox tongue, about
    2.25kg/5–5¼lb
45ml/3 tbsp corn oil
2 onions, finely chopped
2 garlic cloves, chopped
3 or 4 drained pickled *serrano* or
    jalapeño chillies, seeded and chopped
30ml/2 tbsp chopped fresh coriander
2 x 275g/10oz cans tomatillos
    (Mexican green tomatoes)
salt and freshly ground pepper
fresh coriander, to garnish
small new potatoes, to serve

1 Thoroughly wash the tongue and put it into a large saucepan. Cover with cold water and bring to the boil. Remove any scum that rises to the surface. Lower the heat and simmer, covered, for 3–4 hours until tender. Allow the tongue to cool in the stock.

2 Lift out the tongue when it is cool enough to handle, reserving the stock. Peel the skin from the tongue and trim the root end and discard. Cut the tongue into fairly thick slices and place these in a flameproof casserole.

3 Heat the oil in a large frying pan and sauté the onions and garlic with the chillies until the onion is tender. Add the coriander, the tomatillos (with the can juices) and salt and pepper to taste. Stir to mix and pour over the tongue, adding a little reserved stock if the mixture is thick.

4 Cover the pan with foil or a lid and cook over a moderate heat for about 15 minutes until hot. Serve at once, garnished with coriander sprigs and accompanied by new potatoes sprinkled with chopped coriander.

COOK'S TIP

Fresh lamb's tongues can be used – they only need to be cooked for 45–60 minutes.

Pork with Pineapple

INGREDIENTS

Serves 6

30ml/2 tbsp corn oil
900g/2lb boneless pork shoulder or
   loin, cut into 5cm/2in cubes
1 onion, finely chopped
1 large red pepper, seeded and
   finely chopped
1 or more *jalapeño* chillies, seeded and
   finely chopped
450g/1lb fresh pineapple chunks
8 fresh mint leaves, chopped
250ml/8fl oz/1 cup chicken stock
salt and freshly ground black pepper
fresh mint sprig, to garnish
rice, to serve

1 Heat the oil in a large frying pan
and sauté the pork in batches until
the cubes are lightly coloured. Transfer
the pork to a flameproof casserole,
leaving the oil behind in the pan.

2 Add the finely chopped onion,
finely chopped red pepper and the
chilli(es) to the oil remaining in the
pan. Sauté until the onion is tender,
then add to the casserole with the
pineapple. Stir to mix.

3 Add the mint, then cover and
simmer gently for about 2 hours
or until the pork is tender. Garnish
with fresh mint and serve with rice.

COOK'S TIP

If fresh pineapple is not available, use
pineapple canned in its own juice.

Veal in Nut Sauce

Ingredients

Serves 6

1.5kg/3 – 3½lb boneless veal, cut into 5cm/2in cubes
2 onions, finely chopped
1 garlic clove, crushed
2.5ml/½tsp dried thyme
2.5ml/½tsp dried oregano
350ml/12fl oz/1½cups chicken stock
75g/3oz/¾cup very finely ground almonds, pecan nuts or peanuts
175g/6fl oz/¾cup soured cream
fresh oregano, to garnish
rice, to serve

———— Cook's Tip ————

Choose domestically raised pink veal if you can. It has a much better flavour and tends to be more moist than than white veal.

1 Put the cubes of veal, finely chopped onions, crushed garlic, thyme, oregano and chicken stock into a large flameproof casserole. Bring to a gentle boil. Cover tightly and simmer over a low heat for about 2 hours or until the veal is cooked and tender.

2 Put the ground nuts in a food processor. Pour in 120ml/4fl oz/½ cup of the veal liquid and process for a few seconds until smooth. Press through a sieve into the casserole.

3 Stir in the soured cream and heat through gently, without boiling. Serve at once with rice, if liked.

Picadillo

Serve as a main dish with rice, or use to stuff peppers or fill tacos.

Ingredients

Serves 6

30ml/2 tbsp olive or corn oil
900g/2lb minced beef
1 onion, finely chopped
2 garlic cloves, chopped
2 eating apples
450g/1lb tomatoes, peeled, seeded and chopped
2 or 3 drained pickled *jalapeño* chillies, seeded and chopped
65g/2½oz/scant ½cup raisins
1.5ml/¼tsp ground cinnamon
1.5ml/¼tsp ground cumin
salt and freshly ground black pepper
tortilla chips, to serve

To garnish

15g/½oz/1 tbsp butter
25g/1oz/¼ cup slivered almonds

1 Heat the oil in large frying pan and add the beef, onion and garlic and fry, stirring from time to time, until the beef is brown and the onion is tender.

2 Peel, core and chop the apples. Add them to the pan with all the remaining ingredients, except the almonds. Cook, uncovered, for about 20 – 25 minutes, stirring occasionally.

3 Just before serving, make the garnish by melting the butter in a small frying pan and sautéing the almonds until golden brown. Serve the Picadillo topped with the almonds and accompanied by the tortilla chips.

Mole Poblano de Guajolote

Mole Poblano de Guajolote is *the* great festive dish of Mexico. It is served at any special occasion, be it a birthday, wedding, or family get-together. Rice, beans, tortillas and Guacamole are the traditional accompaniments.

INGREDIENTS

Serves 6–8

2.75–3.6kg/6–8lb turkey, cut into
  serving pieces
1 onion, chopped
1 garlic clove, chopped
salt
90ml/6 tbsp lard or corn oil
fresh coriander and 30ml/2 tbsp toasted
  sesame seeds, to garnish

For the sauce

6 dried *ancho* chillies
4 dried *pasilla* chillies
4 dried *mulato* chillies
1 drained canned *chipotle* chilli, seeded
  and chopped (optional)
2 onions, chopped
2 garlic cloves, chopped
450g/1lb tomatoes, peeled
  and chopped
1 stale tortilla, torn into pieces
50g/2oz/⅓ cup seedless raisins
115g/4oz/1 cup ground almonds
45ml/3 tbsp sesame seeds, ground
2.5ml/½ tsp coriander seeds, ground
5ml/1 tsp ground cinnamon
2.5ml/½ tsp ground anise
1.5ml/¼ tsp ground black peppercorns
60ml/4 tbsp lard or corn oil
40g/1½oz unsweetened (bitter)
  chocolate, broken into squares
15ml/1 tbsp sugar
salt and freshly ground pepper

COOK'S TIP

Roasting the dried chillies lightly, taking care not to burn them, brings out the flavour and is worth the extra effort.

---

1 Put the turkey pieces into a saucepan or flameproof casserole large enough to hold them in one layer comfortably. Add the onion and garlic, and enough cold water to cover. Season with salt, bring to a gentle simmer, cover and cook for about 1 hour or until the turkey is tender.

2 Meanwhile, put the *ancho, pasilla* and *mulato* chillies in a dry frying pan over gentle heat and roast them for a few minutes, shaking the pan frequently. Remove the stems and shake out the seeds. Tear the pods into pieces and put these into a small bowl. Add sufficient warm water to just cover and soak, turning from time to time, for 30 minutes until soft.

3 Lift out the turkey pieces and pat them dry with kitchen paper. Reserve the stock in a measuring jug. Heat the lard or oil in a large frying pan and sauté the turkey pieces until lightly browned all over. Transfer to a plate and set aside. Reserve the oil that is left in the frying pan.

4 Tip the chillies, with the water in which they have been soaked, into a food processor. Add the *chipotle* chilli, if using, with the onions, garlic, tomatoes, tortilla, raisins, ground almonds and spices. Process to a purée. Do this in batches if necessary.

5 Add the lard or oil to the fat remaining in the frying pan used for sautéing the turkey. Heat the mixture, then add the chilli and spice paste. Cook, stirring, for 5 minutes.

6 Transfer the mixture to the pan or casserole in which the turkey was originally cooked. Stir in 475ml/ 16fl oz/2 cups of the turkey stock (make it up with water if necessary). Add the chocolate and season with salt and pepper. Cook over a low heat until the chocolate has melted. Stir in the sugar. Add the turkey and more stock if needed. Cover the pan and simmer very gently for 30 minutes. Serve, garnished with fresh coriander and sprinkled with the sesame seeds.

Pheasant in Green Pipian Sauce

INGREDIENTS

Serves 4

2 oven-ready pheasants
30ml/2 tbsp corn oil
175g/6oz/1 generous cup *pepitas*
  (Mexican pumpkin seeds)
15ml/1 tbsp *achiote* (annatto) seeds
1 onion, finely chopped
2 garlic cloves, chopped
275g/10oz can tomatillos (Mexican
  green tomatoes)
475ml/16fl oz/2 cups chicken stock
salt and freshly ground black pepper
fresh coriander, to garnish

COOK'S TIP

Achiote is a typical ingredient in Yucatán. It adds a subtle flavour and an orange-red colour. There is no substitute. Look for it in Caribbean and tropical markets.

1 Preheat the oven to 180°C/350°F/ Gas 4. Using a large sharp knife or poultry shears, cut the pheasants in half lengthways and season well with salt and pepper. Heat the oil in a large frying pan and sauté the pieces until lightly brown on all sides. Lift out, drain and arrange, skin-side up, in a roasting tin large enough to hold them comfortably in one layer. Set aside.

2 Grind the *pepitas* finely in a nut grinder or a food processor. Shake through a sieve into a bowl. Grind the *achiote* seeds and add them to the bowl and set to one side.

3 Put the onion, garlic, tomatillos and their juice into a food processor and purée. Put in a saucepan.

4 Add the *pepita* mixture, stir in the stock and simmer over a very low heat for 10 minutes. Do not let the mixture boil as it will separate. Cool.

5 Pour over the pheasant halves. Bake for 40 minutes, basting from time to time with the sauce, or until tender. Garnish with coriander.

Chicken in Green Almond Sauce

INGREDIENTS

Serves 6

1.5kg/3–3½lb chicken, cut into
  serving pieces
475ml/16fl oz/2 cups chicken stock
1 onion, chopped
1 garlic clove, chopped
115g/4oz/2 cups fresh coriander,
  coarsely chopped
1 green pepper, seeded and chopped
1 *jalapeño* chilli, seeded and chopped
275g/10oz can tomatillos (Mexican
  green tomatoes)
115g/4oz/1 cup ground almonds
30ml/2 tbsp corn oil
salt
fresh coriander, to garnish
rice, to serve

1 Put the chicken pieces into a
flameproof casserole or shallow
pan. Pour in the stock, bring to a
simmer, cover and cook for about 45
minutes, until tender. Drain the stock
into a measuring jug and set aside.

2 Put the onion, garlic, coriander,
green pepper, chilli, tomatillos
with their juice and the almonds in a
food processor. Purée fairly coarsely.

3 Heat the oil in a frying pan, add
the almond mixture and cook over
a low heat, stirring with a wooden
spoon, for 3–4 minutes. Scrape into
the casserole or pan with the chicken.

— COOK'S TIP —

If the colour of the sauce seems a little pale,
add 2–3 outer leaves of dark green cos lettuce. Cut out the central veins, chop the
leaves and add to the food processor with
the other ingredients. This will lift the
colour without altering the flavour.

4 Make the stock up to 475ml/
16fl oz/2 cups with water, if
necessary. Stir it into the casserole or
pan. Mix gently and simmer just long
enough to blend the flavours and heat
the chicken pieces through. Add salt to
taste. Serve at once, garnished with
coriander and accompanied by rice.

Green Lima Beans in Sauce

A tasty dish of lima beans with a tomato and chilli sauce.

INGREDIENTS

Serves 4

450g/1lb green lima or broad beans,
 thawed if frozen
30ml/2 tbsp olive oil
1 onion, finely chopped
2 garlic cloves, chopped
350g/12oz tomatoes, peeled, seeded
 and chopped
1 or 2 drained canned *jalapeño* chillies,
 seeded and chopped
salt
chopped fresh coriander sprigs,
 to garnish

1 Cook the beans in a saucepan of boiling water for 15–20 minutes until tender. Drain and keep hot, to one side, in the covered saucepan.

2 Heat the olive oil in a frying pan and sauté the onion and garlic until the onion is soft but not brown. Add the tomatoes and cook until the mixture is thick and flavoursome.

3 Add the *jalapeños* and cook for 1–2 minutes. Season with salt.

4 Pour the mixture over the reserved beans and check that they are hot. If not, return everything to the frying pan and cook over low heat for just long enough to heat through. Put into a warm serving dish, garnish with the coriander and serve.

Green Bean and Sweet Red Pepper Salad

INGREDIENTS

Serves 4

350g/12oz cooked green beans,
  quartered
2 red peppers, seeded and chopped
2 spring onions (white and green parts),
  chopped
1 or more drained pickled *serrano*
  chillies, well rinsed and then seeded
  and chopped
1 iceberg lettuce, coarsely shredded, or
  mixed salad leaves
olives, to garnish

For the dressing

45ml/3 tbsp red wine vinegar
135ml/9 tbsp olive oil
salt and freshly ground black pepper

1 Combine the cooked green beans,
chopped peppers, chopped spring
onions and chillies in a salad bowl.

2 Make the salad dressing. Pour the
red wine vinegar into a bowl or
jug. Add salt and freshly ground black
pepper to taste, then gradually whisk in
the olive oil until well combined.

3 Pour the salad dressing over the
prepared vegetables and toss lightly
together to mix and coat thoroughly.

4 Line a large platter with the
shredded lettuce leaves and arrange
the salad attractively on top. Garnish
with the olives and serve.

Frijoles

INGREDIENTS

Serves 6-8

350g/12oz/1¼-1½ cups dried red
kidney, pinto or black haricot beans,
picked over and rinsed

2 onions, finely chopped

2 garlic cloves, chopped

1 bay leaf

1 or more *serrano* chillies (small fresh
green chillies)

30ml/2 tbsp corn oil

2 tomatoes, peeled, seeded and
chopped

salt

sprigs of fresh bay leaves, to garnish

─────── COOK'S TIP ───────

In Yucatan black haricot beans are cooked
with the Mexican herb *epazote*.

1 Put the beans into a pan and add
cold water to cover by 2.5cm/1in.

2 Add half the onion, half the garlic,
the bay leaf and the chilli(es). Bring
to the boil and boil vigorously for
about 10 minutes. Put the beans and
liquid into an earthenware pot or large
saucepan, cover and cook over a low
heat for 30 minutes. Add boiling water
if the mixture starts to become dry.

3 When the beans begin to wrinkle,
add 15ml/1 tbsp of the corn oil
and cook for a further 30 minutes or
until the beans are tender. Add salt to
taste and cook for 30 minutes more,
but do not add any more water.

4 Remove the beans from the heat.
Heat the remaining oil in a small
frying pan and sauté the remaining
onion and garlic until the onion is soft.
Add the tomatoes and cook for a few
minutes more.

5 Spoon 45ml/3 tbsp of the beans
out of the pot or pan and add
them to the tomato mixture. Mash to a
paste. Stir this into the beans to thicken
the liquid. Cook for just long enough
to heat through, if necessary. Serve the
beans in small bowls and garnish with
sprigs of fresh bay leaves.

Peppers Stuffed with Beans

Stuffed peppers are a popular Mexican dish. A special version – *Chiles en Nogada* – is served every year on August 28 to celebrate Independence Day. The green peppers are served with a sauce of fresh walnuts and a garnish of pomegranate seeds to represent the colours of the Mexican flag.

INGREDIENTS

Serves 6
6 large green peppers
1 quantity Frijoles Refritos (Refried
  Beans)
2 eggs, separated
2.5ml/½ tsp salt
corn oil, for frying
plain flour, for dusting
120ml/4fl oz/½ cup whipping cream
115g/4oz/1 cup grated Cheddar cheese
fresh coriander sprigs, to garnish

1 Roast the peppers over a gas flame or under a medium grill, turning occasionally, until the skins have blackened and blistered. Transfer the peppers to a plastic bag, secure the top and leave for 15 minutes.

2 Preheat the oven to 180°C/350°F/ Gas 4. Remove the peppers from the bag. Hold each pepper in turn under cold running water and gently rub off the skins. Slit the peppers down one side and remove the seeds and ribs, taking care not to break the pepper shells. Stuff with the Refried Beans.

3 Beat the egg whites in a large bowl until they stand in firm peaks. In another bowl, beat the yolks lightly together with the salt. Fold the yolks gently into the whites.

4 Pour the corn oil into a large frying pan to a depth of about 2.5cm/1in and heat. Spread out the flour in a shallow bowl or dish.

5 Dip the filled peppers in the flour and then in the egg mixture. Fry in batches in the hot oil until golden brown all over. Arrange the peppers in an ovenproof dish. Pour over the cream and sprinkle with the cheese. Bake in the oven for 30 minutes or until the topping is golden brown and the peppers are heated through. Serve at once, garnished with fresh coriander.

Chopped Courgettes

Calabacitas is an extremely easy recipe to make. If the cooking time seems unduly long, this is because the acid present in the tomatoes slows down the cooking of the courgettes. Use young tender courgettes.

INGREDIENTS

Serves 4
30ml/2 tbsp corn oil
450g/1lb young courgettes, sliced
1 onion, finely chopped
2 garlic cloves, chopped
450g/1lb tomatoes, peeled, seeded
   and chopped
2 drained canned *jalapeño* chillies,
   rinsed, seeded and chopped
15ml/1 tbsp chopped fresh coriander
salt
fresh coriander, to garnish

1 Heat the oil in a flameproof casserole and add all the remaining ingredients, except the salt.

2 Bring to simmering point, cover and cook over a low heat for about 30 minutes until the courgettes are tender, checking from time to time that the dish is not drying out. If it is, add a little tomato juice, stock or water.

3 Season with salt and serve the Mexican way as a separate course. Alternatively, serve accompanied by any plainly cooked meat or poultry. Garnish with fresh coriander.

Refried Beans (Frijoles Refritos)

There is much disagreement about the translation of the term *refrito*. It means, literally, twice fried. Some cooks say this implies that the beans must be really well fried, others that it means twice cooked. However named, *Frijoles Refritos* are delicious.

INGREDIENTS

Serves 6–8
90–120ml/6–8 tbsp lard or corn oil
1 onion, finely chopped
1 quantity Frijoles (cooked beans)

To garnish
freshly grated Parmesan cheese or
   crumbled cottage cheese
crisp fried corn tortillas, cut into
   quarters

1 Heat 30ml/2 tbsp of the lard in a large heavy-based frying pan and sauté the onion until it is soft. Add about 225ml/8fl oz/1 cup of the Frijoles (cooked beans).

COOK'S TIP

Lard is the traditional (and best tasting) fat for the beans but many people prefer to use corn oil. Avoid using olive oil, which is too strongly flavoured and distinctive.

2 Mash the beans with the back of a wooden spoon or potato masher, adding more beans and melted lard or oil until all the ingredients are used up and the beans have formed a heavy paste. Use extra lard or oil if necessary.

3 Tip out on to a warmed platter, piling the mixture up in a roll. Garnish with the cheese. Spike with the tortilla triangles, placing them at intervals along the length of the roll. Serve as a side dish.

Pumpkin in Brown Sugar

INGREDIENTS

Serves 4

900g/2lb pumpkin, cut into wedges
350g/12oz/2 cups soft dark
   brown sugar
about 120ml/4fl oz/½ cup water

1 Scrape the seeds out of the pumpkin wedges. Pack the wedges firmly together in a heavy-based flameproof casserole.

2 Divide the sugar among the pumpkin pieces, packing it into the hollows which contained the seeds.

COOK'S TIP

The best pumpkin for this recipe is the classic orange-fleshed variety used to make Hallowe'en lanterns. Choose one which will fit neatly into your casserole when cut.

3 Pour the water carefully into the the casserole to cover the bottom and prevent the pumpkin from burning. Take care not to dislodge the sugar when pouring in the water.

4 Cover and cook over a low heat, checking the water level frequently, until the pumpkin is tender and the sugar has dissolved in the liquid to form a sauce.

5 Using a slotted spoon, transfer the pumpkin to a serving dish. Pour the sugary liquid from the pan over the pumpkin and serve at once with natural yogurt, sweetened with a little brown sugar, if you like.

Buñuelos

INGREDIENTS

Serves 6

225g/8oz/2 cups plain flour
5ml/1 tsp baking powder
2.5ml/½ tsp salt
15ml/1 tbsp granulated sugar
1 large egg, beaten
120ml/4fl oz/½ cup milk
25g/1oz/2 tbsp unsalted butter, melted
oil, for frying
sugar, for dusting

For the syrup

225g/8oz/1⅓ cups soft light
   brown sugar
750ml/1¼ pints/3 cups water
2.5cm/1in cinnamon stick
1 clove

1 Make the syrup. Combine all the ingredients in a saucepan. Heat, stirring, until the sugar has dissolved, then simmer until the mixture has reduced to a light syrup. Remove and discard the spices. Keep the syrup warm while you make the *buñuelos*.

2 Sift the flour, salt and baking powder into a bowl. Stir in the sugar. In a mixing bowl, whisk the egg and the milk well together. Gradually stir in the dry mixture, then beat in the melted butter to make a soft dough.

3 Turn the dough on to a lightly floured board and knead until it is smooth and elastic. Divide the dough into 18 even-size pieces. Shape into balls. With your hands, flatten the balls to disk shapes about 2cm/¾in thick.

4 Use the floured handle of a wooden spoon to poke a hole through the centre of each *buñuelo*. Pour oil into a deep frying pan to a depth of 5cm/2in. Alternatively, use a deep-fryer. Heat the oil to a temperature of 190°C/375°F or until a cube of day-old bread added to the oil browns in 30–60 seconds.

```
——————— COOK'S TIP ———————

Make the syrup ahead of time if you prefer,
and chill it until ready to use, when it can
be warmed through quickly.
```

5 Fry the fritters in batches, taking care not to overcrowd the pan, until they are puffy and golden brown on both sides. Lift out with a slotted spoon and drain on kitchen paper.

6 Dust the *buñuelos* with sugar and serve with the syrup.

Churros

INGREDIENTS

Makes about 24

250ml/8fl oz/1 cup water
15ml/1 tbsp granulated sugar, plus
   extra for dusting
2.5ml/½ tsp salt
175g/6oz/1½ cups plain flour
1 large egg
½ lime or lemon
oil for frying

─────── COOK'S TIP ───────

You can use a funnel to shape the churros.
Close the end with a finger, add the batter,
then release into the oil in small columns.

1 Bring the water, sugar and salt to
  the boil. Remove from the heat
and beat in the flour until smooth.

2 Beat in the egg, using a wooden
  spoon, until the mixture is smooth
and satiny. Set the batter aside.

3 Pour the oil into a deep-frying pan
  to a depth of about 5cm/2in. Add
the lime or lemon half, then heat the
oil to 190°C/375°F or until a cube of
day-old bread added to the oil browns
in 30–60 seconds.

4 Pour the batter into a pastry bag
  fitted with a fluted nozzle. Pipe
7.5cm/3in strips of batter and then add
to the oil, a few at a time. Fry for
3–4 minutes or until golden brown.

5 Using a slotted spoon, remove the
  churros from the pan and drain on
kitchen paper. Roll the hot churros in
granulated sugar before serving.

Sopaipillas

INGREDIENTS

Makes about 30

225g/8oz/2 cups plain flour, sifted
15ml/1 tbsp baking powder
5ml/1 tsp salt
30ml/2 tbsp lard or margarine
175ml/6fl oz/¾ cup water
corn oil, for deep frying
syrup or honey, to serve

─────── COOK'S TIP ───────

Use your imagination when deciding what
to serve with the puffs. Sprinkle them with
cinnamon and sugar, or flavour syrup with
rum. The fat little pillows could even be
served plain, as they taste delicious.

1 Put the flour, baking powder and
  salt into a large bowl. Lightly rub
in the lard or margarine, using your
fingertips, until the mixture resembles
coarse breadcrumbs.

2 Gradually stir in the water, using a
  fork, until the mixture clumps
together to form a soft dough.

3 Shape the dough into a ball, then
  turn out on to a lightly floured
surface and knead very gently until
smooth. Roll out thinly to a rectangle
measuring about 46 x 35cm/18 x 15in.
Using a sharp knife, carefully cut into
about 30 x 7.5cm/3in squares. For a
decorative edge you could use a pastry
wheel to cut out the squares.

4 Heat the oil to 190°C/375°F or
  until a cube of day-old bread
browns in 30–60 seconds.

5 Fry the puffs, a few at a time, in
  the oil. As they brown and puff
up, turn over to cook the other side.
Remove with a slotted spoon and drain
on kitchen paper. It is important that
the temperature of the oil remains
constant during the cooking process.
Serve warm, with syrup or honey or
any sauce of your choice.

Index

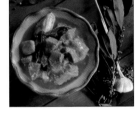